D0874113

Emerging Leadership Vistas

INTERNATIONAL LEADERSHIP
SYMPOSIA SERIES
James G. Hunt, General Editor

Current Developments in the Study of Leadership.
Edited by E.A. Fleishman and J.G. Hunt. 1973.

Contingency Approaches to Leadership. Edited by
J.G. Hunt and L.L. Larson. 1974.

Leadership Frontiers. Edited by J.G. Hunt and
L.L. Larson. 1975.

Leadership: The Cutting Edge. Edited by J.G. Hunt and
L.L. Larson. 1977.

Crosscurrents in Leadership. Edited by J.G. Hunt and
L.L. Larson. 1979.

Leadership: Beyond Establishment Views. Edited by
J.G. Hunt, U. Sekaran, and C.A. Schriesheim. 1982.

**Leaders and Managers: International Perspectives on
Managerial Behavior and Leadership.** Edited by
J.G. Hunt, D.M. Hosking, C.A. Schriesheim, and
R. Stewart. 1984.

Emerging Leadership Vistas

Edited by

James Gerald Hunt
Texas Tech University

B. Rajaram Baliga
Texas Tech University

H. Peter Dachler
Hochschule St. Gallen

Chester A. Schriesheim
University of Miami

Lexington Books
D.C. Heath and Company/Lexington, Massachusetts/Toronto

Library of Congress Cataloging-in-Publication Data

Emerging leadership vistas.

Bibliography: p.
Includes indexes.
1. Leadership. 2. Management. I. Hunt, James G.,
1932–   .
HD57.7.E44   1987   658.4'092   86–46310
ISBN 0–669–15331–1 (alk. paper)

Published simultaneously in Canada
Printed in the United States of America
International Standard Book Number: 0–669–15331–1
Library of Congress Catalog Card Number: 86–46310

The paper used in this publication meets the minimum requirements of
American National Standard for Information Sciences—Permanence of
Paper for Printed Library Materials, ANSI Z39.48–1984.

87 88 89 90 8 7 6 5 4 3 2 1

To leadership normal scientists and interpretists

Contents

Preface and Acknowledgments   xi

1. Emerging Leadership Vistas: An Introduction   1
   James G. Hunt, B.R. Baliga, H. Peter Dachler, and
   Chester A. Schriesheim

I Charismatic and Transformational Leadership   5

2. Charismatic Leadership: A Phenomenological and Structural
   Approach   11
   Kimberly B. Boal and *John M. Bryson*

3. Transformational Leadership, Charisma, and Beyond   29
   Bruce J. Avolio and *Bernard M. Bass*

4. Toward an Organizational Leadership Theory   51
   Marshall Sashkin and *Robert M. Fulmer*

5. Commentary on Part I   66

   Chapter 2 Commentary: Welcome Back Charisma   67
   D. Anthony Butterfield

   Chapter 3 Commentary: Transformational Leadership: Fostering Follower Autonomy, Not Automatic Followership   73
   Jill W. Graham

   Chapter 4 Commentary: The Merger of Macro and Micro
   Levels of Leadership   80
   Patricia Riley

II Leadership in a Dynamic Organizational Context 85

6. The Skills of Leadership 80
    Dian-Marie Hosking and *Ian E. Morley*

7. The Management Team: An Equilibrium Model of
    Management Performance and Behavior 107
    Andrew Crouch and *Philip Yetton*

8. An Organizational Life Cycle Approach to Leadership 129
    B.R. Baliga and *James G. Hunt*

9. Commentary on Part II 150

    Chapter 6 Commentary: Leadership: Nothing but
    Constructing Reality by Negotiations? 151
    Klaus Bartölke

    Chapter 7 Commentary: Leadership Research: A Systemic
    Viewpoint 158
    Gilbert J.B. Probst

III Inside the Heads of Leadership Researchers: Their
Assumptions and Implications on How Knowledge Is
Generated 165

10. Leadership Theory as Causal Attributions of
     Performance 169
     James C. McElroy and *J. David Hunger*

11. Gleanings from a Frustrated Process Analysis of Leadership
     Research Stakeholders 183
     Mark F. Peterson and *Peter B. Smith*

12. Reading Leadership as a Form of Cultural Analysis 201
     Marta B. Calas and *Linda Smircich*

13. Commentary on Part III 227

     Chapter 10 Commentary: On Extending Leadership Theory:
     Leadership Attributions and Beyond 228
     Torodd Strand

Chapter 12 Commentary: Rereading Leadership with
Structural Lenses   235
Walter Nord

IV   Overviews   243

14. Leadership Research: Some Forgotten, Ignored, or Overlooked
    Findings   245
    Robert J. House

15. Constraints on the Emergence of New Vistas in Leadership
    and Management Research: An Epistemological
    Overview   261
    H. Peter Dachler

References   287

Name Index   313

Subject Index   321

About the Contributors   329

Preface and Acknowledgments

This book covers the content of an international symposium on leadership and managerial behavior research held at Texas Tech University, from July 23 to 27, 1985. It comprises volume 8 of the International Leadership Symposia Series, which originated in 1971 and joins the earlier volumes in charting the state of the field. Like its most recent predecessors, it reflects the series' increasing international thrust and consideration of broader aspects of managerial behavior in addition to leadership.

The previous volumes are *Current Developments in the Study of Leadership* (1973), *Contingency Approaches to Leadership* (1974), *Leadership Frontiers* (1975), *Leadership: The Cutting Edge* (1977), *Crosscurrents in Leadership* (1979), *Leadership: Beyond Establishment Views* (1982), and *Leaders and Managers* (1984).

The series was established to provide in-depth consideration of current and future leadership directions and to provide an interdisciplinary perspective for the scholarly study of leadership. Taken as a whole, the books in the series have been designed to build on one another, to show the evolution of the field over time, and to be at the forefront of new developments. The current international focus and broadened managerial behavior emphasis are considered to be at the heart of developments in the field.

The format of the books has encouraged the achievement of these objectives in several ways. First, a mix of work from well-known scholars, widely recognized for many years, and newer scholars, whose work has only recently received attention, has been utilized. Second, expert discussants/critiquers have prepared commentaries for the presentations. Third, interchanges have been encouraged at the symposia and issues emerging from these interchanges have been woven into the introductory part or chapter materials of the books. Fourth, a broad-ranging overview has typically been prepared to put the books' contents into perspective. That perspective has often ranged far afield from the contents of the chapters themselves. Finally, in more recent books, the editors have provided a considerable amount of additional commentary to help balance the content of the books in terms of current directions.

To encourage further scholarship in the leadership area and to recognize the contributions of outstanding individuals, the Ralph M. Stogdill Distinguished Leadership Scholarship Award was established in 1976. Bestowed on an intermittent basis, the award is given to a leadership scholar "in recognition of his or her outstanding contribution to the advancement of leadership research and for devotion to the development of a new generation of leadership scholars." Thus, the award is intended not only for the scholarly research contribution of the chosen individual but, equally important, for the contribution to the development of others in the field. To date, award recipients have been Ralph M. Stogdill himself, 1976; Fred E. Fiedler, 1978; and Rensis Likert, 1980.

This current symposium was sponsored by the Texas Tech University College of Business Administration, Area of Management, and Texas Center for Productivity and Quality of Work Life. We are indebted to individuals in all these units for their encouragement and support.

Planning and arrangements for this symposium involved a number of people. First, there was the symposium organizing committee to participate in planning, paper evaluation, and decision making. The committee was composed of the four editors: James G. (Jerry) Hunt (Texas Tech), B.R. Baliga (Texas Tech), H. Peter Dachler (St. Gallen Graduate School of Economics, Law, Business and Public Administration, Switzerland), and Chester A. Shriesheim (University of Miami, Florida).

Second, to host the symposium and implement travel and lodging arrangements in addition to performing symposium secretarial duties, Jeanna Richards in the Texas Tech Area of Management provided invaluable help. Third, graduate students Gin Seow and Susan Fox along with the Area of Management secretary Carolyn Guess and student workers Alan Davidson and Robbie Floyd, all at Texas Tech, provided support help beyond the call of duty.

The content of this book was obtained as follows. First, a call for abstracts was mailed to a large number of people throughout the world and communicated in selected journals and newsletters. Abstracts from the Americas were sent to Jerry Hunt and those from the rest of the world were sent to Peter Dachler. A review board was established at each location.

Second, the board blind-reviewed the abstracts. With consultation between and across the editors, a group of abstracts was judged to have received ratings indicating they should be considered further.

Third, the authors of this group of abstracts were invited to prepare complete papers. The completed papers then underwent a review process similar to that of the earlier abstracts. Seven of these papers were finally selected for presentation; along with two invited overviews, they appear as chapters in this book. These were supplemented with a workshop on leadership in organizations in transition and a workshop employing Mason and Mitroff's

(1981) Strategic Assumption Surfacing Technique as applied to the assumptions of leadership researchers. The content of these workshops was then used to form the basis of respective chapters by Baliga and Hunt and by Peterson and Smith.

The review process was aided by a longstanding symposium advisory board, augmented by a large number of ad hoc reviewers. Advisory board members are:

Chris Argyris
Harvard University

Bernard Bass
State University of New York at
   Binghamton

David Bower
University of Michigan

Elmer Burack
University of Illinois at Chicago

John Cambell
University of Minnesota,
   Twin Cities

Martin Chemers
University of Utah

John Child
University of Aston in
   Birmingham, U.K.

Larry Cummings
Northwestern University

Martin Evans
University of Toronto

George Farris
Rutgers, The State University of
   New Jersey

Fred Fiedler
University of Washington

Edwin Fleishman
Advanced Research Resources
   Organization, Bethesda, Md.

William Fox
University of Florida

George Graen
University of Cincinnati

Charles Greene
University of Southern Maine

Edwin Hollander
State University of New York at
   Buffalo

James Price
University of Iowa

Marshall Sashkin
U.S. Office of Education,
   Washington, D.C.

Chester Schriesheim
University of Miami

Henry Sims, Jr.
The Pennsylvania State University

John Slocum, Jr.
Southern Methodist University

John Stinson
Ohio University

Peter Weissenberg
Rutgers, The State University of
New Jersey, Camden

Ad hoc reviewers were:

Klaus Bartölke
Bergische Universität-
Gesamthochschule Wuppertal,
Federal Republic of Germany

D. Anthony Butterfield
University of Massachusetts

Ricky W. Griffin
Texas A & M University

Peter Holderegger
Hochschule St. Gallen, Switzerland

Rudiger Klimecki
Institut für Betriebswirtschaft
Hochschule St. Gallen,
Switzerland

Richard T. Mowday
University of Oregon

Richard N. Osborn
Wayne State University

James S. Phillips
University of Houston

Philip M. Podsakoff
Indiana University

Randall S. Schuler
New York University

Thomas Schwinger
Universität Münster
Federal Republic of Germany

John E. Sheridan
Texas Christian University

Henry L. Tosi, Jr.
University of Florida

Gary A. Yukl
State University of New York at
Albany

The advisory board and reviewers have been very helpful in providing a critically important perspective to supplement that of the organizing committee.

The present symposium could not have been held without the assistance of all those mentioned in the preceding. In addition, financial support has been critical. The bulk of this support came from the United States Army

Research Institute for the Behavioral and Social Sciences and Mrs. Helen DeVitt Jones of Lubbock. This was supplemented by support from the Office of Naval Research and Smithsonian Institution, along with the Texas Tech Center for Productivity and Quality of Work Life and the St. Gall Graduate School of Switzerland. Secretarial and other clerical assistance was provided by Texas Tech University and the St. Gall Graduate School.

In terms of editorship, the American editors have been joined by Peter Dachler, their colleague from Switzerland. This has helped ensure an international mix of works. It was agreed that Jerry Hunt, as the founder and principal architect of the symposia series, would be the senior editor and the others would be listed alphabetically. This ordering is followed in all of the editorial pieces in the book. Let there be no doubt about overall contribution, however; both the symposium and this book are based on a team effort by *all* of the editors.

Finally, Donna Hunt should be recognized for proofreading assistance. We are indebted to her and to all those above for their contributions.

J.G. Hunt
B.R. Baliga
H.P. Dachler
C.A. Schriesheim

1
Emerging Leadership Vistas:
An Introduction

James G. Hunt
B.R. Baliga
H. Peter Dachler
Chester A. Schriesheim

L eadership research tends to mirror the organizational research of
which it is a part. Both have been in a state of turmoil for some time.
That turmoil has been reflected in the leadership symposia volumes
since 1975, and is manifested in the metaphorical nature of all the titles
but one.

As editors we see this turmoil as a necessary process to move beyond the
status quo. Hence we are encouraged rather than disturbed by it. Thus, in
this current book on emerging leadership vistas we have encouraged diversity
and controversy and see such diversity and controversy as fairly representing
the state of leadership research today.

Themes reflected in recent volumes are again reflected here. Primary
among these are contrasts between perspectives of U.S. researchers and
others; differences in epistemological assumptions; varying conceptualizations of what is meant by leadership; and contrasts between micro and macro
aspects of leadership.

Perhaps the most controversial aspect of this book is concerned with different and in part contradictory epistemological assumptions that underlie
the study of leadership. Within the traditional "realist perspective" of social
science one sees leadership as a concept independent of the observer and subject to laws and regularities assumed to be inherent in the objective nature of
leadership "out there," waiting to be discovered by the leadership researcher.
In the context of an interpretative, social constructionist perspective of social
science, one experiences leadership as something that emerges out of the complex social-political network of relationships in organizations. Some people
embedded in this network of relationships with its implicit rules, codes,
norms, theories and ideologies are experienced as leaders, based upon the
socially constructed meaning of the specific and wider social and cultural
context. In addition, the community of leadership researchers, which constitutes a complex social system within a particular culture, collectively

constructs on the basis of the dominant discipline paradigm the nature and meaning of leadership and management as much as those who engage in leadership.

It is interesting to note that although this difference in perspectives is partially reflected in the difference between U.S. scholars and those from the rest of the world, it also clearly separates U.S. scholars. It is probably fair to say that differences between perspectives of normal science proponents and subjectivist or interpretist proponents are greater than those between U.S. and non-U.S. scholars. Be that as it may, this book in its entirety (content chapters, commentary chapters, and overviews) reflects a mix of normal science, interpretist, U.S., and outside-U.S. contributions.

The normal science/interpretist split is no more sharply reflected than in the overviews and in the treatment of charisma in part I, but it permeates much of the rest of the book as well.

Let us now take a brief look at the way the book's content is structured. Following this introductory chapter, there are four parts, each containing from two to four chapters.

The mix of authors across content, commentary, and overview chapters comprises a fifty/fifty split between those located in the United States and those outside the United States. There is not a straightforward one for one balancing here; rather people were assigned where they would be the best fit and where they could provide especially appropriate insights. The first three parts contain content chapters with a concluding chapter of comments about each of the content chapters. Part IV contains the two overview chapters mentioned earlier providing dramatically different perspectives of leadership and ways of moving ahead. Each part contains a short introduction by the editors providing a short summary of each of the content and commentary chapters. Also included are some issues for readers to ponder as they read the chapters in the part in question. These issues are a combination of our own insights and highlights of those expressed by the symposium participants.

In part I of this book, three chapters address the still ambiguous notions of charismatic and transformational leadership, where the latter view of leadership tries to focus on that which may make followers exceed their own expectations. All three contributions attempt to make initial steps toward showing that there are aspects of leadership that lie not only within the conscious, rational analyses leaders or managers "do" on people and situations but that leadership also includes more intuitive processes regarding value and cultural processes within work groups and organizations. More importantly, these chapters show that these aspects of the leadership process are not simply mystical "attributes" of a particular leader.

Part II of this book is concerned with leadership in a dynamic, organizational context. Two of the chapters focus on a long-neglected issue in leadership research, namely the embeddedness of leadership in organizations as a whole. Traditional perspectives have reduced the concept of leadership primarily to the narrow interaction patterns between a usually formally assigned leader and his or her followers. The organizational and larger societal context, if it is included in the leadership model at all, is primarily treated as isolated contingency variables which moderate the leader-follower interactions. The third chapter looks at the dynamic, processual aspects of leadership deep within the organization. It centers on dynamic processes between managers and subordinates in work teams.

Part III contains epistemological issues in leadership research which deal with problems that so far have received very little, if any, attention in the previous leadership symposia volumes. Each of the three chapters in this part deals with conceptually separate epistemological issues. But the common thread is the recognition that leadership and management theory and research methodologies are not simply a reflection of the inherent properties of an objective, separately existing leadership reality, but are socially constructed outcomes of the community of leadership researchers and their root assumptions, values, ideologies, and preconceptions.

Finally, part IV of this book contains two overview chapters covering the symposium and fundamental issues in leadership and management research in general. Although originally the idea was to review the symposium from a U.S. and European perspective, during the course of the symposium and its preparation it became quite obvious that the fundamental issue was not one of a U.S. and European cultural tradition in leadership research, although such cultural differences clearly play their part. The fundamental issue revolved around two contradictory epistemological perspectives of social science out of which quite different answers to the questions of "what is leadership" and "what are *new* vistas of leadership" emerge. The two overview chapters approach these questions from the "normal science" perspective on the one hand and the "social construction of reality" perspective on the other. Two very different leadership realities emerge from the two chapters.

Part I
Charismatic and Transformational Leadership

James G. Hunt
B.R. Baliga
H. Peter Dachler
Chester A. Schriesheim

A frequently heard lament in recent years among those studying leadership has been that the research has become sterile and though rigorous misses the real essence of what leadership is all about. The chapters in this part address what seems to be becoming a new focus in leadership research and may allow us to start asking some rather different questions regarding the leadership phenomenon. The discussion of charisma and its cousin transformational leadership in this first part makes it clear that these aspects of leadership are more than a mystical gift that is bestowed on a fortunate few (see Dubin 1979). Although mystical in the sense that charisma and transformational leadership involve interpretational and symbolic processes, the chapters of this part lay some groundwork for dismissing the simplistic idea that charisma is solely (or primarily) a function of the leader's personality.

Chapter 2, "Charismatic Leadership: A Phenomenological and Structural Approach," by Kimberly M. Boal and John M. Bryson, starts the book's look at charisma by considering two kinds of charismatic leaders. The first of these is a leader who obtains charisma by means of extraordinary vision communicated to the followers. The important insight by Boal and Bryson is the fact that it is not the leader as such who creates and communicates an "extraordinary vision"; rather, a perspective or idea of a leader is experienced by the relevant actors as a vision in the context of their phenomenological world. The second, in marked contrast, is a leader who obtains charisma by means of a crisis in the context of which charismatic qualities are attributed to a leader.

Boal and Bryson argue that the two kinds of charismatic leaders will have different effects on the phenomenological worlds (interpretative scheme) of the followers. In both cases the worlds will be different than before. However, with a visionary leader the process begins with an interpretative scheme whereas in the case of crisis-produced charismatic leadership the crisis-related actions of the relevant actors lead to the interpretation of charisma under certain experienced circumstances.

The authors develop a model that combines phenomenological and structural approaches to charismatic leadership. The model is followed by a series of propositions suggesting conditions under which charismatic effects are more likely. The propositions are a beginning step in looking at charisma within a contingency framework.

Boal and Bryson's chapter 2 is followed by Avolio and Bass's, "Transformational Leadership, Charisma, and Beyond." That chapter builds on the earlier work of Burns (1978) and Bass (1985) regarding transformational leadership—that which motivates followers to work for transcendental goals and to perform beyond their expectations. Transformational leadership is defined as including not only charisma but individualized follower consideration and intellectual stimulation as well. The chapter emphasizes the importance of using transactional leadership—that based on traditional leader-follower exchange relationships—as a base, with the truly effective leader using transformational leadership on top of transactional leadership.

Avolio and Bass measure both transactional and transformational leadership using questionnaires and make the point that leaders possess degrees of transformational and charismatic leadership and that these are not simply gifts bestowed on a fortunate few. They then report results of a number of studies that go beyond those earlier summarized by Bass (1985). Finally, they examine the research and practitioner implications of this body of work.

Chapter 3, "Toward an Organizational Leadership Theory," by Marshall Sashkin and Robert M. Fulmer, embeds charismatic leadership within the broader study of leadership in organizations. The chapter is organized around the themes of person, situation, and behavior and explores these themes for both operational (lower level) and executive (top level) leadership. Leaders' motivational needs and cognitive abilities are seen as providing them with the wherewithal needed to focus on relevant situational factors and then to carry out appropriate behaviors for effective leadership. The behaviors are based on recent work by Bennis and Nanus (1985) and are charismatic or transformational in nature. The details of how executive and operational leaders implement this person, situation, behavior model differ but the basic pattern of the model is argued to hold true at both levels.

The three chapters, in combination, approach the study of charismatic leadership from a number of different perspectives. The commentaries and issues raised by symposium participants help highlight these differences and stimulate the reader's thinking while he or she moves through this part.

Anthony Butterfield was chosen as the commentator for chapter 2 by Boal and Bryson for numerous reasons. He is an expert in leadership, he comes from an institution (the University of Massachusetts Department of Management) that emphasizes interpretist views, and he has followed and participated in the symposia series which has provided an important backdrop for his views. His commentary in chapter 5 does several things. First, it lauds the Boal and Bryson chapter for integrating both subjectivist and functionalist approaches. Second, it points out a number of major strengths of the contribution and follows these with some concerns. Finally, Butterfield emphasizes the need for work on charisma and shows the contribution of the Boal and Bryson chapter in this work.

Jill Graham's work on organizational citizenship served as a key reason for her selection as a commentator on the work of Avolio and Bass. That perspective is shown in her differentiation between subordinates as mere automotors responding to the leader's charismatic acts and followers who demonstrate free choice behavior. She draws a parallel between transactional leadership and its development of dependence on the part of subordinates and true transformational leadership and its development of follower autonomy. She argues that House's (1977) charismatic model assumes the former whereas the transformational approach of Avolio and Bass emphasizes the latter—as does organizational citizenship behavior. Citizenship behavior is that behavior on the part of the follower that goes beyond routine response to achievement of organizational goals. For this to take place the leader must provide employee empowerment as opposed to dependence. Graham contends that it would be desirable to measure both transformational leadership and organizational citizenship behavior in one study.

Patricia Riley has an organizational communication background and is thus attuned to both objectivist and interpretist research perspectives. It was this background that caused us to choose her as a commentator for the Sashkin and Fulmer chapter. Although that chapter uses an objectivist perspective, its use of charisma as a key feature could clearly benefit from the perspective of someone familiar with the subjectivist tradition which underlies a good bit of the charismatic literature.

She discusses Sashkin and Fulmer's work in terms of the conceptual framework, epistemological concerns, and future research. In terms of the conceptual framework, she takes issue with the classification of some of the variables. For example, she sees charisma as a person variable whereas Sashkin and Fulmer consider it a behavior. Similarly she takes issue with some of the variables which Sashkin and Fulmer call behaviors. She argues instead that they are metabehaviors that include evaluations of successful outcomes. She also has some concerns about their treatment of culture. Basically she is arguing for a more thorough explication of the variables and a stronger tie with the interpretist literature.

Epistemologically, she cautions against the tendency to use such symbolic terms as *leader* and *charismatic* as mere categories of behaviors. She argues that these should be analyzed using forms of analyses that will pick up their richness as symbols, their creation of meaning, and their dramatic impact.

In terms of future research, she suggests some directions and an approach that allows focusing on leadership *in context* as opposed to treating it as a variable in isolation.

Highlights of Issues Raised at the Symposium

Some issues related to Boal and Bryson's chapter 2 are the following. First, is charisma a gift or a relationship? If it is a relationship there are not charismatic leaders per se but rather charismatic situations or charismatic actions. Crisis situations may invoke different kinds of leadership than non-crisis situations and these lead to leader-follower relationships developing differently in the two situations. Under non-crisis situations, the leader may generate the particular relationship termed charismatic. This question is an interesting one because it challenges the traditional view of charisma as a gift and opens up a way of thinking that can lead to very different implications than the traditional view.

Second, in a crisis situation does the behavior of the crisis-induced charismatic leader change or is it merely perceived differently by the followers? Or is some combination of both at work?

Third, is creating phenomenological validity exclusively a function of charismatic leaders in the context of their groups and their followers or is it a function of all leaders? If the latter, where then does charisma enter in? This really raises the question of the extent to which charisma is necessary in the Boal and Bryson model or whether simply examining crisis versus non-crisis leaders would suffice.

Finally, to what extent may visionary leaders induce pseudocrisis in order to generate conditions necessary for their charismatic efforts to be felt?

Turning to the Avolio and Bass chapter, the following kinds of issues deserve consideration. First, to what extent is the charisma component of leadership simply the residual effect on outcomes which remains after the basic task has been accomplished? In this sense, how does it differ from discretionary leadership (e.g., Hunt and Osborn 1982)? Discretionary leadership is behavior at the leader's volition that is above the behavior required for minimal performance of the leadership role. Also, is it accurate, as some writers such as Graham (chapter 5, this book) argue, to consider transactional leadership the same as management or "supervision" (in Jacobs's 1971 terms) and transformational leadership as "leadership."

Second, this chapter clearly argues that charisma is not a uniquely personal attribute of a few but rather something that everyone has to a greater or lesser degree. If one accepts this, it has extremely interesting developmental implications akin to some of those raised above for Boal and Bryson's work. In combination, the implications are quite far-reaching and suggest that charisma and transformational behaviors or relationships can be taught.

Finally, the work reported by Avolio and Bass does not emphasize contingencies. In this it differs from the Boal and Bryson and Sashkin and Fulmer chapters, where contingencies are considered to be an important aspect of charismatic leadership.

Let us now look at some issues raised by the Sashkin and Fulmer chapter. First, as both Sashkin and Fulmer as well as Riley indicate—and this is worth repeating—the meaning of leader behaviors comes from the subordinates and not from the behavior per se. In other words, meaning adheres to the context of the behavior and not to the simple behavior itself. It is this that creates the major problem in measuring leader behavior and in understanding its meaning and implications for developing a theory of leadership. It is here that an interpretist orientation can provide much insight.

Second, what constitutes leadership may be a function of the particular culture in which it is embedded. To the extent that this is true the conception of, for example, good and bad leaders may be culture specific. If this notion is extended to organizational cultures (an important aspect of Sashkin and Fulmer's chapter), what are the implications for developing leadership theory?

In closing it may be helpful to focus on an issue that cuts across all the arguments about charisma in this part of the book: does charismatic behavior lead to superior outcomes or do subordinates where such superior outcomes exist attribute charismatic or transformation behaviors to the leader after the fact?

2
Charismatic Leadership: A Phenomenological and Structural Approach

Kimberly B. Boal
John M. Bryson

"Some men see things as they are and say, why? I dream things that
never were and say, why not?"
— Robert F. Kennedy as quoted by Ted Kennedy in Ted's eulogy for
Robert[1]

"There are no great men. There are only great challenges which ordinary men are forced by circumstances to meet."
— Attributed to Admiral W.F. "Bull" Halsey, U.S.N.[2]

L eadership has been one of the most researched topics in management,
yet the research results have also been among the most disappointing.
Some researchers, in fact, have gone so far as to suggest that the concept of leadership has outlived its usefulness (Miner 1975). Others argue that
leadership has become a dumping ground for unexplained variance (Pfeffer
1977), or a "romantic" illusion that allows us to believe someone is in charge
when in fact no one is (Meindl, Ehrlich, and Dukerich 1985).

Part of the difficulty lies in the controversy surrounding the appropriate
definitions, measurements, units of analysis, and methods for studying leadership. Yet, in all the confusion, most people agree that some people appear
to make a big difference in the unfolding of events—so big that they are
referred to as *charismatic* leaders. Weber (1947) suggested that these leaders
have a gift of exceptional or even supernatural qualities—a "charisma"—
that helps them lift ordinary people to extraordinary heights. We would agree
such leaders do exist, and describe them as *visionary* charismatic leaders. We
argue, however, that there is another, *crisis-produced,* form of leadership in
which it is extraordinary *circumstances* and *not* extraordinary individuals
that create charismatic effects. The opening quotes capture the difference
between these two types of leadership.

We would like to thank in particular Newman Peery, Gary Yukl, and an anonymous reviewer
for their comments.

Although we believe that the starting points for these two types of charismatic leaders differ, we also believe there is a common thread. The common thread is our belief that the essential function of charismatic leadership is to help create a new or different world that is *phenomenologically valid* (Brickman 1978)—that is, "real"—to the followers. Conditions existing in the larger organizational environment and within the psychological profiles of the followers help to differentiate the two forms of charisma.

The remainder of the chapter is divided into four sections. Phenomenological validity—an individual level concept—is discussed in the first section, including its two aspects, intrinsic and extrinsic validity. The group analog of phenomenological validity—consensually validated interpretive schemes—also is discussed in the first section, along with its two aspects, co-orientation and system effectiveness. The second section focuses on the difference between visionary and crisis-produced charismatic leadership. The two forms of leadership may be distinguished based on their differing starting points and effects on the phenomenological world of the followers. A model of charismatic leadership is proposed in the third section. Particular attention is given in the model to follower characteristics and situational (i.e., task and environmental) variables that are hypothesized to affect phenomenological validity.

Phenomenological Validity

House (1977) suggests that charismatic leadership should be defined in terms of its effects. In other words, *charismatic leaders are those who have "charismatic effects" on their followers to an unusually high degree.* Based on a review of the literature, House suggests the following effects of charismatics as a starting point for development of a more parsimonious scale or set of scales: follower trust in the correctness of the leader's beliefs, similarity of followers' beliefs to those of the leader, unquestioning acceptance of the leader, affection for the leader, willing obedience to the leader, identification with and emulation of the leader, emotional involvement of the follower in the mission, heightened goals of the follower, and the feeling on the part of followers that they will be able to accomplish or contribute to the accomplishment of the mission. What is interesting about these effects is that charismatics appear to be intimately and unusually involved in the creation of a new or different "world"—or interpretive scheme(s)—for their followers that is cognitively, emotionally, behaviorally, and consequentially "real" for them. In other words, charismatic leaders appear to play a crucial role in helping create a phenomenologically valid (real) world for their followers that is new or different from their previous world. This world, the actor's *Lebenswelt,* consists of all the sensory, affective, and cognitive events subjectively experienced by the actor. What we argue is that charismatic leaders help bring order, meaning, purpose, and consequence to these events, and are viewed by their followers as playing a central, "causal" role in the creation of this order, meaning, purpose, and consequence.

Phenomenological validity is concerned with the conditions under which people decide a situation is real.[3] Brickman argues that for a person to decide that a situation is real two correspondences must occur. First, there must be an *internal* correspondence between a person's feelings (we would argue cognitions as well) and their behavior. "This means that a person's behavior expresses feelings that are both substantial and appropriate to the behavior" (Brickman 1978, 11). If this correspondence is high, then the linkage may be called *intrinsically valid.*[4] Second, there must be an external correspondence between a person's behavior and the consequences of that behavior. "This means that a person's behavior elicits responses that are both substantial and appropriate to the behavior" (Brickman 1978, 11). If the correspondence is high, then the linkage is *extrinsically valid.* Situations must be both intrinsically and extrinsically valid for them to be phenomenologically valid for the actors in them.

What happens when one of the correspondences is weak or nonexistent? Table 2–1 outlines four situations based on different possible combinations of internal and external correspondence. As already noted, *real* situations are those in which actions express cognitions and feelings that are both substantial and appropriate to the behavior, *and* the actions elicit responses that are both substantial and appropriate to the actions. In situations where actions elicit consequences, but the actions do not express a person's cognitions and feelings, we have *alienation,* as when a person is "just doing their job." Alienated people, in other words, are those who "just put in time," but whose "hearts are not in the job." In situations where people act based on their feelings, but where the consequences are not substantial—as in the game of Monopoly—we have *fantasy.* We also have fantasy when people avoid doing or saying what they might wish to because they fear the consequences or because the consequences seem impossible to achieve. Walter Mitty, in other words, lived in an intrinsically valid, but extrinsically invalid, fantasy world. Finally, situations in which there is neither internal nor external correspondence involve *role plays,* where people "go through the motions" without affect, reward, or punishment. Of course, effective *educational* role plays strive to create a world that is at least for a time phenomenologically valid for the players. What we have in mind here are not educational role plays, but people who in "real life" play a role with no corresponding affect or effect— people surely well-suited to undergo psychotherapy!

Charismatic leaders appear to have the effect of helping create—at least for a time—unusually powerful degrees of correspondence between a person's cognitions, feelings, behavior, and the consequences of that behavior.

Table 2–1
Phenomenological Validity: Elements of Internal and External
Correspondence

		Internal Correspondence	
		Actions express substantial and appropriate perceptions and feelings.	
		Yes	No
	Yes	1. Real[a]	2. Unreal
		Ordinary interaction	Alienation
External Correspondence			
Actions elicit substantial and appropriate consequences.			
	No	3. Unreal	4. Unreal
		Fantasy	Role play

Source: Adapted from Brickman, P. (1978). Is it real? In J.H. Harvey, W. Ickes, and R.F. Kidd (eds.) *New directions in attribution research* (13). Hillsdale, N.J.: Erlbaum Associates.
[a]Phenomenologically valid situation.

Charismatic leaders, in other words, either help create powerful correspondences where they did not exist before, or else help heighten correspondences where they previously existed in weak form.

Of course there are dangers when either internal or external correspondence becomes very high—to say nothing of the risks when both are high (Brickman 1978, 15):

> If internal correspondence is perfect, actions are unambiguous indicators of feelings and can never be excused. If external correspondence is perfect, actions have irredeemable consequences and [one] can never afford a mistake.

Situations of very high internal and external correspondence thus would appear to be inherently unstable. They would appear to require either that those who cannot handle the high correspondences leave, or else that psychological and structural supports be established to maintain the correspondences in the face of threats to their disestablishment.

Although intrinsic and extrinsic validity are *within-subject* constructs, we believe there is a *between-subjects* analog. We suggest that group behavior can reflect a common *co-orientation* (Newcomb 1953) that is the group analog of intrinsic validity. In this situation, we would argue that the behavior of group members, both individually and collectively, reflects shared interpretative schemes, values, and understanding of the appropriate theories of action (Argyris and Schon 1978).[5] But more than this, not only do individuals share this common belief system, they are *aware* each other shares it (cf., Scheff 1967).

The between-subjects analog of extrinsic validity is *system effectiveness.* Effective systems would be ones where the group's behavior elicits intended consequences. When both co-orientation and system effectiveness are high, we would have a condition of *consensually validated interpretive schemes,* the collective analog of phenomenological validity.

Table 2–2 outlines four situations based on different possible combinations of co-orientation and system effectiveness. In cell 1, the group or organization is co-oriented and is effective in bringing about intended consequences. A successful family-owned business or a company such as Celestial Seasonings might be an example. In cell 2, where actions elicit consequences but do not reflect shared values or understanding, we have alienation. Such a situation would be classified as working, but alienated. The situation in a company prior to a strike might be an example. Cell 3 represents a situation where there is high value congruence and shared understanding, but the system is failing. To the extent the group clings to its beliefs despite their ineffectiveness, it is deluded. A failing family business might be an example at the organization level. Finally, in cell 4 there are situations where there are neither shared interpretive schemes, values, and theories of action nor system effectiveness; anomie or chaos is a likely result.

Table 2–2
Consensually Validated Interpretive Schemes: Elements of Co-Orientation and System Effectiveness

		Co-Orientation	
		Group actions (both individually and collectively) reflect shared interpretive schemes, values, and theories of action.	
		Yes	No
System Effectiveness Group actions elicit intended consequences.	Yes	1. Consensually validated interpretative schemes	2. Working, but alienated
	No	3. Delusion	4. Anomie or chaos

Source: Adapted from Brickman, P. (1978). Is it real? In J.H. Harvey, W. Ickes, and R.F. Kidd (eds.) *New directions in attribution research* (13). Hillsdale, N.J.: Erlbaum Associates.

Visionary and Crisis-Produced
Charismatic Leadership

We have argued that there are two types of charismatic leaders—visionary and crisis-produced—and the common thread to both is that each tries to create a new or different world that is phenomenologically valid for his or her followers. In this section, however, we would like to clarify the differences between the two types of charismatic leadership. We argue that the two types of leaders start by emphasizing different aspects of phenomenological validity.

We believe that *visionary* charismatic leaders are those who produce charismatic effects primarily through helping to heighten *internal correspondence* for individual followers or *co-orientation* within a group of followers. As Berlew (1974, 269) argues, "The first requirement for . . . charismatic leadership is a common or shared vision of what the future *could be.*" Thus visionary charismatics link individuals' needs to important values, purposes, or meanings through articulation of a vision and goals—inspiring interpretative schemes—and also through pointing out how individuals' behavior can contribute to fulfillment of those values, purposes, or meanings. We think that visionary charismatic effects are most likely to develop in cells 2 and 4 of tables 2–1 and 2–2—the cells characterized by the absence of internal correspondence and co-orientation.

We believe, however, that visionary charismatics do more than simply provide new schemata, values, or theories of action. The organizational change literature suggests that in addition: (1) potential followers need to be dissatisfied with the current situation (March and Simon 1958), perhaps through the unselling of old "truths" (Wildavsky 1972); (2) the new vision must provide for a stronger linkage between values, attitudes, and behaviors; and (3) followers must have a chance to successfully practice part(s) of the vision before they will attribute charisma to the leader (Argyris and Schon 1978).

Crisis-produced charismatic leaders create charismatic effects primarily through helping to heighten *external correspondence* for individual followers and *system effectiveness* for groups of followers. Crises exist when a system is required or expected to handle a situation for which existing resources, procedures, policies, structures or mechanisms, and so forth, are inadequate (Bryson 1981). In other words, crises sever the linkage between behavior and the consequences of that behavior—the external correspondence necessary to add "reality" to actions. Continued severance of this linkage would result in a condition of "learned helplessness" (Seligman 1975). Crisis-produced charismatic leaders handle a crisis situation through detailing the actions to be taken and the expected consequences of those actions.

Crises enable leaders to do so in at least two ways. First, as Korten (1968) has pointed out, under conditions of stress and ambiguity, group members give power to individuals who promise to remove the ambiguity and stress. Thus, crises empower a leader to act in ways that would otherwise be constrained, and allow the leader to base his or her own behavior on his or her own ideologies and values. Charismatic effects, however, will be short-lived in crisis situations unless the crisis is favorably resolved from the standpoint of the followers. Furthermore, charismatic attributions will be short-term unless the leader remains in a prime focal position and can relate to handling of the crisis to a higher purpose that has intrinsic validity for the actors. Focal position allows the leader to continually influence the feelings and behaviors of followers (Roberts 1985). As Beyer (1981, 187) points out, "People behave in accordance . . . with the ideologies and values of powerful superiors." Tapping higher purposes will improve the favorable perceptions of the leader by the followers, arouse follower needs, and improve follower acceptance of challenging goals. Crisis-produced charismatics, in other words, can be expected not to stop with efforts to reestablish external validity, but also can be expected to work for the establishment of the psychological supports necessary to maintain high degrees of internal correspondence in their followers as well. For as Kaufman (1960, 222–23) points out, "all influences on . . . behavior are filtered through a screen of individual values, concepts, and images. . . . To the extent the leaders of an organization can manipulate the screen, they can increase the receptivity of personnel to organization directives and decrease their receptivity to outside influences."

A second way that crises help leaders detail new actions and consequences is by promoting unlearning and the search for new actions by followers (Hedberg 1981). Hewitt and Hall (1973, 370) note that in disorderly situations, "people evoke quasitheories that first postulate a cure, which is followed by an analysis of the cause and effect that supports the cure." This suggests, as Hedberg (1981, 196) states, "If ambiguity is high, solutions are chosen before the value and ideological commitments they represent become clear." Thus crisis-produced charismatic leaders differ from visionary charismatic leaders in one important respect. Crisis leaders start with action and *then* move to interpretative schemes, values, or theories of action, to support or justify the action. Visionaries, on the other hand, start with "theory" and move to action.

We believe, in other words, that crisis-produced charismatic effects are most likely to be produced in cells 3 and 4 of tables 2–1 and 2–2—the cells characterized by the absence of external correspondence and system failure. Cell 3 is thus the sole province of the crisis-produced charismatic, whereas cell 2 is the sole province of the visionary charismatic. *Either* type of charismatic, on the other hand, might be expected to emerge in cell 4; whereas *neither* might be expected to emerge in cell 1, as conditions favoring the production of charismatic effects would not exist (although a leader who had helped move a situation from cells 2, 3, or 4 to cell 1 might be able to maintain charismatic effects in cell 1).

A Model of Charismatic Leadership

In this section we propose a model of charismatic leadership that represents a synthesis of House's (1977) work, Brickman's (1978) development of the concept of phenomenological validity, Gidden's (1979) attempt to link phenomenological and structural approaches, and our own efforts to adapt these writers' efforts to the question of how charismatic leadership develops in organizational settings. The model is summarized in figure 2–1. Several propositions will be presented in this section that summarize the relationships that constitute the model. Due to a lack of prior theory and empirical research, only a few speculative propositions primarily at the individual level of analysis will be offered.

The model consists of six basic components. The first component consists of leader characteristics and behaviors and is based on House (1977). The second component is the perceptions and feelings of the followers. The third component is the behavior of the followers, and the fourth component is the consequences of the behavior of the followers. The fifth and sixth components of the model are follower characteristics and task and environmental variables that are hypothesized to affect internal and external correspondence.

At this point we must address directly the question of whether phenomenological and structural approaches are compatible. We argue that they are—that they represent two sides of the same coin of social life (cf., Sanders 1982). Giddens (1979) provides persuasive support for this position. The key to his argument is his concept of *structuration,* based on what he asserts to be the three fundamental elements of social life, and three necessary levels of analysis. He argues that all social life involves three essential elements: the creation and communication of meaning (in this case between leader and followers), the exercise of power (in this case the power of a charismatic leader to get followers to do what they otherwise would not), and the evaluation of conduct as measured against normative standards (in this case the sanctioning and reinforcement of leader and follower behavior based on normative criteria). He goes on to differentiate three levels of analysis. He argues that interaction (the primary province of phenomenologists, ethnomethodologists, and hermeneutic specialists) is linked to structure (the primary province of structuralists and logical positivists) through the concept of modality. The modality level consists of all the modes, media, or methods through which structure is drawn upon to create interactions, and through which structure is recreated by those interactions.

Acceptance of Giddens's approach allows one to do three things: (1) bracket structure and focus on patterned regularities in interaction as the phenomenologists do, (2) bracket interaction and focus on structure—seen as impersonal properties of social systems—as the structuralists do, or (3) attend to interaction, modalities, and structure in a structurational analysis. The model presented in figure 2–1 may appear to bracket interaction and present a structural and positivist approach, but the model clearly invites—even requires—phenomenologically based understanding and methods to apply it in any given setting. That is, *our model provokes attention as much to patterned regularities in interaction as it does to impersonal properties of social systems.* Thus we argue that our model represents a step toward the reconciliation of phenomenological and structural approaches.[6]

Now we return to the model. We have argued that the primary impact of charismatic leadership is through facilitation of the creation of a new or different world that is phenomenologically valid to the follower. We propose that the most direct impact of the visionary charismatic's characteristics and behaviors is on the perceptions and feelings of the follower—their interpretative schemes and what flows from them purposefully, emotionally, and motivationally. In this line of reasoning affect is viewed as an antecedent to behavior. We argue further that the most direct impact of the crisis-produced charismatic's characteristics and behaviors is on the follower's behaviors and the consequences of those behaviors. In this line of reasoning, behavior is an antecedent to affect (Staw 1980).[7]

Intrinsic and extrinsic validity, however, are experienced whenever perceptions and feelings are congruent with behavior and behavior is congruent with consequences. Changes in follower perceptions, feelings, or behavior, or in the consequences of that behavior therefore could establish the necessary conditions for phenomenological validity to be experienced. The linkages between perceptions and feelings and behaviors, and behaviors and consequences, thus should be viewed as reciprocal or interactive in terms of creating conditions for internal and external correspondence.

In addition to the direct impact of leader behavior on the feelings of followers, we believe that leaders may also have an indirect impact on phenomenological validity through fostering conditions that enhance internal and external correspondence. This impact could occur when leaders change task or environmental variables that are hypothesized to affect internal and external correspondence, such as task design, reward systems, and organizational structure (Kerr and Slocum 1981, 122).

The rest of this section consists of propositions based on the model. The propositions are summarized in table 2–3.

Proposition 1 is true by definition if our model is valid. House (1977) argues that most writers on charisma—including himself—believe it must be based on the articulation of an ideological goal. We do not fully agree,

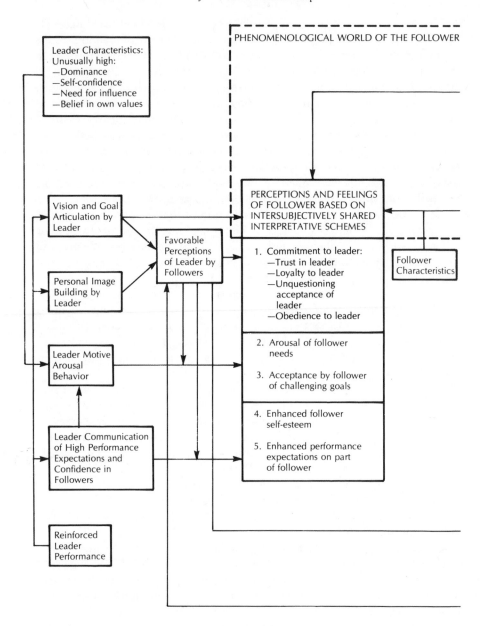

Source: Based in part on House (1977) and Brickman (1978).

Figure 2–1. A Model of Charismatic Leadership in Organizations

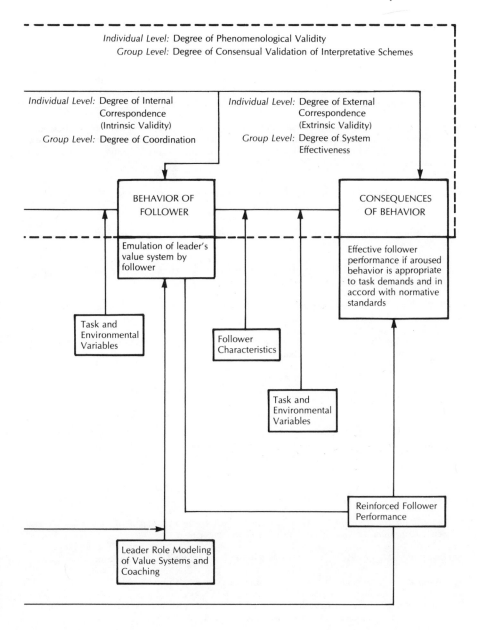

Table 2–3
Propositions on Charismatic Leadership

Proposition 1. There must be a high degree of internal correspondence between the perceptions and feelings of the follower and the behavior of the follower, and a high degree of external correspondence between the behavior of the follower and the consequences of that behavior for the "charismatic situation" to be real to the follower and for charismatic effects to be produced.

Proposition 2. For long-lasting charismatic effects to be produced, effective follower and leader performance (that is, behavior appropriate to task demands and in accord with normative standards) must be reinforced; successful performance is probably especially important in the case of maintaining crisis-produced effects.

Follower characteristics and situational task or environmental variables that affect intrinsic validity (that is, the correspondence between internal states and behavior)

Proposition 3. Individuals with high job involvement will experience their jobs as more intrinsically valid.

Proposition 4. Individuals who are high in organizational commitment, especially in successfully handled crises, will experience their roles as more intrinsically valid.

Proposition 5. Long-linked technologies and tasks low in job scope, that is, variety, autonomy, identity, significance, and feedback, will decrease internal correspondence.

Proposition 6. Individuals with strong growth need strength will experience tasks high in job scope as more intrinsically valid than individuals with low growth need strength.

Proposition 7. Mediating technologies with pooled interdependence and intensive technologies with reciprocal interdependence will enhance internal correspondence.

Proposition 8. Bureaucratic structure decreases intrinsic validity.

Follower characteristics and situational task or environmental variables that affect extrinsic validity (that is, the correspondence between behavior and consequences)

Proposition 9. Individuals high in job involvement will experience their jobs as more extrinsically valid.

Proposition 10. Individuals early in their role involvement will emphasize external correspondence more than individuals late in their role involvement.

Proposition 11. Tasks low in job scope will diminish external correspondence.

Proposition 12. Bureaucratic structures enhance extrinsic validity.

Proposition 13. Individuals with an internal locus of control will experience greater intrinsic validity than individuals with an external locus of control.

Proposition 14. Individuals characterized by a condition of learned helplessness will experience reduced extrinsic validity when compared with those not so characterized.

Proposition 15. When task performance is a function of group cohesiveness, the greater the group cohesiveness, the greater the external correspondence for members of the group.

because we do not think it is necessary in crisis situations, and because the concept of ideology is too restrictive unless we broaden it to include cognitions, values, and need structures (e.g., Hall 1976, Kohlberg 1969, and Rokeach 1973).

We do believe, however, that individuals must see their behavior in terms of the fulfillment of some underlying purpose, meaning, or value that transcends the particulars of the moment if they are to experience the leader as charismatic (cf., Frankl 1959). If individuals are to see their behavior as meaningful and consequential, internal and external correspondence must be established, thus allowing the person to experience his or her own behavior as "reality based."

A long tradition of theorizing and research in motivation theory suggests the importance of linking behavior to its consequences. Thorndike's "law of effect" is an example from reinforcement theory and instrumentality perceptions are an example from expectancy theory (Porter and Lawler 1968). Thus we believe, for long-lasting charismatic effects to be produced effective follower and leader performance (i.e., behavior appropriate to task demands and in accord with normative standards) must be reinforced (proposition 2). This is especially important, we think, with respect to crisis-induced charismatic leadership.

The leader in a crisis who produces no effect or negative effects will not command support over any length of time. Note also that proposition 2 does not preclude followers from vicariously experiencing the leader's and others' behavior as well as their own. Thus, extrinsic validity is experienced not only as a result of the actor's own behavior but through the behavior of others as well.

The remaining propositions focus on factors that we believe influence the creation of a charismatic Lebenswelt. In some cases, the factors are viewed as residing within the follower in the sense that they represent individual differences. In other cases, the factors arise in the situation and are not dependent on which actor is involved. It is our contention that the leader can enhance the likelihood of producing charismatic effects either by changing the task or environmental variables in which behavior is embedded or by selecting individuals who are more likely to prefer a particular environment.

In suggesting factors that influence the experience of intrinsic and extrinsic validity, one would normally draw upon existing theory and research. Unfortunately, there is a paucity of both. We thus must rely on our intuition and hunches derived from our knowledge of other areas. We also admit that the suggested moderating variables are not necessarily inclusive or even necessarily likely to turn out to be the most important.

Propositions 3 to 8 primarily concern factors that influence whether cognitions and feelings and behaviors will be high on *internal* correspondence, and thus be experienced by the followers as intrinsically valid. Propositions 9 to 15, on the other hand, concern factors that are primarily thought to affect *external* correspondence.

Although job involvement and organizational commitment may be viewed as effects of charismatic leadership, we argue that they also may be viewed as preexisting conditions characterizing a group of subordinates who acquire a new leader. Individuals may be viewed as high on job involvement if at least one of three conditions exist.

First, they view their own performance as central to their self-esteem. Second, they view work as a central life interest. And third, they actively participate in and influence the way things are done (Saleh and Hosek 1976). The first two dimensions of job involvement emphasize the linkage between attitudes and behaviors (i.e., internal correspondence), whereas the third dimension emphasizes the link between behavior and its consequences (propositions 3 and 10). We think that job involvement, as active participation, would be especially important for a visionary leader. This is so because active participation may serve to bind a follower to a course of action, and change the follower's perceptions and attitudes to be in accordance with the vision put forth by the leader (cf., Staw 1980).

Organizational commitment, when conceptualized as an attitude, also is generally characterized by three factors: (1) a strong belief in and acceptance of the organization's goals and values, (2) a willingness to exert considerable effort on behalf of the organization, and (3) a strong desire to maintain membership in the organization (Mowday, Porter, and Steers 1982). All of these facets emphasize the linkage between attitudes and behavior.

We believe that organizational commitment, as an individual difference, will have special significance in times of crisis. A natural tendency is to withdraw when faced with a crisis. Thus, a leader in a crisis situation might not have the necessary support inside the organization to deal successfully with the crisis. Leaders who have subordinates high in organizational commitment, however, would have greater potential to mobilize the necessary people and resources to deal successfully with the crisis than would leaders with followers who are low in commitment. Crises provide three opportunities. First, crises make the subordinates more receptive to leader influences. Second, a crisis allows subordinates to demonstrate their commitment, which will be self-reinforcing. And third, if the crisis is handled successfully, additional external reinforcement will be provided. All will lead to enhanced internal correspondence (proposition 4).

Long-linked technologies (Thompson 1967) with serial interdependence and low job scope, that is, low degrees of task autonomy, variety, identity, significance, and feedback (Hackman and Lawler 1971, Hackman and Oldham 1976), do not allow actors to fully utilize valued skills and abilities. Research suggests that workers on these kinds of jobs experience low job satisfaction (cf., Pierce and Dunham 1976). Thus, we suggest that long-linked technologies and jobs low in task scope decrease internal correspondence (proposition 5).

Task significance for the follower (a component of job scope) can be especially important when visionary charismatic leadership is involved. We would argue that visionary charismatics would help followers see their jobs as more meaningful—and therefore more intrinsically valid—by linking their jobs to higher purposes. These effects would be especially strong for individuals with high growth need strength (Hackman and Oldham 1976, Pierce and Dunham 1976) (proposition 6).

In addition, Blauner's (1964) research suggests that tasks low in job scope result in a sense of powerlessness, thus diminishing external correspondence as well (proposition 11). On the other hand, mediating and intensive technologies, which emphasize person, as opposed to task specialization (Thompson 1961), and which tend to be larger in job scope (Rousseau 1977), would increase internal correspondence (proposition 7).

We assume that most actors prefer states that allow control and discretion (cf., Brehm 1966, White 1959). Further, we assume that the greater the freedom an actor has, the more likely behaviors will reflect internal states and thus be experienced as intrinsically valid. Organizational factors that we believe would reduce control and discretion are high standardization, formalization, and centralization. These are characteristics commonly associated with bureaucratic organizations (Pugh, et al. 1969). Under these conditions, we think the message of the visionary may be lost. At the same time, however, we recognize that the ideas that are acted upon may be more effectively implemented (e.g., Zaltman and Duncan 1977, Bradley 1984), thus creating greater extrinsic validity (propositions 8 and 12).

Propositions 9 to 15 concern factors that are thought to primarily affect *external* correspondence. For example, Rotter (1966) suggests that individuals develop generalized expectancies regarding the linkage between their behavior and the outcomes they experience in life. Individuals who believe they control their own fate are said to have an internal locus of control. Those who believe, on the other hand, that external factors (e.g., luck, other people) are the primary determinants of their fate are said to have an external locus of control. Thus, individuals with an internal locus of control would be more likely to experience their behavior as extrinsically valid than would individuals with an external locus of control (proposition 13).

In a similar vein, Seligman (1975) has found that when individuals are unable to affect consequences they display decreased motivation, impaired learning, and increased emotionality. He refers to this state as "learned helplessness." Thus, individuals who are characterized by a state of learned helplessness would not experience external correspondence (proposition 14).

These two traits or states, external locus of control and learned helplessness, are important with respect to both visionary and crisis-produced charismatic leadership. Persons characterized by either state would see visionary causes as utopian and without substance. In the case of a crisis, such persons would see the situation as impossible and without hope. Such persons thus would be unlikely to respond to either type of charismatic leadership. However, to the extent they did, we would postulate that a shift in locus of control, from external to internal, would occur.

Research suggests that when cohesiveness is relevant for group performance (e.g., when intensive technologies are involved), cohesive groups are more effective in achieving their goals than are noncohesive groups (Seashore 1954, Stogdill 1972). Thus, when cohesiveness is relevant to performance, individuals who are members of cohesive groups are more likely to experience high external correspondence (proposition 15). Both visionary and crisis-produced charismatics are likely to echo messages of solidarity (i.e., the need for cohesiveness). The visionary does it to build the critical mass necessary for mobilization, whereas the crisis-produced charismatic does it to maintain membership and enhance performance.

Conclusions

We have argued that the primary function or impact of charismatic leadership is to help create a new or different world—or interpretive scheme and what flows from it purposefully, emotionally, motivationally, and consequentially—that is phenomenologically valid for the follower.

We have gone on to present a model of charismatic leadership in organizations. Although we do not present any data based on a direct test of our model, we do think that the propositions are testable and consistent with existing empirical findings. Further, an implication of our model is that charismatic effects may not be limited to a few who are endowed with exceptional gifts or supernatural qualities. Rather, our model implies that the potential for charismatic effects may be widespread. For example, leaders who successfully handle minor crises or engage in such seemingly mundane activities as job redesign may come to be seen as charismatic.

We have also argued that our efforts represent a step toward reconciliation of phenomenological and structural approaches to charismatic leadership. In other words, we feel our model invites an *understanding* of meaning, reasons, motivations, and intentions as much as it seeks *explanatory* connections between formal structural arrangements and behavior. A complete marriage between these nominally opposed approaches requires complementary methodologies, such as the use of interviews, case histories and participant observation in concert with more formal structural analyses. But consummating such a marriage also requires further theoretical development. In particular, more attention should be given to the modes, media, and methods through which structure is drawn upon to create charismatic interaction, and through which those structures are created and recreated by those actions. We feel that our model represents a useful first step in the direction of such a reconciliation and theoretical advance.

Notes

1. Ted Kennedy's eulogy for his brother will be found in *The New York Times,* 9 June 1968, p. 53.

2. The Halsey quote is from Beirne Lay, Jr., and Frank D. Gilroy, *The Gallant Years,* a United Artists movie, 1959.

3. The scholarly tradition of research in phenomenology is quite long, and has been influenced by symbolic interactionism (Blumer 1969) and ethnomethodology (Garfinkel 1967), as well as seminal works within phenomenology itself (Schutz 1967). These historical-hermeneutic (Habermas 1971, 309–10) approaches have aimed at understanding meaning, reasons, motivations, and intentions. Good reviews of the application of these approaches to organizational studies may be found in Burrell and Morgan (1979) and Astley and Van de Ven (1983); see also Sanders (1982).

Obviously we are not able to draw upon the full richness of the phenomenological tradition in a chapter as short as this. Of necessity we have been forced to limit ourselves. We have chosen in particular to utilize two aspects of the phenomenological tradition. The first is the concept of *interpretive schemes.* These are abstract, cognitive frameworks of organized experiences which establish relations among specific events and entities. They serve as an initial frame of reference for perception and action (Schutz 1967, Jermier 1985). The second is the concept of *phenomenological validity.*

4. Intrinsic and extrinsic validity, as used here, are not to be confused with other concepts of validity, for example, internal, external, construct, and statistical conclusion validity, as used from a positivistic science point of view. See Cook and Campbell (1976), among others, for a discussion of these.

5. "Theories of action . . . are for organizations what cognitive structures are for individuals" (Hedberg 1981, 7).

6. An anonymous reviewer suggested that there is an inherent contradiction between a phenomenological interpretation of social reality which seeks a wholistic understanding and the epistemological assumptions of positivistic science. Thus, our attempt at understanding charismatic leadership by examining component parts or variables is at odds with a phenomenological interpretation. We do not, however, see these positions as mutually exclusive but rather as complementary. To begin with, both approaches are concerned with phenomenal experiences, both are empirical, and both bracket experience to focus attention. Further, we assume that "different" types of individuals can experience "similar" situations similarly, and that "similar" types of individuals can experience "different" situations as similar as well. Thus, we believe that common task or environmental structures promote common experiences. At the same time we recognize the influence of individual differences. Thus, the assumptions of positivistic science help us "explain" the pattern of regularities in behavior across

individuals and situations, whereas phenomenological strategies aid in "understanding" the meaning of those regularities to the individuals involved.

A fully *structurational* approach to charismatic leadership awaits more attention to the modes, media, or methods through which action is linked to structure and vice versa in charismatic situations.

7. Recent arguments between Zajonc (1984) and Lazarus (1984) over the primacy of affect or cognition raise the issue of the independence and causal connection between affect and behavior. For us, this is not an issue. We recognize, as does our model, that the leader may have a direct or indirect impact on either perceptions or affect or behavior. Also, we agree that action produces feeling and vice versa. For us, the key issue is whether the actor's Lebenswelt is internally consistent and meaningful to the actor.

3
Transformational Leadership, Charisma, and Beyond

Bruce J. Avolio
Bernard M. Bass

> "Ah, but a man's reach should exceed his grasp."
> —Robert Browning

A young senior executive found himself moving to take over a new division. Tradition called for a lengthy inaugural address. He redrafted his speech from 1½ hours to 7 minutes! "I prophesize . . . I expect . . . You can expect . . . and I believe . . ." Immediately upon completion of his speech his group members stood up and cheered.

Much of the leadership research since World War II has concentrated on how to maintain or achieve results as expected or contracted between the leader and the subordinate. Yet, there are many examples of leadership that clearly do not conform to the ever popular exchange models of leadership. The young executive above is one such example, but clearly each and every one of us has experienced leadership that cannot be neatly classified as a simple transaction between leader and follower. Our purpose in this chapter, therefore, is to build upon existing models of leadership which have focused on readily observable, short-term leader-follower relations in order to present a new paradigm of leadership, and preliminary evidence, to account for variance in subordinate effort and performance that goes beyond the boundaries or predictions of current leadership theories. We intend to build upon the current body of research that addresses the transactional processes of leadership by examining transformational leadership as defined by Burns (1978) and Bass (1985). Armed with a model that attempts to explain how leaders draw the attention of their subordinates to an idealized goal and inspire them to reach beyond their grasp to achieve that goal, we hope to account for the actions of leaders that result in higher order changes in subordinates.

In the remaining sections we attempt to show how Bass's (1985) paradigm of leadership builds on previous models of leadership. We will also review preliminary work that led to the model's current status, discuss research completed to date that has addressed propositions in the model, and suggest the many avenues and opportunities we foresee for leadership research in this area. Some detail will have to be omitted due to space limitations. More information on the model itself can be found in Bass (1985).

Building the Base: Transactional Leadership

Theory and research has concentrated on leadership as an exchange process in which the subordinate is rewarded for enacting a role to accomplish agreed-upon objectives (e.g., Bass 1960, Hollander 1978). The leader clarifies for the subordinate what will facilitate the successful attainment of those objectives. Simply put, transactional leadership is contingent reinforcement. Subordinates are the actors who accept the leader's promises of reward or avoidance of punishment for enacting agreed-upon roles. Contingent avoidance reinforcement may be seen in management-by-exception. The leader only intervenes when standards are not being met by the subordinate. Transactional leadership is dependent upon the subordinate's perception that the leader can reinforce the subordinate for successful completion of the "contract."

As shown in figure 3–1, transactional leaders help subordinates recognize what the role and task requirements are to reach a desired outcome. The transactional leader helps clarify those requirements for subordinates, resulting in increased confidence that a certain level of effort will result in desired performance. By recognizing the needs of subordinates, and clarifying how those needs can be met, the subordinate's motivational level should be enhanced. This form of leadership is also essentially rooted in path-goal theory (Evans 1974, Graen and Cashman 1975, House and Mitchell 1974). Subordinates learn what they must do to gain rewards and to avoid punishments through an exchange process with their superior. In the current model of leadership we propose that there are two transactional factors of relevance to a leader's exchange with a subordinate: contingent reward and management-by-exception. These factors were empirically derived by Bass (1985) and are addressed in greater detail in the discussion of our leadership survey.

There is support in the literature concerning the effectiveness of leadership-by-contingent reinforcement (e.g., Hunt and Schuler 1976; Luthans and Kreitner 1975; Oldham 1976; Podsakoff, Todor, and Skov 1982; Reitz 1971; Sims 1977; Spector and Suttell 1975). Using contingent reinforcement, leaders have been shown to increase subordinate performance and job satisfaction, and to reduce job role uncertainty. Nevertheless, the transactional leadership approach only captures a portion of the leader-subordinate relationship. Often, its effectiveness is marginal. It can also be counterproductive.

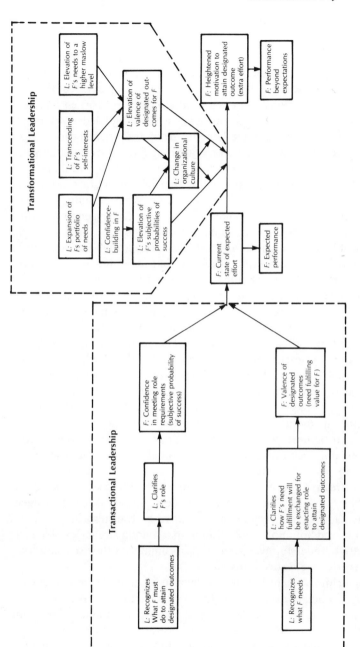

Note: L = leader; F = follower.

Figure 3–1. Transforming Leadership: Add-On Effect

Problems with Transactional Leadership

Although potentially useful, transactional leadership appears underutilized. In an interview study of a representative national sample of 845 U.S. workers, Yankelovich and Immerwahr (1983), found that only 22 percent of the participants saw a direct relationship between how hard they worked and how much they were paid. Again, 73 percent felt that working harder would not result in their receiving any greater benefits from the organization. Most important, 61 percent would prefer to see a closer link established between pay and performance. Time pressures, poor performance appraisal systems, doubts about the fairness of the reward system in the organization, constraints outside a manager's control, or lack of managerial training may partially account for the failure to make more use of contingent rewarding despite its popularity with organizational psychologists.

Another problem concerns the reward. Reward is often in the form of positive feedback from the superior, feedback that may also be counterproductive. What managers view as being valued feedback for the subordinate is not always perceived by the subordinates as being relevant and may be weighted less than feedback received from the job or coworkers (Greller 1980). As for contingent reproof, reprimand or worse, managers appear to avoid giving negative feedback to followers. They distort such feedback to subordinates to protect them from the truth (Ilgen and Knowlton 1980).

A transactional leader who views leading others solely from a contingent reinforcement perspective, may find that subordinates will circumvent a better way of doing things to maximize short-term gain to reach their goals in the most expeditious manner possible, regardless of the long-term implications. This system by itself would seem to support and reward the creative subordinate, but not necessarily the long-term goals of the organization.

Ironically, in some situations, noncontingent reinforcement has been shown to be as effective a motivator as contingent reinforcement (Podsakoff, Todor, and Skov 1982). The impact may be negative when contingent rewards by the superior are seen as manipulative by the subordinate. Bass, Valenzi, Farrow, and Solomon (1975) found that among five styles of leadership, manipulative leadership was seen by subordinates as the least satisfying and the most ineffective leadership style.

Contingent reinforcement has been shown to be an effective strategy for reducing job role uncertainty. This suggests that contingent reinforcement may have more of an effect on learning than on performance. For some groups of employees, reward contingent on performance is probably an effective extrinsic motivator for increasing effort and performance. But overall, positive and particularly aversive contingent reinforcement may fail to generate the desired higher levels of motivation or performance. Hence, contingent reinforcement must be augmented.

Adding in Transformational Leadership

How do we motivate people to do their best or to maintain peak effort? Since most of the leadership research to date has concentrated on affecting lower order changes in subordinates, a new paradigm was sought to help account for both lower and higher order changes brought about by transformational leadership. Burns (1978) conceptualized the transformational leader as one who motivates followers to work for transcendental goals instead of immediate self-interests and for achievement and self-actualization instead of safety and security. The transformational leader gains heightened effort from subordinates as a consequence of their self-reinforcement from doing the task.

To an extent, transforming leadership can be viewed as a special case of transactional style leadership with respect to exchanging effort for rewards. In the case of transformational leadership, the rewarding is internal. Each approach is linked to the achievement of some goal or objective. The approaches differ, however, with regards to the process by which the leader energizes a subordinate's effort to accomplish the goals, as well as in the type of goals set. For example, a transformational leader may communicate a mission or vision to the subordinate that is exciting and in theme alone is able to motivate the subordinate to work hard and long to achieve that mission. The vision itself suffices as a motivator of increased effort. By working towards a vision or mission, and its eventual accomplishment, subordinates may also improve their personal skills, give themselves a broader picture of the problem, or merely question their own values or attitudes which they had failed to question previously. The leader communicates a vision to the subordinate and in return the subordinate is self-rewarded for efforts to convert the vision into reality. Understanding and development which are also rewarding are enhanced in the subordinate.

Simply viewing the exchange between leader and subordinate as a lower order change ignores the effects personal qualities of leaders have on higher order changes in followers. Consider how much of the variance one could account for in the impact of Mahatma Gandhi's leadership on the Indian people by using a simple contingent reinforcement model. Clearly, the Indian people were willing to offer considerable sacrifice to make real the vision that Gandhi espoused.

It should be kept in mind, however, that transformational leadership cannot be effective if it stands alone. As Tosi (1982) correctly notes, supporting most successful charismatic/transforming leaders is their ability to effectively manage (transact with subordinates) the day-to-day mundane events that clog most leaders' agendas. Without transactional leadership skills, even the most awe-inspiring transformational leader may fail to accomplish his or her intended mission. History is strewn with visionaries and revolutionary leaders whose lack of managing skills or disciples with such skills resulted in the rapid demise of their movements. Jesus without Paul might have been lost to history as a minor Jewish rabbi about whom a transient minor sect was founded.

Measurements

Development of the transformational leadership factors was based on both quantitative and qualitative procedures. Using Burn's (1978) definition of transformational leaders, Bass (1985) surveyed senior male executives to determine those attributes that would best describe transformational and transactional leaders. Items developed from this survey as well as those gene-rated from the leadership literature were subjected to a response allocation analysis in which raters assigned each item to one of two categories of leader-ship, that is, transactional or transformational. Items that raters could reli-ably place in each category were retained and placed in a survey given to senior U.S. army officers who rated their immediate superiors in terms of how frequently they exhibited each leadership characteristic. Principal com-ponents factor analyses of the final items resulted in five primary leadership factors which accounted for approximately 90 percent of the common vari-ance. Two leadership factors, all of whose items had previously been labeled by the response allocation analysis as transactional, were contingent reward and management-by-exception. The three transformational factors, all of whose items had previously been labeled as transformational, were charis-matic leadership, individualized consideration, and intellectual stimulation. These same five factors have emerged in an independent factor analysis of 360 managers not used in the derivation sample. High scores on each of the five factors indicate the following.

Transformational Leadership

1. *Charisma.* The leader instills pride, faith, and respect, has a gift for seeing what is really important, and has a sense of mission (or vision) which is effectively articulated.

2. *Individualized consideration.* The leader delegates projects to stimulate and create learning experiences, pays personal attention to followers' needs—especially those who seem neglected—and treats each follower with respect and as an individual.

3. *Intellectual stimulation.* The leader provides ideas that result in a rethinking of old ways, and enables followers to look at problems from many angles and resolve problems that were at a standstill.

Transactional Leadership

(4) *Contingent reward.* The leader is seen as frequently telling subordinates what to do to achieve a desired reward for their efforts.

(5) *Management-by-exception.* The leader avoids giving directions if the old ways are working; the leader intervenes only if standards are not met.

The Multifactor Leadership Questionnaire (MLQ)—Form 5 (revised) is the primary instrument currently used by our research team to measure transactional and transformational leadership. For 728 respondents the following coefficient alphas, estimates of internal consistency, have been obtained for ten-item scales: charismatic leadership (.88), intellectual stimulation (.83), individualized consideration (.86), contingent reward (.78), and management-by-exception (.67). Procedures used to estimate the interrater reliabilities associated with each of the five scales have also provided very promising results. Using analyses of variance, in which each leader is rated by several subordinates (see Bass et al. 1975 and Dansereau, Alluto, and Yammarino 1985 for a more detailed description of this procedure), eta values have ranged in the high 70s and 80s for the transformational leadership factors and low 70s and 60s for the transactional factors. Even in situations where nine raters have evaluated a single leader, we found a high degree of consistency across leadership ratings. It is interesting to note that in two independent samples the highest levels of interrater agreement have been with the charismatic leadership scale.

To summarize, respondents completing the MLQ are asked to judge how often their leader displays each of seventy items of behavior or attitude, using the following scales: 4, frequently, if not always; 3, fairly often; 2, sometimes; 1, once in awhile; 0, not at all. These options bear a magnitude estimation-based ratio to each other (Bass, Cascio, and O'Connor 1974).

In the following section, we briefly examine how Bass's transformational leadership model fits in with other leadership approaches and also how it builds on House's (1977) theory of charismatic leadership.

Expanding the Boundaries

Figure 3–1 also displays how transformational leadership adds on to transactional factors previously discussed in this chapter. Although conceptually distinct, these two styles of leadership can be displayed by the same individual to varying degrees. For example, Franklin D. Roosevelt was able to transform this country with his vision of a "New Deal," but in turn, was often viewed by his closest subordinates as highly transactional, arranging political deals and encouraging competitiveness among his associates. Accordingly, we support the notion that leadership, as we have conceptualized it here, can be captured in a five-factor profile.

A One-Minute Review

The leadership work at Ohio State in the 1950s and 1960s brought forth two factors, initiation and consideration, which subsequently received the lion's share of research interest. This is true even though many other scales were developed for the Leader Behavior Description Questionnaire (e.g., LBDQ— Form XII). The two factors in one form or another can be identified in most current models of leadership behavior and/or style (i.e., Fiedler's Hi/Lo-LPC; Path-goal theory; Blake and Mouton's managerial grid; Vroom and Yetton's Decision-making/Delegation model; and Hersey and Blanchard's Situational Leadership Theory). Bass's model cuts across these two dimensions, Initiation can be transactional or transformational. So can consideration. The transformational leader may provide a new strategy or vision to structure the way to tackle a problem. The transactional leader may clarify the "right" way of doing things. Likewise, consideration for a subordinate's current needs and self-interests is likely to be transactional, whereas consideration for a subordinate's long-term personal development in alignment with organizational needs is transformational leadership.

Transformational leaders strive to make subordinates more self-confident. The leaders, themselves, are models of such self-confidence. Although clarifying the path to an objective may result in increased confidence and self-esteem, showing greater concern for the subordinate and flexibility in how the situation is structured has two additional benefits. First, it helps the subordinate to take a longer range view of his or her own needs, leading to potential elevation of those needs. Second, the leader, through acts of individualized consideration, and articulation of the "big picture," models a style of leadership that will help the subordinate as he or she takes on leadership responsibilities.

Although it is not fully represented in figure 3–1, we agree with Fiedler, Hershey, and Blanchard, and Vroom and Yetton, in particular, that the situation often can be a determinant of leader effectiveness; however, we differ on one fundamental point. We view the leader as being as dynamic in terms of having the ability to change the situation as Fiedler views the situation as being the major factor in determining how effective a leader can be. More specifically, transformational leaders do not necessarily react to environmental circumstances—they create them. Rather then trying to be a leader in the situation, as given, John F. Welch is leading General Electric by changing its culture and encouraging subordinates to take the risks entailed to join in the change efforts. Of course, we are not arguing that the situation, as given, should be ignored or that transformational leaders are not reactive to environmental determinants. We merely suggest that with their ability to concretize a vision, to excite others, to change the way problems are thought about, the transformational leader is able to get others to react over time in ways that earlier models neither anticipate nor elaborate upon. The understanding of leadership requires expansion.

Relation to House's Theory of Charisma

House (1977) ended his discussion of his theory of charismatic leadership by quoting Hebb (1969, 21): "A good theory is one that holds together long enough to get you to a better theory." Although empirical testing was slow to emerge (Smith 1985), probably because of the difficulties involved and the resources required, we are witnessing an upsurge in research on charismatic leadership (e.g., Howell's 1985 and House's 1985 contributions).

Based on preliminary factor analyses of the MLQ leadership scales, charismatic leadership accounted for a large portion of the variance in transformational leadership. As we define and measure charismatic leadership this factor also takes into account what Yukl (1981) defined as inspirational leadership. Similar to House's model, charismatics are viewed as attracting strong feelings of identity and intense feelings of love and hate. Charismatic leaders generate excitement and increase the expectations of followers through their visions of the future and, as Weber originally conceptualized, the leader's special gift. The fact that charisma has been viewed as an endowment, however, may have deterred others from further conceptualizing and evaluating this construct. We therefore question previous views of charismatic leadership that consider charisma solely as an inborn trait and operationalize charisma as being a function of how followers view their leader. That is, the leader is charismatic because we think he or she is so. In light of recent evidence produced by Howell (1985), there is strong empirical support for the idea that charismatic leadership is a function of what followers perceive, and most importantly that such leadership can be trained in a laboratory setting. Perhaps some are born with this gift, but most leaders probably attain it the hard way—they learn it and earn it!

Bass (1985a) agreed with House (1977), Oberg (1969), Dow (1969), and Shils (1965b) that charisma is widely distributed in organizational settings. In fact, as reported later, we have found charisma at all organizational levels. It is not limited to world-class leaders. Bass expanded on House's model in terms of how charisma fits in with transformational leadership. Charisma is one component, albeit an important one, in the transformational process. Transformational leaders also need the ability to recognize the needs, aspirations, and values of their followers and the skill to conceive and articulate strategies and goals that will predispose the followers to exert their best efforts. These skills seem to embody what we referred to earlier as individualized consideration and intellectual stimulation, both of which are helpful, but not sufficient even when joined with charisma to achieve successful outcomes for the transformational leader. For example, the transforming leader who operates within a highly bureaucratic structure that resists change may fail to inspire others to join in his or her vision no matter how compelling it may be, regardless of the leader's determination or self-confidence, and irrespective of the leader's ability to engender trust and affection from followers.

From a transforming perspective, the leader must be able to read situations to determine when the time is right for changing individuals, organizations, and/or societal perspectives. It is here that earlier contingency and situational leadership models will play a significant role in furthering our understanding of the importance of contextual factors on the success (or failure) of transformational leadership. Transforming leaders must be able to diagnose what can be feasibly done given the formal and informal constraints of the environment within which they operate. Those who do not or who cannot may succeed through sheer perserverance, but the likelihood of success is probably lower.

As Bennis (1982) concluded following his study of ninety directors and chief executive officers, successful transformational leaders are able to create a compelling vision and have the self-determination to see it through no matter how difficult things become. However, they *must* be adaptable and willing to change as demands change within their environments. Where self-determination turns to insensitivity (declining consideration), the resulting effect may be a failure to endure and an inability to achieve one's mission. This particular abuse of self-determination was noted by McCall and Lombardo (1983) as being the major contributor to a "rising star" becoming metaphorically an "organizational nova."

Purely Charismatic or Transformational?

The purely charismatic leader may fail to be transforming for other reasons. Lacking in individualized consideration, a purely charismatic leader may strive to keep followers from personally growing as individuals. As long as followers support a leader's message, any further change in the follower may be perceived as threatening by the leader. The purely charismatic leader may want followers to adopt the charismatic's worldview and go no further; the transformational leader will attempt to instill in followers the ability to question not only established views, but eventually those espoused by the leader. Relatively speaking, the charismatic leader who is transformational will rely more heavily on rational intellectual persuasion to build into the subordinate the ability to do the same. The purely charismatic leader will depend more heavily on emotional appeals.

The difference we propose is one of both immediate and long-term process and outcome. The process differs in that transformational leaders excite subordinates, but go further in coaching them to think on their own and to develop new ventures that will further the group's goals while also developing the subordinate. Although the outcomes may be identical in the short term, transformational leaders ideally build in subordinates the willingness and motivation to question future systems and rules that even the transformational leader never dreamed of in his or her original vision.

Charisma, Cognition, and Emotional Arousal

House's model of charismatic leadership does not deal with two additional areas: first, how cognitive and emotional factors play a role in explaining the arousal levels of subordinates engendered by the charismatic leader; second, the extent to which situational factors moderate the arousal levels of subordinates working with different charismatic leaders.

By arousing emotional responses in followers, the charismatic can reduce inhibitions to change. We suggest that this does not only come about through role modeling or impression management but through an idolization of the leader and a belief in the leader's conception of what the future can and must be, not what others will allow it to be. The leader is viewed as being larger than life. How this excitement is created by the leader, under what circumstances, how different individuals react or the same individuals at different times react, are some of the issues that deserve closer scrutiny. Most important, the link between charismatic qualities and follower excitement has not been adequately explained either from a cognitive or an emotional perspective. When theory and evidence is available to explain this linkage, the "gift" of charisma will probably be more available to all of us.

Charismatic leadership has a strong emotional effect on followers—it is enlivening and arousing—however, to thoroughly understand the less explicable emotional components of charisma, a further analysis of the relation between cognitions and subsequent emotional states is warranted. A good starting point for this analysis is in recent work in social psychology (e.g., Scherer 1982, Smith and Ellsworth 1985).

A Cognitive Process View of Charisma

For some time, many authors have suggested that emotional differences or subjective states of feeling should be examined with respect to how the individual cognitively appraises his or her environment (James 1890/1950, Lazarus 1968, Schacter and Singer 1962, Scherer 1982, Clore and Ortony 1984, Abelson 1983). These authors have argued that by viewing emotions as simply ranging from positive to negative, we ignore how individuals interpret different emotionally charged situations and how that interpretation affects the type of emotional response observed. One view is that all emotional responses to external events have some cognitive antecedents. In this regard, Smith and Ellsworth (1985) state, "We believe that people must answer certain fundamental questions about changing sensations that impinge upon them not only so as to know what to do, but also so as to know what they feel." (Smith and Ellsworth 1985, 819). Even pleasantness, which is seen by Zajonc (1980) as being so automatic as to appear to precede cognition, most likely has some cognitive antecedents.

Of particular import are the cognitive dimensions which have been identified over the years to explain the range of emotions. Smith and Ellsworth (1985) identified six such cognitive dimensions from past literature and empirical analyses of their own that help explain how one emotion differs from another. The six dimensions of consequence are attention, novelty, uncertainty, responsibility for events, anticipated levels of effort, and situational control factors. By using these dimensions, which are by no means all-inclusive, we can begin systematically analyzing how charismatic leadership results in the emotional arousal in followers often attributed to this dimension of leadership. For example, the first step in analyzing the emotional reaction of a follower to a leader is to determine if the leader (and the leader's message) was noticed; i.e., the follower can choose to attend or not attend to a leader. Here is where the follower's interpretation of the leader's message begins—or abruptly ends following the choice of the follower (if such a choice is feasible) to ignore the leader. Contributing to whether the leader is ignored or not is the novelty of the leader's message or vision. A novel message (the fact that a vision can be novel or not with respect to human emotions necessitates some cognition) can grab the attention of the follower because of its content or the leader's skill in presenting the argument. These factors can also motivate the follower to ignore the leader's future messages when the same message repeated time and time again loses its appeal for the follower.

Uncertainty can also play a significant role in the type of emotional response evoked by the charismatic leader. The more the current situation either does not fit with any prior expectations or violates prior expectations of the follower, the greater the follower's hopes and/or fears become, which in turn result in greater attention to what the leader has to say. This fits with the conception that charismatic leadership will have its greatest impact (cognitively and emotionally) in situations where threats to "steady state" are eminent. Hence, if after appraising his or her environment the follower does not perceive any degree of uncertainty, the follower's emotional response to a charismatic's message may be less intense if we hold constant the novelty of the message and the extent to which the follower is turned on by other personal qualities of the leader (e.g., the leader's intelligence, good looks, presentational style, and so on).

Particularly relevant to our analysis of how transformational leaders energize their subordinates into action is Smith and Ellsworth's discussion of activation level. Level of activation is viewed as being a function of our estimating how much effort will be needed to deal with our current situation. Cannon (1929) referred to this as "fight or flight." Emotional responses can be viewed as being a function of how much effort we anticipate is needed to do something, ranging from an extreme expansion of our effort to just sitting back and enjoying the scenery. By articulating their vision, charismatic leaders can affect the subjective estimates of effort made by followers in at least several plausible ways. First, by concretizing a vision that followers view as being worthy of their effort, the charismatic leader excites followers and in turn, raises their anticipated levels of effort. Rather than reflecting a simple exchange and a lower order of change, the leader raises the anticipated level of effort, resulting in the follower performing beyond "expected" levels of performance. Using this scenario the leader creates a "Pygmalian effect" (Eden and Shani 1982) that inspires followers to greater levels of effort than were previously considered necessary for achievement of a goal. Second, transformational leaders bring to a situation a feeling that there is greater control over events than previously perceived by followers. This revised analysis of the situation can result in a reformulation of anticipated effort. Numerous "real world" examples exist to support this position. For instance, Lee Iacocca was able to convince Chrysler's employees, Congress, and the banks, that Chrysler's survival was feasible by changing the expectations of those parties that Chrysler could again be a profitable corporation. His message clearly led to a change in activation level among employees that has subsequently resulted in a Chrysler corporation that has performed beyond all expectations.

Finally, the transformational leader can offer followers alternative solutions to problems by using intellectual stimulation. The use of intellectual stimulation by the leader results in a cognitive reappraisal of current circumstances involving the subordinate that shifts the subordinate away from feelings of frustration to feelings of there being a challenge. The challenge then results in higher levels of activation and effort as opposed to feelings of helplessness.

The Charismatic Relationship

Some additional antecedents to the success of charismatics bear mentioning. Having a shared sense of purpose and common norms between follower and leader should help facilitate charismatics in successfully completing and communicating their mission. If norms are not common to both leader and follower, then the first step toward transforming subordinates may involve the leader presenting alternative views which stimulate followers to question not only the way they perceive problems and solutions, but the very attitudes, values, and norms that may have resulted in those problems. Charismatics must unfreeze subordinates' attitudes and values and then gain conformity with their own value systems to increase the likelihood that the mission will conform or transform previously obeyed norms that would inhibit success. It is not simply unquestioning acceptance nor is it a basic disagreement with the leader's values that will necessarily result in the desired transformation by the leader, and the highest order of change in followers. It is the fact that subordinates have gone through a reexamination of their position in relation to the one espoused by the leader that motivates them to reconsider their needs and elevate their goals.

Research Progress

Since Bass (1985, chapters 11 and 12) published some introductory survey findings, a number of studies have been partially or fully completed regarding the effects of transformational and transactional leadership on individual, group, and organizational effectiveness. The results are encouraging both in terms of the basic propositions of the model and in regards to the overwhelming evidence supporting the notion that transformational leadership seems to exist at many levels in a variety of organizational settings.

We have continued to find in our data from military, industrial, and educational settings indications that transformational leadership is not at all rare. Many superiors were identified as exhibiting transforming behaviors fairly frequently. In industrial settings, we found some degree of transformational leadership being practiced at the most senior levels down on through to nonmanagerial employees, but as hypothesized, more of it was seen at higher levels.

Additional evidence supporting the frequent occurrence of transformational leadership was obtained in studies of U.S. Army colonels and U.S. Army officers ranging from captain to colonel. Similar results have been obtained for squadron commanders in the U.S. Air Force.

High-scoring transformational leaders also turn up among students and among women. In fact, a female graduate student (in one study) received close to the highest transformational leadership factor score of all leaders rated thus far. Her scores were based on a composite of ratings by nine peers participating with her in a semester-long management simulation game and on an impartial rater who evaluated the leadership qualities of each leader based on a review of videotapes of the leader in action.

In a workshop for twenty-four managers in a high-tech firm, half of whom were women, the four whose subordinates described them as most charismatic were women. It suffices to say, that sufficient data are now available to show that transforming leadership is not uncommon in organizational settings nor is it limited to males, top management executives, and world-class leaders.

Transformational Leadership and Organizational Effectiveness

Transformational leadership relates positively to how effective the leader is perceived to be by subordinates, how much effort subordinates expend for the leader, and how satisfied subordinates are with the leader's performance. Transformational leaders are viewed as being more effective at communicating the needs of subordinates to higher-ups, as having more effective work groups, and as contributing more to the organization's overall effectiveness. Subordinates also view themselves as putting in greater amounts of effort for the transformational leader.

Although contingent reward has also been positively correlated with the aforementioned factors, the magnitude of the relationship is generally much lower. Passive transactional leadership (management-by-exception) is consistently negatively correlated with ratings of leader effectiveness and extra effort in industrial studies and only marginally in the military. These findings support survey results reported by Yankelovich and Immerwahr (1983) concerning the frustration employees express over the current absence of active transactional leadership. In and of itself management-by-exception is not very favorably perceived as a leadership style, although we can imagine a situation in which a group of highly "independent" individuals would not only prefer but would seek out a manager who would intervene in worker affairs in rare situations—for example, research scientists.

Subordinate Satisfaction

Subordinates rate their satisfaction with the leader as being higher the more frequently the leader displays transformational leadership qualities. This finding is consistent across all organizational settings. Thus the transformational leader not only gets subordinates to put forth greater effort, they also are seen as being more satisfactory to work for whether in the military, industry, or in educational settings.

Leadership by contingent reward was also positively correlated with subordinate satisfaction with a leader, whereas management-by-exception was negatively correlated with subordinate satisfaction.

Analysis with and without Common Methods Bias

Overall, individual ratings of leader effectiveness, satisfaction with the leader, and the degree to which the leader is able to get extra levels of effort from subordinates were all positively correlated, and most highly, with transformational leadership. But interpreting these results as definitive had to remain problematic due to the common methods bias associated with much of the collection of rated leadership and criteria of effectiveness, satisfaction, and extra effort. However, a number of other studies have been completed without such bias present. These studies are briefly summarized below.

1. Performance was measured separately from leadership ratings by Waldman, Bass, and Einstein (1985) to examine how transformational leadership combines with transactional leadership to affect individual and group performance. They examined the incremental effect of transformational leadership over transactional for predicting individual performance levels of 256 managers from a manufacturing firm. The theoretical basis for this analysis came from Bass (1985, chapter 2), which postulates the add-on effect of transformational leadership to transactional leadership style in predicting differences in individual and group performance.

A two-step hierarchical step-wise regression analysis resulted in the transformational leadership factors accounting for a significant amount of unique variance in performance above and beyond transactional leadership.

2. In an independent series of analyses of transforming/transactional leadership in a commercial firm, the proposition was tested for 360 managers, that higher performers in the organization, who were placed by superiors in high management potential groups, would be viewed by their subordinates as being more transformational. MLQ scores were collected from subordinates independently of the superiors' evaluations of the managers. In contrast to a random sample, the high-potential managers according to their superiors were rated significantly higher on transformational leadership factors by their subordinates.

3. Avolio, Waldman, Einstein, and Bass (1985) have recently examined the effects of transformational leadership on group performance. Eighteen MBA student groups, comprised of nine members each, participated in a management simulation game. Leaders were chosen in each group using a peer nomination procedure.

The groups begin with equivalent assets at the start of the term and compete with each other for market share in their respective industries. The game has high external validity in that the typical factors that influence how firms do business are incorporated into the game, such as current inflation rates, interest rates on loans comparable to current rates, realistic limitations on resources and available capital, having to abide by employment laws in personnel actions, avoiding hostile takeovers by other firms, and gaining approval from boards of directors to begin new capital ventures. Competition is rather fierce among teams since each student's six credit hour grade is dependent on how that student's team performs relative to other teams in his or her industry.

Although the game runs for one full semester, it actually simulates eight full quarters of performance. Ratings of each team's president were collected in the latter part of the spring semester at a group meeting where all nine members of the team rated the president on the MLQ (Form 4). Performance data were collected at each quarter and reflect common financial indices of performance typically used to measure organizational effectiveness, for example, stock price, debt/equity ratio, return on assets, and so on.

Analyses indicated that those teams who had leaders with higher ratings of transformational leadership (i.e., 3.0 and above) had significantly outperformed those teams with presidents rated lower in transformational leadership. As expected, the transformational leaders were viewed as being more effective and team members had greater levels of satisfaction with their leadership.

It is important that we point out several issues regarding the interpretation of our findings. First, the transformational factor scores of leaders in the game were comparable to those obtained in industrial settings. Second, unlike in most organizational settings, the followers on these teams had ample opportunity to observe their leaders close-up, and yet they still viewed some leaders as being highly charismatic. This contradicts the notion that distance between leader and follower is a necessary precondition for one to have the mystique of a charismatic leader. Perhaps our most important point is the conclusion that transformational leaders have more effective organizations.

There is a less plausible alternative hypothesis which cannot be ruled out. Since ratings of leadership were collected at the end of the semester, the possibility exists that more successful teams attributed transformational qualities to their leaders—qualities which the leader may not have exhibited to the extent perceived by followers. In other words, charisma or intellectually stimulating qualities are attributed to a leader because a team is successful. It should suffice to say that the current data do not allow for a definitive test of the hypothesis of whether transformational leaders augmented the team's performance or leaders were merely ascribed transformational qualities.

To summarize, preliminary data are now available to support the notion that transforming leadership can significantly contribute to performance above and beyond transactional leadership. Further, transformational leadership may impact on group and individual performance in a similar, positive fashion.

Reflections and Recommendations

Our preliminary research on transformational and transactional leadership has merely scratched the surface in regards to the potential for empirical inquiry in this area. As we expressed earlier, very little is known regarding the process by which individuals become energized and under what circumstances a transforming leader will be most effective. In our opinion, this is one of the most important questions raised by Bass's model in that it not only focuses on how individuals are energized by a leader, but how the individual becomes the source of energy for others. Accordingly, we have much to gain by viewing leadership as a dynamic development process. Consequently, one clear message we wish to leave the reader with is that leadership is a more dynamic process than the boundaries of transactional leadership theories allow for or even consider.

One recommendation we have for future research on transformational and transactional leaders involves the type of methodology used for analyzing these styles of leadership. Psychohistorical analyses of "famous" leaders, for example, is an approach which has rarely been used by social and organizational psychologists to systematically study leadership behavior and attributes. In general, past leadership research has failed to take advantage of the wealth of information in biographies of world-class leaders to evaluate leadership behaviors—behaviors we often attempt to simulate in laboratory settings.

Recently, Bass, Avolio, and Goodheim (1987) reported evidence that supported the usage of biographical accounts of world-class leaders as a reliable method for evaluating leader behavior and attitudes. Students were instructed to choose a world-class leader whom they would enjoy reading about. During the course of a semester, students read a biographical account of a leader and wrote a short term paper to document their observations. At the end of the semester they completed the MLQ (Form 4) as if they were a subordinate of their chosen leader.

Several interesting findings emerged from this process. First, multiple raters evaluating the same leader tended to agree with each other similar in degree to estimates of interrater reliability presented in the previous section. Second, the pattern of relationships among the empirically derived leadership factors were virtually identical to those obtained in more traditional survey research settings. Finally, in most cases, leadership ratings characterized the reputations of world-class leaders. For example, Andrew Young, Dag Hammarskjold, and Mahatma Gandhi were rated very high on charisma; Eleanor Roosevelt was rated highest on individualized consideration—Adolph Hitler was lowest; Gerald Ford was rated low on intellectual stimulation, whereas David Ben-Gurion was rated high. In general, this pattern appeared to hold true for most leaders.

Obviously, there is much more that can be done to improve on current psychohistorical procedures. For instance, the actual biographers could complete a leadership survey on the leader they wrote about to determine if different biographers would agree on ratings of the same leader. Another approach currently being developed by House (1985) is to content analyze biographies of leaders. The content analysis can then be used to evaluate the quality of behavioral information in the biographer's account of the leader and also as a means of evaluating the type of leader that person was in his or her time period. Since a psychohistorical approach is so rarely used in organizational research, it is difficult to determine its validity in comparison to other more traditional methodologies. It suffices to say, that the limited evidence that is available does support a further examination of psychohistorical approaches for studying world-class leaders.

A second recommendation for future research on transformational leadership is to use longitudinal designs to determine the antecedent conditions that cause a leader to be more (or less) successful. Both House (1977) and Bass (1985) make specific recommendations in their models of charismatic and transformational leadership, respectively, that necessitate a longitudinal design for examining the influence of leadership. For example, in both models, self-confidence is identified as being an important attribute of the leader, in addition to the leader's ability to instill greater confidence in the subordinate. The process by which one builds confidence in oneself and others is time-bound and cannot be accurately examined by relying upon static cross-sectional designs. Other examples exist that also support giving greater attention to longitudinal analyses of leadership factors, particularly those factors that take more time to have an impact.

One basic premise throughout this chapter has been that leadership can also affect higher order changes in subordinates. It is therefore imperative that future research in this area consider a broader spectrum of criteria. This relates to the idea of adding on to path-goal theory, and examining criteria that represent performance beyond expectations. Hence, it is necessary that we consider the criterion deficiencies in prior research on transformational leadership.

Specifically, there are many situations where performance data can be easily collected and correlated with ratings of transformational leadership; however, many performance appraisal systems do not emphasize performance beyond expectations—higher order change. This particular criterion problem may result in attenuating the model's ability to predict the consequences of transformational leadership. There are several ways to deal with this type of criterion deficiency. One way is to develop criteria that assess how much reserve capacity the follower is willing to expend to complete a mission. Take for instance the following example: A doctoral student recently completed her dissertation in the coal mining industry, where she analyzed teams of miners performing on the job. During the course of her investigation she noted that some teams would continue to work on their equipment even after the main drills had broken down, while other teams would pass the time by playing cards or exchanging stories.

The outcomes of this dissertation offer a good example of what we mean when we refer to performance beyond expectations. We are recommending that one alternative to developing appropriate criteria for studies on transformational leadership is to partition the task into primary and secondary tasks. In our example above the primary task was to remove coal from the face of the mine. The secondary task was choosing how to occupy one's time while the machinery was being fixed. Those groups who continued to work could be viewed as transcending their own immediate self-interests—to relax—for the good of their organization. From an energizing perspective, the residual effort left unaccounted for in many appraisal systems may be extremely critical to testing the predictive validity of Bass's leadership model.

As was mentioned in our discussion of residual effort, greater emphasis needs to be placed on developing reliable intermediate criteria. Intermediate criteria such as a willingness to delay immediate payoffs for the good of the group or organization, an interest in developing oneself to achieve higher standards, estimating the levels of excitement created by the leader and how that excitement manifests itself, and even the degree to which leaders instill within subordinates the willingness to consider taking greater risks are potential criteria one could develop.

The willingness of a subordinate to take risks as a criterion measure is worth expanding on. The idea that transformational leaders can influence the risk propensity of their followers is intuitively appealing given the historical emphasis placed on great leaders who were able to impel their followers to metaphorically and literally charge up the hill at great personal risk to themselves. We are suggesting that further concentration needs to be directed towards understanding the cognitive and emotional components of such actions. This idea actually parallels one finding of Peters and Waterman's (1982) in that more successful companies had leaders and organizational cultures that supported risk-taking behavior (and thought). However, we need to develop a clearer understanding of the process underlying the development of this type of culture, as well as the leader's role in getting subordinates to contemplate riskier ventures.

The examples cited previously emphasize both the importance of focusing on secondary or residual measures of performance to determine the degree of impact that a transformational leader has had on his or her followers or organization and the need for leadership research to put greater emphasis on determining the effects of transforming leaders on process variables, for example, the way one thinks. Each is needed to provide a fairer test of the model.

There are many additional questions that need to be answered: What type of organizational environments breed the transformational leader and how many can one system handle? Are there any similarities across transformational leaders in terms of personality, intelligence, values, attitudes, family background, or education? What type of subordinate reacts positively (or negatively) to a transformational leader? How does the influence of transformational leadership spread throughout an organizational system and to what extent can it be observed impacting one organizational level to the next? To what extent can we train this form of leadership? At what point will followers "burn out" on the transformational leader and rebel against the leader's vision?

These are just some of the issues neglected in our overview of the model and our findings to date. Clearly, there are many avenues for research in this area that we have overlooked; however, if we have gotten the reader excited about a new approach to understanding leadership, an approach that provides for a clearer vision of how to explain higher order change, but does not overlook one's personal needs for effective leadership, then we have achieved our primary objective of getting the reader to think about leadership in a way that had not been previously considered and thus a transformation has occurred.

4
Toward an Organizational Leadership Theory

Marshall Sashkin
Robert M. Fulmer

Top-level managers take on many roles. This has been documented by various observational and diary-type studies of executive behavior. The most recent and popular of these was Mintzberg's (1975) intensive observational report of the activities of several CEOs, whose behaviors were sorted into ten emergent categories. One of these role categories, "leadership," seems—when defined only a bit more broadly than did Mintzberg—to account for a rather large proportion of executive behavior, as well as including what many scholars see as some of its most important aspects. Katz and Kahn (1966, 1978), for example, consider the "origination"—creation and development—of organizational structures and policies as the unique and identifying aspect of executive behavior. Mann (1965) carried this further by noting the CEO's role as manager of the organization-environment interface, a sort of top-level boundary spanner.

The sort of organizational approaches to the leadership role that we have been noting have always been off the track of primary research on leadership. Leadership research and theory has centered on the leader-follower relationship, either dyadically or in the context of the small group, rather than on organizational leadership. This has been true from the classic lab and field studies to the most recent work of Fiedler and his associates. (See Bass, 1981, for a review of this work.)

In our view, the study of leadership from an organizational perspective has been neglected, in favor of a focus on what might be called "supervisory management"—the role of the leader at middle and lower levels of the organizational hierarchy. This has led to considerable nontheoretical but practical understanding of leadership at these "operational" levels. Katz and Kahn (1966) refer to leadership activities at these levels as "interpolation"—adding to and interpreting structures and policies developed at the top—and, at the lower levels, as "administration," simply operating within defined structures and carrying out policies. With a few prominant exceptions, such as Mintzberg or Katz and Kahn, organizational psychologists have failed to pay attention to top-level executive leadership as an organizationally relevant phenomenon. This has left the study of organizational leadership to psychologists who write Freudian interpretations of "charismatic" leadership (e.g., see Schiffer 1973), and to sociologists whose interests lie in the mass-movement effects of such leadership (e.g., see Burns 1978 or Weber 1947).

The present argument returns to the organizational level concepts of leadership pioneered by Katz and Kahn (1966, 1978) and Mann (1965, 1968), while integrating within this system-level framework some new concepts about leaders' personality structures (Jaques 1985) and behaviors (Bennis 1984). This leads to an effort to include within such an argument what is known about "lower level" leadership traits (e.g., McClelland 1975) and behavior (e.g., Stogdill 1974). A simple yet useful framework for both contrasting and integrating individual and organizational leadership concepts can be found in Kurt Lewin's classic paradigm which states that behavior is a function of personality factors in interaction with certain important aspects of situations: $B = f(P,S)$. This framework is used in figure 4–1, to outline the theory to be presented here, specifically comparing and contrasting the way the theory treats top-level "executive" leadership and mid- to lower level "operational" leadership.

The discussion that follows is organized around the three themes shown in figure 4–1: person, situation, and behavior. Each of these themes is explored with respect to operational as well as executive leadership. One aim is to present some new concepts regarding leadership and how it works. Equally important, however, is the attempt to develop clear connections between the "micro" variables that are typically associated with the study of leadership and more "macro" variables at the organizational level of analysis.

Leadership and Personality

For many years it was thought that the secret of leadership was some special characteristic of the "born leader," some unknown—but real—trait that gave such leaders a key to success. This myth was demolished in the late 1940s by a major integrative review and synthesis of research on leadership by Stogdill (1948). He found that of over 100 research studies, *none* showed any clear evidence that leaders were strikingly or substantially different from nonleaders. There were some consistent (but minor) differences: leaders are a bit taller, a bit heavier, a bit brighter, and so on. But none of these "bits" was especially significant, nor did they come together to form a picture of a "special" leader personality.

One result of Stogdill's review of leadership traits was, perhaps, unfortunate. Stogdill (personal communication, October 1976) said that he never intended to close off research on the personality of leaders (he hoped to focus it better), but that was essentially what happened. Since 1950 only a very few

Executive Leadership

Vision: Effective executive leaders can think in time spans of at least five years and, more typically, over periods of fifteen years and more. Such leaders see how their plans fit together, can clearly explain the process or sequence of action, know how to apply plans in various situation and can see opportunities for expanding their plans across organizational structures (Jaques 1985).

Change, Goals, People: On the broad organizational level, three issues can be seen as key aspects of the organization's "culture." These issues are: action-emphasis for effective adaptation, focus on goals of importance to clients, and involvement of employees. They represent the critical functions any organization must deal with effectively in order to survive: adaptation, goal attainment, and coordination (Parsons 1960). The effective executive leader understands these key aspects organizational culture and is always assessing their strength as well as looking for new ways to strengthen them (Peters and Waterman 1982).

Charisma: The effective executive leader understands and is skilled in using a set of key task- and relationship-centered behaviors that produce in others the feeling of charisma—being inspired, wanting to perform beyond "standard" expectations, having high self-worth, and belonging to the organization. Some of these behaviors are: effective communication, focused attention, consistent actions, expressed concern for people, and creating sensible risks and opportunities that involve others (Bennis 1984). The leader uses these behaviors and the resultant charismatic feelings to create and reinforce shared beliefs that define and sustain the three key aspects of organizational culture (concerning change, goals, and people).

Operational Leadership

Power: The effective mid- and lower-level leader has a high need for power. Such power is used not just to satisfy the leader's own personal desires but to have a significant impact on the organization and benefit its members (McClelland 1975).

Authority, Task Structure, Employees: On the level of specific jobs and tasks, the most potent situational factors seem to include the leader's authority of position, the ways tasks are set up or structured, and the ability and willingness of employees to actually do the job (Fiedler 1967, Hersey and Blanchard 1982, House 1971, Yukl 1981). The effective mid- and lower-level leader looks for and consciously assesses these situational factors, as a basis for deciding what specific behavioral actions to take.

Consistent Versatility: The effective mid- and lower-level is aware of the two broad basic types of leadership behavior, task-directed and relationship-centered, as well as the more specific behaviors within each category. Such leaders "tailor" their behavior to fit the different needs of different situations. When effective, such a tailored approach leads subordinates to see the leader as being both highly task-directed *and* highly-relationship-centered. Academics often misconstrue this to mean that effective leaders physically engage in high levels of both sorts of behavior, as could be identified by an objective observer.

PERSON

SITUATION

BEHAVIOR

Figure 4–1. Organizational Leadership

researchers have studied personality factors that characterize successful managers. And, their focus has been on issues rather different from the sort of traits examined in the studies reviewed by Stogdill. These early studies looked at traits like "emotional stability," "absence of modesty," "fortitude," or "insight." Oddly enough, however, personality factors included in the present model and based on recent research are highly consistent with Stogdill's integrative synthesis, briefly detailed in the concluding section of his 1948 review paper. Stogdill speaks of *capacity* (intelligence, judgment), *achievement* (scholarship, knowledge), *responsibility* (dependability, aggressiveness, self-confidence, desire to excel), *participation* (activity, sociability, cooperation, adaptability), and *status* (position, popularity) as five basic themes identified by personality research as important for effective leadership. Some of these themes are reflected in the present framework, in terms of the two personality variables we will discuss in depth.

Responsibility: The Need for Power and Impact

It is suggested that effective leaders must be motivated to make an impact on the world around them. This may relate to Miner's (1965) concept of "motivation to manage," but it seems most closely connected to McClelland's (1975) "pro-social power need." McClelland and Burnham (1976) discuss how their initial notion that effective leaders are high on need for achievement was off-track; individuals with such high need for achievement (nAch) will, if pressed, go out and do the job themselves because they so value the associated achievement. But, notes McClelland, this is quite the opposite of effective leadership, which implies success in getting *others* to accomplish goals.

McClelland's work suggests that effective leaders are only moderate in need for achievement. Instead, they are high on need for power (nPow). This need may be exhibited in behavior as dominance, and that may be why research (see House 1977, House and Baetz 1979, Stogdill 1948) seems to consistently show aggressiveness, power-orientation, or high dominance need as a trait characteristic of leaders. McClelland, however, argues that when nPow is expressed as dominance the outcomes are quite negative, and the ultimate consequences for the individual often include depression and alcoholism in addition to failure as a leader (McClelland et al. 1972). According to empirical evidence offered by McClelland and Burnham (1976), successful leaders use their high need for power to influence others to attack goals that benefit their subordinates and the organization, not just the leader.

Thus, classic as well as modern research on leader personality seems consistent in suggesting that effective leaders have a strong need to "make a difference," as well as a need for the power and influence to do so. More tenuous in terms of research base, but surely consistent with any rational thought and observation on leadership, is the view that effective leaders express their need for power and influence in ways that benefit everyone in the organization.

Capacity: Level of Cognitive Development

A second personality factor might be termed "cognitive ability," but we do not mean to simply suggest a general intelligence factor. Again, this factor is quite consistent with Stogdill's synthesis, which included intelligence, "knowing how to get things done," and "alertness to, and insight into, situations." The source of the variable used in the present framework is the work of Elliott Jaques (1985), who has recently extended his earlier research and theory on "time span of discretion" (Jaques 1964).

In prior work Jacques demonstrated that people in organizations differ in the length in time of their longest term responsibilities. The longer the time span the higher the management level. But to function effectively at high levels, over longer time spans, requires higher levels of cognitive development. Thus, Jaques (1985) has developed an extension of Piagetian theory, arguing that at higher organizational levels individuals require more advanced cognitive development in order to "see" over longer and longer time spans.

A foreman typically needs no more than a year of such a long-range vision, in terms of thinking about work that Katz and Kahn would term "administration": application of rules, policies, and standard procedures. Middle managers, however, who must "interpolate" their own notions of how to make top-level policies actually work, will typically require time spans of two to four years. And executives, who "originate" policies and programs, must think, in concrete terms, over spans up to ten years. Jaques observes that truly "visionary" chief executives will often have time spans of twenty years and more.

Summary

It is suggested that effective leaders believe they can have an impact on the world and have a high need for power in order to create such impacts. This need is then expressed through pro-organizational actions, rather than as personal dominance. And, effective leaders are at a level of cognitive development appropriate to the time span requirements of their positions. In terms of evidence, the research of McClelland and his associates on *n*Pow (McClelland 1975, McClelland and Burnham 1976), as well as classic (Stogdill, 1948) and recent research on personality traits of leaders (Mann 1959, Stogdill 1974), provides support for the present argument.

Jaques' views on time spans of leaders at different organizational levels are supported by extensive research evidence (Jaques 1961, 1964, 1976, 1979).

His views regarding cognitive development (Jaques 1985) are clearly more theoretical than proven, although he and his associates have conducted research studies on the theory as well as developed individual measures. Although further work is clearly called for, the bulk of trait research, from Stogdill's classic review and synthesis to Jaques' on-going work, provides a solid grounding for the concepts of leadership and personality put forth in the present model.

Leadership and the Situation

Our view of the situation is based on Parsons' (1960) "action framework." Using the classic work of Weber (1947) as a basis, Parsons added the concept of a system with inputs from the environment, internal action, and outputs to the environment. Parsons identified certain critical functions that *any* system must effectively attend to, in order to survive. One has to do with *adapting* to change in the environment. A second concerns attaining *goals* that clients or customers want and will pay for. A third function centers on the coordination of ongoing activities, that is, "integrating" the various behavioral actions of the *people* who operate the organization. Finally, Parsons proposed a fourth and most basic function, that of maintaining the pattern of actions with respect to adapting, attaining goals, and coordinating people's activities. This pattern of actions is maintained through the shared development of a set of common values, beliefs, and behavioral norms, an organizational "culture." These elements define the culture and determine how (and if) the organization adapts to change, what goals are aimed for (and how these goals relate — or fail to relate — to what clients and customers want), and the way people are dealt with and deal with one another in order to coordinate their organizational activities.

The first three functions are relevant at the "micro" level, the level of the middle- or lower level operational leader, as well as at the "macro" (whole organization) executive leadership level.

Macro-Variables: Executive Leadership and Culture

In agreement with Schein's (1985) recent argument, we suggest that executive leaders are directly concerned with creating culture, with designing organizational functions that promote organizational effectiveness. These large scale or "macro-level" variables are the situational factors they attend to. As noted earlier, executive leaders have a long-range "vision" or time span; this enables them to deal conceptually with the long-term issues involved in creating a culture.

Just what sort of a culture does an executive leader try to create? To answer, we return to Parsons' (1937, 1951, 1960; Parsons, Bales, and Shils 1953) concepts and his action framework. In those terms, one can say that executive leaders must develop organizational beliefs and value systems that make it more likely that the critical adaptation, goal attainment, and integration (coordination) functions will be carried on effectively. Thus, the organizational culture is the fourth and most important function, the "pattern maintaining" function, as Parsons called it. A primary task of executive leaders is creating an effective culture, that is, one that supports the other three key functions (e.g., see Schein 1985).

We suggest that in order to deal effectively with issues and problems of adaptation, executive leaders encourage internal entrepreneurs to develop new ideas, programs, and even mini-businesses. They create norms of risk-taking, of freedom from fear of punishment if a risk does not pan out. They make it clear that when in doubt one takes action, that asking forgiveness is more desirable than going through procedures to get permission in advance.

The goal attainment function calls for executive leaders to focus organization members on the significance of matching organizational outputs with the needs and desires of clients. These "output goals" (Perrow 1970), the goals of the public in contact with the organization, are critical. *Unless* "system goals," the ways the organization chooses to operate, and "product goals" (what we normally think of as goals, such as volume, quality, etc.) are consistent with output goals, clients and customers will *not* be satisfied. They will take their business elsewhere, and the organization's survival (let alone prosperity) will be threatened.

Executive leaders foster an organizational belief in the importance of people, in order that the organization can better deal with issues of integration or coordination. It is patterns of employee behavior that define coordination, and such coordination is logically likely to be more effectively accomplished when people are more committed and involved (e.g., see Thompson 1967). A basic belief in the importance of people means involving them, directly and to the greatest possible extent, in the operation of the organization.

Micro-Variables: Operational Leadership and Context

Although the culture-defining variables are the responsibility of executive leaders, operational leaders look to the micro-management issues, the day-to-day context in which organizational activities occur. At this contextual level we can identify a set of three variables that are analogous to the three culture-defining factors just discussed. These variables also appear in several of the best-known approaches to leadership, both practice-models (such as Hersey and Blanchard's [1969] Situational Leadership Theory) and academic research-based theories (such as Fiedler's [1967] Contingency Model).

The first variable is *leader authority,* which is taken from Fiedler (1967) and appears also in House (1971). The leader's formal authority is important because it determines the sorts of extrinsic motivators the leader can bring to bear in a situation. It also defines the limits of intrinsic motivation through the delegation of authority (and thus of control or autonomy) to subordinates. That is, the leader can delegate only to the extent the leader has the authority to do so. This notion is similar to Maier's (1948) "area of freedom" concept. Effective adaptation requires control—authority—but also calls for leaders who can, as appropriate, share their power.

A second variable is the degree to which the *task* is *structured.* Task structure and the effect of highly structured versus relatively ambiguous tasks have been discussed in detail by House (1971) and House and Mitchell (1974). Task structure is also critical in Fiedler's (1967) model, although in this case task structure more typically refers to the group or unit's task rather than to an individual's task, as is most often the case for House's theory. Fiedler also places more conceptual emphasis on the leader's control and manipulation of task structure. Kerr and Jermier (1978) suggest that a carefully structured task can, to a degree, be a substitute for active leadership behaviors, in terms of manager-employee face-to-face interaction. Task structure is, of course, closely related to goals and goal attainment. Indeed, House's approach is called the "path-goal theory of leadership."

A recent meta-analysis of research on Fiedler's model (Peters, Hartke, and Pohlmann 1985) concluded that although the model received substantial support, it was incomplete, requiring specification of additional major variables. We suggest that "subordinate capability" would be one such useful addition. Hersey and Blanchard (1969) first proposed the task competency and cooperation of employees as a key situational factor for leadership effectiveness. Various studies of House's path-goal leadership theory have examined the proposition that enhancing the performance of workers at very different skill and experience levels requires different leadership approaches. Some support has been found for this hypothesis, providing a degree of confirmation for the inclusion of subordinate capability as an important situational variable. Subordinate capability is, in our view, a "micro-level" expression of the function defined by Parsons (1960) as critical for integrating or coordinating people's work activities and task-related interactions.

Although there are surely other important situational factors, it is interesting to see how consistent three well-known situationally-centered leadership theories are in identifying the same basic situational variables as important. House's path-goal theory considers task structure and subordinate capability as key situational factors, with leader's authority an important secondary variable. Fiedler's contingency model treats leader authority and task structure as critical, whereas subordinate capability plays a small part in Fiedler's third factor, leader-member relations. Hersey and Blanchard's situational leadership theory treats subordinate capability as the single key factor but recognizes leader authority as important for designing task structures and developing subordinates' capabilities. We suggest that these similarities are not due to chance, or even to academic inbreeding. Rather, it is because the situational context can be most clearly defined in terms of the critical functions in Parsons' (1960) action framework: adaptation, goal attainment, and integration (or coordination). Adaptation implies the exercise (or sharing) of control or power. Goal attainment is the focus of task structure issues. And people—and their capabilities—*are* the coordination/integration issue.

Summary

For both middle-to-lower-level leaders and executive leaders, the key situational factors relate to Parsons' critical functions. Leaders at different levels concern themselves with different manifestations of these functions. Executive leaders are concerned with *cultural* factors, with creating beliefs and values that support the other three functions, whereas operational leaders deal with the specific *contexts* in which the functions are played out on a "microscopic" level.

Note that we first see some indications here of the interaction between leaders' personality characteristics and situational variables. Managers who feel neither a need to have an impact nor a need for the power that can be used to make positive organizational impacts are not likely to be leaders, at any organizational level. Such managers may not be especially concerned with situational factors, for lack of motivation. But even when managers do exhibit the needs and motives characteristic of leaders, they may not have the cognitive capacity to identify and deal effectively with the situational factors we have defined, especially when this requires conceptual planning over a relatively long term scale (as is true for the case of creating organizational cultures).

Let us examine the sorts of behaviors that are a product of the personality and situational factors we have defined.

Leadership and Behavior

The behavioral research inaugurated in part as a reaction to Stogdill's review of trait research and, in part, by Stogdill himself (along with his Ohio State colleagues), identified two very clear dimensions of leader behavior. One type of behavior concerns *task* activities and involves setting goals, giving directions, providing materials, organizing the work setting, and so on. Another broad category centers on *interpersonal* activities, such as cooperating with coworkers, providing psychological support, and guiding the work group's interactions.

These two dimensions have been shown to account for a very large proportion of all leadership behavior (Stogdill and Coons 1957, Yukl and Neme-roff 1979) and have been studied by many researchers, often under different labels. The Ohio State researchers called the dimensions "consideration" and "initiating structure." For convenience we will label them *T* for task-focused and *R* for relationship-centered behavior.

An obvious inference, made both by scholars (Fleishman 1953) and prac-titioners (Blake and Mouton 1962), was the idea that effective leaders exhibit high levels of both types of behavior. This notion was supported by early laboratory research directed by Bales (1958), who found that "great man" leaders—individuals consistently observed to emerge as leaders of four-person discussion groups, regardless of group composition or topic—did, indeed, engage in very high levels of both T and R behavior. Such persons, however, represented a very small fraction of all emergent leaders in those studies—less than 5 percent, in fact.

As we show in the next section, many years of subsequent research on the relationships between leader behavior and subordinate performance, in both field and laboratory settings, have consistently failed to demonstrate any con-sistent relationship between levels of the two major leader behaviors and subordinate performance. At the same time, non-observational studies have shown strong relationships between high levels of both behaviors (as reported by subordinates) and leader effectiveness measures.

We will suggest a relatively simple explanation for this puzzle, with respect to the behaviors of operational leaders. We will also suggest that, as Bales found, "great" leaders do actually engage in high levels of both T and R behavior, in terms of specific behaviors required for the creation of an organi-zational culture.

Versatility: Operational Leadership Behaviors

Early hopes that leaders might be taught to exhibit high levels of both T and R behaviors and thus become more effective (as measured by subordinates' performance and satisfaction) were not fulfilled. For one thing, it turned out to be more difficult than anticipated to get trainees to exhibit the desired behaviors when "back home" (Fleishman 1953, Stogdill and Coons 1957). Even more serious, research studies consistently failed to confirm the sensible notion that effective leaders actually engage in high levels of T and R behav-ior (Fleishman and Harris 1962, Stogdill 1974).

This situation was made puzzling (in addition to being disappointing) when subordinate reports (unconfirmed by actual observation) continued to describe effective leaders as engaging in high levels of both T and R behavior (Blake and Mouton 1962, 1964). As if to compound the puzzle, a major study directed by Hall and involving almost 2,000 managers showed striking differences in subordinates' reports of the behaviors of fast-, average-, and slow-advancing managers (Hall and Donnell 1979). Managers promoted more rapidly than their peers were reported to engage in high levels of T *and* R, both in absolute terms and in comparison to their less successful peers. Those promoted with average "speed" were high on T but low to average on R, and the least successful managers were quite low on both.

Our explanation is deceptively simple. Although effective leaders are seen or *perceived* by subordinates as highly task-focused *and* highly relationship-oriented, at the same time, their actual physical *behavior* varies. As we see it, the same behavior can mean very different things, depending on the situation, and that is the key. The effective leader is skilled in terms of behavior and changes his or her behavior with what Blake and Mouton call "versatility," to take into account important factors in the situation. By doing so, the leader is *seen* as highly focused on both the task and on relationships. Note that we are not implying that the leader's behavior is not "real" or that the leader tries in any way to be manipulative, giving only the appearance of caring about the task (or about the people), when he or she is really only concerned about the people (or about the task). What the leader is doing is carefully designing his or her actions, to convey to subordinates the accurate and true meaning of the leader's behavior, that is, a high concern for *both* the people and the task.

We do not mean to oversimplify; it is obvious that a wide range of specific behaviors falls within each of the two broad T and R categories (e.g., see Benne and Sheats 1948). The specific behaviors an effective operational leader chooses to engage in (as well as the T/R balance) will be determined by situational factors as those factors interact with the leader's own needs and abilities (conceptual, as well as behavioral). The advantage of the operational leadership framework we have developed (and summarized in figure 4–1) is that it focuses on key factors, both with regard to the leader's personality and with respect to the situation, as derived from earlier theories of leadership and based on a variety of research investigations not well integrated into current leadership theory.

Charisma: Executive Leadership Behaviors

The task of executive leaders is creating an organizational culture incorporating shared values, beliefs, and norms that help the organization effectively carry out the functions of adapting, attaining goals, and coordinating activities. Executive leaders do this through their actions, of course, not by some mystical or magical process. Three sorts of actions seem important: creating an organizational philosophy, establishing policies and programs, and personal interactive behavior. The first two actions are clear examples of what Katz and Kahn (1966) mean by the term "origination." The first is a relationship-focused action, aimed at creating strong affectively-based value bonds between individuals and the organization. The second is a task-centered action, involving policy formulation and the actual establishment (and funding) of structures to carry out those policies. Ouchi (1981) deals with these approaches to creating organizational cultures.

The third and most complex activity calls for the executive leader to create elements of the organization's culture by means of his or her own behavioral interactions with organization members. This is the essence of what some have called "charismatic leadership," for it involves the creation of shared values, beliefs, and norms through strong affective reactions to the leader's behavior. In other words, the executive leader engages in certain task- and relationship-centered behaviors that produce in followers the affect we call "charisma." The specific content of the leader's behavior deals with actions that establish or confirm specific values, beliefs, and norms that support adaptation, goal attainment, and integration functions.

Through intensive clinical interviews with ninety reputedly charismatic leaders, Bennis (1984, Bennis and Nanus 1985) identified a set of specific behavior strategies used by these individuals. Sashkin (1985a) turned these into specific behaviors and developed an instrument to measure them, the *Leader Behavior Questionnaire* (LBQ). The LBQ includes a separate measure of charismatic affect toward the leader. This permits an hypothesis test: if the behaviors are in fact linked to charisma, then higher levels of such behavior should be associated with stronger charismatic affect among followers. Use of independent observations of the same leader, one to report behavior and the other to report charismatic affect, eliminates the sort of same-source bias common to questionnaire studies of this type. Such a process, using a sample of 69 leaders reporting on their own behaviors and 108 followers reporting charismatic effect, yielded an $r = .256$ ($p < .05$). (In most cases the reports of two followers were averaged to increase reliability; for thirty leaders only one follower report was available.) As might be expected, when behavior and charismatic affect reports are correlated for the same observer, the correlations increase greatly, to .638 for leaders and .585 for followers ($p < .001$). It seems clear from this exploratory work that leaders who engage in those behaviors to a greater extent *are* seen as more charismatic than leaders who engage in them to a lesser degree.

The five specific executive leadership behaviors that Sashkin (1985a) derived from Bennis's (1984) studies are the following:

1. *Focusing attention* on specific issues of concern, concentrating communication on key points to involve others in analysis, problem solving, and action planning.
2. *Taking risks,* but only on the basis of careful calculation of the chances of success, and in ways that create opportunities for others to join in.

3. *Communicating* skillfully, with understanding and empathy; insuring that effective two-way communication takes place through the use of active listening and feedback skills.

4. *Demonstrating consistency* and trustworthiness by one's behavior, openly expressing positions and sticking with them, and following through on action commitments.

5. *Expressing active concern* for people including one's self, thus modeling self-regard, and reinforcing feelings of self-worth in others, by action (such as involving others in important decisions and activities) as well as words.

Notice that the first two behaviors—focusing attention and taking risks—are special types of task-oriented activity, whereas the latter three—communicating, showing trust, and showing concern for people—are types of relationship-centered behavior. Thus, these charismatic leadership behaviors fit within the broader frame of reference of leader behavior established by the Ohio State studies.

We suggest that it is through these charismatic behaviors that effective executive leaders go about putting their long-range organizational plans into practice, on a "microscopic" level. On an organizational level the executive leader is creating a "culture," a set of shared values, beliefs, and norms that can guide the organization and the actions of its members over relatively long periods of time (Sashkin 1985c). As noted earlier, key to an effective culture, on nothing more than a definitional basis, are the functions identified by Parsons (1960) through his "action framework." Parsons argued that *all* systems must deal with adaptation, goal attainment, integration (internal coordination), and "latent pattern maintenance." The latter consists of culture-defining values, beliefs, and norms. It is proposed here that organizations characterized by sustained high performance are also characterized by certain sorts of values regarding each of the other three functions, values that foster sustained high performance.

The integration function should be strengthened by the value of high concern for people, as the coordination of individuals' and groups' behaviors is the essence of this function. It should also be facilitated by increased involvement of organization members, since such involvement helps to achieve what Thompson (1967) calls "coordination by mutual adjustment," the *only* way to coordinate effectively in many complex interdependent organizations. We see the three relationship-centered charismatic behaviors as all acting to create and reinforce values supporting the importance of people and of involving employees.

The goal-attainment function is, we propose, supported by a value that places client or customer goals above all else. This is of benefit because, at least for private sector organizations, it is through satisfaction of clients' goals that the organization prospers (by future resource inputs; see Sashkin 1985b). The charismatic leader task-centered behavior of focusing attention on key issues can be directed toward emphasizing this task-goal-related value.

Finally, the adaptation function is, we suggest, strengthened by a value that says, "take action, do *something*!" When faced with rapid change, as so many organizations are, and the need to confront such change and adapt to it, taking action, taking sensible risks, is a critical issue. And this is exactly what the charismatic leader behavior of risk-taking aims to instill.

We are, again, oversimplifying. First, it is rather doubtful that Bennis— or we—has identified "the" five charismatic leader behaviors. It is not, however, unreasonable to hypothesize that many or most of our five are among a larger set of such behaviors. And, unless one believes in magic or mental telepathy, it is *surely* through specific leader behaviors that the affective result we call "charisma" is created. Our argument is a hypothesis, but it is an interesting one, for it attempts to link macro organizational issues to micro executive leadership behaviors. We suggest that it is indeed, as Schein (1985) and Sashkin (1985c) argue, executive leaders who create organizational cultures.

And we hypothesize that they do this through specific behaviors that create charisma and thus instill the values, beliefs, and norms that create cultures in the minds of organization members.

Summary

Leaders' motivational needs and cognitive abilities provide them with the reason and wherewithal needed to focus on relevant situational factors and then determine and carry out behavioral strategies associated with effective leadership. Although the details are rather different for lower-to-middle-level operational leaders, versus high-level executive leaders, the basic pattern described by Lewin's equation, $B = f(P,S)$, holds true for both types of leader.

Identification of effective leadership behaviors, for either operational or executive leaders, is bound to provoke disagreement, for there is at present little enough agreement as to just what behaviors *are* effective. With respect to both sorts of leadership, we have tried to rely on empirical evidence to help identify effective behaviors, but we are fully aware of how limited that evidence is, as well as of the methodological arguments it has inspired. We mean our specifications to be tentative and open to change, based on future research. Our focus has been to look for organizationally-relevant leadership behaviors, for both operational and executive leadership, using Parsons' action framework as our base. It is this organizational focus that may be our most important contribution.

Conclusion

We believe that one challenge for leadership theory and research is the identification of a limited number of variables in each of the three areas—personality, situation, and behavior—that nonetheless explain a maximum degree of variance in leadership effectiveness. We feel that substantial progress has been made over the past decade toward this aim, and that in this sense the present chapter is more of a synthesis than it is a new treatment of leadership. A second and perhaps more difficult challenge is the development of an organizational approach to leadership, an approach that is not confined to the dyad or small group and that can deal with leadership as origination as well as interpolation and administration. If we have produced new ideas and a new approach to leadership it is with regard to this second challenge.

Over the past decade we believe there has developed a degree of convergence of the work of various research scholars and practitioners in the field of leadership. The leading edge of this work is in the domain of organizational concepts of leadership, concepts that do not ignore the individual or individual-level variables but that relate such factors to organizational issues and phenomena. It has been our aim to sketch some broad outlines of this new organizational approach to leadership. To the extent that we have succeeded we will stimulate discussion, disagreement, and new syntheses with regard to the issues we have tried to address.

5
Commentary on Part I

Chapter 2 Commentary: Welcome Back Charisma

D. Anthony Butterfield

For about the last ten years, we leadership researchers have been very critical of the research knowledge generated in our field. Indeed, the 1975 leadership symposium book, *Leadership Frontiers,* in which John Miner suggested doing away with the leadership concept (Miner 1975), can be seen as the stimulus for all sorts of self-flagellation. The next symposium book was even more self-critical. It was called *Leadership: The Cutting Edge* (Hunt and Larson 1977), and cutting edge turned out to mean cutting up each others' work rather than a ship's bow knifing ahead through the waters. It has since become fashionable to dump on the output of mainstream leadership research, and to call for new ways of approaching the study of leadership, and new theories to account for the leadership phenomenon — if, indeed, there is such a phenomenon. Thus, we have *Emerging Leadership Vistas,* the title of this book.

To this presumed sorry state of leadership research has been added in recent years a general disaffection, on the part of a growing number of social scientists and organizational behavior researchers in particular, with the whole approach to the study of organizational behavior based on functionalism and logical positivism. Now, it is not just leadership research that is in the doghouse, it is practically the whole body of knowledge in organizational behavior generated by the functionalist paradigm.

The chapter by Boal and Bryson ambitiously tackles both fronts simultaneously. It offers a new and comprehensive model for looking at leadership in terms of charisma, and it does so from a broad epistemological perspective that includes the increasingly popular interpretivist approach without, happily, rejecting the structuralist.

Contributions of the Boal and Bryson Chapter

The Boal and Bryson chapter offers several important contributions to the field of leadership theory. First, it explains the dynamics of the charismatic leadership process, in ways more thorough than other current charismatic approaches such as Bennis and Nanus (1985) and Tichy and Ulrich (1984), and even the Avolio and Bass, and Sashkin chapters in this book. It does this through the notion of phenomenological validity, which charismatic leaders create in the minds of followers. Second, it posits two types of charismatic leadership—visionary and crisis-produced—each with its own type of phenomenological validity: intrinsic validity (balance between the individual's internal states and behavior) for visionary charisma, and extrinsic validity (balance between the individual's behavior and its consequences) for crisis-produced charisma. These explanations and distinctions are useful, as long as one accepts the notion that the charisma exists in the minds of the followers. The psychologist in me has no problems with that, although the logical positivist in me squirms a bit.

In defining charismatic leadership in terms of its effects on followers, Boal and Bryson borrow directly and openly from House's 1976 charismatic theory, presented in an earlier symposium volume (House 1977). Although their explanation of charismatic leadership goes well beyond his, it gets to be a bit confusing, and I am not yet convinced that crisis-produced charismatic leadership ought to be called charismatic, or even, for that matter, leadership, since it is so temporary and situation-bound. "Crisis-produced problem solving" might be more correct; but I like their explanation of crisis-produced charismatic leadership as enabling followers to see positive connections between their behavior and outcomes.

A third contribution is Boal and Bryson's accounting for charismatic leadership at both the individual and group level. Groups achieve phenomenological validity through the process of co-orientation, for visionary leadership, and system effectiveness, for crisis-produced charismatic leadership. Although this goes well beyond House's work, which focused primarily on the individual, their presentation for the group level is much less thorough and convincing than that for the individual level of analysis. They hint that this could be due to space limitations. It may also be more difficult to pull off.

A fourth contribution of Boal and Bryson is their merging of the phenomenological and structural approaches. Although most of what I have mentioned of their work thus far deals with the phenomenological, their stress on patterned regularities in moving from the individual to group level, and their explicit incorporation of task and environmental variables, even though as perceived by the follower, makes an integration with structural approaches possible. Although I am not convinced that they have pulled it off, it is a worthy attempt, and a welcome relief from our tendency to entrench ourselves in one paradigmatic approach versus another.

Concerns about the Boal and Bryson Chapter

On the whole I admire their effort. Nevertheless, there are some concerns I have, some of which I have hinted at. First, as already suggested, calling crisis-produced leadership charismatic may do a disservice to the notion of leadership and charisma because of the short-term nature of most crises. As Boal and Bryson themselves point out, the term *charisma* is derived from "gift." I am not sure what gift crisis-produced charismatic leaders possess, other than being in the right place at the right time. Thus, Boal and Bryson may have unnecessarily created a contingency theory of charismatic leadership, when one may not yet be needed. Visionary leadership evolving from crisis, such as Lee Iacocca's rescue of Chrysler, can be seen as charismatic. But I would not call TWA stewardess Uli Derickson charismatic for her magnificent performance in handling the group during the recent highjacking of flight #847. Thus, although adding the crisis dimension makes their model more comprehensive, I am not sure it makes it better.

Second, the sixth element of their model, task or environmental variables, is the weakest. Although it highlights their interest in integrating interpretive and structural perspectives, it really has little to do with leadership, except that the leader can manipulate such variables. Their propositions are worthy, testable propositions, but they do not have much to do with leadership. They could as easily be propositions for a theory of job design.

This fact leads to a third concern. Propositions should spur new research. Yet, their first two are essentially definitional:

> Proposition 1: There must be a high degree of internal correspondence between the perceptions and feelings of the follower and the behavior of the follower, and a high degree of external correspondence between the behavior of the follower and the consequence of that behavior for the "charismatic situation" to be real to the follower and for charismatic effects to be produced.

> Proposition 2: For long-lasting charismatic effects to be produced effective follower and leader performance (i.e., behavior appropriate to task demands and in accord with normative standards) must be reinforced; successful performance is probably especially important in the case of maintaining crisis-produced effects.

Proposition 1 is the core of theory and proposition 2 is a charismatic leadership version of Thorndike's Law of Effect. The remainder of the propositions do not deal with leadership per se. In other words, although there is much that is new in the chapter, we do not really have any new or test-worthy propositions regarding charismatic leadership among the fifteen they list.

A fourth concern is that their explication of group-level charismatic process is not thoroughly carried out. Their identification of both individual and group charismatic effects shows promise, but is not realized. I would rather have seen some propositions dealing with charisma at the group level, than those on the task and environment which have so little to do with leadership.

A fifth concern is not so much a concern as an observation. Despite its title, this chapter is not really so much a chapter on charismatic leadership as it is on the general process of attribution, and of understanding our worlds at work. It is about epistemology in organizational research. In fact, of their roughly seventy references, only about fifteen deal directly with leadership. The rest deal primarily with issues of research methodology and philosophy of science. Indeed, theirs is one of the few pieces on leadership I have read in recent years that does not cite Stogdill's *Handbook of Leadership* (Stogdill 1974a) or Bass's update of it (Bass 1981). Thus this chapter is much more than a contribution on leadership; therein lies much of its weightiness, I suspect.

I have a sixth concern, and it is probably unfair. The Boal and Bryson piece is a very academic contribution. It is a perfect example of a paper written for academics to talk to each other, which is of course why it was written in the first place and why these volumes are published—for academics to talk to each other about our work. Nevertheless, given the topic of leadership, which is so pervasive in our society and which will not go away no matter how much some academics might want it to, I was hoping to see something of explicit practical relevance for real-world leaders. Even a few examples would help get the authors' point across now and then. Again, this comment may be unfair, given the nature of the intended audience; and I am sure some leaders would find this piece a help to their understanding of their own leadership process. Perhaps I should just wait for the version to come out in *Organizational Dynamics*.

Need for Research on Charismatic Leadership

The last several years have witnessed the emergence of charismatic approaches to scholarly work on leadership. The Boal and Bryson chapter is a strong example of this movement. It is a movement to be welcomed. Charismatic leadership has always been of interest in the popular press, especially during the time of presidential elections in the United States. As a society we seem to search for explanations for social outcomes in terms of what leaders did or did not do, just as attribution theory says (cf. this book's chapter 10, by McElroy and Hunger). We also seem to look for solutions to social problems in terms of what leaders can do for us, particularly at election time. This is in spite of John F. Kennedy's inaugural command that we do otherwise.

Until recently, however, charisma did not receive much scrutiny from leadership researchers in organizational behavior, although it has remained of interest in other disciplines, such as political science (e.g., Barber 1977, Burns 1978). This avoidance on the part of scientific researchers is due to several factors. First, as leadership research progressed in full force in the 1960s and early 1970s, quantitative studies increased, as did psychometric concerns with measuring leadership. Charisma was difficult to study because it seemed almost impossible to measure (Butterfield 1972). (The Boal and Bryson chapter has deftly sidestepped this problem, in part by remaining a conceptual model without having to resort to ways of operationalizing variables.) Indeed, we became very expert, and still are, at criticizing methodological weaknesses, especially measurement.

Second, starting with Fiedler (1967), contingency theories arrived on the scene and became paramount. All sorts of other factors had to be taken into account before leadership could be understood. It was almost as though the leader was being taken out of theories of leadership. If the leader was of limited importance anyway, then surely charismatic theories were out of step with mainstream contingency approaches.

Today there is a third factor at work, seeming to discredit charismatic approaches to the study of leadership. Elements of this factor are reflected in much of the content of this book. Behind this factor is the notion that studying leadership directly is inappropriate because the very concept of leader is the result of our social construction of reality. We have been studying the wrong thing, or studying something that does not really exist except in our heads. Even if that is true, and the latter may well be true, that does not make the concept of leader or leadership unimportant, or necessarily consigned to the research junkyard as obsolete, particularly if one's paradigm assumes, in essence, that all social reality is socially constructed.

So why should we welcome back attention to charismatic leadership, and be glad that there are not one but *three* chapters on charisma in this book? Simple. The language of charisma and expectations for it are around us everywhere and every day. It is high time we leadership researchers caught up with everybody else.

Conclusion

Boal and Bryson's chapter is a very good effort toward finding new ways of thinking about leadership. It is comprehensive, integrative, and very sophisticated in its elaboration of the charismatic leadership process. As I suspect most of us do, I believe the field of leadership research is better off if we have new models, and new methodologies. It is better to have alternative perspectives, indeed, alternative paradigms. I believe it is better yet to have models that can integrate alternative perspectives, which the Boal and Bryson model does. For that they have my admiration.

According to brainstorming theory, it is better to generate many new and different ideas in order to increase the probability of getting a good one. However, it does not necessarily follow that any given new idea is better than an old one. New and different may be just that, but not *better* than the old or similar. At times in our clamor for new approaches to the study of leadership

I fear we have become like marketers, who are always trying to come out with new products, just to increase sales. It may say new on the box, but is it really new inside, and is it really any better than the old?

The new perspective in the Boal and Bryson chapter does not reject the old, it builds on it. It does not throw out the old paradigm, it integrates it with the new. Charisma does deserve some scientific attention these days, as does leadership per se. Although their chapter is certainly not without problems, I find it an insightful and constructive stimulus to our thinking about leadership.

Chapter 3 Commentary: Transformational Leadership: Fostering Follower Autonomy, Not Automatic Followership

Jill W. Graham

One approach to understanding leadership, especially charismatic leadership, is to study followers, but there are two fundamentally different ways to do that. One highlights followers' dependence on the leader, the other, followers' capacity for independence. Exemplifying the first approach is House's (1977) seminal work on charismatic leadership, in which "unquestioning acceptance" and "willing obedience of the leader" are cited as responses by followers to charismatic leaders. That perspective has been dominant ever since, but Graham (1982) offered another point of view when she suggested that fostering follower *autonomy* is the hallmark of effective leadership. The present commentary elaborates on the latter position by focusing on the creation and support of good organizational citizenship. In this way it helps elaborate on and extend the Avolio and Bass chapter, which, it is argued, supports the idea that the appropriate product of leadership is follower autonomy rather than automatic followership.

A basic premise of this commentary is that the measure of good leadership is the work done by followers. It makes no sense to say that a leader did a good job of leading, but that followers did not do their part. A "good job of leading" is shown exactly *by* followers doing their part. That simple truth highlights followership as even more tightly linked to organizational effectiveness than is leadership. From that perspective, leadership within the organization is but an instrument to achieve followership, which in turn serves the goal of organizational effectiveness. As Meindl, Ehrlich, and Dukerich (1985) recently demonstrated, the tendency to focus on leader rather than follower behavior to account for organizational success or failure is a romantic simplification of reality which threatens to diminish rather than deepen our understanding of how to make organizations work better.

This commentary, then, focuses on followers and the relationship between leaders and followers, rather than on any heroic vision of leader behavior. The first section defines leader-follower relations in terms of follower autonomy. Avolio and Bass's distinction between transactional and transformational leadership is discussed. The next section considers two issues concerning followers: the nature of their attachment to the organization, and the nature of their performance within it. Organizational citizenship as a descriptor of autonomous follower behavior is introduced. The dangers of inattention to follower autonomy are explored in the third section, as is the role of transformational leadership in promoting autonomous followership. The commentary closes with some methodological caveats about doing research on transformational leadership. The possibility of combining research on organizational citizenship and transformational leadership is also suggested.

Leader-Follower Relations

Definitions of leader-follower relationships typically draw a distinction between voluntary acceptance of another's influence, on the one hand, and coerced compliance, on the other (Graham 1982, Hunt 1984, Jacobs 1971, Jago 1982, Katz and Kahn 1978). That distinction rests on the degree of free choice exercised by followers. Specific instances of obedience which stem from the fear of punishment, the promise of rewards, or the desire to fulfill contractual obligations are examples not of voluntary followership but of subordination, and the range of free choice available to subordinates is relatively small. Appropriate labels for the person giving orders, monitoring compliance, and administering performance-contingent rewards and punishments include "supervisor" and "manager," but *not* "leader." As noted by Jago (1982, 330), following Jacobs (1971):

> *Leadership* involves the influence of group members through interpersonal processes *without resort* to the authority or power derived from an employment contract. *Supervision,* on the other hand, involves the influence of group members through the use of formal rewards and punishments and through the exercise of contractual obligations. (emphasis added)

Hunt (1984, 21), referring to French and Raven's (1959) typology of bases for social power, makes a similar argument when he claims that "leadership is the use of personal-power bases (expert and referent)" whereas supervision "is the use of position-power bases (reward, coercion, and legitimacy) to influence group members."

The distinction between transactional and transformational leadership in the Avolio and Bass chapter bears a striking resemblance to what is now the well-established difference between supervision and leadership. Certainly a transactional leader's use of contingent reinforcements is nothing more than supervision. Research on supervision, moreover, is in the same conceptual category as theories of organizational control and the operant paradigm for employee motivation (Jago 1982, 330). Only transformational leadership occupies a conceptual category that is independent of those other topics, that is, leadership standing alone.

Followers' Organizational Attachment and Performance

Here, two issues concerning followers are discussed: the nature of their attachment to the organization, and the nature of their performance within it. Followership is considered as distinct from subordination, just as leadership is distinct from supervision. Using O'Reilly and Chatman's (1984) adaptation of Kelman's (1958) trichotomy (compliance, identification, and internalization) to describe an employee's psychological attachment to the organization, we can posit that *subordinates* are linked to organizations in order to obtain specific, extrinsic rewards; the nature of their involvement is instrumental compliance. *Followers,* on the other hand, are psychologically linked to the organization because of identification (that is, involvement based on pride in affiliation) and/or internalization (that is, involvement based on a congruence between individual and organizational values).

Interesting parallels are plausible between those types of employee attachment to organizations and the bases of leader influence discussed by Hunt (1984). Position-based power for supervisors is plausibly linked to instrumental compliance by subordinates. Person-based power for leaders, on the other hand, may correspond to identification and internalization in followers, with referent power most closely linked to identification and expert power to internalization. Those hypotheses might be tested with the help of Podsakoff and Schriesheim's (1985) recent advice on improved measurement of French and Raven's (1959) power bases.

The second issue to be raised about followers (again in contrast to subordinates) concerns their behavior on the job. What separates excellence from adequacy in regard to followership and subordination? This is a topic that a number of researchers are currently studying under the title of "organizational citizenship" (see Graham 1985, for a review). The essential requirements of organizational participation and task performance form the core of an employment contract.

Compliance with those essential requirements, however, can range from minimal maintenance of appearances, through grudging performance of assigned duties, to cheerful obedience. Beyond those varieties of compliance with the employment contract, moreover, lie several kinds of *superior* performance that can be called good organizational citizenship. Compliance in this case is not with regard to what a job contract requires or a supervisor has instructed, but rather what the employee supposes *would be* desired if the present situation had been foreseen or were now known by higher-ups in the organization. The employee engages in what might be termed "anticipatory compliance," fulfilling the spirit as well as the letter of organizational policy, supervisory instruction, or just plain common sense.

The criteria for good organizational citizenship, as proposed by Graham (1985), are threefold:

1. It is represented by observable behaviors, not private attitudes.
2. It is discretionary, that is, it goes beyond the minimum requirements of a job description or supervisory instruction.
3. The primary beneficial impact is on the organization, not on the employee's own immediate interests.

Initial work at Indiana University done on the organizational citizenship concept led to two published studies (Smith, Organ, and Near 1983, Bateman and Organ 1983), the first finding a two-factor description of organizational citizenship (factors the authors labeled "generalized compliance" and "altruism"), and the second a single factor.

Feeling that citizenship involves more than voluntary helping behavior, and certainly more than mere compliance, another group of researchers (Cummings, Dunham, Graham, and Pierce) are currently engaged in an effort to develop a reliable multidimensional measure of organizational citizenship. The general categories being explored include extraordinary compliance with rules and instructions; initiative and innovation on the job; interpersonal helpfulness within the organization; support of the organization to outsiders; and responsible political involvement in organizational affairs (including principled dissent). The results of the effort to develop measures of citizenship should be helpful in providing a way to test Avolio and Bass's predictions about the effect of transformational leadership on followers' levels of activation and effort.

Follower Free Choice

A theme common to the familiar distinction between supervision and leadership, on the one hand, and the definition of organizational citizenship, on the other, is follower free choice. Followers freely choose to be influenced by those who lead them (that is, their allegience is not coerced, bought, or owed), and organizational citizens volunteer organizational service beyond job requirements. Supportive leadership, in fact, was found to be one of the determinants of organizational citizenship by Smith, Organ, and Near (1983).

But consider what would happen if either of those wells ran dry, if obedience became habituated subordination, or if superior performance were redefined as the new standard of required performance. Superficially we would have a semantic problem: by our definition, leadership is impossible unless followership is problematic, that is, unless subordinates have it within their power *not* to accept a leader's influence. Similarly, when what were once extra-role behaviors become expected of a role incumbent, performance of those behaviors is no longer discretionary and hence loses its status as evidence of organizational citizenship. Without follower free choice, leadership and citizenship would both disappear — to be replaced, respectively, by supervision and routine performance.

At a deeper level and going beyond semantics, however, the dry-well problem raises a more profound question: once subordinates are successfully conditioned to follow instructions without question, can they ever regain the capacity to think for themselves, to innovate, to contribute at a level "over and above mechanical compliance with the routine directives of the organization" (Katz and Kahn 1978, 528)?

Although House's theory of charismatic leadership (1977) does not address that issue directly, his list of charismatic effects on followers emphasizes their dependence on the charismatic leader, rather than their capacity for independence. By that account, once followers surrender themselves to a charismatic leader, follower autonomy is gone for good.

Avolio and Bass's multidimensional analysis of transformational leadership reveals features that support a more optimistic view. They found three factors within transformational leadership:

1. *Charisma:* Possessing gifts of insight and inspirational communication; instilling faith, respect, even awe in followers.

2. *Individualized consideration:* Creating learning opportunities tailored to individual needs; treating each person with respect.

3. *Intellectual stimulation:* Facilitating radical thinking, even to the extent of inviting followers to challenge the positions of the leader.

Individualized consideration and intellectual stimulation are the pump primers used by transformational leaders to make followers more self-confident, self-reliant, and critical people, all of which reduces the likelihood that followers will fall into habituated subordination. Adding the latter two factors to purely charismatic leadership provides the theoretical safeguard against the well of follower free choice running dry.

Followers who, as autonomous organizational citizens, utilize their critical skills to assess organizational issues, communicate their analyses to others, and participate in devising and implementing constructive responses to organizational problems and opportunities, are at one and the same time engaging in political citizenship within the organization, contributing to organizational effectiveness, and demonstrating the effects of transformational leadership as outlined by Avolio and Bass. That sounds great, but how and when could it ever happen? Can real leaders contribute to organizational citizenship in followers, or does the human need for control and desire for personal power preclude empowerment of others?

Although there is certainly room for some cynicism on that matter, there are also reasons for optimism. The notion of leadership as employee development and empowerment has most recently been popularized in the "Excellence" books (Peters and Waterman 1982, Peters and Austin 1985), and also in Bennis and Nanus's (1985) book on leaders, all of which contain many real-life examples of transformational leadership.

Peters and Austin (1985) highlight five different activities engaged in, each under particular circumstances, by exceptionally talented leaders. They include educating, sponsoring, coaching, counseling, and confronting employees.

All of those activities build the self-esteem and confidence of employees, as well as facilitate their growth and independence, and they do so in a way that is collaborative rather than condescending. In the terminology of transactional analysis (Berne 1961), leader and follower relate as adult-adult rather than as parent-child. Individualized consideration and intellectual stimulation are certainly among the behaviors recommended by Peters and Austin (1985).

Bennis and Nanus (1985, 82–83) touch on many of the same themes when they identify four components of employee empowerment, which is the outcome of effective leadership: feelings of *significance* (making a difference to the organization and/or the world at large), *competence* (skill development and learning on the job), *community* (joining with others in common purpose), and *enjoyment* (having fun).

At least in the popular business press, then, transformational leadership is all the rage. Reports in scholarly journals will doubtless follow as the research program of Avolio and Bass (and others) reveals important relationships between transformational leadership and other concepts in organizational behavior.

Conducting Research on Transformational Leadership

In closing, I want to raise again the issue of organizational effectiveness and its relationship to leadership. I argued at the outset that the test of good leadership is effective performance by followers. But that is *not* to say that employees only perform well in the presence of good leaders. There are certainly other contributing factors to effective performance besides leadership.

Employees might be intrinsically motivated, be part of self-managed work teams, or have available to them other technical or organizational "substitutes for leadership" (Kerr and Jermier 1978; Pierce, Dunham, and Cummings 1984) which contribute to their effective performance. Because of the potential importance of factors other than leader behavior, Avolio and Bass's proposal to study transformational leaders by means of psychohistorical analysis must be viewed with considerable caution.

In proposing to identify transformational leaders by reference to the success of their groups or organizations, Avolio and Bass risk making the attributional error discussed by Meindl, Ehrlich, and Dukerich (1985), namely, exceptional group performance may cause observers to attribute socially desirable characteristics to group leaders quite apart from their actual possession. If that is the case, psychohistorians would be collecting popular myths about leadership rather than learning about actual leader behavior, let alone about the factors contributing to success that are unrelated to leadership.

That would mean a retreat to the unedifying oversimplification of charismatic leadership as mesmerizing mystery and magic. Avolio and Bass's singular contribution is to focus on specific dimensions of leader behavior that go *beyond* glitter and excitement, to those that empower followers to serve as autonomous organizational citizens. A promising way to do research on that form of leadership is to measure both transformational leadership and organizational citizenship behavior in a single study.

Chapter 4 Commentary:
The Merger of Macro and Micro Levels of Leadership

Patricia Riley

The impetus for Marshall Sashkin and Robert Fulmer's chapter, "Toward an Organizational Leadership Theory," is relatively simple—theory and research have focused on the "supervisory management" level of leadership to the exclusion of "top-level" leadership. By utilizing Lewin's constructs of person, situation, and behavior, Sashkin and Fulmer suggest a model that provides parallel interpretations of effective leadership for both the "operational" and "executive" levels of leadership.

These comments regarding Sashkin and Fulmer's work address three general areas: (1) the conceptual framework, (2) epistemological concerns, and (3) future research.

Conceptual Framework

The model presented in their chapter blends previous findings on effective management/leadership with several rediscovered issues in organizational research (i.e., culture and charisma). An attempt to integrate such diverse concepts is both intriguing and timely. Sashkin and Fulmer, first, focus on the distinction between "management" and "leadership." Recent literature indicates that distinctions between these activities have been obscured and that the differences are significant. Bennis (1984) believes that "managers do things right while leaders do the right things" and Riley and Finney (1986) state that "bureaucrats invoke rules, managers create rules, and leaders transform rules." Although separating these forms of "leadership" is not new (e.g., James MacGregor Burns's separation of transformative leaders from transactional ones [Burns 1978], and Max Weber's argument that charismatic leaders launch enterprises and bureaucrats run them [Weber 1947]), conceptualizing both forms of leadership behavior as "a function of personality factors in interaction with important aspects of situations" is new.

What is needed, however, is a clearer assessment of the extent to which Lewin's formulation is actually being used to explain the functioning of effective leadership. It seems to exist primarily as a category scheme that allows comparisons to be made across the two types of leadership.

Sashkin and Fulmer, second, successfully synthesize previous research within their tripartite model. Many leadership studies in the organizational behavior literature focus on person, situation, or behavior factors, or some combination thereof, particularly at the operational level of leadership. The "variable" structure of the framework, however, is less well suited to the more symbolic aspects of executive level leadership, as the concepts tend to be more elusive than traditional social science constructs.

For example, "charisma" is the dominant element in the "behavior" category for executive leadership. Although Sashkin and Fulmer are referring to the actions of "charismatic leaders," a more faithful representation of this concept would place it in the person category. For Weber, charisma is a complex interaction of leader, follower, crisis, etc., but first and foremost, charisma exists because of the unusual, transcendental qualities possessed by an individual (Shils 1965). This does not deny that there are similarities in the actions of charismatics; there are (House 1977). The issue, however, is that if an individual models these characteristic behaviors, he or she may become a better manager, or perhaps even a better leader, but it is difficult to imagine that engaging in such actions simultaneously endows one with charisma. Thus charisma should first be considered a personal attribute.

The complexity of identifying "behaviors," in the sense that Lewin used the term, certainly adds to the confusion. Sashkin and Fulmer note that perceptions of an operational leader's behavior, and observations of physical actions by that same leader, can vary greatly (they attribute this to flexibility and situational planning by the leader; however, an analogy to equifinality in systems theory may be just as accurate). Bennis (1984) similarly states that the styles and actions of the "charismatic leaders" he interviewed were quite disparate. Thus the "behaviors" Sashkin and Fulmer present are often meta-behaviors—not descriptions of what these individuals actually do, but categories and patterns of action that include evaluations of successful outcomes (i.e., effective communication; creating sensible risks and opportunities that involve others). A clearer understanding of the relationship between these implicit effectiveness outcomes and behavior—whether observed, perceptual, or intersubjectively understood—is needed.

The "person" and "situation" categories fare much better in the synthesis of executive leadership research, as the current literature is replete with provocative examples. For instance, "vision," or the capacity to see connections that are not obvious or are unprecedented, is clearly a personal ability, although it obviously is affected by other organizational factors.

Organizational culture, as the "situation" example, represents the shared values and patterns of activity that enable and constrain executive leaders. There is some conceptual slippage, however, in the explanation of "culture." Sashkin and Fulmer give paramount attention to the actions of "culture creation" and "pattern maintaining" under the situation category. Such activities seem more appropriate to the behavior category (certainly more appropriate than charisma). Aspects of culture such as cultural types (e.g., "Z" cultures, Ouchi 1981) or the depth and breadth of cultures or subcultures would be more congruent with the notion of "situation."

The notion of subcultures is a necessary addition because the chapter has a tendency to treat cultures as monolithic. (The problems with this viewpoint are given by Lewis (1985), among others.) In addition, although Sashkin and Fulmer's position that leaders are the primary force in culture creation has intuitive appeal, other researchers have suggested that leaders may be able to influence cultural development only at certain periods in an organization's history (see Martin, Sitkin, and Boehm 1983 for a review of this literature).

In summary, the model presented by Sashkin and Fulmer synthesizes numerous studies on leadership and illuminates the consistencies between the two types of leadership across the three components of effective leadership. The theoretical underpinnings of this model need to be explicated with respect to leadership and reconciled with the more "interpretive" literature on executive leadership. Finally, a more concrete way of operationalizing "effectiveness" is needed to better conceptualize the relationship between behavior and the person and situation factors.

Epistemological Concerns

In the conclusion of their chapter, Sashkin and Fulmer call for the identification of a limited number of variables that will someday explain a maximum degree of variance in leader effectiveness. This may be a fruitful enterprise; however, the nature of the phenomena under investigation—particularly the concepts described under executive leadership—also points to lines of research that are neither variable analytic nor parsimonious in the traditional sense.

The notions of charisma, vision, and culture all share a sense of the aesthetic—the art form of leadership (another Bennis term). This requires some forms of analysis that are sensitive to style, to the creation of meaning, and to the dramatic edge of leadership. Symbols like "leader" and "charismatic" have power in and of themselves because of their ability to evoke expressive and nonrational images and feelings. To utilize these terms as mere categories of behaviors runs the risk of stripping them of this power and moving them to the level of the mundane—plain-label symbols.

Future Research

Although current research into these areas is primarily interpretive (storytelling, metaphor analysis, etc.), this need not be the case. Empirical studies can be undertaken within compatible research traditions—for example, social cognition, structuration, discourse analysis, rules theory. What is important is that leadership remains embedded in the social structure in which it is enacted. Isolated from the systems that create and recreate leadership, theory will never advance to some of the more compelling questions: How do certain forms of leadership emerge? How are organizational cultures and leadership related? What circumstances give rise to transformative leadership? And what leads to the success or failure of either particular individuals or certain forms of leadership?

One of the most interesting areas for future research lies in pedagogy. If, indeed, executive leadership is different in kind from management, can it be taught? Can executives develop "vision," for example, and does it differ from long-term strategic planning?

In looking at the relationship between leadership and culture, assessments must be made regarding various levels of leadership. To what extent do cultures reproduce themselves with little or no regard to top-level leadership? To what extent is culture maintenance or culture change dependent on leadership activities at many levels and in many subgroups in the organization? Another area that needs more research is the influence of culture on perceptions of leadership (both organizational and national culture).

Theoretical advancements are also needed to bridge micro- and macro-levels of analysis (the theory of structuration—e.g., Giddens 1979—is one promising avenue of research), and to better integrate the "nonrational" or political components of leadership.

The list could go on ad infinitum. What is important is that through the spotlight on organizational culture, interest in leadership *in context* was reborn. This should create theoretical and practical advancements beyond our present understanding.

Part II
Leadership in a Dynamic Organizational Context

James G. Hunt
B.R. Baliga
H. Peter Dachler
Chester A. Schriesheim

T his part brings together different aspects of leadership in a dynamic organizational setting. It consists of three content chapters and a commentary chapter.

"The Skills of Leadership" (chapter 6), by Dian-Marie Hosking and Ian Morley, argues that a key problem with leadership is that leadership phenomena typically have been divorced from the organizational processes of which they are a part. Accompanying this has been a neglect of the significance of leadership skills as they accompany leadership processes.

The authors develop a conceptual model around these processes and skills. Leadership is seen as the process by which social order is constructed and changed. It relies heavily on negotiation and the accompanying skills as leaders negotiate descriptions of threats and opportunities (their political environment) or as they negotiate a particular interpretation of events and what to do about them. The leader contributes to social order both within his or her group and in relation to other groups or even organizations. This is called organizing, and the authors argue that it needs to be contrasted with traditional macro-oriented leadership approaches (e.g., Hunt and Osborn 1982) which concentrate on what they call the "condition of being organized." Hosking and Morley discuss in detail the nature of the skills needed to carry out the processes of leadership and suggest some ways of testing their model.

Continuing the dynamic processual aspects of leadership, but from a very different espistemological perspective, is Andrew Crouch and Philip Yetton's chapter 7, "The Management Team: An Equilibrium Model of Manager and Subordinate Performance and Behavior." The authors develop a dynamic model tested with six-person management subordinate work teams. According to the model, the behavior and performance characteristics of a team tend to evolve toward either a high manager-subordinate, mutual trustworthiness condition or the opposite. The model also provides an explanation for the adjustments that occur in group membership. Furthermore, it examines the likely performance gain or loss from replacing a manager and/or subordinates in their particular groups.

The model's major tenets are supported by the authors' empirical data, and traditional strategies for team development are discussed in light of the model.

Hosking and Morley consider the process aspects of leadership to be needed at both the micro (within group) and macro (between groups and even between organizations) levels. Crouch and Yetton's chapter concentrates on process aspects at the group or team level. Chapter 8, "An Organizational Life Cycle Approach to Leadership," by B.R. Baliga and James G. Hunt, looks at differences in leadership/management requirements at different phases of the organization's life cycle.

The Hosking and Morley chapter conceptualizes leadership as a process, as does the Crouch and Yetton chapter. The Baliga and Hunt chapter conceives of the organizational life cycle as a four-phase process with each phase including a transition and a stage. Leadership as such is a variable within the life cycle process. Propositions are formulated to cover each phase. Thus, empirical work to test these propositions would consist of a series of tests done during each phase of the processual life cycle. In Melcher's (1979) terms, this would be a comparative statics approach, analogous to taking a series of snapshots rather than a dynamic processual approach, which would be analogous to using a movie camera.

The Baliga and Hunt chapter develops a model that looks at both transformational and transactional aspects of leadership and posits that the impact of these on organizational outcomes will differ as a function of the organization's phase in its life cycle, from inception to revitalization or death. Thus, in addition to its kinship with the other chapters in this part, the Baliga and Hunt piece also has linkages with the transformational and charismatic aspects of leadership treated in part I.

Klaus Bartölke was chosen as a commentator for Hosking and Morley's chapter 6 because of his broad background and work in areas related to but different from those in traditional leadership research. He focuses on the importance of Hosking and Morley's treatment of leadership as a social construction of reality. He provides a perspective beyond that of Hosking and Morley with respect to the place of negotiation in providing for the social construction of reality. Basically, his commentary extends and further develops the concepts in Hosking and Morley's chapter. Bartölke's knowledge of ways of constructing reality helps provide additional insights into the strengths and weaknesses of Hosking and Morley's innovative chapter. He also has something to say about the model's potential usefulness to practitioners.

Gilbert Probst was chosen as a commentator for the Crouch and Yetton chapter primarily because of his background and research in general systems theory. Like a number of others in this book (e.g., Bartölke, Calas and Smircich, Dachler, Hosking and Morley), he approaches his contribution using a non-functionalist perspective. Indeed, he argues strongly that the positivist approach of Crouch and Yetton is insufficient, even inappropriate, to really understand the kind of systemic thinking on which the Crouch and Yetton chapter is based in part.

To him trying to isolate the relationships as Crouch and Yetton have done simply does not reflect the essence of systemic thinking. He argues that we have to understand patterns of interactions and patterns of orders as they emerge and that concentrating on equilibrial states is too narrow a concept. Probst's commentary illustrates clearly the vast difference in perspective that exists between him and the authors in terms of how research should be conceptualized and conducted.

The Baliga and Hunt chapter developed as an offshoot of a symposium workshop session devoted to examining leadership in organizations in transition. It extended many of the ideas brought out in that session but because of the way in which it developed, it does not have a separate commentary as do the other chapters in this part.

Additional Concerns

What follows are some points beyond those contained in the commentary on the chapters in this part that may be of some interest to the reader. First, is the question of Hosking and Morley's conception of leadership. They see it as constructing social orders that foster the values and interests of the group to which group members belong in order to help group members deal with complexities. It is useful to compare this definition with the more traditional influence conceptualizations of leadership. What similarities and differences are there between the different conceptualizations? Hosking and Morley argue that a key difference is their emphasis on leadership as a process and in turn on ways of studying leadership. What are other implications of the different conceptualizations?

Second, is the model put forth by Hosking and Morley really a paradigm for scientific study of leadership (thus connoting a paradigm shift)? Or, on the other hand, is it, instead, a heuristic to guide case studies for descriptive purposes? Both are important but the implications for the field are quite different.

Third, how does one determine effectiveness in the Hosking and Morley approach? If, as is implied, the criteria have to be grounded in the particular context of a study, what are the implications for generalizability?

Fourth, the authors' conceptualization looks at leadership as a distributed (among group members) as opposed to a focused (appointed leader only) phenomenon. What are the implications of this in studying leadership in organizations?

Finally, as units are embedded in larger systems what is the relative impact of the unit leader(s)? To what extent does the larger system constrain or enhance the leadership actions?

Turning now to the Crouch and Yetton chapter, first, the model looks at the influence subordinates can have on the leader. This is a relatively neglected area in current leadership literature and thus enhances the value of the study.

Second, and related to Probst's concerns, what are process and context implications of this study of groups abstracted from their setting? In other words, in addition to examining leader-member relationships, an important issue is what do leaders do to develop desirable group processes? Also, how does one broaden this to include realistically the knowledge of the context within which the group operates?

Finally, to what extent does the cross-sectional nature of the study limit the processual conclusions that can be drawn? What are the implications for the inferences of Crouch and Yetton?

6

The Skills of Leadership

Dian-Marie Hosking
Ian E. Morley

The potential value of the leadership concept can be realized only by taking it seriously. The existing literatures do not "add up" (Argyris 1979), partly for the reason that diverse phenomena have been studied in the name of leadership. Here it will be argued that the concept can be made useful when used with greater care and rigor than has typically been the case. However, this, of itself, will not be enough. Decisions must be made about what kind of concept leadership should be. Shortcomings of the existing literatures again suggest what is required. It will be argued that the literatures do not add up because leadership phenomena have been divorced from the organizational processes of which they are a part (Child and Hosking 1979). One important consequence of this is that the political quality of leadership has received insufficient attention. Finally, it will be argued that additivity is lacking because the significance of *skills,* as they characterize leadership processes, has been largely ignored.

Although gloom and despair seem to characterize the comments of most critics, the view taken here is essentially one of optimism. The concept of leadership can be made to work through a social-psychological perspective in which it is intrinsically connected to the concepts of skill and organization. This may be achieved through attention to interlocking cognitive, social, and political processes. A model will shortly be outlined which does just this. However, it is first necessary to indicate what kind of model is intended and why.

Leadership, Skill, and Organization: Some Preliminary Remarks

A truly social-psychological approach requires premises and arguments concerning three components: participants, processes, and contexts. Each needs to be theorized in ways that implement existing knowledge. Further, and this is crucial to the arguments that follow, each component must be theorized in ways that are commensurate with the other two.

Participants

Our opening argument was for taking the concept of leadership seriously. This requires an explicit definition that can be employed to interpret existing literatures and to direct subsequent research and theory. We argue for a definition of leaders as those who consistently contribute certain kinds of acts to leadership processes. More precisely, we define participants as leaders when they (1) consistently make effective contributions to social order, and (2) are both expected and perceived to do so by fellow participants. In this sense, leaders' contributions represent a "special variety of ordinary member behavior" (Douglas 1983, 72). As will be shown, what makes the contributions "special" is their achievement of skillful leadership processes.

This conceptualization has three general and important implications. The first is that we prefer *not* to follow the common practice of using the terms *leader* and *manager* interchangeably (see Dubin 1979). This practice is becoming more widespread, resulting in a "leadership-management controversy" (Hunt, Sekaran, and Schriesheim 1982). In our view, studies of managerial behavior should not be assumed necessarily to inform our understanding of leadership. Of course they may; however, it is always necessary to establish that the managers concerned were also leaders in the sense the term is used here. Later, a model will be presented which was partly induced from certain studies of managers at work. Other research and theory led to the inference that such findings were of relevance to leadership. Of course this interpretation requires independent validation.

The second and related point is that the only sure means of identifying leaders is through the analysis of leadership processes. The reason, quite simply, is that leaders achieve their status as a result of their contributions, and the ways these are received, relative to the contributions of others. Therefore, the question of a participant's possible status as a leader cannot be resolved without reference to these processes. In other words, to study leaders must be to study leadership, that is, the processes by which "social order" is constructed and changed.

Third, and last, our conceptualization recognizes that significant leadership contributions may come from a minority, including a minority of one; equally, they may be expected and contributed by the majority. Either way, the processes are performed with a degree of skill that is likely to make a difference between effective improvement, maintenance, or decline of participants' social order.

Clearly, more must be said to even approximate a sufficient model of participants. However, this may be better achieved once processes and contexts have been discussed. For the present, it is sufficient to say that participants (whatever their formal or informal status) are understood as active, constructive, interpretive agents. They are argued to negotiate descriptions of their political environment (e.g., in terms of "threats" and "opportunities") and methods for dealing with it. They may differ in their values and interests, knowledge bases, and other resources; they may differ in the frequency with which they contribute acts that are influential in structuring leadership processes, and therefore, their social order.

Processes

In the symposium book, *Crosscurrents in Leadership,* Edwin Hollander called for "more attention to the study of process and to perceptions of context by the participants in leadership events" (Hollander 1979, 102). To some extent, this has occurred (see Hunt and Larson 1979; Hunt, Sekaran, and Schriesheim 1982). However, with one or two exceptions, this research has not attended to the processes implied by our concept of leadership. This is because they have focused on manager-subordinate relations within a recognizable task group.

By our definition, it is necessary to study the processes by which particular acts come to be perceived as contributions to social order, and therefore, come to be perceived as leadership acts. Studies are required of, for example, the means by which participants might attempt to maintain or destroy their status as leaders, having earned it; of status competition; changes in the status quo, and so on. Our conceptualization implies that these processes are endemic to leadership whether or not there are appointed managers involved. In other words, the position taken here is that leadership, properly conceived, is emergent. For these reasons, there is an urgent need for studies of the processes by which social order is constructed, while "simultaneously" and "implicitly" particular acts come to be defined as leadership contributions (see Stein et al. 1979).

We take the view that leadership processes represent a special kind of organizing activity. The organizing activity is political decision making, construed in the widest possible sense. This activity has the effect of constructing more or less stable social orders which, in turn, are more or less effective in protecting and promoting the values of participants. Social orders are, to some significant degree, negotiated; some are more negotiated than others. They are characterized by systems of both power, and value.

There are many reasons why power is an inevitable characteristic, one being that participants differ in their values; in consequence, some desire change, and some do not. This is also true of social orders. Differences in values are often accompanied by differences in resources to promote them. Further, some leadership processes will be more skillful, and therefore, more likely to protect and promote the values of that social order at the possible expense of others. In sum, leadership is an inherently political process.

Degrees of social order are revealed in both social and interrelated cognitive processes; higher degrees are present to the extent that participants are able to negotiate an "adequate guide to the use of knowledge and the conduct of human affairs" (Kelvin 1970, 226). Social order is grounded in considerations of value as these arise both with respect to means, i.e., "modes of conduct" (Lovejoy 1950), and ends (Brown and Hosking 1986).

The process of negotiation to which we have referred is a more or less collective process in which issues are agreed, solutions developed, and policies put into effect. These are referred to later as the "core processes" of leadership. They will be discussed using the abstract terms of information search, interpretation, choice, and influence. The terms are deliberately abstract so as to accommodate variations in their content.

Finally, while on the subject of processes, it is important to note that we do not restrict these to face-to-face, within-group interactions. Almost all leadership research has been of this kind. Although such processes provide some evidence of leadership, they are only part of the picture. Groups exist in the context of other groups, individuals simultaneously belong to many groups, and, group memberships overlap. Order is negotiated both within and between groups; negotiations result in tacit and explicit agreements concerning "threats" and "opportunities," the terms on which participants will do business, accept influence, and so on. Interactions within and between groups provide the means for, for example, building and mobilizing resources, building interpretations of what is going on, and what to do about it, and so on. Activities of this kind may make all the difference to the degree of skill with which values are promoted. Processes of this kind have rarely been contemplated in the leadership literatures. They are the subject of our model.

Contexts

It was asserted earlier that leadership has typically been abstracted from the organizational processes of which it is a part, and that this is one reason why the literatures do not "add up." The lack of attention to organizational variables has been noted in previous leadership symposia (Hunt and Larson 1979; Hunt, Sekaran, and Schriesheim 1982). Few researchers have investigated empirical relationships between leadership and organization (but, see Meyer 1975). More importantly, there is little in the way of theory which would effectively guide research of this kind. The few attempts that exist either imply, or explicitly argue, a perspective that has the effect of divorcing organization from social action (e.g., Hunt and Osborn 1982). Elsewhere, we have described this general approach as "entitative," as one that emphasizes the "condition of being organized": organization is treated as a macro object which exists independently of the activities, interactions, and evaluations of participants; the concept of organization is static and apolitical (Hosking and Morley 1985).

Criticisms of this perspective or "paradigm" have only recently gained force (see, e.g., Zey-Ferrell and Aiken 1981) and have largely been expressed outside the leadership literatures (but, see Hosking and Morley 1983, 1985). This is not the place to examine the range and substance of this critique. For our purposes, it is sufficient to note that the entitative perspective does not allow satisfactory conceptualization of links between organization and leadership processes. Such links can only be achieved through a "bottom-up," "processual" approach that stresses "acts of organizing" (Hosking and Morley 1985; Hosking, in press). It is within the context of this larger critique of the traditional concept of "organization" that our arguments concerning leadership take their full significance.

It is for reasons such as these that we argue for a view of leadership as a special kind of organizing activity (see earlier). Our concepts of leadership and organization imply that leaders and their groups, through their leadership processes, attempt to create and maintain a sense of social identity and social order for themselves. They do so in relation to other groups. Order is negotiated both within, and between, groups of participants whose values and interests, sense of identity and order are likely to vary, and sometimes, to conflict. In other words, "organization" is found in the cognitive-social and social-political processes through which leaders and groups enact, socially construct, and influence their social order, and that of interdependent others.

We shall argue that these processes may be performed with more or less skill. The degree of skill depends on participants' practical understanding of the systems of power and value in which they are involved (within and between groups); it depends on the abilities of leaders to "invent a formula" and "negotiate detail" (Zartman 1977), that is, to negotiate "frames" (Huff 1984). The skills are, to some extent, the skills found in negotiation, reflecting a sensitivity to the prevailing systems of power and value (Wrapp 1984), demonstrating a concern to reach agreements that will "stick" (Morley 1983). We shall have more to say about what these skills look like.

Existing Approaches to Social Skill: Description and Comment

Previous research on social skills may be described under the following four headings.

The Traditional Regression Approach

Work of this kind represents normal science within the "ruling orthodox paradigm" of North American research. Leadership effectiveness is defined as an outcome, and is typically investigated in relation to input, and moderator, or contingency variables using regression analysis. Leadership skills, if considered at all, are treated as traits of the leader, that is, as inputs (see Martinko and Gardner 1984). Aspects of organization are treated as contingency variables: variables which are viewed as independent of the activities and interpretations of leaders and other participants in leadership processes.

Theories of this kind exemplify the traditional emphasis on the condition of being organized. For this reason, they have little to say about the skills of organizing. For example they say little about what must be learned, or about the processes of learning that characterize leadership; they ignore the ways in which participants, particularly leaders, may be active agents in such processes. In contrast, the approach to be taken here emphasizes social learning: what has been called learning with descriptions (Minsky and Papert 1972). Broadly, the process of leadership is, in part, a process of learning how to describe contextual features, and how to make inferences based on those descriptions. The process is *social* because participants learn from others, and because they *influence* the ways other participants describe their context and act upon it. This is how leaders influence social order: by negotiating with others a particular interpretation of events and what to do about them.

Skill as a Resource

Heller and his colleagues have conducted longitudinal studies of decision making in organization (Drenth and Koopman 1984, Heller 1984). Their joint emphasis on skill and on decision making is of considerable interest in the present context. However, their attention has largely focused on the development of a contingency model of participation. They have not attended to the kinds of skills implied by a perspective that stresses leadership as an organizing activity.

The model to be presented discusses leadership as a *process of complex decision making*. Following Steinbruner, decisions are understood to be complex when a given policy has several effects, some beneficial, and some not. Complex decisions are characterized by a special kind of uncertainty which is structural, where the achievement of a sufficient sense of order, so that possible outcomes can be described, "is itself a matter of uncertainty" (Steinbruner 1974, 18). When placed in the context of organizing processes, decisions can be seen to be made more complex by being negotiated between interdependent participants who are likely to disagree about the "values at stake, the weight to be given to them, the resolution of major uncertainties" (Steinbruner 1974, 18). This leads to certain important "dilemmas." An understanding of these dilemmas is central to an understanding of leadership skills and yet they have been almost entirely ignored. We shall have more to say on these matters.

Micro Communication Skills

Explicit attempts to train managers in the micro-skills of communication have been employed in the context of interview training at the University of Bradford, in England. The essence of this approach is well captured by two of the researchers involved:

> Although we were ostensibly training people to carry out a particular kind of interview, we were in fact training people in skills which . . . would be useful in virtually any interaction between managers and subordinates. Rather to our surprise . . . we came to the conclusion that, implicitly, we were training people in leadership skills. (Wright and Taylor 1984, xi–xii)

This research is both interesting and important in its own right. However, it can contribute little understanding of leadership processes as they are defined here. The model to be presented is founded on the premise that leadership is primarily a matter of macro rather than micro skills. In contrast with the existing work in this area, we assume that leaders have a basic competence in the kinds of micro skills outlined by Argyle (Argyle 1969, 1978). Instead, the issues are seen as being whether or not participants "know their way around" their decision-making environment, how they achieve this understanding and make it practical, and what contributions leaders make to such processes. To quote Argyle, "In order to function effectively one needs a good map, showing how the system works" (Argyle 1984, 97). The model to be presented attempts to map the leadership processes by which this is, more or less, skillfully achieved.

Studies of Managerial Behavior

The last fifteen years have seen a marked increase in studies of managerial behavior, identifying what managers do, how they do it, the contacts they make, and so on (e.g., Kotter 1982, Sayles 1979, Stewart 1976). Although excellent in many ways, this work has not been directed by an explicit and systematic treatment of the skills involved. Further, the authors have not implemented a distinction between leadership and management, and have not been concerned with leadership as an organizing process in the sense employed here.

Despite these features, some of the empirical work seems to provide evidence of the leadership skills implied by an organizing perspective. For example, certain studies suggest that effective managers recognize and deal with "dilemmas," which are endemic to the relationships, and issues, in which they participate. In particular, they suggest the importance of networking, and begin to explore the skills involved (see, e.g., Kanter 1984, Kotter and Lawrence 1974). What is needed is a systematic account in which the concept of skill serves to integrate the discussion of relations between leadership and organization. Such an account will now be offered.

The Skills of Leadership

The main purpose of this chapter is to present a general model of leadership skills which integrates talk about leadership with talk about organization. The most important elements in the model are summarized in figure 6–1.

The elements are taken from Morley's analysis of the skills of formal negotiation (Morley 1981a, b; 1983) and from Hosking's analysis of leadership as skillful organization (Brown and Hosking 1986; Grieco and Hosking 1985; Hosking 1983a, b; Hosking, in press; Hosking and Morley 1983, 1985). The model emphasizes leadership processes as those of "complex" decision making (see earlier) in which participants recognize and respond to actual or potential changes in the status quo—changes that imply that they may have something significant to lose (a stake) or gain (a prize). Leaders are defined as those who are both perceived, and expected, to make consistent, influential contributions to such processes.

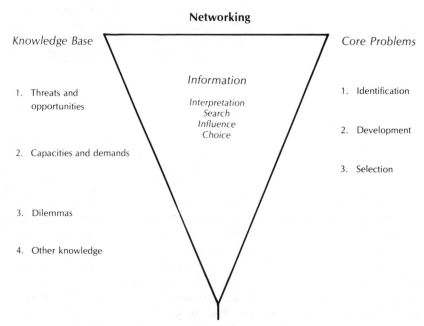

Networking

Knowledge Base

Information

1. Threats and
   opportunities

*Interpretation
Search
Influence
Choice*

2. Capacities and demands

3. Dilemmas

4. Other knowledge

Core Problems

1. Identification

2. Development

3. Selection

Protect and pursue values and interests through understanding

Figure 6–1. A General Model of Social Skill

Figure 6–1 is intended to describe the elements necessary for the analysis of *any* social skill that involves complex decision making in the sense described. It is assumed that the processes will vary in their content, that is, in the particular values, interests, and so on, under study. In other words, a social situation is recognized as different to the extent that it requires changes in the content of the elements in figure 6–1.

Social skills may always be described in terms of the "core processes" identified inside the triangle of figure 6–1. This being so, any process of complex decision making may be interpreted in terms of the processes of information interpretation, information search, influence, and choice. To focus on "core processes" is to focus on one unit of analysis. Three additional units are required in order to describe the more or less skilled ways in which these core processes may be structured: knowledge bases, networking, and core problems. No one of these can be understood without understanding its relation with the other two, or without considering its significance in relation to core processes, and to the values of the social order. This makes separate discussion of each element less than satisfactory. Even so, this is what will be done.

Knowledge Bases

Recent work in cognitive science has shown the degree to which intelligent, or skilled, performance depends on a variety of different kinds of knowledge (e.g., Minsky and Papert 1972). Further, other areas of inquiry, such as symbolic interactionism, political psychology, and cognitive sociology, indicate some of the interrelations between cognitive, social, and political processes.

The Perception of Threats and Opportunities. Decision making begins when leaders recognize and respond to actual or potential changes in the status quo—changes that are inherently ambiguous. They are interpreted, that is, given meaning, by relating them to cognitive frameworks such as "operational codes," "frames," or "scripts" (see Holsti 1970, Huff 1984, Gioia and Poole 1984). In this sense, skilled leadership depends on skilled perceptions: leaders have a significant influence over such processes. They achieve this, in part, through contributing higher-order constructs which help systematically to organize understandings of the environment, and how to work in it. What this amounts to, is that leadership involves the management of meaning. Leaders promote persuasive scripts that help others to interpret actions, and events, in relation to the "core values" of their social order (e.g., Selznick 1957, Weick 1978). Further, by definition, leaders are *expected* to make contributions of this kind, and to do so consistently (Huff 1984, Morley and Hosking 1984). "Effective leadership depends on the extent to which the leader's definition of the situation . . . serves as a basis for action by others" (Smircich and Morgan 1982, 262).

Leaders achieve the preceding through negotiating acceptance of persuasive scripts—scripts that are motivating because they engage central values, and suggest ways in which participants should mobilize resources to protect their "stakes," or gain a "price." They are able to do so primarily because cognitive frameworks, such as scripts, define, *in ordinary language,* threats and opportunities in relation to values; they bring certain values sharply into focus, at the expense of others. Further, frameworks of this kind exemplify the "reasoning of practical syllogism" (Eiser 1980, 43). That is, they show what kind of action is appropriate in the circumstances.

Scripts are not imposed; they will rarely provide detailed specifications, nor are they "permanent." Leaders arrive at appropriate scripts by engaging in trial arguments with themselves, and with others. They encourage others to launch "trial balloons," and then monitor their progress (Huff 1984, Wrapp 1984). Endorsement, and implementation, of a script, results from a process of negotiation, a process in which influential participants sponsor different scripts, and "acceptable" terms are established (Hosking, in press). Thus, skillful perceptions and negotiations promote *flexible* social order, not a "rigid perpetuation" of doing things the way they have always been done (Kelvin 1970).

Capacities of Participants and Demands of Tasks. Perhaps the best-known approach to the study of social skill is that outlined by Welford (1980). It derives from ideas central to the information processing paradigm in cognitive psychology. At its heart is the recognition that certain mental processes are resource limited. People have limited capacities for processing information and performing mental work. Skilled leaders recognize that this is so. Our arguments concerning threats and opportunities imply that leaders help others to work through the core processes of information search and interpretation, influence, and choice.

Some of the ways in which managers may do this have been described by Stewart (1976) and Kotter (1982); they will be discussed in the context of "networking." Otherwise, what we have to say is somewhat speculative. To the extent that the skills of leaders are the skills of negotiators, it may be supposed that leaders facilitate the matching of capacities with the demands of complex decision making by making moves designed to reduce ambiguity, clarify communications, and generally slow things down. Some of the ways this is done in the context of formal negotiations have been identified (see Morley 1981b, 1983; Rackham and Carlisle 1978a). Direct evidence that skilled leaders do this is hard to find. However, some descriptions of effective executives suggest that they employ skills similar to those of negotiators (Drucker 1970). Both appear to remove unnecessary obstacles to decision making, and therefore, to the promotion of social identity and social order. They do so by helping others to handle the core processes identified in figure 6–1. We argue that skilled leaders do the same.

Dilemmas

Dilemmas are fundamental to an understanding of social skills because they represent choices inherent in the social-political processes by which decisions are made. They occur because leadership is a process of complex decision making. Decision making of this kind is stressful, because choices have to be made between courses of action that will satisfy some important values, and not others (see earlier). In such circumstances, participants may be aware that important decisions have to be made, and that whatever they do will probably be wrong. This poses particular problems for those perceived as leaders; they run the risk of being seen to make ineffective contributions, and so, risk loss of status.

Brown and Hosking (1986) have identified four kinds of dilemmas. First, there are those that derive from difficulties in managing relationships, for example, "being demanding with superiors without being perceived as uncooperative" (Kotter 1982, 16). Second, there are those that derive from difficulties in managing resources, for example, balancing long-term and short-term considerations. Third, there are those arising from activities: figuring out what to do, when, how, for how long. Finally, there are those that result from possible relationships between valued "end states" and valued "modes of conduct."

Taken together, these difficulties pose a higher-order dilemma, perhaps *the* dilemma for social organization in general. The dilemma arises because leadership is effective to the degree it achieves *flexible social order*. The dilemma is one of how to achieve a degree of order that is, on the one hand, sufficient to provide the basis for coordinated social action, although, on the other hand, not too much, thus perpetuating a rigid way of doing things as they have always been done (Kelvin 1970). This dilemma is observable in the dynamics of "groupthink" (Janis and Mann 1977), and is particularly vivid in the case of certain social movements (Brown and Hosking 1986).

Let us look at some of the ways in which leadership processes might handle these dilemmas. Broadly, it seems vital that disagreement is a valued mode of conduct, and that disagreement is used in particular ways, and for particular purposes, that change in relation to the core problems. In other words, the skills lie, in part, in the content and sequencing of contributions. Also, it seems that skilled participants learn to label their contributions, so that when they disagree, this is not interpreted as dislike, which would present an obstacle to decision making.

Other Kinds of Knowledge. For a social order to be flexible, one or more participants must have a great deal of specific knowledge about their decision-making environment. For example, large, family-based employment networks have been found to accumulate a considerable knowledge of alternative jobs, employers, and places of work. This has been a necessary element in the skillful process of moving the network from one place of (threatened) employment to another (Grieco and Hosking 1985). It seems likely that skillful leadership will often involve what might be called "technical" components of this kind, components which may, or may not, be transferable to a new context (see also Kotter 1982).

Networking

Constructs such as "script" or "operational code" help to explain what otherwise might be rather puzzling. Participants clearly deal with mixed evidence, and uncertain environments, yet they form strong, categorical judgments (Steinbruner 1974). Evidence to confirm a script is quickly found, thereby implicating certain threats and opportunities, and possibly, certain courses of action. Equally disconfirming evidence is denied, distorted, or ignored (Nisbett and Ross 1980, Steinbruner 1974).

Risks of this kind have been argued to be endemic to all kinds of perception; "ordinary seeing" is veridical because people move around and are forced to recognize that "inputs" have changed (Neisser 1976). What is "ordinarily seen" in the social context must be similarly evaluated. Somehow participants must "move around" their decision-making environment, and so test out their interpretations. Leaders make especially important contributions to such processes, both in moving around themselves, and in influencing others accordingly.

One of the ways skilled performers move around their environment is by networking. For example, the general managers rated as excellent in Kotter's research "created networks with many talented people in them and with stronger ties to and among their subordinates" (Kotter 1982, 71). Similarly, in the case of women's centers in Britain, evidence shows that networking may be skillfully employed to obtain information and achieve influence, processes without which survival would have been unlikely (Brown and Hosking 1986).

Certain kinds of "close relationships" are especially important in this context (Morley and Hosking 1984). They are exchange relationships in the sense of Homans (1951). Of particular note, are the *political aspects,* features which receive little prominence in existing literatures. First, there is exchange of information that is often confidential or quasi-confidential. Second, there is exchange of activities such that participants help each other to work out how (a) values can be satisfied, and (b) agreements can be grounded in an appropriate historical context so as to accommodate previous agreements, rules of custom and practice, and the like (Batstone, Boraston, and Frenkel 1977). The information and activities function as resources that have political significance in the context of competing values.

There is a sense in which relationships of this kind are "collusive" (Morley and Stephenson 1977); they are so, both within, and between groups. They are important because they allow participants to identify obstacles to decision making, and to communicate them to others. They are important because they help participants mutually to identify threats and opportunities in the context of interdependent values. As a result, skillful networking facilitates the development and implementation of "knowledge bases" and other resources (see figure 6–1).

Core Problems

Leaders initiate or respond to changes in the status quo. That is, they manage "violations of tolerance" by structuring leadership processes so as to handle the core processes of information interpretation, information search, influence, and choice (Snyder and Deising 1977). In plain language, leaders have to work out what is going on, why, and what to do about it. What is important, is that the core processes take different forms, depending on whether the problem is identification, development, or selection.

"Identification," is the identification of problems (what is going on), whereas "development" concerns the generation of alternative solutions; "selection" is made of a policy. The core processes involved in the first two problems are at least partially antagonistic to those involved in selection. More precisely, although each of the core processes is characterized by bargaining, the bargaining involved in identification and development is more often "integrative," whereas that involved in selection is typically "distributive" (see Walton and McKersie 1966).

We have argued that the skills of leaders are, to some extent, the skills of negotiators. They are implemented, to a lesser or greater degree, in the core processes by which core problems are handled. We have also argued that these processes occur both within, and between, interdependent groups. Skillful negotiators are those who make negotiations as hard as they need be, but no harder; in so doing, they structure processes so as to remove obstacles to agreement. This is, in part, achieved because skilled negotiators are not afraid to disagree. Rather, disagreement is organized to indicate the strengths of differing interpretations of core problems, and to draw attention to the differing values involved. Further, disagreement is used to clear up ambiguities concerning core problems and differing values. This increases the likelihood of stable agreements—that is, agreements that are stable until the status quo changes in ways felt to represent threats or opportunities.

Values and Interests

Figure 6–1 is intended to indicate that "core processes" are found in the development and implementation of knowledge bases, in the processes of networking, and in the handling of core problems. Further, figure 6–1 is intended to show that knowledge bases, networking, and core problems, are themselves interrelated. For example, making things no harder than they need be involves complex interrelations between networking, the building and implementation of knowledge bases, and the handling of core problems.

It has been argued that successful leadership processes are those in which the capacities of participants are matched to the demands of complex decision making. Core problems are revealed in an active, sometimes aggressive, search for information and understanding; especially from those involved in close relationships. As a result, leaders are better able to negotiate a process that facilitates the skillful handling of core problems. This, in turn, is argued to increase the probability that the values of the social order are protected and promoted (figure 6–1).

In sum, it is skillful processes of the sort described which further "flexible social order," and positive social identity. Contributions of a particular kind, that is, those which are consistent and influential contributions to order, may be perceived and expected from a minority, or from the majority, of participants. Our principal concern has been with leadership processes, and the skills with which they are performed. However, underlying this has been the important question of who makes what kinds of contributions, and in particular, who makes those contributions that define a leader. As we have indicated, there is no such thing as a leaderless group, at least, not for long. Whether there be one, or many, leaders in a group, the crucial question concerns the degree to which leadership processes reflect skills of the kind described.

Putting the Model to Work

Our major purpose has been the attempt, systematically and explicitly, to articulate the skills of leadership. The model presented in figure 6–1 shows the concepts we think necessary. To put the model to work is to use it (primarily) to facilitate "appreciation" of the skills of leadership as the skills of "organizing" (Weick 1979a).

Organizing of this kind has two major aspects; these are reflected in the principal sources of the model. The first concerns the general nature of intelligent social action. Here we drew on insights from a variety of disciplines. From individual psychology we took the idea that people have limited mental resources; skilled leaders are argued to recognize this in various ways which we have attempted to specify. From cognitive science we took the understanding that mental life is concerned with the manipulation of symbols, and borrowed the concept of script. Furthermore, we recognized that intelligent performance requires appropriate knowledge to be represented in appropriate ways. From cognitive sociology we took the central themes of symbolic interactionism, relating actions to meanings. The literature of social psychology and political science also facilitated our understanding of these processes.

Our second major theme came from empirical studies of effectiveness in management and negotiation. A detailed treatment of the relevant literatures is given in Hosking (in press). The findings mainly derive from techniques such as activity analysis, diaries, network analysis, and behavioral observation. Figure 6–1 represents our attempts to incorporate them within a single conceptual framework. We would add that such a framework showed little sign of emerging from the texts on leadership (see Bass 1981).

Figure 6–1 outlines the kind of analysis which we believe must be at the heart of any attempt to understand the skills of leadership. We also believe that a framework of this kind illustrates the defining characteristics, and the strengths, of a truly social psychological approach, one able to integrate the analysis of participants, processes, and contexts without losing sight of their political qualities.

To put such a model to work is to return social psychological analysis to center stage. This is likely to result in three kinds of activity. First, the model may be used to throw new light on old research. For example, certain managerial activities such as answering the phone, unplanned meetings, and the like, have been interpreted as reactive, time-wasting conditioned responses that "need to be brought under control" to "increase effectiveness" (Davis and Luthans 1980, 72–73). However, from our perspective, differences in effectiveness are more likely to be found in the more or less skillful use of such activities. For example, we would expect skilled performers to use chance meetings as opportunities for networking and building strong relationships. Similarly, they may take the opportunity to "gather gossip," which, in turn, keeps them informed of the political possibilities in the world of work (Feldman and March 1981, Kotter 1982).

Second, the model may be used to guide research into the skills of leadership. However, it suggests only the kind of analysis that will be necessary. The model will need to be instantiated in each particular case. In other words, the *content* of the elements will be a matter for empirical research, as will be the nature of the relationships between them. Only by doing this will it be possible to identify leadership processes and leaders. Our conceptualizations of these terms reflect our abstractions, inference, and interpretation; the concepts focus on underlying processes rather than surface phenomena.

Like other "second degree constructs," they are relatively difficult to translate into simple measurement procedures. However, we think the attempt worthwhile, and certainly preferable to continuing to miss the point. We would add that there are a variety of methods and measures which seem likely to be of use in this respect. For example, many of the techniques employed by Kotter and Lawrence (1974), and Kotter (1982), along with existing measures of "operational codes" (Holsti 1970), seem likely to be of use.

Third, the model may be used to direct a "case" or "anthropological" approach, and/or interpret its results. Such an approach provides an essential methodology for identifying the social and political processes of leadership and organizing (e.g., Sayles 1964). It does so by allowing the use of a wide variety of methods having the potential, not only to describe the content of participants' norms, values, interests, and so on, but also, to provide "thick" description, facilitating new understandings concerning our central concepts and arguments. Examples are drawn from two case studies to illustrate these points: both employed a variety of research methods, and both produced findings that, when interpreted in terms of our model, produced important new insights.

The first example concerns the earlier-mentioned study of women's groups (Brown and Hosking 1986). The principal method was participant observation over a period of approximately two years. This was supplemented by the use of semi-structured interviews, both with participants and with others who had an interdependent relationship with the groups concerned. Documentary sources provided further information.

A proper understanding of these groups was found to come from the recognition that common decision-making dilemmas were, for them, especially acute. The reasons lay with their egalitarian values concerning both "modes of conduct" and "end states of existence." These values needed to be understood in relation to the values of other societal groups. For example, the women's groups' values were both different, and more radical. As a result, such groups had major difficulties in handling the dilemma of how to achieve a degree of order sufficient to provide the basis for collaborative social action, but not too much. The latter would be reflected in grooved thinking, and in procedures that maintained the existing social order, solidarity, and cohesion. Our arguments imply that this dilemma will demand especially skillful leadership, without which the groups' values are unlikely to be "protected and pursued."

Our model provided further appreciation of the case material by directing attention to the potential appearance and significance of the distinction between "leaders" and "leadership." The egalitarian values of the women's groups implied a derogation of leaders, yet contributions to leadership processes continued to be vital, and indeed, required considerable skills of participants in order that their values be protected and pursued.

A related insight came from application of the model to case studies of family-based employment networks (Grieco and Hosking 1985). Case methods included snowball interviewing of network members, plus semi-structured interviews and documentary evidence from personnel departments and the Employment Bureau in Britain. The case material showed the existence of family networks moving into, and out of, employment settings over a period of forty years or more. Often, achievement of this collective presence in a place of work required migration from one part of the country to another.

Our model seems to provide a useful appreciation of the processes by which such families organized their employment *as a network*. At the same time, we have gained an insight into the ways in which "organizing" can be practiced, regardless of the boundaries of "formal organization." This, in turn, helped us to realize the weaknesses of the concept "organization," as compared with the concept of "organizing."

In going about their organizing, it is evident that many networks moved in anticipation of "threats" to the status quo: threats of imminent redundancies or factory closure. It was crucial to our understanding of these moves, and of the network's activities more generally, that we understood their central values, norms, and interests. Briefly, it was, for them, of great significance to be a "good worker," and to be known as such; the family reputation on this matter was of central importance. For these reasons, certain norms were "enforced" concerning acceptable behavior at work, mutual aid, and so on. Organizing was, in this sense, all about harnessing and maintaining employment *for the network*.

Some family members were especially influential in relation to these values and, indeed, were expected to be so. Further, consistent with the model, there was evidence that they networked more than others, better understood potential threats, and so on. In sum, certain individuals made especially significant contributions to leadership: they built-up and integrated the network's knowledge bases; facilitated an understanding of the processes by which employment might be harnessed; and, were able to help network members to translate these understandings into action. This is what skilled leadership is all about.

Concluding Remarks

We have attempted to provide a systematic and explicit treatment of the nature of the skills of leadership. It is to be hoped that the attempt to link leadership and organization, and the use of social skill as an integrating concept, will have a number of beneficial consequences. First, we hope to have helped overcome the naive separation of individual and social units of analysis; second, to have done so in ways that recognize the political qualities of relationships; and third, to put the study of leadership where it belongs—that is, at the center of organizational analysis.

Our emphasis on the *negotiated* quality of cognitive-social, and social-political processes, is critical. Negotiation is very much more than influence through direct contact at a "bargaining table"; it extends beyond explicit agreements between representatives of formal bargaining units. Negotiation is generally recognized to involve both intragroup and intergroup processes of influence and exchange. Further, these processes can be seen to combine indirect, as well as direct, relationships in which, for example, *A* may influence *B* by getting *C*'s support. Networking, and other processes, facilitate the achievement of indirect influence and indirect exchange.

Perhaps the essence of our argument is captured by saying that organization and negotiation involve *change,* actual or potential. Skillful leadership achieves a social order in which *certain kinds of change are seen to make sense.* Leaders are importantly understood as change agents whose skills are vital in the success of organization development. This is because their skills concern the "creative" and "political" aspects of innovation (Kanter 1984). The creative aspects of the process arise because the sense making is active, interpretative, and fundamentally social (Hosking and Morley 1985). The political aspects arise because policies (or projects) compete for resources and other kinds of support. Thus, to understand leadership, it is necessary to understand the cognitive, discretionary, and politically problematic aspects of leadership processes. It is these aspects that are fundamental to a shift from "mechanistic" to "non-mechanistic" views of knowledge (Clark 1984, 376–77). This is what it will take to achieve a "paradigm shift" (Hosking et al. 1984) in the study of leadership.

7
The Management Team: An Equilibrium Model of Manager and Subordinate Performance and Behavior

Andrew Crouch
Philip Yetton

One of the major developments that has emerged from current research in leadership is the increasing emphasis being placed on process issues. In the 1982 leadership symposium volume, for example (see Hunt et al. 1984), a number of chapters, including those prepared by Rauch and Behling (1984), Huff (1984), and Heller (1984), deal in different ways with process-induced changes in social structures. The present chapter is a further contribution in that direction. The values adopted in pursuing the current investigation are positivist in a North American tradition. Although we are aware that other interpretations might well be made of both the questions and their answers, for reasons of space these issues are left to be considered elsewhere.

The unit of analysis is the management team comprising a manager and a number of subordinates. We ask how manager and subordinate task performance and behavioral characteristics are related to one another and how these patterns change in response to disturbances originating outside the team. These questions concern the maintenance of team social structures and structural transitions following changes in team membership.

Over the past decade or so there has been a clear shift away from traditional stimulus-response models of leadership process. The contingency models advanced by Fiedler (1967), House (1971), and Vroom and Yetton (1973) have given way to a serious questioning of their one-way causal linkages. A more complex and process-oriented view is now emerging. For example, Greene (1979) has investigated two-way relationships involving manager and subordinate behavior. Graen describes role-making processes through which the social structure of a management team develops (Graen and Cashman 1975). Relationships of mutual dependence also underly manager-subordinate exchange and reciprocal influence as described by Hollander (1978).

In this chapter another step in the development of explanatory models is proposed. Our primary concern is the *form* of the explanatory model. We develop an equilibrium model to explain processes of pattern maintenance and transition in group social structure. The model specifies a set of transitions by which teams evolve towards one of two stable equilibrium states, which are therefore predicted to occur with high frequency. Their incidence among a cross-sectional sample of 165 management teams is analyzed.

In addition, the model predicts the changes in social structure that occur when a team is disturbed from an equilibrium state by a disturbance originating outside the group. In particular, the model explains how team responds to the replacement of some of its members: the manager, subordinates, or both. Managers are often surprised by the new patterns of behavior that develop in a team after its membership is changed. The degree to which such unanticipated consequences can be predicted and avoided is central to both the theory and practice of selection, promotion, and team building.

Finally, rather than comparing these findings and predictions with the existing literature, their implications for team building are discussed. Although both skill training and the replacement of team personnel are used in organizations to upgrade team performance, the team-development literature deals nearly exclusively with behavioral skill training and pays little attention to the alternative strategy of replacing team members. Here we examine the frequently exercised alternative options of replacing a team's manager or subordinates. The analysis shows that high team performance is vulnerable to changes in composition. A return to low team performance is a frequent outcome of composition changes initiated in an attempt to upgrade an initially low performing team. These conclusions highlight the sensitivity of team performance to poor promotion decisions.

An Equilibrium Model of Team Performance and Behavior

Two characteristics differentiate the model presented here from both the bivariate stimulus-response and reciprocal causal models typically described in the leadership literature. First, the model deals with stability and change among a restricted cluster of variables. No simple causal ordering is assumed to exist among the variables. Rather, they form a mutually dependent cluster. This means that a change in any one is likely to alter the joint characteristics of the variables in the cluster.

The second distinguishing aspect of the model is the centrality of the concept of equilibrium to the analytical framework adopted. Consistent with definitions advanced elsewhere (e.g., Homans 1951), a stable state within an equilibrium process model is defined as a configuration among variables whereby the pattern among the variables is restored after any small externally-induced change in any one of the component variables.

Within traditional North American models of leader and subordinate performance and behavior, two particular domains of behavior are frequently studied. These are supportiveness, that is, helpful cooperative behavior, and conflict legitimization, the encouragement of open expression of differences of opinion. Both of these behaviors are necessary to develop and sustain high-performing groups (see, for example, Likert 1961). Support provides a basis for trust, mutuality, and reassurance among group members. It helps the achievement of interdependent tasks and provides a buffer for the ambiguities and uncertainties associated with open communication in an uncertain task environment. Conflict legitimacy promotes this free flow of task information, while avoiding inhibiting group processes such as "groupthink" (Janis 1982). In general, candor within a supportive group setting is a necessary condition for building trustworthiness and trusting behavior (e.g., Johnson 1981).

A large number of other variables from different frames of reference could also have been considered. No claim is made that the variables in the model are either exhaustive or new. They were selected to illustrate the application of an equilibrium process model and are a small number among those available in the field of small group dynamics. Furthermore, we accept that the individual relationships linking these variables are not new.

However, although the constructs are familiar, the form of the model is less familiar. The notion of equilibrium has received little attention as an analytical tool in the leadership literature. Elsewhere, the converse is the case. For example, Bales (1953) refers to the equilibrium characteristics of behavior patterns in small groups. Homans (1951) also uses the concept of equilibrium to explain how group members adhere to social norms. Indeed, the idea of an equilibrium as developed by Becker, Parsons, and others (see, for example, Loomis and Loomis 1965) is a widely accepted sociological concept. The point to be made here is that although equilibrium analysis is not new, its potential in the context of managed work groups has not yet been fully investigated.

Interdependencies among Manager and Subordinate Performance, Support, and Conflict Legitimacy

The following equilibrium model specifies the relationships among four variables: manager and subordinate performance and manager and subordinate trustworthiness, where trustworthy (untrustworthy) behavior is defined as congruent high (low) support and conflict legitimization (see figure 7–1). In figure 7–2, manager and subordinate performance are also dichotomized

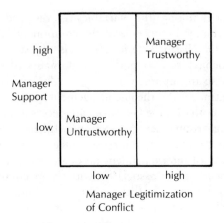

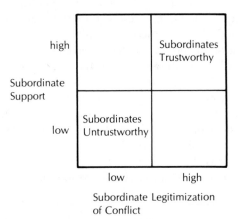

Figure 7–1. Manager and Subordinate Trustworthiness as a Function of Supportive Behavior and Legitimization of Conflict

(high versus low), and the sixteen possible configurations of performance and trustworthiness are represented as cells in a 2 × 2 × 2 × 2 matrix. Each of the four 2 × 2 tables in this diagram represents a unique combination of

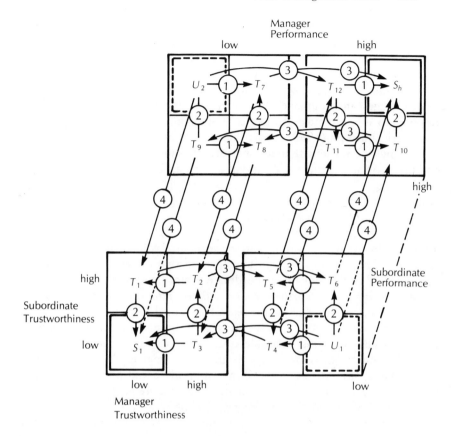

Figure 7–2. An Equilibrium Model Relating Manager and Subordinate Performance and Trustworthiness

manager and subordinate trustworthiness for each of the four combinations of manager and subordinate performance. This representation has two advantages. First, although a dichotomous classification is an oversimplification, a team can be described in terms of a unique configuration of manager and subordinate behavior and performance. Second, it simultaneously presents both the configuration of a team (cell characteristics) and the direction in which that structure is likely to change (transition dynamics). The former allows us to analyze the relative frequency with which certain structures occur. The latter facilitates the examination of different developmental interventions.

The arrows in figure 7–2 represent the tendency for teams with certain social structures (cell characteristics) to evolve different structures. This is presented as a shift from one cell into another. The arrows are numbered 1 to

4. They represent four team dynamics that have received extensive support in the literature. These are reviewed as follows. Only a brief discussion of each dynamic is presented because their interactions are the primary issue in this chapter, not their individual validity.

1. *Subordinate performance and manager trustworthiness.* A number of studies suggest that a manager acts supportively and legitimizes conflict as a response to subordinate performance. For example, Lowin and Craig (1968) and Farris and Lim (1969) report that managers behave more supportively toward high-performing than low-performing subordinates. Similarly, Graen and his associates (Dansereau, Graen, and Haga 1975, Graen and Cashman 1975) argue that access to information and influence by subordinates is largely based on the subordinates' performance. In figure 7–2, this linkage between subordinate performance and manager trustworthiness is represented by the arrows numbered 1. The arrows are interpreted as follows. In all four cells for which subordinate performance is high, teams have a tendency to shift from low to high manager trustworthiness. The reverse tendency occurs in the four low subordinate performance cells.

2. *Manager trustworthiness and subordinate trustworthiness.* Social learning theory argues that people select role models because they have desirable social characteristics such as status and success. Subordinates perceive their manager as having desirable status and success in an organizational hierarchy and are therefore likely to imitate the manager's behavior (Weiss 1977). Thus, subordinates behave in a supportive and open manner when their manager acts in this way. Similarly, they imitate untrustworthy behavior if it is displayed by their manager. This process is represented in figure 7–2 by the arrow marked 2, linking manager behavior and subordinate behavior.

3. *Subordinate trustworthiness and manager performance.* In complex task environments, a manager's performance is a function of the efficient and effective upward flow of information from subordinates (Jablin 1979). Subordinates who openly express their opinions in a supportive manner facilitate information flows which then enhance manager performance. In contrast, information manipulation by subordinates in a defensive and/or politically aggressive way reduces the flow of relevant information to a manager. For example, the research on the behavioral aspects of budgetary control systems reports numerous cases of such information restriction and distortion, and their dysfunctional impact on manager performance (Argyris 1951, Libby and Lewis 1982). In a dynamic and interdependent task environment, this unsupportive and closed subordinate strategy has an adverse impact on manager performance. This process is represented in figure 7–2 by the arrow marked 3, linking subordinate trustworthiness and manager performance.

4. *Subordinate performance and manager performance.* A manager's ability to acquire resources from his or her own supervisor and from his or

her management team's external environment depends, in part, on the manager's own demonstrated task performance. A high-performing manager is much more likely to be successful in negotiating increases in both resources and discretion than a low performer. High resources and discretion help subordinates to perform more successfully than a relatively resource-deprived group with little discretion. Furthermore, a high- relative to a low-performing manager is more likely to deploy these resources and exercise this discretion in ways that enhance subordinates' performance. This relationship is consistent with the evidence, for example, from the contingency theory of intraorganizational power (Hinings et al. 1974, Salancik and Pfeffer 1977). This process is represented in figure 7–2 by the arrow marked 4, linking manager performance and subordinate performance.

The complete pattern of transition tendencies in figure 7–2 gives rise to three types of team configurations. Two of the sixteen configurations are stable, two are unstable, and the remainder are termed transition states:

Stable states. The change tendencies represented by the arrows in figure 7–2 show that groups located in the cells labeled S_h and S_1 are stable. Four arrows lead into them and none lead out. These cells are stable because any externally-induced shift to another cell results in a tendency for the team to return to one of the two stable cells. Once a team achieves either the high (S_h) or low (S_1) performance pattern, it is unlikely to change through its own internal social dynamic.

Unstable states. The pattern of change tendencies also shows that two configurations of team characteristics are unstable (U_1 and U_2). In both cases there are no arrows that lead into these cells. The only paths associated with them are those leading into adjacent cells. U_1 and U_2 are unstable because a group is unlikely to change toward these characteristics in the course of a developmental process. Such characteristics can only be produced by exogenous intervention.

Transition states. The remaining patterns of behavior and performance represent transition states. These cells are labeled T_1 to T_{12}. They are considered transition configurations because each has two paths leading into it and two leading out. This means that a team whose configuration of variables coincides with one of these cells is unlikely to sustain this pattern. Rather, it will change its structure in one of the directions shown by the outward arrows.

Incidence of Stable and Unstable States

A major feature of the equilibrium model is the predicted change in team characteristics. A test of the theory would require an assessment of the direction of these change tendencies using an experimental or quasiexperimental design. Without the immediate opportunity to conduct this type of research it was nevertheless possible to undertake a cross-sectional study to assess the incidence of stable and unstable configurations of behavior and performance among management teams. The hypothesis derived from the model is that teams tend to adopt the two equilibrium conditions and move away from the unstable patterns. Therefore, the incidence of teams in cells S_h and S_1 should be higher than expected by chance and the incidence of teams in U_1 and U_2 should be lower.

Survey

The subjects are managers and their subordinates comprising 165 established managerial work teams. While attending management development programs, the managers were asked to complete a large questionnaire and to allow five of their subordinates to be approached by the researchers for the same task. The questionnaire, a covering letter explaining the purpose of the survey and a guarantee of confidentiality signed by their manager and one of the researchers, was then mailed to each subordinate. Completed questionnaires were returned directly to the researchers. Subordinates were promised confidential feedback and assured by the researchers that their manager would only receive aggregate team data while attending the course. The response rate was 100 percent for the managers and 82 percent for subordinates.

This survey procedure introduces two sources of potential sample bias. Since the managers were unrestricted in their nomination of subordinates for inclusion in the study, they could have chosen those with whom they were on friendly terms. There could also be a similar bias among subordinates who responded. However, few managers had more than five subordinates and, therefore, few subordinates were excluded by a manager's choice. This, combined with the high response rate among subordinates, indicates that these selection effects are likely to be weak. Furthermore, any range restriction arising from selection effects would inflate the Type II Error rate rather than constitute a validity threat to the results reported here.

The data were collected using the Crouch (1982) Behavioural Inventory. This instrument collects perceptions of a number of dimensions of behavior, including support, conflict legitimacy, and task performance. All measures are unit weight averages across five items using seven-point Likert scales (see table 7–1 for item content). Manager scores are the average subordinate perceptions of a manager's supportiveness, legitimization of conflict, and performance. Subordinate scores are their manager's perceptions of their average supportiveness, legitimization of conflict, and performance. Table 7–2 reports mean values on a 0–10 range, standard deviations, and both individual and group alpha coefficients.

Table 7–1
Behavior and Performance Items

Support

Is reluctant to cooperative with others (R)

Cannot be trusted (R)

Goes out of way to help

Is interested in the feelings of other people

Cooperates in an agreeable manner

Conflict Legitimization

Is willing to listen to others

Encourages suggestions

Takes a negative approach to suggestions offered (R)

Resents criticism (R)

Maintains an open mind

Performance

Needs constant prodding (R)

Makes many mistakes (R)

Does exceptionally good work

Adapts quickly to situations

Gets things done without delay

Note: (R) denotes reverse scoring.

Table 7–2
Scale Characteristics

			Coefficient Alpha	
	Mean	*SD*	*Individual*	*Group*
Manager support	7.44	1.04	0.84	0.89
Legitimization of conflict	7.08	1.04	0.80	0.87
Performance	7.74	0.92	0.77	0.81
Subordinate support				
Legitimization of conflict	7.63	1.08	0.80	0.85
Performance	7.01	1.09	0.84	0.83

Analysis

Dichotomizing the manager and subordinate performance and supportiveness and trustworthiness behavior using a median split produces a $2 \times 2 \times 2 \times 2 \times 2 \times 2$ contingency table with sixty-four cells. The model presented in figure 7–2 is a submatrix (see figure 7–3) of this more general matrix. The within-manager and within-subordinate conflict and support behaviors are restricted in the submatrix to cells in which the two behaviors are congruent (both are either high or low).

In practice, these behaviors are highly correlated. Two contingency tables (see figure 7–4) show that supportiveness and conflict legitimization are positively related for both managers ($\chi^2 = 67.2$, $p < 0.01$) and subordinates ($\chi^2 = 28.7$, $p < 0.01$). The weaker relationship for subordinates relative to managers is probably a function of measurement error. A manager's score is an average across a number of raters' judgments about a single stimulus (manager behavior), whereas the average subordinate's score is the average of a single rater's judgments about multiple different stimuli (subordinates' behavior).

To test whether the end points to the dynamic, namely cells S_1 and S_h, occur more frequently than expected, we compare their observed frequencies with their expected cell frequencies. Cell frequencies were estimated using a log linear modeling procedure which controls for (1) the marginals, (2) the congruence between supportiveness and conflict legitimacy, and (3) any response consistency effect arising from the fact that managers code both the behavior and performance of their subordinates and, similarly, subordinates code both the behavior and performance of their managers. (For those unfamiliar with this procedure, it is essentially a generalized χ^2 model used for the analysis of multidimensional contingency tables [see Bishop, Fienberg, and Holland 1975].)

Figure 7–3 reports the observed cell frequencies, the expected frequencies, and their standardized residual differences for the variables in figure 7–2. Note, the expected frequencies are compared for the complete $2 \times 2 \times 2 \times 2 \times 2 \times 2$ matrix. Only cell frequencies for the matrix presented in figure 7–2 are reported in figure 7–3. The combined cell frequencies for S_1 and S_h are 44 out of a sample of 165. The expected cell frequency, controlling for within-person behavior effects and response consistency, is 28.8. The observed frequencies as a proportion of the total sample is significantly greater than the expected proportion (binomial test: $Z = 3.04$, $p \le 0.01$).

A similar procedure shows that the unstable configurations, cells U_1 and U_2, occur less frequently than expected. Their combined frequency is 20. This is significantly less than the expected frequency of 28.7 (binomial test: $Z = 1.70$, $p \le 0.05$). Given the size of the matrix (sixty-four cells), these two tests can be treated as essentially independent of each other.

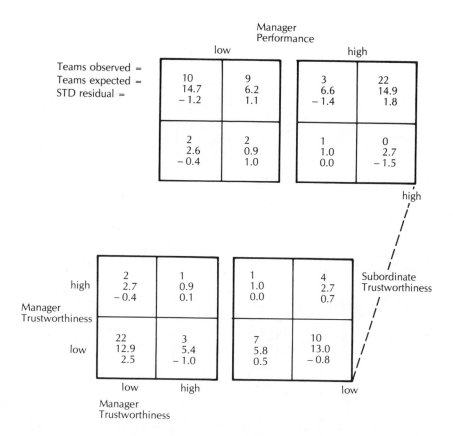

Note: Expected cell values, control of marginals, and response consistency effects. This figure is a submatrix of the full six-dimensional figure which includes manager and subordinate support, conflict legitimization, and performance.

$n = 99$

Figure 7–3. Observed and Expected Configurations of Manager and Subordinate Performance and Trustworthiness among Managerial Work Teams

Within the restrictions imposed by the use of cross-sectional data, the preceding tests report strong evidence in support of the equilibrium model. It seems likely that (1) managerial teams do cluster in the two stable equilibrium configurations, and (2) managerial teams move away from the two unstable configurations.

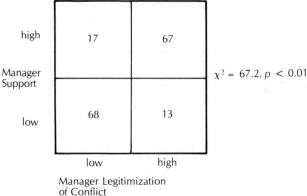

$\chi^2 = 67.2, p < 0.01$

Manager Legitimization
of Conflict

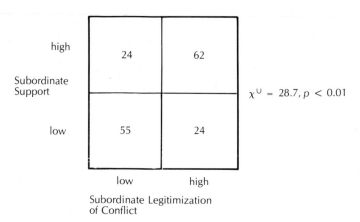

$\chi^{\cup} = 28.7, p < 0.01$

Subordinate Legitimization
of Conflict

Note: Cell values refer to number of managerial work teams in which the combinations of behaviors were observed.

Figure 7–4. Relationships between Manager Support and Legitimization of Conflict and Subordinate Support and Legitimization of Conflict

Implications: Responses to Changes in Team Membership

Although the equilibrium model predicts that management teams evolve towards one of the two stable configurations, a number of organizational procedures have the effect of displacing a team from either cell. Here, the adjustments resulting from changes in manager or subordinate behavior and performance due to changes in team membership are traced through the model presented in figure 7–2. This allows us to speculate on the most likely transition paths and their outcomes. To simplify the discussion, changes in leader and subordinate membership are explored independently.

Replacing the Manager

Consider first the appointment of a high-performing but untrustworthy manager to a low-performance team (S_1). This is shown in figure 7–5 as a shift to T_4. The new manager may find he or she cannot get on top of the task, in which case, the transition is likely to be back to S_1. Alternatively, the manager may "take charge," and lift subordinate performance by directing subordinate effort. Such behavior is typical of Blake and Mouton's (1964) task-focused manager. The gains are likely to be temporary. To consolidate high performance in the long term, such a manager would need to change his or her behavior and be open and supportive rather than directive. Given that he or she was promoted on the basis of previous directive behavior and that opening up requires releasing control in a dangerous situation, it is unlikely that the manager would change his or her behavior. Instead, behavioral and communication problems would accumulate and both manager and subordinate performance would eventually suffer.

The latter transition is the pattern typically followed when a high-performing but untrustworthy manager is appointed to S_h. Initially subordinates continue to cope with the task interdependencies among their roles without their manager's legitimacy and support. Unless the manager can change and encourage conflict and act supportively, subordinates will become independent and defensive. Subsequently, both manager and subordinate performance decline.

Of course, declining performance is not inevitable. A new high-performing and trustworthy manager can sustain high performance and improve low performance in a team. Obviously, he or she is a stable match in cell S_h. For a low-performing team (S_1), the new manager's appointment results in a shift to U_1 (see figure 7–5). This is a highly unstable configuration. A rapid change will occur and its direction depends largely on the attributions made about previous poor performance. If the previous manager is seen as responsible for the depressed team performance, then it is likely that the subordinates would respond positively to both the manager's high performance and trustworthiness. The team will quickly establish a stable high-performing configuration. Alternatively, if the manager judges that the subordinates are weak and blames them for the previous low performance, the manager would respond by attempting to take charge and this behavior

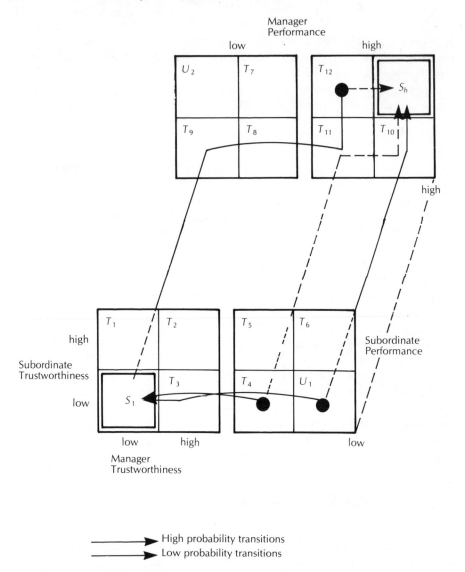

Figure 7–5. Responses to Changes in Manager's Membership of the Team

would be perceived by subordinates as untrusting. Over time, this configuration is eroded into a stable low-performing team.

Replacing Subordinates

Instead of replacing the manager, one or more of the subordinates could be replaced. Again, the response to a change in team composition depends on the initial form of the equilibrium from which the team is disturbed.

Consider first a team that initially had a stable high-performing equilibrium (S_h). The promotion of high-performing and trustworthy subordinates into such a team does not disturb the team from its stable high-performing configuration. In contrast, if the new subordinates do not display trustworthiness, then information restriction leads to a reduction in manager performance and a subsequent decline in subordinate performance. The manager then withdraws his or her own supportive behavior; and the team shifts towards the unfavorable poor-performance equilibrium (S_1) in figure 7–6. If, instead, the subordinates model themselves on the manager's and the other subordinates' high trustworthy behavior, then the high-performing team equilibrium is reestablished. It follows that, to maintain a stable high-performing pattern, the manager should isolate and replace a subordinate who cannot learn trustworthy behavior before long-term damage is done.

A second departure from the high-performance cell involves a change in subordinate composition toward reduced task performance, while maintaining a high level of openness and trustworthiness. This is shown in figure 7–6 as a shift to cell T_6. This occurs when high-performing subordinates are themselves promoted and replaced by less successful subordinates. Since subordinates' task performance is less dependable, the manager's behavior becomes less supportive. The subordinates realize that they are not trusted, and they also become less trustworthy. The manager's performance suffers as restrictions are placed on the flow of information. This sequence of changes brings the team into a stable, low-performing equilibrium.

The changes in subordinate composition for teams with an initially high performance equilibrium suggest that sustained high team performance is a somewhat vulnerable state. Furthermore, compared with the apparent ease with which a high-performing team can decline into an unfavorable equilibrium, we show below that it is difficult to upgrade a poor team.

Consider the case of a low-performance team (S_1) in which subordinate composition is altered to bring about an increase in subordinate trustworthiness. This is shown in figure 7–6 as a shift to cell T_1. Such behavior simply cannot be sustained under the leadership of an untrustworthy manager in a team in which both manager and subordinate task performance are below average. Suspicion, defensiveness, and distrust would quickly return the team to the unfavorable and stable equilibrium (S_1). A similar outcome is the most likely result of a change in team composition that improves only subordinate

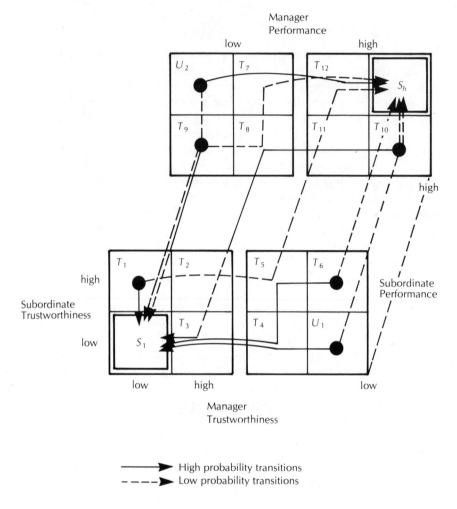

Figure 7–6. Responses to Changes in Subordinate Group Composition

performance. This is shown as a shift to cell T_9 in figure 7–6. In an environment characterized by defensive behavior, subordinate performance would soon erode. It is theoretically possible, though in practice somewhat unlikely, that the manager would become more trusting of the higher-performing subordinates, which in turn, if imitated by subordinates, would lead to a high-performance team equilibrium.

The change in subordinate composition that is most likely to lead to a high-performance team pattern is an increase in both task performance and trustworthy behavior. This is shown as a shift to cell U_2 in figure 7–6. Where the prior performance was a function of subordinate behavior, this combination is likely to bring about an initial increase in manager performance, followed by an increase in manager trustworthiness, and a stable high-performance equilibrium is attained by the team. In contrast, with an incompetent and directive manager, subordinate performance and behavior would be eroded. The manager's performance would not increase.

The transitions previously described are those considered likely within the equilibrium model. This is not to say that other paths are theoretically impossible. Indeed, a number of other paths which reverse the overwhelming tendency for teams to shift toward the low-performance configuration are theoretically feasible, but the very substantial effort and resources required of team members to achieve a favorable pattern makes them less likely than those shown in figure 7–6.

Team Building and Changes in Membership

The preceding analysis of team dynamics demonstrates the vulnerability of management teams to both inadequate leadership (leader behavior) and followership (subordinate behavior). In addition, it suggests two strategies, one for sustaining an effective team, the other for rebuilding an ineffective one. Both strategies are frequently observed in practice. As often happens, the theory clarifies our understanding of good practice, and, we hope, helps us replicate it elsewhere. The analysis also highlights the underlying cause of one of the classic organization promotion dilemmas, namely, the promotion of a functional specialist into a role with general management responsibilities.

The simplest way to maintain a successful team (S_h) is to promote a manager who has had task experiences similar to those of the previous manager. This can be achieved by establishing standard career routes which are followed by a high proportion of senior managers. It would also help to match their behaviors if the departing manager is given a major say about his or her replacement. This is often the case in organizations.

To rebuild an ineffective team, a powerful strategy is to combine two of the changes described in the previous section: to appoint a high-performing and trustworthy manager and replace at least one low-performing and untrustworthy subordinate. The replacement should be someone who can seed the team with the desired high-performing and trustworthy behavior. As shown in figure 7–7, the new subordinate facilitates the shift from U_1 to a stable high-performance equilibrium. In this case, both the manager and the new subordinate act as role models for the existing subordinates. Naturally, the new manager would expect and be given a major part in choosing the

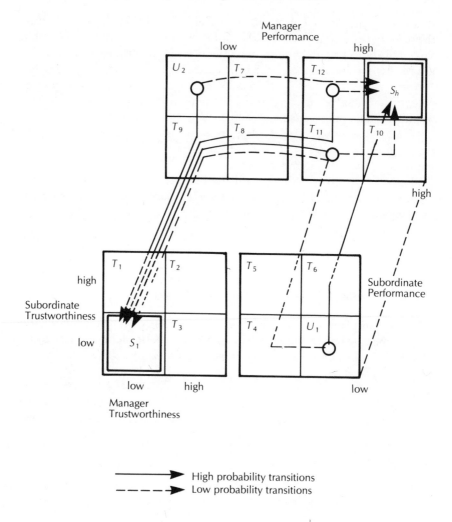

Figure 7–7. **Strategies for Rebuilding an Ineffective Team**

replacement subordinate. The major risk to this strategy is that the new manager and subordinate can work so easily together that they exclude the others and the team development process is stalled before it begins. The outcome is then an unbalanced ineffective team with one powerful dyad.

Finally, consider the classic organization problem of promoting a functional specialist into a position with general management responsibilities.

This promotion is often from a head office staff functional area with cost accountability to a divisional management position with profit accountability. It is the change in task environment which is the critical factor. In the staff function, conflict is primarily about means rather than ends and the team members share a particular professional ideology. The manager is seen as an expert exercising expert judgment in a relatively well structured task environment. The need for trust and openness is low and is, when needed, made easy to achieve through the shared ideology and mutual respect for recognized expertise. In contrast, a divisional role is characterized by high conflict over ends, competition for scarce resources, and a lack of any shared recognized expertise.

Some of the problems can be identified by exploring such a promotion to both high- and low-performing teams. In the former case, there is a risk that the functional expert would not only be seen as untrustworthy, but his or her technical skills would also be only partly relevant and, therefore, his or her performance would be low. At best, this is a shift from S_h to T_{12} in figure 7–7. Alternatively, it is a shift to U_1. Reestablishing stable high performance requires the manager to simultaneously learn new task skills and new behavior. More likely, the new manager would employ a one-on-one structure (professional review process) to manage. For subordinates who are used to a collaborative group style, this is likely to be seen as a divide and control, if not divide and conquer, strategy. The subordinates would use the manager's behavior as a role model and reduce cooperation among themselves. The problems due to a lack of task coordination would then reduce their performance.

The prognosis for a promotion into a low-performing team is also poor. At best, the manager takes control and by refocusing individual subordinates' efforts increases their performance. The team is shifted from S_1 to T_{11} in figure 7–7. The problems of task coordination are likely to erode this performance gain. In this instance, it does not help for the manager to take one of his or her own subordinates with him or her to the new team. Frequently, this actually means promoting one of the manager's former subordinates into the manager's previous job. The temptation for both people to focus on the area in which they are both highly competent would be very great and, in the long term, counterproductive. Because other areas are afforded insufficient influence and attention, overall team performance is unlikely to increase.

Of course, functional specialists, like other managers, want promotion opportunities. Unfortunately, the preceding prognosis is not good. The organization risks a loss of motivation by ambitious managers if it restricts their opportunities. It risks maintaining and even creating ineffective teams if they are promoted. It is obvious why this remains a classic problem endemic to many organizations.

Team Building and Process Training

As noted at the beginning of this chapter, both practice and theory have focused nearly exclusively on training managers and subordinates. Strategies of selection and replacement are conspicuous by their absence. Furthermore, within the conventional team development approaches management training in behavioral skills is also divorced from training in task skills. In contrast, both areas of skill development are integrated in the model presented previously.

The prevailing bias towards training the existing management team members rather than replacing them is easy to understand. Organization development managers and consultants have cultivated a "counseling psychology" within which it is assumed that team members rather than the organization are the clients. From this perspective, dismissing one's client, even for the client's own good, is bad for business. Skill development is much more attractive than team wastage and replacement.

Unfortunately, the results for process training are at best mixed. For example, Kaplan's major survey found little evidence for gains in performance as a result of process training (Kaplan 1979). Although traditional simple causal models predict performance gains from behavioral skill training, the findings arising from the equilibrium model predict minimal performance gains.

Consider three illustrative cases. First, analyze the consequences of providing behavioral skill training to members of a team with a high-performing configuration. This training simply serves a maintenance function. It helps sustain and perhaps marginally increases the level of team support and conflict legitimization which reinforces its existing high performance.

Second, training could be offered to high-performing but untrustworthy managers before they are promoted. Of course, the key issue here is how well new behavior can be learned. Typically, such training is conducted in a supportive training environment, and the effective transfer of learned behavior from such a supportive environment to a work setting is unlikely for two reasons. One is that the new behavior is learned in an environment in which there are no performance pressures or emphasis on formal authority. The other is that few managers could cope with the pressures and stresses of a new job sufficiently well to attempt new "experimental" behavior. Unfortunately, if the new behavior is not attempted until the manager has been in the job long enough to know that change is needed, the damage to a high-performing team will already have been done. In addition, any untrustworthy behavior by subordinates would have been reinforced and made more difficult to reverse later.

Finally, consider training the manager of a team with a low-performance configuration. Subordinates commonly doubt the long-term effectiveness of such training and they would probably be reluctant to imitate it. Sooner or later the manager would revert to his or her previous untrustworthy behavior, rationalizing that the effort had been made and the subordinates had failed to respond.

Instead of training either the manager or the subordinates, it is frequently argued that both the manager and the subordinates should be trained. This amounts to a shift by the team to T_2 in figure 7–7. Two transitions are possible. One occurs if the manager's performance improves as a result of the increased cooperativeness of the subordinates. Alternatively, the manager's support declines if he or she experiences no performance gains and gives up the experiment.

Typically, such team training takes place away from the workplace and focuses on personal growth and interpersonal relations, rather than task performance. No doubt it is easier to openly discuss these issues than to accept the responsibility for poor work performance. For this reason the training increases social satisfaction rather than task performance. It is difficult to transfer such learning back to the work context where social satisfaction is insufficient to sustain the new behavior in the face of the pressures from continued poor performance.

To stimulate a transition to a high-performance equilibrium, simultaneous training in both task and process skills is required over an extended period, with increased performance rather than social satisfaction as the primary goal. Although this might show promise of being a successful strategy, it typically requires a consultant to act as a surrogate leader to undertake the task of completely retraining and structuring the team, including the manager. Even the cost advantage of such a strategy over simply replacing the manager and one or two subordinates is not clear. Certainly replacement has the advantage of being quick and simple.

Conclusion

In contrast to the optimism of the traditional organizational development team-building literature, the preceding prognosis is pessimistic. Not only are successful teams vulnerable to change in their membership, but unsuccessful teams "resist" development. However, these somewhat bleak predictions are consistent with both current management practice and the mixed success of team building based on the recommendations and optimistic claims of the traditional literature.

8
An Organizational Life Cycle Approach to Leadership

B.R. Baliga
James G. Hunt

C urrent mainstream approaches to leadership tend to emphasize the importance of the interaction between both leadership and the situation in determining leadership effectiveness. Fiedler's (1967) theory, for example, argues that work group effectiveness depends on an appropriate match between leadership style and the demands of the situation. House's (House and Mitchell 1974) approach assumes that a leader's key function is to act in ways that complement the work setting or situation in which subordinates operate. If this function is done well, subordinate satisfaction, motivation, and performance will increase. Vroom and Yetton's (1973) model looks at how participative a leader should be in terms of subordinate knowledge and the attributes of the problem to be dealt with.

Each of these situational approaches and others like them are more sophisticated than earlier trait or behavioral approaches which examined leadership effects without considering the situation. However, these situational approaches tend to concentrate on:

1. Leadership at lower levels in the organization
2. Group or individual subordinate performance
3. Leadership, which implicitly assumes a static organization

In this chapter we discuss a framework that goes beyond these situational approaches. Specifically, we examine leadership in the context of organizationally-derived managerial tasks in different phases of the organization's life cycle (Greiner 1972, Katz and Kahn 1978, Kimberly and Quinn 1984, Lippitt and Schmidt 1967, Quinn and Cameron 1983). Also, in terms of our exposition of the framework, we focus most heavily on top-level managers, in Mintzberg's (1983) term, "the strategic apex." Following this, we extend the framework, albeit briefly, to mid-level managers and supervisors.

Consistent with the concepts advanced by Stewart (1982) and Hunt and Osborn (1982), managerial tasks are visualized as having an element of discretion which provides managers the opportunity to exercise leadership. Instances in which organizational members create and exercise discretion in tasks that have limited or no discretionary elements are also treated as "exercising leadership." It is our contention that as one moves up the organizational hierarchy, discretionary components of the manager's job increase dramatically. This is consistent with arguments advanced earlier by Simon (1976) and Jaques (1956).

At the highest level of the organization, that is, at the strategic apex, discretion can be so great and the leadership component of managerial roles so large that one can speak of the strategic apex manager(s) or organizational leaders in virtually synonymous terms. We tie these discretionary notions together with our conceptualization of leader effectiveness in a later section.

The Organizational Life Cycle

Organizational scholars (Kimberly and Quinn 1984, Quinn and Cameron 1983, Quinn and Rohrbaugh 1983, Tichy 1983), among others, have advanced the notion that organizations move along a life cycle in a manner analogous to biological organisms. Though there are some differences in conceptualization in terms of the number of different stages through which organizations move, there appears to be an underlying consensus that the key stages are birth, growth, maturity, decline, revival/death. (See figure 8–1).

If the organization is successful in reviving itself then this revival is generally considered to give rise to a new life cycle. Unfortunately, no definitive empirical studies exist that provide an indication of the average span of these life cycles. Also, it is conceivable that organizational demise can occur abruptly (either from leadership failure or some catastrophic environmental shocks), truncating the organizational life cycle. That is, the organization can die without ever having grown.

Each stage in the life cycle can be visualized as one of organizational equilibrium, and movement from one stage to the next as involving a "transition." Miller and Friesen (1980, 271) define transitions as "the packet of changes that occur between the onset of imbalance or stress in one stage and the time when equilibrium or tranquility is reached in the adjacent stage."

For our purposes, we conceptualize an organizational life cycle as having four major phases. We define each phase as the combination of a particular state in the organizational life cycle and the transition preceding the stage. The four phases and the stages and transitions they incorporate are:

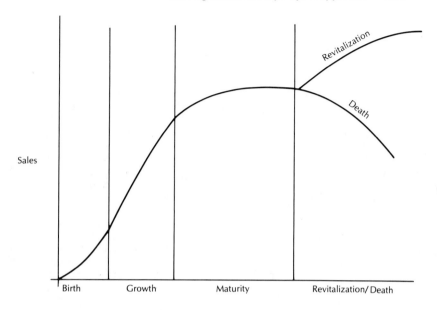

Figure 8–1. Organizational Life Cycle

Phase	Transition	Stage
Phase 1	Gestation to Birth	Birth
Phase II	Birth to Growth	Growth
Phase III	Growth to Maturity	Maturity
Phase IV	Maturity to Revitalization	Revitalization
or	or	or
Phase IV'	Maturity to Death	Death

These are shown in figure 8–2.

Phase I is concerned with the establishment of the organization. Phase II is characterized by an increase in organizational outputs. Phase III is characterized by a decrease in the rate of growth of oganizational outputs. Phases IV and IV' correspond to the phases that result from the organization following a maturity-to-revitalization transition (Phase IV) or a maturity-to-death transition (Phase IV'). In our conceptualization, the maturity-to-death transition could also include such activities as the focal organization being acquired by, or merging with, another organization, as the focal organization would then cease to have a distinct identity. Strategies in which the focal organization acquires another organization or merges with another (while maintaining identity), despite changes in form, we regard as revitalization.

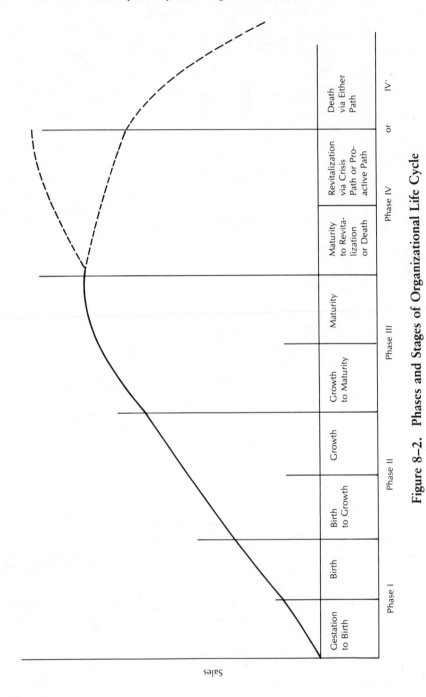

Figure 8–2. Phases and Stages of Organizational Life Cycle

We do not take the position that death is necessarily bad for the organization. That is, under certain circumstances, it may be to the benefit of the majority, if not all, of the stakeholders (entities who can influence the organization and be influenced, in turn, by the organization, e.g., shareholders and employees) to let an organization die proactively.

Organizational Life Cycle and Effectiveness Considerations

Demands, Constraints, and Choices

So far we have looked at our framework in terms of what we mean by the organizational life cycle and its phases. For the framework's next aspect we are concerned with looking at the manager's role in terms of demands, choices, and constraints, and their influence on effectiveness. Following Rosemary Stewart (1982), we can think of a manager's job in terms of three components: *demands* (what anyone in a given managerial job absolutely must do), *choices or discretion* (opportunities for managers in similar positions to do both different work and the same work in different ways than their counterparts), and *constraints* (factors such as monetary or human resource constraints, etc., inside and outside an organization, that limit what a manager can do).

The demands, choices, and constraints change over the organizational life cycle as a function of managerial actions and environmental changes. Although these may be different in terms of the specific demands, choices, and constraints between different organizations, we argue that there is a great deal of similarity in *generic* terms. For example, for all organizations in Phase I, demands center around establishing the organization; choices center around what constraints exist in terms of the resources that the organization can acquire. Also, in most instances, although the demands associated with a particular phase tend to be more easily identifiable, the choice and constraint sets tend to be greatly influenced by the manager's cognitive abilities and emotional makeup and account for variations in responses to demands. Over time, there is a give and take across these demands, constraints, and choices such that in meeting an earlier set of demands a manager's choices will influence the demands, choices, and constraints of a later period.

Managers, Leaders, and Effectiveness

When is a manager a leader? Bennis and Nanus (1985) and Zaleznik (1977) assert that managers are people who "do things right" and leaders are those who "do the right thing." If one accepts this assertion, then people are either managers *or* leaders but not both. It is our contention that managers can certainly be leaders as well (i.e., do the right thing). The conceptualization of the manager's job in terms of demands, choices, and constraints, in conjunction with the notion of slack, enables us to demonstrate how this is feasible. (According to Thompson (1967), organizations seek to protect themselves from environmental fluctuations that are detrimental to organizational survival and growth. One way in which this can be accomplished is through the creation of slack—that is, by generating an excess of resources over and above those required to meet demands.)

Consider the case of a sales manager who has to ensure that certain goals are met. This, in effect, is the sales manager's primary demand and is organizationally-induced. In addition, the sales manager is given a budget to work with and told that the production department should not be adversely affected by the actions of the sales department. These, in effect, are the sales manager's major constraints. If the sales manager consistently fails to meet these goals, not only has he or she failed as a leader but also as a manager. The sales manager would probably be labeled an "ineffective manager" and in all probability lose his or her job.

Now assume that the manager consistently meets his or her sales targets operating at the limit of the assigned constraint set but fails to generate slack. Furthermore, the manager neglects to determine whether customers could have been handled differently in order to generate customer loyalty, whether the operations could have been run more efficiently, whether more organizationally-favorable targets could have been set and met, and the like: that is, fails to modify demand and constraint sets through exercising initiative. The sales manager might now be considered a reasonably effective manager but an ineffective leader. If, in the process of meeting the demands, the sales manager is also able to create organizational slack and favorably modify constraints and choice sets and future demands, the manager can be considered to be acting more as a leader than as a manager in the Bennis and Nanus (1985) sense.

Using such logic, we define managerial and leader effectiveness as follows:

1. Very ineffective manager: unable to fulfill demands consistently

2. Effective manager/marginal leader: fulfills demands but is not able to make beneficial modifications to the constraint and choice sets

3. Effective manager/effective leader: fulfills demands; also is able to favorably modify the constraint, choice, and future demands sets and create some organizational slack

4. Effective manager/very effective leader: fulfills demands with a minimum level of resources while simultaneously *minimizing* constraints, *maximizing* choices, and creating favorable future demands in order to generate *maximum possible slack* for the organization

We asserted earlier that different phases of the organizational life cycle generate different demands, constraints, and choices. It is likely that leaders who are very effective in dealing with a particular set of demands, constraints, and choices may be less effective in dealing with another set of demands, constraints, and choices encountered in a different phase of the organizational life cycle. In other words, the traits, skills, and behaviors appropriate for effectiveness in one phase of the organizational life cycle may be inappropriate in other phases. This has important implications for manager selection, promotion, and training; that is, managers have to be matched to the organizational life cycle.

If a manager is being promoted at a time when the organization is going through a transition, then it may be useful to assess the manager's traits, skills, and behaviors to see whether they are going to be appropriate *for the phase into which the organization is moving* and provide the appropriate training. Texas Instruments is an organization that recognizes the merits of such an approach and changes managers based on a life cycle approach; risk-taking, entrepreneurial managers are assigned to start-up (Phase I) situations and the like. (Tichy 1983, 222).

Leadership Aspects

In the preceding, we have described briefly the phases used in our organizational life cycle framework. We have also linked the framework to effectiveness and to the concepts of demands, choices, and constraints. We examine the kinds of leadership aspects relevant to the framework and its varying demands, choices, and constraints. Once we have considered these expanded leadership aspects we incorporate these into the life cycle framework in the next section.

Leadership as Superior-Subordinate Influence

The most common way of treating leadership has been as influence from a leader to one or more followers or subordinates (Bass 1981). Typically this superior-subordinate influence has been concentrated on a fairly narrow range of task-oriented and relationship-oriented behaviors or, more recently, on leader/subordinate exchange relationships involving various forms of reinforcement. (See, e.g., Avolio and Bass, this book, ch. 3.)

To deal with the activities required across the organizational life cycle we need to expand the typical superior-subordinate treatment of leadership to include behaviors that are not restricted to superior-subordinate influence only and behaviors that go beyond task- or relationship-oriented and exchange behaviors.

Representation Behaviors

Representation behaviors involve behaviors representing some aspect of an organization or unit to people who are not the leader's immediate subordinates. Thus, they include behaviors with people over whom a leader has no direct authority. Typically these will be with people at or near the leader's own organization level. They can also include behaviors from a leader directed toward a superior.

For the strategic apex, these behaviors will be those external to the organization. For mid- and supervisory-level managers these activities are more likely to be across units within their own organization or, less frequently, with superiors.

Following recent work (Glauser and Bednar 1986, Schermerhorn, Hunt, and Osborn 1985), we can think of these activities in terms of: (1) resource acquisition, (2) network development and support, (3) organizational advocacy, (4) interface management, and (5) environmental scanning.

Resource acquisition consists of securing required budget, personnel, equipment, information, and materials, and obtaining necessary approval. *Network development and support* consists of establishing an inside track to those on whom the leader is dependent, encouraging and facilitating interorganizational (interunit) communication, and nurturing important contacts outside the organization. *Organizational (unit) advocacy* consists of public relations work to create and maintain high visibility for the organization (unit), seeing that organizational (unit) members receive equitable rewards and development opportunities, and taking stands to support the organization's (unit's) activities. *Interface management* consists of clarifying the organization's (unit's) role vis-à-vis other organizations (units), negotiating satisfactory solutions in interorganizational (interunit) conflicts, solving resource bottleneck problems, and protecting the organization (unit) from overload from other organizations (units). *Environmental scanning* consists of engaging in activities to identify organizations (units) playing a key part in the success of the leader's organization (unit); and engaging in activities to predict future political and economic conditions in the environment.

Expanding Superior-Subordinate Behaviors

Besides considering representation behaviors, we pointed out earlier that we need to broaden the traditional superior-subordinate leader behaviors to go beyond task- or relationship-oriented and exchange behaviors. We are interested in those strategic apex behaviors in dealing with different aspects of the organizational life cycle that have recently been called visionary (Sashkin and Fulmer, this book, ch. 4) or transformational behaviors (Avolio and Bass, this book, ch. 3).

These include or are related to those behaviors usually termed charismatic leadership. Until recently, charisma was considered to be a gift that only a few possessed. Furthermore, it was seen as having such a mystique or aura that although people knew it if they saw it, it was considered virtually impossible to measure. Fortunately for us, there is now evidence that although some people have more charisma than others, it does appear that it is possible for nearly everyone to exhibit at least some degree of charismatic behavior (this book, ch. 3). A corollary of this is that charisma can be measured in fairly straightforward ways (this book, ch. 3).

Avolio and Bass (this book, ch. 3) and Bass (1985) argue that transformational leadership (leadership that broadens and elevates goals and instills subordinates' confidence to go beyond ordinary goals) is "higher order" leadership that moves beyond what they term transactional leadership (that that gets things done through leader-follower exchange relationships). Transactional leadership is seen as necessary to accomplish day-to-day activities. However, for a leader to go beyond the ordinary, transformational leadership is seen as necessary.

Avolio and Bass see transformational leadership as consisting of: (1) *charisma* (the leader instills pride, faith, and respect, has a gift for seeing what is really important, and has a sense of vision which is effectively articulated); (2) *individualized consideration* (the leader delegates projects to stimulate and create learning experience, pays attention to followers' needs, especially those followers who seem neglected, and treats each follower with respect and as an individual); and (3) *intellectual stimulation* (the leader provides ideas that result in a rethinking of old ways, that is, the leader enables followers to look at problems from many angles and to resolve problems that were at a standstill).

We can see, then, that charisma is a necessary but not sufficient component of transformational leadership.

This is similar to Sashkin and Fulmer's (this book, ch. 4) recent work, which deals with "visionary leadership" in terms of focusing attention, communicating skillfully, expressing active concern for subordinates, demonstrating trustworthiness, integrity, and consistency of behavior, and taking risks. Here the earlier transformational leadership is extended to include the consistency and risk-taking notions.

Avolio and Bass see the transactional leadership base as involving *contingent reward* (the leader is seen as frequently telling subordinates what to do to achieve a desired reward for their efforts) and *management-by-exception* (the leader avoids giving directions if the old ways are working and intervenes only if standards are not met). Transactional leadership is seen by Avolio and Bass as being consistent with that used in most of the traditional approaches and is necessary but not sufficient for the highest levels of performance. Higher order transformational leadership is argued to provide the sufficient condition.

It is important to keep in mind that although these behaviors are indeed primarily concerned with extending traditional superior-subordinate influence, they are also relevant for those other than followers or subordinates. In other words, they may be used to influence external stakeholders, for example.

Linking Life Cycle, Demands, Constraints, Choices, and Expanded Leadership Aspects

We will now breathe life into our framework by first analyzing explicitly the changing demands during each of the life cycle phases. Choice and constraint changes are not explicitly identified since they are considered to be much more organizationally specific than are demands. Readers should keep this point in mind and should not lose sight of the importance of choices and constraints even as we explicitly discuss demands.

Next, for each phase of the life cycle we use the strategic apex demands (and implied choices and constraints) as a base to formulate research propositions using the previously discussed leadership aspects. For illustrative purposes we do this for both the gestation-to-birth transition and the birth stage in Phase I. For the remaining phases, because of space constraints, we emphasize the stage within each phase and do not consider transitions.

We then take a brief look at mid- and lower-level manager demands, although, again, space constraints prevent us from considering leadership propositions at these levels. Nevertheless, we invite the reader to develop these.

Finally, we should note that the leadership propositions are stated in general terms. That is, they are not broken down by the previously discussed specific leadership dimensions. We do not feel that enough is yet known to make specific dimensional predictions. However, it is important to note that we propose that the leadership measures be made operational by inclusion of these dimensions. Some readers may notice that inclusion of these specific dimensions could lead to a tautological relationship with demands, depending upon how the leadership dimensions are conceptualized and made operational. For example, there might be a demand for environmental scanning. One might then argue that it is tautological to hypothesize that leaders with a high score on the environmental scanning leadership dimension will be more effective. For now we simply want to let the reader know that we are sensitive to this issue. In the section on methodological concerns we discuss how we propose to deal with this issue.

Phase I

Figure 8–2 shows that this first phase incorporates the gestation-to-birth transition that culminates in the birth stage. We see the primary demands in this transition as: (1) developing a viable strategy, and (2) acquiring the necessary financial, material, and human resources to translate the idea and strategy into organizational reality. If these demands (particularly the second demand) cannot be met, the strategic apex leader is clearly ineffective and the "organization" is aborted.

One criterion for leader effectiveness here is the cost-benefit ratio of resource acquisition. Other criteria are suggested by the process of resource acquisition. If the process generates a number of constraints and limits current and future choice sets, then leadership can only be considered "marginal" in terms of our conceptualization.

An example would be where the financing is made available by a bank/ venture capital firm but stringent conditions—such as the repayment schedule, and so on—are attached to the strategy that the company is allowed to pursue.

On the other hand, if the leader can acquire resources above those anticipated as necessary for creating the organization (i.e., generate organizational slack) and have a favorable impact on choice and constraint sets we would classify the leader as very effective.

Human resource acquisition tends to be particularly crucial. As an organization does not yet exist, effectiveness in this area is demonstrated by readying a number of "key" people to come on board once the organization materializes. Here again we can consider leadership to be less than effective if the constraints created in the readying process (in terms of lucrative contracts, signing bonuses, etc.) are great.

Leaders are seen as being in a better position to keep their choice/constraint options open if they have had past success in similar ventures.

We see the leader's primary role here as that of a "salesperson," as the organizational possibility has to be sold to those stakeholders who can provide the organization with necessary resources. The basic skills are the ability to interact with a wide range of stakeholders and communicate effectively the vision of the proposed organization. The task becomes all the more difficult if the vision is radically different from the norms, technologies, and so on that the stakeholders are familiar with.

Leadership Proposition: Gestation-to-Birth Transition. The previous discussion leads to the following proposition for the gestation-to-birth transition: The previously discussed representation leader behaviors and transformational behaviors toward external stakeholders will be more important than other leader behaviors (transformational behaviors toward subordinates; transactional behaviors) and will be more strongly related to effectiveness than will these other leader behaviors.

Birth Stage. Assuming appropriate strategy development and resource acquisition in the gestation-to-birth transition, the organization then moves into the birth stage. This stage commences at the moment the nascent organizational structure takes form. Typically the structure is likely to be "simple" (Mintzberg 1983). It will have little specialization, a loose division of labor, few rules and procedures, few members, and will rely on direct supervision as its primary means of coordination. The stage is probably characterized by extreme scrutiny by the external and internal stakeholders (financiers, suppliers, governmental agencies, employees, etc.), who want to know how likely it is that the nascent organization can deliver on its gestation promise.

We see primary demands in this stage as:

1. Maintaining stakeholder confidence
2. Recruiting the key personnel identified and readied in the gestation-to-birth transition
3. Obtaining commitment from key personnel to the leader's vision and objectives

Just as the external stakeholders and key personnel place demands on the strategic apex leader, their expectations and aspirations also impose constraints. As before, the leader needs to try to incorporate these while maintaining as many future choices as possible.

Because of the initial excitement of building a new enterprise, motivation and morale are not likely to be problems here (e.g., Tichy 1983). The strategic apex leader needs to have as much time as possible to deal with external stakeholders. Thus, once the personnel have been socialized, and are committed to the leader's vision, the apex leader should delegate as much as possible to set in motion a process of "dispersed strategic leadership" in order to spread the organizational gospel.

As a result of the fluid nature of the nascent organization and the newness of the personnel, one can inevitably expect mistakes. Because of the importance of developing the organizational growth mass and maintaining external stakeholder relations, the leader must guard against responding to these mistakes by emphasizing an internal operations-oriented focus. It is crucial for long-term organizational effectiveness that the leader be successful in creating requisite conditions to foster an innovating and nurturant organization.

Our discussion thus far has focused on new organization start-ups. However, a number of start-ups are undertaken by existing organizations. Many of these, especially those in areas that are very different from the start-up organization's core business, typically fail to meet the expectations of the start-up. We contend that this is primarily due to the phase of the organizational life cycle and history of the founding organization intervening in the start-up. Most start-ups appear to be undertaken when organizations are either at the end of their growth phase (Phase II) or in the maturity phase (Phase III). The strategic apex leader who is assigned to head the start-up is probably one who has been successful in dealing with the Phase II or III demands of the organizational life cycle. The behaviors that the leader is likely to depict in the start-up stage are likely to be similar to those that have been successful in these (Phase II and III) phases. These are likely to be ineffective for Phase I of the cycle.

Leadership Proposition: Birth Stage. The preceding discussion leads to the following proposition for the birth stage: Representation behaviors and transformational leadership behaviors toward both external stakeholders and internal stakeholders (subordinates) will be more important than other leader behaviors (transactional behaviors) and will be more strongly related to effectiveness than will these other leader behaviors.

Mid-Level and Supervisory-Level Managers. The primary demands on mid-level managers in this stage are seen as:

1. Communicating and socializing their subordinates to organizational objectives and goals and establishing a social architecture for the organization
2. Designing information, control, and performance appraisal systems
3. Selecting technology appropriate for producing desired organizational outputs

It is easy to see that mid-level managers have a fairly wide range of choices from which to meet these demands. Constraints are likely to be primarily resource constraints along with some organizational constraints emanating from the fluidity of the structure. It is important for mid-level managers to understand that the choices they make not only create future constraints for themselves but also for the other parts of the organization. For example, if special purpose technology is selected for operations this could create a significant constraint for the strategic apex in terms of future strategic choices.

The primary demand on supervisory-level managers in this phase is seen as putting in place manufacturing and operations systems. Training of operatives is also a concern and progress in this area is seen as having crucial implications for success in Phase II.

Phase II

After the organization has successfully overcome the pangs of birth, it enters Phase II, comprising the birth-to-growth transition and the growth stage. If growth is rather explosive, organizations generally experience a great deal of confusion during the transition primarily because there is an imbalance between the resources required to sustain the growth and the rate at which resources become available. Furthermore, the simple structure developed in Phase I increasingly becomes a liability as a result of its looseness and amorphous tasks. The net result is likely to be a decline in member motivation and morale. As a consequence of these changes, the following demands are seen as being created at the strategic apex

1. Maintaining output in the face of resource constraints while simultaneously increasing the flow of resources
2. Creating the processes necessary to move the organization to a more formal structure
3. Maintaining motivation and morale
4. Sustaining organizational credibility with stakeholders
5. Assisting mid- and lower-level managers in setting up technical systems to ensure that growth demands can be sustained
6. Involving mid- and lower-level managers in strategic issues such that strategic thinking is dispersed across the organization
7. Emphasizing the strategic importance of operations to subordinates

As may be gathered from the preceding list, the primary demands tend to shift from the mainly external ones of Phase I to an almost equal proportion of internal and external ones. The absolute number of demands also is seen as growing considerably. The sheer number of demands forces the strategic apex leader to choose between dealing with the internal or external demands based on his or her particular predispositions. Unless compensated for, focusing on either the external or internal demands could lead to poor organizational performance. Effective leaders, recognizing the constraints in meeting all the demands by themselves, set in motion a process of dispersing some of the tasks associated with the demands to other parts of the organization, thus generating demands for mid-level and supervisory leaders.

This dispersal process can create its own set of demands on the strategic apex, viz. the need to ensure that the dispersed activities are consistent with those required of the demands at the strategic apex. This reinforces the notion that delegation and coordination are particularly critical for the strategic apex leader in this phase.

Leadership Proposition: Growth Stage. The preceding discussion leads to the following proposition for the growth stage: Transformational leadership behaviors toward external stakeholders and transactional leadership behaviors toward subordinates will be more important than other (representation behaviors, transformational behaviors toward subordinates) leadership behaviors and will be more strongly related to effectiveness than will these other behaviors.

Mid-Level and Supervisory-Level Managers. Hayes and Abernathy (1980) assert that a primary factor in the decline of global competitiveness of U.S. business has been the failure of the strategic apex to adequately deal with the earlier stated demand to emphasize the strategic importance of operations to subordinates. They further assert that strategic apex leaders in Japanese organizations are particularly adept at reinforcing, on an organization-wide basis, the strategic importance of operations and that this accounts for their substantial competitive edge in world markets.

The primary demands on mid-level managers in this phase are seen as:

1. Ensuring that operations take place as optimally as possible
2. Communicating and reinforcing the strategic importance of operations to personnel directly involved in operations
3. Communicating and reinforcing organizational values to their subordinates
4. Dealing with their counterparts in supplier and consumer organizations
5. Scanning the environment (particularly the competitive environment) in order to remain abreast of evolving technologies (systems that can influence the organization's strategy)

From the previous list, it is evident that mid-level manager demands in this phase broaden to include some that have an external orientation. If the demands are met effectively, mid-level managers can help alleviate the pressures on the strategic apex created by the demand set discussed earlier, leading to increased organizational effectiveness.

Unfortunately, most U.S. organizations do not seem to have recognized the potentially crucial role that mid-level managers can play in this phase, preferring to see them essentially as conduits of information who can be easily replaced by the evolving information systems hardware. Nance (1984) asserts that a primary cause of Braniff's failure was the lack of an adequate core of mid-level managers to deal with the demands encountered in the growth phase—a direct result of the failure of the strategic apex to meet one of its primary demands in this phase.

The primary demand confronting the supervisory level is seen as ensuring that operatives clearly understand their tasks and their goals. Simultaneously, they need also to be concerned with motivating their subordinates and communicating subordinate concerns to upper levels of management. Leadership notions such as initiating structure, consideration (Bass 1981), task, maintenance (Bass 1981), and Fiedler's Least Preferred Coworker (LPC) concept (Fiedler 1967), probably have considerable relevance at this level in this phase of the organizational life cycle.

Phase III

The growth-to-maturity transition is an insidious type of transition. In many instances the strategic apex fails to recognize this transition. A primary reason behind this failure is that those at the apex are generally so caught up in the internal operations complexities of Phase II that they fail to recognize shifts in environmental forces that contribute to this transition.

The growth slowdown also tends to reduce advancement opportunities for lower-level managers and subordinates. Thus, morale and motivation may suffer unless potential new revitalization opportunities can be communicated.

Because of demands of the previous phase, the organization is likely to be quite formalized and its structure firmly entrenched. In short, we might expect a fair amount of inertia.

The primary demands during this phase are seen as:

1. Scanning the environment to determine the domain to be used following Phase III (i.e., determining strategies for revitalization or proactive death)
2. Activating processes to move toward the new domain without disrupting current operations
3. Communicating and reinforcing potential opportunities for personal advancement and growth in order to rekindle and maintain motivation and morale in mid-level and supervisory personnel

Leadership Proposition: Maturity Stage. The previous discussion leads to the following proposition for the maturity stage: Representation behaviors and transactional leadership behaviors toward subordinates will be more important than other (transformational behaviors toward external stakeholders and subordinates and transactional behaviors toward external stakeholders) leadership behaviors and will be more strongly related to effectiveness than will these other behaviors.

Mid- and Supervisory-Level Managers. At mid- and supervisory-levels the demands center around running operations as efficiently as possible. Constraints result from the slowdown in the organizational growth rate which can rapidly lead to inefficiencies in operations from reduced equipment utilization, decreases in economies of scale, and so on. Innovative solutions generated by mid- and supervisory-level personnel can be of immense value in maintaining the desired level of efficiency. To the extent that mid-managers and supervisory personnel can deal with problems emanating from below without having to refer them up the hierarchy to the strategic apex, then the strategic apex is free to concentrate on the externally-generated demands alluded to earlier.

Phase IV and Phase IV'

We see these as the most crucial of all the phases. As indicated earlier, actions undertaken in the transition can lead to organizational revitalization (Phase IV) or organizational death (Phase IV'). The organization can enter these phases either through a crisis path or proactive path.

Crisis Path. The crisis path results from either ineffective leadership in Phase III or from an intense environmental shock. A vivid example of ineffective leadership in Phase III creating crisis is provided by the failure of the managers of steel mills in the United States to recognize and deal with changes in technology and foreign competition (Lawrence and Dyer 1983). A graphic example of environmental shock leading to organizational crisis was the Arab Oil Embargo of 1973 in numerous firms world wide. Yet another cause leading to the crisis path is "the failure of success syndrome" (Marrow 1974). In this syndrome, past successes blind organizational leaders to changes that can have adverse impacts on continuing organizational effectiveness.

If the crisis has been created by either leadership failure or the failure of success syndrome, then a change in leadership may be the only way for organizational revitalization. Also, the organizational culture established by the previous leaders may necessitate drastic changes in the strategic apex or dominant coalition. New leaders from within the organization may emerge during the course of the transition or new leaders may have to be hired from the outside. A recent example of this was the hiring of Lee Iacocca at Chrysler when it became apparent to Chrysler's board that its current leaders were incapable of dealing with the declining organizational performance that was threatening the survival of Chrysler (Iacocca and Novak 1984).

The key task confronting the strategic apex is seen as that of ensuring survival and growth. In some senses this is similar to the demand confronting the leader in Phase I of the organizational life cycle. However, there are major differences that make the task considerably more difficult than was the case in Phase I. Major constraints arise from the substantial loss of credibility among the various external stakeholders, demoralized organizational employees, noncompetitive product/service lines, and limited financial resources. Also, the time available for turnaround and revitalization is likely to be very limited. We see strategic apex primary demands in this phase as:

1. Reestablishing credibility with the various stakeholders and obtaining the requisite resources, particularly time, for turning the organization around

2. Scanning the environment and making product/service decisions grounded in the firm's distinctive competencies

3. Creating and communicating clearly a plan of action for dealing with the crisis and creating a new vision for the organization

4. Laying the groundwork for a culture consistent with the new vision of the organization. This would require creating and sustaining a double loop learning process (Argyris and Schon 1978) within the organization

5. Rapidly overcoming the negatives of past organizational cultures and accentuating the positives. Cherished symbols of the past would have to be phased out and replaced with new symbols consistent with the desired organizational culture (Kanter 1984)

6. Instigating technical changes

Revitalization along the Crisis Path Leadership Proposition. The previous discussion leads to the following proposition: Transformational leadership behaviors toward external stakeholders and subordinates, representation leadership behaviors, and transactional leadership behaviors toward subordinates will be more important than transactional behaviors toward external stakeholders and will be more strongly related to effectiveness than will these other behaviors.

Mid- and Supervisory-Level Managers. Expected demands on mid-level managers in this phase are to:

1. Provide the necessary technical assistance to strategic leaders in creating the new vision and translating it into more focused objectives and goals that can then be used in operating the organization

2. Demonstrate appropriate behaviors indicating confidence in the organization's ability to deal with the crisis

3. Maintain organizational morale, particularly when cuts have to be made differentially across individuals, groups, and departments

4. Take control of many of the day-to-day operational activities in order to permit the strategic apex time and flexibility in dealing with external stakeholders

The primary demand expected at the supervisory level is to create conditions that facilitate adaptation to the new technology. This may require the creation of training programs and the gradual phase-over of personnel from the old technology to the new. The major constraints at both mid- and supervisory-levels arise from an organizational culture that is increasingly dysfunctional for revitalization (Tichy 1983). Also, resources are likely to be highly constrained and worker morale low.

Proactive Path. The proactive path to revitalization should be a considerably less threatening path than the crisis path discussed earlier. The critical assumption underlying this path is that the strategic apex has been relatively effective in the earlier phases of the organizational life cycle in recognizing changing conditions, acknowledging them, and striving to deal with them. A recent example is GM's move into electronic data systems and aerospace (*Business Week* 1984).

As opposed to the crisis path, stakeholders should not have lost their confidence in the organization; rather, they should have abundant faith. Consequently resource acquisition is likely to be less of a constraint and time available for the transition is likely to be much greater than along the crisis path. A critical decision facing the strategic apex along this path is determining whether or not their style and the current organizational culture are consistent in dealing with the new demands. If they deem that this is not the case and that they cannot either reorient themselves or their organizational culture in the required direction, then they should consider stepping aside and handing over the reins to others who can adapt and direct the organization appropriately. An excellent example of such behavior was shown by the former Chairman of AT&T, John de Butts, who permitted Charles Brown to succeed him a year before de Butts's mandatory retirement upon recognizing that his leadership skills, honed in a regulatory environment, were likely to be unsuitable in the highly deregulated environment (*Business Week* 1980). Resistance to such changes create the major constraints in this phase. However, the resistance encountered in the proactive path is likely to be of a different kind and intensity than that encountered along the crisis path. In the crisis path, resistance is likely to be grounded in those members who perceive themselves to be vulnerable to layoffs, dismissals, and the like during the course of strategic reorientation. Support for the change is likely to come from those who perceive their position being strengthened as a result of the change. In contrast, in the proactive path, the very lack of crisis is likely to increase resistance to change as the majority of the organizational members may well feel quite comfortable with their situation and perceive any change to be unwarranted.

Primary demands here are seen as:

1. Ability to scan the environment and make product/service decisions based on the firm's distinctive competencies

2. Ability to develop and communicate a vision to persuade and motivate organizational personnel in new directions

3. Ability to modify the old culture or create a new culture to reinforce the new vision

Revitalization along the Proactive Path Leadership Proposition. The previous discussion leads to the following proposition for the proactive path: Representation leadership behaviors and transformational leadership behaviors toward subordinates will be more important than other leadership behaviors (transformational behaviors toward external stakeholders; transactional behaviors toward external stakeholders and subordinates) and will be more strongly related to effectiveness than will these other leadership behaviors.

Phase IV'

Occasionally, it may be better for organizational stakeholders if managers make the choice to liquidate the organization. That is, effective strategic apex leaders would select the proactive death path. This would be true of organizations that are confronted with very hostile environments (e.g., many companies in the asbestos industry) or whose future prospects are gloomy at best. The primary demand, under such conditions, at the strategic apex is to recover as much value as possible for internal and external stakeholders.

Leadership Proposition. The previous discussion leads to the following proposition for the proactive death path: Representation leadership behaviors and transactional leadership behaviors toward subordinates will be more important than other leadership behaviors (transformational behaviors toward external stakeholders and subordinates and transactional behaviors toward external stakeholders) and will be more strongly related to effectiveness than will these other leadership behaviors.

Mid- and Supervisory-Management Demands. The primary demand at mid- and supervisory-levels is to assist the strategic apex in this process. The major constraints here is that most managers would perceive moving along the proactive death path as indicative of their ineffectiveness and thus would be unwilling to move along this path.

Methodological Concerns

It is beyond the scope of this chapter to present a detailed methodology for testing our framework. Suffice it to say that we think multiple methodologies are necessary and that the methodologies would have to recognize the dynamic nature of the model. However, one methodological issue is so important that it does need to be addressed in this chapter. That issue is the demands/leadership potential tautology mentioned earlier. We gave the example of a possible tautology if one hypothesized that where there were a demand for environmental scanning, leaders who scored high on the environmental scanning leadership dimension would be more effective than those who did not. We think that such a tautology could occur with this as well as other dimensions from the leadership questionnaires as currently measured. To deal with this issue, we will need to reoperationalize the traditional dimensions.

Conceptually we can use a power analogy with regard to demands and leadership dimensions. Power is often considered as the *force* or *capacity* that makes things happen. That force is activated in the influence process. (Influence is the behavioral response; see, e.g., Carroll and Tosi 1977.)

We see demands in our framework as analogous to power. We see the demands "activated," if you will, through the behavioral response exemplified by a particular leadership dimension.

To return to the environmental scanning example, we need to measure the environmental scanning leadership dimension in an active or behavioral mode. Thus, rather than simply using an item such as, "the leader obtains information about governmental regulations," more behaviorally-oriented measures are needed. Examples might include such measures as estimates of the amount or proportion of time spent on this information-seeking activity as well as other activities typically involved in environmental scanning. Similar kinds of changes would also be made in the other dimensions, as needed.

In this way tautological relationships could be minimized if not totally avoided.

Summary and Conclusions

The leadership literature almost entirely neglects leadership requirements of organizations as they move from one phase of the life cycle to another. Tending to this neglect shows promise of providing important new knowledge to help strategic apex leaders in their jobs.

We have developed an organizational life cycle approach to leadership which specifies: (1) some key explicit demands and implicit constraints and choices faced by the strategic apex in each of five phases in the life cycle, and (2) strategic leadership behavioral propositions believed appropriate for the demands, constraints, and choices at each phase. The leadership behaviors involve a number of dimensions within comprehensive transformational, transactional, and external leadership categories.

The next step is to test and refine this framework and to make that information available to researchers and eventually to strategic apex leaders.

9
Commentary
on Part II

Chapter 6 Commentary: Leadership: Nothing but Constructing Reality by Negotiations?

Klaus Bartölke

Some Assumptions

Commenting on a major attempt, such as that of Hosking and Morley, to provide a new perspective on a rather controversial research area such as leadership requires that one clarify one's own position with respect to the questions at stake. Leadership—understood here as formation and implementation of will—is part of social reality. How it is discussed will therefore be dependent on the conceptualization of social reality.

My basic assumption is that social reality as the playground, or the battlefield, on which leadership occurs is socially constructed reality (for earlier discussions of this concept in the context of the leadership symposia, see, e.g., Dachler 1984; Hosking et al. 1984). It is a reality in the making, the construction of which often will not be completely understood because of interplays of different construction attempts directed at change as well as preservation. Interplays in the passing of time lead to highly complex developments (that some are inclined to interpret as evolution in an almost biological sense). The resultant constructed reality will not necessarily be effective, in fact—apart from unintended consequences and chance—functionality might be a conflictual issue since with different construction attempts contradictory aims will be pursued. Thus, social reality cannot be defined as nature but has to be conceptualized as culture and as such can and does take very different forms. To understand them, it should be possible to reconstruct in cultural terms the dominant principles on which they are based. Furthermore, such different forms are not determined by, although they may in degrees be dependent on or limited by, the natural environment or habitat.

This assumption has been confirmed by my own research on the kibbutz as a specific social reality, the construction of which is very visible (Bartölke, Bergmann, and Liegle 1980, Bartölke et al. 1985). It represents a perspective nicely summarized by a student of the Indians of Texas:

It is the conviction . . . that by knowing and understanding tribes and nations far removed from ourselves in time or space, we can gain perspective and objectivity in evaluating ourselves and our age . . . Knowledge of others forces us to realize that our way, our beliefs and ideals, are only our own solutions to what may be common human problems. We come to see that there are many ways of thinking and acting, and that simply because other ways are different from our own does not inevitably make them inferior or wrong (Newcomb 1980, v. VIII).

Feyerabend (1984) cites Herodot for an impressive example of how differently cultures might deal with the same phenomenon.

When Dareios was king, he had convened before him all the Greeks living in his vicinity and asked them for what price they would be ready to eat their fathers' corpses. They answered they would on no account do so. Then he called the Indian Kalatiers who do eat their parents' corpses and asked them—the Greeks being present and kept informed by an interpreter—for what price they would be ready to burn their dead fathers. They screamed and beseeched him to refrain from such impious words. So it is with the customs of nations, and Pindar is right in saying that custom is king of all being (p. 53, my translation).

It is custom that is king, acknowledges King Dareios, leading the way to socially constructed reality.

To understand a specific socially constructed reality, a number of only artificially separable levels of analysis might apply. Using a rather familiar distinction reflected in academic disciplines, there are the levels of society at large, organizations of different kinds, and groups and individuals. All these levels may be characterized by values, norms, legal codes, rationalities, rationales, and myths, describing qualities of social relationships as bases of social actions such as leadership. These characteristics are not necessarily identical across or within levels at any point in time. There will be dependencies and interdependencies. However, the degree of homogeneity or heterogeneity between or within levels will be influenced by characteristics of society at large more than by characteristics of the other levels as parts of the respective society.

Such a perspective of describing socially constructed realities is a theoretical construction of reality in highly abstract terms. It is incomplete concerning concrete situations. It is incomplete too, with respect to the philosophy of describing and explaining socially constructed reality or, more precisely, theoretical reconstruction of socially constructed reality.

Researchers might adhere to different premises and focus on different topics in their reconstruction of constructed reality. To make such an assumption implies that there is no unambiguous access to reality. Researchers theoretically construct reality dependent on their specific conception of the world (which, in turn, is dependent on the characteristics of the reality they are living in and their involvement in or alienation from leadership performed in this reality). For example, are they looking for scientific knowledge defined as valid independent of time and space or do they modestly focus on the here and now? Do they adhere to a more descriptive rather than a prescriptive understanding? Do they focus more on dissimilarities and less on similarities of different constructed realities (examples for such a struggle are provided by Lammers and Hickson 1979)? The ways such questions are answered will determine the theoretical construction of reality.

I am more convinced than not about the limits of the validity of general theoretical constructions of reality. In the social sciences I rarely see any area where it appears possible to create theories at the same time encompassing large parts of constructed reality and being sufficiently specific to allow understanding, explanation, and perhaps, handling of concrete situations.

Leadership: Nothing but Negotiations?

It is with this kind of skepticism that I address the question of leadership. As already mentioned, I define (reconstruct) leadership in functional terms as formation and implementation of will in terms of attempts to construct reality. Functional means that leadership itself is part of socially constructed realities and that it might take different forms under different societal conditions. The question of how leadership is institutionalized remains open. It is a question of research, how the function of leadership is performed taking into account values, norms, legal codes, rationalities, and the like. That particular individuals are permanently recognized as leaders is only one case among possible others and would have to be analyzed in terms of ideologies (Neuberger 1984) used to justify their dominance in reality construction. Along with the existence of such specified conditions, leadership takes its specific form of institutionalization, personification, justification, and legitimation.

Leadership as a theoretical construction of a socially constructed reality finds its conceptual boundaries in the researcher's perspective and in the aspects of socially constructed reality that are outside of that perspective. Such perspectives are necessary and unavoidable in any theoretical construction because, for a number of reasons, reality cannot be completely described. Therefore, the questions can only be what are the characteristics of the perspective and how would the theoretical construction look if different perspectives had been chosen. Such an analysis concerns the problem of whether the content of the perspective results in theories with some commonality or whether different perspectives for a given time period lead to theories that are incommensurable.

What is the perspective that Hosking and Morley have chosen when discussing "The Skills of Leadership?" I assume that their perspective is defined by the concept of social order. Social order is interpreted as negotiated order (e.g., Bazerman and Lewicki 1983). Leaders are the individuals who are considered by those concerned (the followers?) to contribute effectively to negotiated social order within groups and between groups. What makes them effective are specific skills.

This view seems to be based on the assumption that there are independent individuals or coalitions of individuals who enter into negotiation arenas. Although there might be some differences in power between them, everybody has a chance to participate in the negotiation process concerning the establishment of social order. Such a picture comes close to a liberal market model applied to exchanges of nonmonetary goods. In these exchanges the skillful persons (skillful in terms of relationships with followers as well as relationships with other groups or organizations) are the agents of social control. Social control thus is negotiated control and open to change by renewed negotiation processes dominated by skillful leaders.

Leadership in this sense means social construction of reality and formation and implementation of will. Therefore, I can easily agree that it is a theoretical construction that is worthwhile. I have doubts, however, whether it is an approach with a potential for general theory, applicable to all forms of socially constructed reality. These doubts, as compared with the authors' convictions, might be partly grounded in the comparatively strong German practical and theoretical tradition of thinking and acting in terms of structures and institutions rather than in processes of events, a more British way of looking at and constructing reality. Can it really be assumed that there is one process or one principle underlying all realities on all levels of analysis?

A first question to be raised concerns the conditions of society at large and its mechanisms of social control (Türk 1981) in terms of the possibility of considering negotiation as a general construction principle. For example, pre-organizational socialization and general and occupational education as mechanisms of social control might be built on quite different concepts of the individual. In socialization, there might be strong emphasis on socially constructed structure, understood as processes that are repeated over and over. Structure then might be taken for granted and become a non-negotiable part of a society's perception of reality including leaders' roles. Or, there might be a concept of rationality with regard to production and distribution of commodities that assigns and legitimates the prerogative to lead quite apart from any necessity to negotiate with the holders of specific resources like capital. Under such conditions, specific negotiation skills might be helpful though not necessary to define the situation and to construct reality.

Regarding the level of the organization, the type of governance as a structural and/or cultural characteristic should be considered. Ouchi (1980) has suggested distinguishing among markets, bureaucracies, and clans. The concept of a leader as a skillful negotiator appears to apply more to governance by market as the dominant mechanism than to bureaucracy (of which hierarchy is a main component) or clan. Put into such a perspective, other mechanisms of social control, besides negotiation, appear, namely authority and power, manipulation, and persuasion.

Etzioni's (1961) distinction between coercive, utilitarian, and normative organizations might be of relevance, too. Also, it might be appropriate to differentiate between negotiation and problem-solving in interaction processes that involve coalition formations. In a zero-sum situation, interactions can be rightly called negotiations; under non-zero-sum conditions, the term joint-problem-solving appears to fit better (Bass 1983).

On the individual level, the motivation to enter into a situation where leadership is exercised might make a difference. Negotiation skills are more likely to be a condition for acceptance as a leader when calculative orientations prevail. However, in the case of normative orientations (for the distinction between value orientations, see Kluckhohn 1951 and Rokeach 1973), conformity with central values might be more important.

In summary, conceptualizing leadership and leaders in terms of negotiated order and negotiation skills seems to be a useful theoretical construction. However, what is needed, on such a road is a closer examination of the conditions of constructed reality to which the concept of negotiation might apply.

Usefulness to Practitioners

Hosking and Morley attempt to theorize in ways that make their thinking useful to practitioners. The hope for usefulness of theory often leads to theoretical constructions of socially constructed realities in terms of cause and effect, or intention and action relationships that focus on variables easy to manipulate and neglect other aspects that in the short run must be taken as given (for example, characteristics of society at large). Therefore, I wonder whether skills are easier to change by training than are attitudes or broader value orientations. For practitioners, at the organizational and group levels, attitudes and value orientations are more likely to be controlled by mechanisms of social control apart from negotiations such as selection and self-selection.

The training of leaders as a topic of decision making may be called an ill-structured problem (e.g., Bass 1983) in terms of the following:

No common understanding of the concept of leadership

No agreement on appropriate solutions and methodology to develop them

Obscurity of what are controllable and uncontrollable variables

At least partly unpredictable and unknown interdependencies

Missing consensus on ethical implications with respect to outcomes for leaders and followers, organizations, and society at large

Social construction of leadership in actual constructed reality deals with such ambiguities and uncertainties using judgment, intuition, and experience along with the exercise of power or authority. Theoretical construction of reality as a perscriptive enterprise tries to deal with these ambiguities and uncertainties from the outside, in fact transforming leadership into a well-structured problem (a more precise discussion about the relationships between theoretical constructions by scientists and actual practice is provided by Ridder [1986]). If scientists are successful in convincing practitioners about the validity of their theoretical constructions, they become leaders themselves but without being directly affected by the consequences of their suggestions. Thus, they become leaders without applying negotiation skills.

According to Hosking and Morley, scientists as leaders or potential leaders provide descriptions for others of a reality in construction. Thus, they might help to prevent followers or potential followers from a social construction of reality of their own.

A theory of leadership skills (not just a practical guide—e.g., Adair 1984) in the context of negotiated order as a basis for training leaders perhaps is less vulnerable to ethical problems than other social-technological theories. This is so because such a theory appears to be based on a model of active human beings, not one where a majority is assumed only to behave reactively or even passively. Under such conditions, voluntary acceptance of rather than forced compliance with social order could be expected. However, ethical questions need to be raised when not everyone has the opportunity to participate in the dialogical process of reality construction, and when training is focused on those already better equipped to influence the result of negotiations.

The model of human beings previously described is one that I favor too. Nevertheless, it would lead me down a different road for examining leadership and thinking about change in concrete situations. I would not attempt to construct general theories and social technologies but would rather suggest inquiry into the attributions and theories in use (Argyris 1979) of actors of reality construction and those subject to it. Their attributions and theories, in combination with mine, would be a starting point for working out choices available, their consequences, and their ethical implications.

It is a road in the direction of understanding the world as a human possibility by a process that explores theoretical and practical views of reality on the basis of a common reconstruction of socially constructed reality. By attempting to clarify the construction principles applied in a concrete situation, those involved in the reconstruction might become conscious of the process of leadership, its underlying conditions, and its boundaries in ways that lead to changes in reality construction.

The decision on how to perform and to train leaders would be in the complete authority of those who will have to live in the reality that they are constructing. Regarding the researcher, she or he can only hope that consciousness results in reality construction that is improved for all concerned.

Chapter 7 Commentary: Leadership Research: A Systemic Viewpoint

Gilbert J.B. Probst

A Difference That Makes a Difference?

Recent research results show that organizations in crisis often remove their top managers or sometimes subordinates as a way to erase dominating ideas, to repudiate past programs, to become receptive to new ideas, and to symbolize change. The literature on symbolic or cultural management suggests a similar pattern (cf. Nystrom and Starbuck 1984; Pfeffer 1981; Smircich 1983; Starbuck 1982; Starbuck, Greve, and Hedberg 1978). Therefore the alternative strategy of replacing team managers proposed by Crouch and Yetton is of special interest.

Managers' ideas, values, goals, motives, or interests have a remarkable influence on a system's behavior, a system's learning, sense-making processes, and the structuring of organizations but they also prevent behavior, structures, unlearning, and so on. Certainly the results and consequences of such analysis of teams have to be discussed by managers and taken into account. As Peters and Waterman (1982) have nicely shown, teams, and especially the ongoingness and a capacity for continued ongoingness of teams, has a crucial meaning.

Crouch and Yetton present an interesting look at work teams that signals a change in leadership research. They accept complexity as a phenomenon and try to give an alternative to simple one-way causal models. Their interests have a systemic basis—even if it is not explicitly called systemic—and they focus on equilibrium models. The authors do not look at one individual only, for example, the leader. Their research is built on an interactive and diachronic viewpoint, which takes into account not only the characteristics of the leader, but also those of the subordinates. They emphasize processes in social systems and their complexity. They deal with stability and change and assume no simple causal ordering, but rather, forms of mutually dependent clusters. This is a very systemic basis indeed.

However, they also stay with a positivistic perspective, claiming to develop an explanatory model and aiming to predict consequences or behavior.

In their project, accepting complexity means to model one aspect of that dynamic complexity. The main question stated by Crouch and Yetton is whether developmental processes in teams continue indefinitely or whether stable states exist towards which teams predictably evolve. But this raises another question, namely, whether or not the notion of "complexity" to identify a phenomenon in social systems degenerates to lip service when used for modeling one isolated aspect of social systems.

Complexity is not something purely objective but always includes subjectivity. Based on our interest, we draw the boundaries of a system and therefore perceive complexity. Modeling hundreds of variables does not necessarily include complexity (there is a clear distinction between complicated and complex systems). It is relationships and interactions, the dynamics of a system, that makes us perceive or construct complexity. Moreover, one may ask whether a dichotomy is valid where there are either stable states or development processes continuing indefinitely.

This commentary is embedded in a broader perspective and some epistemological questions. Often it involves not so much a critique as a hint to go further and accept all the consequences a systemic approach entails. The main question is whether the underlying assumptions by Crouch and Yetton provide a satisfactory basis for the research of teams as systems or whether their conceptual and epistemological foundations do not unduly constrain one from dealing adequately with a team's nature and its complexity.

From Leadership to Management of Social Systems

Leadership in its traditional, most fundamental meaning denotes the art of leading people. To be sure, ideas, values, goals, and the like are realized by human action, and to motivate or lead people to act in a certain way is a classic view of leadership. But this cannot be understood by simple analysis of the characteristics of the leader, as motivation theories have demonstrated extensively. To see the followers (or leaders) as isolated beings is too great a reduction for the understanding of human social systems behavior. Human beings act in a network of actions, in interactive communication.

A narrow understanding of leadership tends to explain what happens in a social system and the behavior of the leader in terms of goals, intentions, motives, and interests of the leader. But leaders do not (only) act out of personal goals, intentions, and the like, but in the light of the viability of a system (a group, department, organization). They are not to be isolated from a system as a whole, as in a traditional meachanistic, cybernetic view (controller). Leadership can only be understood as part of an open, interrelated network, or as a part of the system, where the system itself is a part of a larger system or context, interrelated with its environment. In Koestler's (1948) language, social systems are holons with an integrative tendency and expansive, assertive aspects. We cannot reduce the complexity of the whole without changing the nature of the system.

Thus, when leadership is used in the context of heading a team or a larger human social system, and we agree on a systemic view, then the concept of leading people in an individualistic sense turns into a metaphorical meaning, that does not reflect adequately the complexity implied in leading social systems. Rather, we have to take into account the team as a system with its fundamental relationships in a network and with intrinsic or organic control. Such a system does not allow the separation of the leader from the team or the reduction of explanations to cause-effect relationships in a linear sense. When leadership is seen as individualistic, properties of a social system are then reduced to properties of individuals as leaders and followers. That is why the consequences are often dismissing chief executives or starting training programs for individuals.

Kurt Lewin introduced the notion of a group as a dynamic whole (cf. Lewin 1948), and further research has shown that groups display phenomena that are not attributable to individual actions. Thus, it is important to create adequate research designs. Social systems, such as a corporation, a hospital, and so on, cannot be analyzed as groups; they are systems of another category. And neither their origination nor their behavior is explicable on the basis of group research results. Nor can one explain group phenomena solely on the basis of the characteristics of the participants (cf. Ulrich 1984).

Modeling just one aspect of a relatively complex system becomes very unsystemic, for example, when we use an interactive relationship in which the one participant (leader), in order to achieve self-established goals, motives, ideas, and the like, generates and maintains directed behavior of the other participant. Thus, in Crouch and Yetton's rationale there is the danger that management of a team could be understood as nothing more than leadership of people.

Questions about the Methodology

Some reflections on the consequences of the perspectives and assumptions chosen raise doubts about the adequacy of the empirical basis and the methodology as well as the questions posed compared with a systemic approach. Elements such as performance, trustworthiness, conflict legitimacy, support, and the like are ambiguous. Thus, it is essential that they be properly researched. The lack of a clear definition of any of these elements may well be a phenomenon closely related to research on complex social systems but hinders empirical research in the traditional way. Obviously the use of questionnaires gives an idea of the interpretations of the leaders and the followers but I doubt whether we can get a systemic understanding of a system in that way. In addition I would still agree with Barry Staw, who recently commented:

> One problem with data in the field of organizational behavior is that it may merely feed back to administrators their own lay theories of effectiveness. Research data, for example, show that questionnaire responses to items of influence, openness to change, cohesiveness, and satisfaction correlate significantly with organizational performance. Recent research, however, has shown that beliefs about performance also influence our beliefs about other processes that occur in social situations. Once we know that an individual, group or organization is a high or low performer, we are prone to make attributions consistent with this evaluation along many other dimensions. For example, regardless of the actual level of functioning of various processes in a group, research has demonstrated that knowledge, that the group performed effectively, will lead to the conclusion that it was also cohesive, high in communication, high in mutual influence, and highly satisfied (Staw 1977, 5).

Self-reports only reflect the interpretations of the people asked, not true causal relationships, and generalizations or representations of the results are the researcher's interpretation of *a* reality. In this context, one must ask what legitimates the rationale given in the Crouch and Yetton chapter 7. One can find some rationale for why any linkage can lead to another state. For example, if a manager is highly competent or performs well, a subordinate may imitate the manager, but on the other hand one can also find other rationales depending on the context.

Different structures can produce the same outcome and the same or similar structures are capable of producing different outcomes, as has been shown by Singer (1924), Ackoff (1981), Churchman (1971), and Emery (1977). But the claim that there are just two equilibrial states does not fit with a systemic view. If one chooses a wider context and imagines that a team in an unfavorable equilibrium gets into competition with another team, the whole situation, the rationale, may change. But in this empirical research, the teams are not in their work environment; they are in a different context that is not further discussed.

Again, the focus in questionnaire research is on individual properties and behavior. The nature of a team as a system is difficult to understand from an aggregation or calculation of average numbers. As mentioned previously, social systems have to be understood as holons in an inner and an outer integration. Neither the embeddedness of a team within its context, nor the training program situation (which is a very special situation that does not fit with the actual work situation), nor the social, political, cultural, economic, technological, aesthetical, or ethical context are recognized.

Observing Social Systems

Constructivism sheds new light on the question of how we know what we believe we know. Reality is no longer something out there that has to be discovered objectively. "Any so-called reality is—in the most immediate and concrete sense—the construction of those who believe they have discovered and investigated it" (Waltzlawick 1985, 9). However, from the fact that our brain produces the images we perceive, it follows that all experience is subjective. The world as we perceive it is our construction; we are constructing a reality (cf. Von Foerster 1985).

This is not the place to give an overview on constructivism but there is no way to neglect its contents. It leads to a fundamental critical reflection of an empiricist position as it is proposed by Crouch and Yetton. Any discourse about the world is not a reflection or map of *the* world; thus, theory is not dictated by the objective experience of the world but is an emergent outcome of communal interchange (cf. Gergen 1985, Berger and Luckmann 1966, Von Glasersfeld 1985). This does not mean that objectivity becomes odd or useless. Experience can only be compared with experience. But objectivity can then be discussed as a successful insinuation—*Unterschiebung* in the sense of Kant—of our own successful experiences (that means they fit) to others. We need others therefore to construct objectivity (Von Glasersfeld 1984).

But the "objective basis of conventional knowledge" is challenged; it is no longer a description or explanation of the world out there. An absolute distinction required by a positivist viewpoint between subject and object is no longer viable. "Everything said is said by an observer, and, everything said is said to an observer," as Heinz Von Foerster (1979) paraphrased Humberto Maturana. And Gergen gives a very good summary of the consequences:

> What we take to be experience of the world does not in itself dictate the terms by which the world is understood. What we take to be knowledge of the world is not a product of induction, or of the building and testing of general hypotheses. The mounting criticism of the positivist-empiricist conception of knowledge has severely damaged the traditional view that scientific theory serves to reflect or map reality in any direct or decontextualized manner (Gergen 1985, 266).

By far the clearest description of a radial constructivism is given by Ernst Von Glasersfeld.

We have to include the observer in our description of social systems and acknowledge that not only the researcher but all the human beings included in the researcher's research compute a reality. In describing social systems the observer role is a crucial one. It has to be recognized that concepts such as equilibrium, feedback, trustworthiness, performance, conflict legitimacy, support, and so on are not properties of the systems but of the description of those systems by an observer. Thus, we no longer can accept that by an accumulation of empirical research results we get closer and closer to truth. If we construct realities we have to include ourselves. Knowledge is taking part in constructing realities that may be shared or "insinuated by others."

Patterns of Order—A Result of Equilibrial States and Transitions

The core view of today's systems thinking is not equilibrial states, but change, self-organization, evolution, becoming of order, non-equilibrial processes. The ability and desire to change as manifested in learning, self-adapting, self-organizing, and self-developing social systems have become a core concept of systems and cypernetic research in recent years. But it is a necessity to have a close look at traditional and new cybernetics, equilibrial states and transitions, stability and change alike. To concentrate on equilibrial states is too narrow a concept. Equilibrium systems are closed systems, they demand a formulation of a norm of equilibrium, and preferential views are a bias of the observer (or user, describer . . .). "A norm of equilibrium may be thought of as a part of the very definition of an equilibrium-system, but equilibrium alone will not suffice to distinguish the degree to which a particular system achieves its proper purpose; nor is it sufficient for comparing one system with another" (Cowan 1965, 126).

A further danger is that we end up with an aggregate of the properties and behavior patterns of individuals, even if in an interactive and diachronic way. If we do not take into account the system as a whole we miss the idea that the whole is something different from the sum of its parts. I think that from a systemic point of view we have to acknowledge that the interrelationships and interactions among the participants of a team are interwoven in such a way that it is not possible to trace single attributes or reduce the analysis to one aspect of the whole to reach understanding of the leadership of teams.

We have to understand patterns of interactions and patterns of order as they emerge. The properties of social systems as teams or other larger collective phenomena cannot be reduced to their parts (a leader or follower) or isolated interactions or relationships between parts. The properties are of a different kind in a social system than those of the individuals and their interactions (cf. Dachler 1985a).

The question is how order in social systems as a whole arises, how these systems become, grow, and so on—the processes by which social systems are designed, controlled, and developed (Malik and Probst 1984, Probst and Scheuss 1984). Interactions and relationships are very important indeed.

However, often they are explained not on the basis of the attributes of the actors in a complex network-system, but as the attributes of the one actor and his or her cognitive schema, personal skill, trustworthiness, intelligence, power, conflict legitimacy, and so on.

These single attributes act as a sort of stimulus and affect the other person (and this process goes on in that linear mode). The whole is reduced to attributes of one actor. I do not believe that we can predict states in a complex social system (thus, the term *pattern* is well chosen by Crouch and Yetton); we rather have to deal with pattern predictions. "We have in fact learned enough in many fields to know that we cannot know all that we must know for a total interpretation (or understanding) of phenomena" (Von Hayek 1967).

Research projects may be designed differently depending on the reference frame, paradigmatic rules, or perspectives. We can measure more precisely the attributes of leaders, the motifs, goals, intentions, attitudes, trustworthiness, and so on with ingenious instruments without questioning the reference frame, the paradigmatic rules, or the perspectives. But as long as we do not question the latter we are not able to define a system adequately and research hardly makes a difference that makes a difference.

Part III
Inside the Heads of Leadership Researchers: Their Assumptions and Implications on How Knowledge Is Generated

James G. Hunt
B.R. Baliga
H. Peter Dachler
Chester A. Schriesheim

The three content chapters in this part focus in very different ways on the thought processes of those involved in conducting leadership research. As such, they are representative of a newfound respectability in looking at the cognitive processes of behavioral science researchers (see, e.g., Blair and Hunt 1986, Cummings and Frost 1985). They also reflect the introspection that has come about in response to disappointments with the way the content of the leadership field is developing (see, Hunt and Larson 1975, 1977, 1979; Hunt, Sekaran, and Schriesheim 1982; Hunt et al. 1984).

Chapter 10, "Leadership Theory as Causal Attributions of Performance," by James C. McElroy and J. David Hunger, sensitizes us to the importance of researcher attributions. The argument is that researchers carry implicit alternative causal antecedents of performance in their minds as they examine leadership. The authors contend that these alternative attribute causes should be made explicit and in so doing one can examine systematically the *assumptions* underlying leadership theories as opposed to debating the *mechanisms* of such theories (see also chapter 15, by Dachler, in part IV). They propose an attributional framework for classifying these assumptions and propose that performance rather than leadership be the focus of attention. The question would then become what is the role of leadership among other variables in performance as opposed to using leadership as the central focus and making various attributions about its role.

The McElroy and Hunger chapter admonishes leadership researchers to examine systematically their implicit causal attributions to enhance leadership research. Calas and Smircich's (chapter 12) "Reading Leadership as a Form of Cultural Analysis" asks leadership researchers to go much further in reflecting on the state of and assumptions made in the leadership literature. The authors ask researchers to examine their traditional normal science approach to leadership research within the context of narrative literature. They argue that leadership researchers exist in a narrative culture that has scientific knowledge as its preferred mode of discourse, but that the researchers are unaware of this.

The authors anchor this discussion within the context of the dissatisfaction with the state of the field that has been articulated in all leadership symposium volumes from 1975 on (Hunt and Larson 1975, 1977, 1979; Hunt, Sekaran, and Schriesheim 1982; Hunt et al. 1984). They conclude that leadership researchers need to recognize explicitly that they are really doing narrations whose content is scientific discourse. Once that is recognized, researchers will be freed to expand their horizons, connect their community with the rest of the world, and learn from themselves. Narratives legitimize these directions in a way that hard-core normal science does not.

Peterson and Smith's chapter 11, "Gleanings from a Frustrated Process Analysis of Leadership Research Stakeholders," is also concerned with leadership researcher introspection. Here the focus is on identifying the stakeholders and the assumptions of these stakeholders as they affect the direction taken by the leadership field. The authors established a series of task forces and used a variation of Mason and Mitroff's (1981) Strategic Assumption Surfacing and Testing (SAST) technique to explore these stakeholder issues and assumptions and their potential impact on research directions. Peterson and Smith's chapter does provide some of this information but has its primary focus on the strengths and limitations of the SAST technique as designed and used in the present context. The authors discuss the potential of the technique and their less than full success in using it to accomplish the goals of better understanding the role of differing stakeholders in influencing research directions in leadership.

Torodd Strand is the commentator for the McElroy and Hunger chapter. His commentary is basically concerned with continuing McElroy and Hunger's spirit of extending leadership theory by breaking out of traditional ways of thinking. Strand does this by arguing for an integration of psychological and organization theory. He is concerned about attributional errors in one camp and lack of interest in leadership and intervention in the other. Though his arguments are not new, they reflect the view that many researchers outside of the United States appear to hold about leadership. Strand's commentary essentially uses McElroy and Hunger's chapter as a backdrop against which to argue for broader conceptualizations of leadership.

Walter Nord's normal science training as a social psychologist and his interest and expertise in interpretist perspectives allow some interesting commentary for the Calas and Smircich chapter. He argues that a major contribution of their chapter is its emphasis on being reflexive (developing an understanding of ourselves as leadership researchers). As Nord sees it, Calas and Smircich go beyond mere reflexive admonitions and actually do reflexive social science complete with a model based on narrative analysis for others to examine. He takes issue with the authors for not being even more self-reflexive in using their self-reflexive approach. At the same time, he is concerned that they did not make clear how they arrived at some of their conclusions. He also makes the ironic point that in revealing the shortcomings of normal science, the authors themselves used a normal science type of analysis. They were not able to abandon completely the normal science paradigm and they wrote as normal scientists.

Finally, he argues that more than Calas and Smircich's recommendations for getting individual researchers to reeducate themselves and broaden their vision is needed if the research endeavor is to change. He contends that structural changes are necessary as well. The structural changes would involve a much higher degree of specialization among researchers than at present and would need to provide sufficient differentiation and integration.

As with Baliga and Hunt's chapter in part II, the Peterson and Smith chapter does not have an accompanying commentary. The chapter itself includes elements of such a commentary in its content.

Issues to Ponder

As one reads the McElroy and Hunger chapter, a number of points are worth pondering. First, to what extent would a focus on performance miss the essence of the raison d'être for many organizations? Too narrow a conception would rule out social groups formed for member interaction enjoyment. Also, an emphasis on performance implies a certain researcher value system that should be made explicit. In other words, researchers should be reflexive here as elsewhere in conducting research.

Second, and related to the earlier point, to what extent is the selection of performance as a key variable a function of our attributional biases? Are we "attributionally bound" as it were?

Third, to what extent do immediately identifiable leader behaviors keep us from trying to get at deeper structures which may be operating? Are researcher attributions causing a neglect of these deeper structures in leadership research? To what extent does normal science allow a researcher to deal with these deeper structures?

Calas and Smircich also provide some points to ponder. First, their chapter argues for going beyond typical positivist science methodology in doing leadership research. To what extent is the field so biased in that direction that their arguments will fall on deaf ears? As they say, narrative discourse is tolerant of scientific discourse but not vice versa. Both the authors and Nord make recommendations for dealing with this perceived positivist bias. What would be necessary for these recommendations to be taken seriously? Does the fact that they appeared in this book suggest that there is some likelihood of serious consideration?

Second, to what extent are social science paradigms monolithic enough so that one can draw the inferences about leadership research that the authors drew? If there are many paradigms, what are the implications for the kind of analysis done by Calas and Smircich?

10
Leadership Theory as Causal Attributions of Performance

James C. McElroy
J. David Hunger

L eadership is one of the most talked about, written about, and researched topics in the area of management and organizational behavior (Bass 1981). A vast number of articles and books about the leadership phenomenon have been written from a wide variety of perspectives over the years. The most common method of categorizing and discussing the many theories and conceptualizations of leadership is by taking a historical orientation. Textbooks, for example, typically group theories according to whether they focus on traits (popular in the 1930s), behaviors (popular in the 1950s), or on the situation (popular in the 1970s). Interestingly, this method of classifying leadership theories runs the gamut from a focus on the leader in terms of that person's enduring qualities to a focus on the situation in terms of possible substitutes for leadership.

The purpose of this chapter is to examine the leadership literature from a somewhat different perspective. It is proposed here that each of the many theories and conceptualizations of leadership can be more usefully classified as theories of performance. That is, given the existence of an outcome (i.e., performance), theories of leadership can be viewed as alternative explanations used by theorists to explain that outcome. Some leadership theories, therefore, begin with the assumption that effective leadership is an (if not *the*) important determinant of good performance, whereas others do not.

Some of the ambiguity surrounding leadership (Pfeffer 1977) may be the result of variations in the causal attributions used by theorists to explain group and/or organizational performance. Thus, the perspective taken here is that leadership theory can be viewed as a product of the causal attributions employed by theorists in their search for the antecedents of performance. Throughout the chapter, the term *theory* is used rather broadly to include the many different conceptualizations of the phenomenon referred to as leadership. This is done merely to simplify discussion and not to suggest that all the various constructs used to describe leadership are actually theories in the pure

The authors would like to thank Steven Kerr and Paula Morrow for their comments on an early draft of this manuscript.

sense of the term. Moreover, no attempt is made to assess the validity of the various theories being advanced.

The Nature of Causal Attributions

Attributions are defined as interpretations of the causes of behavior. Originally developed by Heider (1958), attribution theory is based on the assumption that individuals have an inherent need to explain events that surround them. Following the occurrence of an event, individuals will attempt to explain why it occurred. The cognitive process of assigning causes to events is called the *attribution process*.

Attribution theorists propose that in achievement-related contexts, success or failure can be cognitively attributed to four basic factors: ability, effort, task difficulty, and/or luck (Weiner et al. 1972). These four types of ascriptions are commonly used in empirical attribution research and have been shown by Frieze (1976) to account for a large portion of the causal inferences made by individuals. Weiner and others (1972) placed these four factors on two general dimensions: internal-external and stable-variable, as shown in figure 10–1. The internal-external dimension refers to the degree to which individuals attribute success or failure to personal versus situational characteristics. The stable-variable dimension refers to the degree to which the perceived causes for performance are of a variable or relatively permanent nature.

Attribution Dimensions		Locus	
		Internal	External
Stability	Stable	Ability	Task difficulty
	Variable		Luck

Source: Adapted from Weiner, B., Heckhausen, H., Meyer, W., and Cook, R. (1972). Causal ascriptions and achievement behavior: A conceptual analysis of effort and reanalysis of locus of control. *Journal of Personality and Social Psychology* 21: 240. Used with permission, © 1972 by the American Psychological Association and the author.

Figure 10–1. Basic Attribution Dimensions

In making attributions, people use information, and the resulting attributions depend on the nature of the information available to the attributor. The existence or absence of such information results in two cases, or what Kelley (1967) calls *systematic statements,* of attribution theory.

The first case is that involving an absence of information available to the attributor, beyond the observation of a single event or outcome. In this case, individuals will rely on what Heider (1958) refers to as one's "naive psychology of action" in assigning causes to events. This naive psychology may come from one's personal experiences or as a result of the conventional wisdom of the time. The particular attribution used to explain success or failure (figure 10–1) is simply a by-product of the attributor's implicit theory of performance.

In some instances, however, an individual has access to more than a single observation of a behavior or event. In this case, Kelley (1967) proposes that three types of information are used in making causal attributions. These information cues are known as consistency, consensus, and distinctiveness. *Consistency* refers to the extent to which an event is repeatedly associated with a particular individual over time. *Consensus* refers to the degree to which an event is associated with other individuals. *Distinctiveness* refers to the degree to which an event is associated with the same individual across different tasks.

For example, any individual in a position to evaluate a supervisor would use whatever information cues are available in order to appraise the leadership effectiveness of that supervisor. Consistency cues would provide information concerning the performance of the work group during the time the person has been supervisor. For example, has the work group continually had high performance under this person's supervision? Consensus cues would allow one to compare this supervisor with other supervisors. That is, do all other supervisors have high-performing groups? Finally, distinctiveness information would allow someone to judge the performance of this supervisor when this person has been in charge of different work groups.

To the degree that this information is available, individuals will utilize it in the assignment of causality for an event. That is, certain combinations of information lead to particular attributions (Mowday 1983). For example, high consistency (this group's performance has always been high during this supervisor's tenure), low consensus (other supervisors' groups are not all high performing), and low distinctiveness information (this supervisor has been successful on other jobs as well) will result in current performance being attributed to the personal qualities of the leader (i.e., an internal-stable attribution).

On the other hand, high consistency, high consensus, and high distinctiveness information cues would result in attributing current performance to the nature of the particular task being accomplished (i.e., an external-stable attribution). Finally, low consistency, low consensus, and high distinctiveness information yields circumstantial attributions or attributions of a variable nature (i.e., internal-variable or external-variable attributions).

To summarize, the placement of these attributions along the two dimensions, as shown in figure 10–1, is the result of a conclusion, based upon available information, on the cause of the work group's performance. Informational cues leading to an external attribution will result in the conclusion that the group's good performance was due either to an easy series of tasks or to luck. If information results in an internal attribution, the group's good performance may still be seen as due either to the supervisor's inherent leadership ability or to the effort expended by the supervisor.

Leadership Theories as Causal Explanations

Figure 10–2 illustrates how Weiner and others' (1972) two-dimensional taxonomy of the perceived causes of success and failure can be used to categorize the various theories of leadership on the basis of causal explanations for group or subordinate performance. The premise for this classification scheme is that the assumption underlying attribution theory—that individuals have an inherent desire to explain observed events—is applicable to theorists as well.

It should be noted that no attempt was made to survey leadership theorists concerning their personal attributional assumptions underlying their theories. Instead, the theories themselves were used as public statements of theorists' causal assumptions. Whether these public statements represent privately held beliefs is subject to debate; however, the analysis of public statements has proven insightful in a wide variety of settings, ranging from corporate annual reports (Bettman and Weitz 1983) to the sports pages (Lau and Russell 1980).

As shown in figure 10–2, leadership theories vary in the fundamental assumption that is made concerning the causal explanations for performance. For example, some theories focus on the leader (an internal attribution) as the dominant cause of group or subordinate performance, whereas others, viewing performance as caused by factors external to the leader, focus on the situation.

Moreover, leadership theories that assume that the causes of performance are relatively stable, propose relatively fixed, specific traits, behaviors, or situational factors as determinants of performance, regardless of time or place. Other theories, based on variable causal explanations for performance, propose that the important behaviors, situational factors, and the like change over time and place.

This view of leadership theory, representing alternative attributed causes

Attribution Dimensions		Locus	
		Internal	External
Stability	Stable	—Great-man theory —Trait theory —Charismatic theory —Styles-to-behavior theory (Lewin and Lippitt) (McGregor) (Blake and Mouton) *I*	—Contingency theory —Strategy manager matching models —Substitutes for leadership *III*
	Variable	*II* —Path-goal theory —Situational leadership theory —Decision-making theory —Operant conditioning theory	*IV* —Leader as a symbol

Figure 10–2. Leadership Theories as Causal Attributions of Performance

for performance, allows us to examine the assumptions underlying leadership theories as opposed to debating the mechanics of such theories. The remainder of this chapter, then, discusses theories of leadership in light of their commonly held attributions for performance. Following this analysis of figure 10–2, the current status of leadership theory will be discussed.

Quadrant I

Within this quadrant are placed those theories of leadership based upon an internal-stable assumption concerning the causes of performance. Performance is seen to be a result of the leader's presence or activities. Other variables are of minor consequence. The causal connection is such that leadership is assumed to directly affect performance ($L \rightarrow P$). Implicit in these theories is the assumption that there is a specific set of stable traits, characteristics, or behaviors that make for good performance regardless of time or place.

The *great-man theory* briefly states that "history was shaped by the leadership of great men" (Bass 1981, 26). Ignoring "great women," this theory suggests that a certain number of people are born with inate leadership qualities that enable them to directly change the world around them regardless of the situation.

Trait theory is a more sophisticated, specified version of the great-man theory. It states that certain clusters of characteristics differentiate leaders from followers, effective from ineffective leaders (Bass 1981, 81). These qualities or traits are assumed to be stable in nature. An effective leader in one situation is thus assumed to be an effective leader in any situation.

House's *charismatic theory* is similar to trait theory in that it proposes the existence of a stable set of personal qualities that have a profound and extraordinary effect on followers (House and Baetz 1979, 399–400). These qualities or characteristics include dominance, self-confidence, need for influence, and a strong conviction in the moral righteousness of one's beliefs. Since it is proposed that these people can create major social change, this theory appears to be a refinement of the great-man theory.

A number of theories can be grouped under the *styles-of-behavior theory* of leadership. Initiated by the famous study of boys' clubs by Lewin, Lippitt, and White (1939), this research concluded that a democratic style of leader behavior is superior in terms of group performance to autocratic or laissez-faire styles. Later, McGregor (1960) conceptualized (and advocated) this democratic style as a function of the leader's theory Y assumptions about subordinates. Blake and Mouton (1964) also propose the existence of "one best style" of leader behavior, based upon the classic Ohio State studies revealing initiating structure and consideration as two independent dimensions of leader behavior. They argue that the best style of leadership, regardless of situation, combines a high concern for production with a high concern for people (the 9–9 style). Although Blake and Mouton propose that all organizations can use the "managerial grid" to generate team-oriented leaders, this development process is long-term oriented. Thus, in the short term, behavior is seen as stable. Even though these latter approaches all focus on leader behavior rather than leader characteristics, they share the same assumptions: that the leader is the primary determinant of group performance, and that a stable set of qualities or behaviors results in desired performance.

Quadrant II

The theories grouped in quadrant II also assume the leader to be the primary determinant of performance; however, the qualities (in this case, behaviors) that result in performance are not inherently stable ones. Rather, effective leader behavior varies with situational demands. The causal relationship is one of leadership affecting performance through its influence on a series of intervening situational variables ($L \rightarrow xyz \rightarrow P$). The leader thus continues to be the primary actor and decision maker, but must be prepared to vary behaviors with the time and the place.

Path-goal theory as developed by Evans (1970) and House (1971) proposes that a leader must adjust his or her behavior on the basis of situational factors, such as characteristics of the subordinates and the task. Identifying four kinds of leader behaviors (House and Mitchell 1974), path-goal theory assumes that leaders can and should vary their style of behavior to meet the demands of a particular situation. Performance will thus be determined by the subordinate's motivation to perform as manipulated by the leader.

Situational leadership theory, as proposed by Hersey and Blanchard (1982), agrees with the other theories in this quadrant that there is no one best way to lead. Also assuming that the leader is primarily responsible for group performance, Hersey and Blanchard state that the most appropriate style of leader behavior is the one "right combination" of task and relationship behavior given the "maturity level" of the group. A particular leader must therefore be prepared to vary leadership style as the job maturity and the psychological maturity levels of the group change. Like path-goal theory, situational leadership theory contends that the primary determinant is the leader's ability and willingness to alter behavior depending on certain variables.

Vroom and Yetton (1973) propose that effective performance is a function of the leader's ability to select the most appropriate style of decision making given the nature of the problem and the willingness of the subordinates to implement the decision. This *decision-making theory* of leadership recommends that the decision maker (i.e., the leader in a managerial role) adopt one of five decision styles ranging from autocratic to participative based on answers to seven questions. Like path-goal and situational leadership theory, the Vroom-Yetton decision-making theory suggests that a leader must be prepared to vary behavior from one point in time to another and from one job to another. The leader has the option of selecting the appropriate decision-making style based upon the least amount of time needed for problem solving or upon team development considerations. The cause of group performance is thus primarily in the hands of the group leader.

Operant conditioning theory (otherwise known as behavior modification), as proposed by Scott (1977), Sims (1977), and Mawhinney and Ford (1977), proposes that leadership can be best explained as a process of managing reinforcement contingencies in the work environment. It assumes that the leader is able to manipulate stimuli, rewards, and punishments in order to cause the subordinate behavior needed for the desired performance. As with the other theories in this quadrant, performance is assumed to be a result of leader behaviors which will need to vary with the situation.

In summary, each of the theories in quadrant II is based on an internal-variable assumption concerning the causality of performance. Although they offer varying explanations on how the leader achieves effective performance, each views flexible leader behavior as the key determinant of performance.

Quadrant III

Contained in this quadrant are those theories of leadership that are based on the assumption that the cause of performance lies in the stable properties of the situation. In contrast to theories in the first and second quadrants, these theories assume that performance is primarily due to situational factors which are (at least in the short run) generally independent of leader behavior. Leadership is simply one of the many variables that cause performance. These variables are assumed to be identifiable and reasonably stable, at least in the short term. The causal connection is that a number of situational variables (including the leader) determine performance ($XYZL \rightarrow P$). The focus of these theories, therefore, is on identifying those variables or factors that tend to account for group or subordinate performance.

Fiedler (1967) advances his *contingency theory of leadership* using the interaction of leader personality (as measured by the least preferred coworker scale) and situation favorability to predict group performance. Similar to trait theory, Fiedler's contingency theory argues that the style of leader behavior is a reflection of the leader's personality and is basically stable for any person. In contrast to trait theory, however, other aspects of the situation play an important part: leader-member relations, task structure, and the power position of the leader are stated as being "of utmost importance in determining the leader's control and influence" (Fiedler and Chemers 1974, 69–70).

The focus of the theory is thus on three specific characteristics of the situation, with the leader being considered only insofar as he or she fits the situation. The leader cannot change his or her personality and thus assumes a position of secondary importance to the situation. Although Fiedler does recommend "engineering" the job to fit the leader, and even leadership training to facilitate this, these three situational variables are generally stable in the short term. Consequently, Fiedler's theory advocates matching the leader and the situation, and if a match is present, performance follows. If a mismatch exists between the leader and the situation, there is not much that can be done about it, in the near term at least, short of replacing the leader.

Similar arguments have been made from a macro point of view in various *strategy-manager matching models* as summarized by Szilagyi and Schweiger (1984). Research in the field of strategic management is concluding that organizations should match key attributes of the strategic manager to the requirements of a particular business unit strategy. Portfolio analysis prescribes specific strategies based upon industry attractiveness and the business unit's competitive position. The strategy-manager matching models attempt to identify specific skills, backgrounds, and personality traits which best match the desired business unit strategy.

The underlying assumption is that those managers with certain characteristics are better able to implement a strategic plan than are those without these characteristics. For example, Wissema, Van Der Pol, and Messer (1980) propose six strategic management "archetypes" for six different strategic directions. Some support for this approach has been provided by Gupta and Govindarajan (1984), who found that strategic business units (SBUs) with a "build" strategy as compared to SBUs with a "harvest" strategy tend to be led by managers with a greater willingness to take risks and a higher tolerance for ambiguity.

As with Fiedler's theory, the strategy-manager matching models focus on the characteristics of the situation, with the leader being considered only insofar as he or she fits the "right" strategy. Strategic managers are perceived as types, such as "professional liquidators," "turnaround specialists," or "mature entrepreneurs" (Hofer and Davoust 1977) who cannot change their leadership style or personality (at least in the short run). They thus assume a position of secondary importance to the situation and must be replaced if the desired strategy for the unit changes.

Recently, leadership has been conceptualized by Kerr and Jermier (1978) in terms of *substitutes for leadership.* Arguing with the assumption implicit in most leadership theories that some leadership style is necessary for effective performance, this approach proposes that many individual, task, and organizational characteristics have the capacity to substitute for hierarchical leadership. Some of these characteristics are the ability, experience, and professional orientation of the subordinates; routineness, feedback availability, and intrinsic satisfaction present in the task; and formalization, group cohesion, and reward structure of the organization. The theory implies that to the extent certain characteristics are present in a work unit, the presence of a leader is unnecessary. The situation alone may cause performance provided it accommodates functions normally provided for by the leader. The theory also implies that such substitutes are knowable and merely need to be identified and used in order to achieve specific performance results (Kerr 1983).

To summarize, the theories in quadrant III place less emphasis on the leader's role as a determinant of performance. The assumption that the relatively stable aspects of the situation cause performance places leadership in the position of a variable that can be superceded by other, situationally stable, factors.

Quadrant IV

Quadrant IV represents the perspective that leadership may, in fact, have very little to do with the causation of performance. Epitomizing this is Pfeffer's (1977) work on the *leader as a symbol.* This perspective received impetus from two sources: (1) the inconsistent results of research testing traditional leadership theories (quadrants I and II), and (2) the success of research on substitutes for leadership (quadrant III). Examples, of the former include Mintzberg (1975) and McCall's (1983) arguments that the pace of managerial work precludes systematic application of those theories grouped in quadrant II. Additional contradictory evidence is provided by research from a variety of field and laboratory studies demonstrating that leader behavior may, in fact, be a result rather than a cause of subordinate attitudes and performance (Greene 1973, Lowin and Craig 1968, Lowin, Hrapchak, and Kavanaugh 1969). With respect to the latter source of impetus, a natural extension of the substitutes for leadership research is the question of whether leadership is a necessary prerequisite for performance at all.

Citing research that found little evidence of the effects of leadership on performance, Pfeffer (1977) argues that leaders are very constrained in what they can do. Derived from attribution theory, the belief in the leader as causal agent is accepted and promulgated because it serves to maintain the social order. Just as firing a baseball manager serves a scapegoating effect, the firing of a chief executive officer and his or her staff sends a clear message to all in the organization that previously held attitudes and behaviors are no longer acceptable. Viewed from this perspective, and coupled with evidence that leadership is not closely related to measures of performance (Tosi 1982, 227) or organizational effectiveness (Farris and Butterfield 1973), leadership assumes the status of a myth, existing only in a post hoc manner. The successful leader, then, is one who is able to attach him or herself to successes and disassociate him or herself from failures.

To summarize, in the perspective of quadrant IV, performance is assumed to be caused by unstable situational variables. This external orientation prevents making a causal connection from the leader to performance but does not prevent a reverse causal connection. Thus, leadership in this quadrant is viewed as a dependent rather than as an independent variable $(XYZ \rightarrow P \rightarrow L)$.

A Historical Perspective

As may be seen in figure 10–2, most of the leadership literature generally assumes a causal link between leadership and performance. Given that the phenomenon of interest (leadership) is personal in nature, and given the lack of previous information, it is attributionally logical for the process of explaining performance to begin with an examination of the inherent characteristics of leaders, particularly in light of attribution research indicating the existence of an actor-observer bias in the assignment of causality for events (Jones and Nisbett 1972). That is, actors tend to look to the environment for causes of performance whereas observers tend to focus on the actor, per se. From an attributional perspective, being observers of the phenomenon they are seeking to explain, it would be natural for researchers to initially look toward the dispositional characteristics of the leader as a means of explaining group and/or subordinate performance.

The research generated, however, concerning the efficacy of trait/behavior theories (quadrant I) produced data inconsistent with this dispositional (internal-stable) view of leadership. It became apparent that the performance level of a group or subordinate was subject to within-leader variability (low consistency), between-leader variability (low consensus), and that the same leader was not always successful with every group or subordinate (high distinctiveness). According to attribution theory, this information combination is posited to lead to variable attributions for performance (e.g., Mowday 1983); however, these explanations could be either of an internal or external nature. Again, coupled with the actor-observer bias, it is attributionally logical that researchers then turned their attention to the variable behaviors of leaders (quadrant II). Only recently, with the exception of Fiedler, have researchers begun to look beyond leadership for the causes of performance (quadrants III and IV).

Discussion

In an earlier symposium volume, Miner concluded that "the concept of leadership itself has outlived its usefulness" and suggested that "we abandon leadership in favor of some other, more fruitful way of cutting up the theoretical pie" (1975, 200). We would argue that unless we consciously examine the assumptions underlying our current theories and research on leadership, this is unlikely to occur. Indeed, as equivocal information has been gathered on current leadership theories, researchers appear content to search for other means of operationalizing the leader's role as a cause of performance as opposed to turning their attention toward other possible causal explanations for performance.

To illustrate, most of the new conceptualizations of leadership, such as the vertical dyad linkage approach (Dansereau, Graen, and Haga 1975), Yukl's multiple linkage model (Yukl 1981), and Wofford's integrative theory of leadership (Wofford 1982), are each based upon the same causal assumptions common to quadrant II, and could be so categorized. The point being made here, however, is not one of cataloging leadership theories. Rather, it is simply to illustrate the constraints that assumptions of causality may bring to bear on the direction of leadership research. Only in those instances where leadership has not been perceived as the major cause of performance have radically new theories of leadership resulted (e.g., symbolism). Perhaps, as advocated by Miner in the preceding quotation, a more fruitful way of cutting up the theoretical pie would be to focus our attention on theories of performance rather than on leadership, per se.

Theories of Performance: The Marginal Utility of Leadership

What is needed are fewer theories of leadership and more theories of performance. Turning attention to performance (or some other behavioral outcome of interest; for example, turnover, absenteeism, and so on) would result in changing the nature of leadership as a research variable. With performance as the dependent variable, leadership would assume independent or intervening (moderating/mediating) variable status.

This should serve to eliminate some of the ambiguity surrounding what leadership is (that is, traits, behaviors, attributions) by, in effect, making it a moot question. Instead, the emphasis would be on the impact of leadership. Or, as noted to Tosi, it will allow us to determine "what portion of the predictability (variance) in behavior patterns is accounted for by interpersonal influence and what portion is accounted for by other factors" (1982, 228).

Some of this type of work is already taking place at both the micro and macro levels of analysis. At the micro level, Mitchell's (1982) review of attribution research exemplifies the approach advocated here in that his analysis focuses on actions as the dependent variable rather than attributions. His conclusion is that attributions play a minor role, explaining only small proportions of the variance in actions, with many instances in which attributions are completely bypassed. At the macro level, there is some evidence that leadership plays a role in organizational performance (e.g., Smith, Carson, and Alexander 1984), but much of the evidence suggests a role of minor importance for leadership compared to the impact of other factors (e.g., Lieberson and O'Connor 1972, Salancik and Pfeffer 1977).

A "theories of performance" perspective holds several implications for leadership researchers. First, and most basic, is the notion that simply assessing what type of leader behavior is called for under a particular set of circumstances is perhaps a necessary but not a sufficient research design. An emphasis on explaining performance requires broad enough research paradigms such that other possible causes of performance can be assessed concurrently with leadership.

By way of analogy, Mitchell (1982) noted a series of studies in which the impact of attributions on responses to a poor-performing administrative assistant was reduced from 20 to 30 percent of the variance explained to only 5 to 10 percent by the inclusion of information on the costs/benefits of various responses. This latter information accounted for 62 percent of the variance in responses. The point being made is simple: attributions may affect people's behavior if there is no additional information available. The presence of additional data may, however, not only directly affect behavior more than attributions; it may actually reduce the effect of attributions on behavior. Thus, leadership research must recognize and take into account other possible variables affecting performance in addition to leadership.

A second implication concerns the need to report statistics showing the proportion of variance explained by leader behavior relative to the proportion of variance explained by other factors. In this way, the role of leadership can be assessed across studies not only in terms of leader behavior but also in terms of the context in which leaders operate.

Finally, consideration of leadership as an independent or intervening variable requires that researchers develop adequate measures of actual leader behavior. Recent research on leader behavior questionnaires has severely criticized their veridicality (e.g., Lord et al. 1978; Mitchell, Larson, and Green 1977; Phillips and Lord 1981; Rush, Thomas, and Lord 1977).

Lord and others (1978) caution that as the behavior component of leadership becomes more ambiguous, leadership questionnaire ratings become more susceptible to being influenced by other informational cues, particularly performance data. The result is a reliance by the rater on a global impression of leadership (Phillips and Lord 1981, Rush, Phillips, and Lord 1981) as opposed to perceptions of leader behavior *per se*.

Although this categorization process (Lord, Foti, and Phillips 1982) may be relevant for understanding how judgments about leaders are formed—that is, selection decisions—research on the effects of leadership on performance requires more accurate descriptions of actual leader behavior. To illustrate this point, consider the work of Fiedler (1967). He utilized a research design that focused on performance. His results, however, would have had greater utility had he utilized a measure of leadership that focused on actual leader behavior rather than one that simply categorized leaders into those with high versus low least-preferred coworker (LPC) scores.

Conclusion

The purpose of this chapter has not been to develop and propose the precise typology of leadership theorists' causal attributions. As noted earlier, figure 10–2 represents *our* assumptions, attributions if you will, concerning the positioning of each leadership perspective rather than those of the authors of each theory. As such, one might debate the placement of any particular theory.

What is more important, however, is that the perspective offered here demonstrates that most leadership theory presupposes leadership as having a dominant role in causing group or subordinate performance. Meindl, Ehrlich, and Dukerich (1985) argue that this "romance" with the concept of leadership results in using our faith in leadership to account for variance in performance that is, in fact, beyond the leader's control. The view taken here is that this faith in leadership restricts the nature of the questions asked about leadership. We advocate that turning attention from leadership per se to performance will allow us to determine the marginal utility of leadership as a construct of interest.

To date the debate surrounding leadership has been too dichotomous in nature. Either leadership is assumed to be *the* cause of performance, or it is eliminated entirely as being insignificant or substitutable. The question as we perceive it is not an either/or question. It is simply one of attempting to ascertain the degree to which leadership contributes to performance.

11
Gleanings from a Frustrated Process Analysis of Leadership Research Stakeholders

Mark F. Peterson
Peter B. Smith

"Ready. Fire. Aim."
—Peters and Waterman (1982, 119)

The Leadership Symposia series has encouraged innovation and experimentation in the leadership field. It has provided a structure for leadership researchers to interact about their work in ways that are not possible through the formal journal review process. Some of what goes on is reflected by a "paper trail" of symposium books. Given that compiling these books requires that the manuscripts presented be very substantially edited after the symposium, they are an intentional distortion of what actually occurs. In a sense, the symposium books are a post hoc rationalization of the conference process.

But even a sound track, including the laughter and publically made asides, of all sessions would be a distortion of much of the substance of the symposium. The leadership symposia, like other conferences, provide an opportunity for informal social processes to occur which contribute as much, if not more, to the leadership field than do either the oral, living research reports or the nicely dressed, written remains that you are looking at now.

The symposium provides an opportunity for socializing and integrating newcomers to the field. (For example: Who are Mark Peterson and Peter Smith? Of what significance are they to me?) It provides an opportunity for people whose research perspectives are compatible to express support for new initiatives and to pledge continuing commitment to a preferred methodology or perspective, or indicate a movement away from one. For example:

As authors, we would like to thank the symposium coordinators for inviting us to conduct the session, especially B.R. Baliga for directing us to the SAST technique. We also appreciate being given permission to name names by the people involved. As session chairs, we would like to thank all participants for allowing us to carry out, more or less, the main thrust of our agenda for the session.

What were Marshall Sashkin and Chet Schriesheim planning in the dorm lobby all evening?) The symposia also provide opportunities for confrontation between parties representing perspectives that are incompatible at some theoretical, methodological, or empirical level. (For example: Did anyone who bore the brunt of the Schriesheim and Kerr critical review of 1977 come to the 1986 symposium?) It also provides an opportunity for those who disagree to offer friendship. (For example: After the session being described here, two people gave Tony Butterfield some flowers after he had professed friendship toward them, even though he belonged to an "enemy" group.)

Constructing a series of symposia with a knowledge that such processes will occur is a bold experiment. The afternoon session described in the present chapter was even more brash. It was based on the premise that many of the informal socialization, collaboration, confrontation, and healing processes that occur informally could constructively be made just as explicit and formal as the presentations. Relying on an informal process of socialization assumes that the skills justifying professional acceptance have a larger interpersonal component.

Informal collaboration assumes that people whose perspectives are similar know one another, are also comfortable together, and are able to recognize the similarities in their perspectives. Confrontation and, especially, subsequent healing may occur to a much smaller degree than is optimal for the field to develop. Attempting to structure such processes has some justification.

A formal process was sought to promote some of the informal processes that otherwise occur simply because of the collection of people assembled at the symposium. A technique was selected that seemed likely to structure some of these informal processes. However, the purposes previously noted are largely a post hoc rationalization and justification of the reasons for selecting the technique. The justification for the session provided in the present chapter reflects to some degree the implicitly held, but never well explicated opinions of various planners of the symposium and of the session. Perhaps because of this lack of clearly explicated purpose to guide the planning, but perhaps for other reasons as well, the session using the technique described in the following was less than fully useful for its original purpose. Nevertheless, its treatment here may help us learn something about the strengths and weaknesses of the approach as structured in the symposium session.

Openness, Epistemology, and the Philosophy of Science

The session described in the following is an applied extension of developments in modern epistemology and the philosophy of science. Epistemological perspectives and philosophies of science differ in the openness attributed to the knowledge acquisition process. Rationalist and idealist philosophies, such as Descartes' rationalism (Haldane and Ross 1955) and Locke's empiricism (Nidditch 1979), assume a largely closed relationship between an isolated observer, abstracted from context, and discrete, separate objects of observation. European epistemology phenomenology recognizes that object perception is an actively constructive process open to a broad domain of context (Carr 1970, Merleau-Ponty 1962). Although phenomenology recognizes the context of the observer in a broad sense, greater attention is given to the effects of an object's context on the qualities perceived in it. The same emphasis is reflected in the figure-ground interrelationships described in gestalt psychology (Koehler 1930).

Modern logical positivism, as applied in leadership research, reflects a sophisticated recognition of the proactively constructive aspects of scientific knowledge formation. This implicit recognition is applied in carefully conceived methodological controls intended to circumscribe these constructive processes. In effect, rational empiricism is taken as a goal to be achieved in a world where naive experience and "nonrigorous" research is subjected to phenomenological biases. Modern positivism recognizes the phenomenological positioning of the social scientist as a proactively perceiving actor who experiences complex social phenomena embedded in a complex social context. However, this situation is treated as an undesirable one, the adverse affects of which are to be avoided. Much of the dialogue at the leadership symposium occurred among researchers who generally accept a phenomenological perspective on science, but who disagree about how its realities should be taken into account in social science investigations.

Social Systems Philosophies of Science

The social systems philosophies of science advocated by Kuhn (1970), and Polanyi (1966), among others, incorporates an additional element of openness into the scientific process—the scientific community. Openness is extended beyond the physical context of an object, and the general psychological context of the observer. The social context surrounding scientists as individuals and as cliques begins to be structured and explicated.

The field of leadership study can be viewed from a social philosophy of science perspective. The field is an amalgam of partially complementary and partially competing researchers and research groups. The boundaries of the field resist definition. Individuals' interest in being associated with the field are reflected in reference to other leadership researchers' work, use of the term *leadership* in article titles, and participation in leadership conferences. The products of this social system are published propositions and research results as well as an oral tradition. Social systems philosophies of science point out the significance of competition among paradigms as opposed to rationalistically logical incremental accumulation of facts.

The experimental session conducted at the leadership symposium was based on the assumption that paradigm debate should be fostered. It assumed that a constructive approach to facilitating the leadership research field would need to overcome the same limitations that characterize traditional approaches to strategic planning. Strategic planning has often had the same rationalistic qualities that characterize positivistic social science. It requires a singular construction of corporate reality in goal setting, and follows a deductive process of working out the implications of this construction in implementation. Implementation becomes the incremental normal science of management.

SAST as a Social Systems Approach to Science

The analogy between strategic planning and social science paradigm competition has limitations. Since social science, at least in most of the world, does not require concerted action by all parties, the last step in strategic planning of developing a working consensus is unnecessary. However, a strategic planning process that recognizes and structures the social process underlying strategy formation was considered a useful basis for designing an experimental session to clarify and debate assumptions. One approach that places strategic social processes above strategic rationalism is the Strategic Assumption Surfacing and Testing (SAST) process designed by Mason and Mitroff (1981).

The kind of devoted, soul-searching strategic planning toward which the SAST process is directed assumes a substantial external motivating force. Otherwise, the time investment by managers required by the process is not worthwhile. For example, a strategic planning process motivated by the crisis of responding to a competitor's recently automated production technology, as it occurs in the context of a complex, changing network of financial, market, and societal conditions, warrants substantial strategic reevaluation. Such a situation is similar to the crisis associated with scientific paradigm formation. During a management strategy crisis, the development, refinement, and applications of standard operating procedures, the corporate equivalent of "normal science," ceases to be appropriate. Through a political struggle to establish a new strategy, culture, and production technology supported by a new dominant coalition of executives (Goodman and Pennings 1977), a new corporate "paradigm" emerges.

Kuhn's (1970) suggestions about the natural processes addressed by the scientific paradigm formation process are similar to Mason and Mitroff's (1981, 12) analysis of the environmental processes that generate policy planning and strategy problems. Mason and Mitroff describe these as "wicked" problems. They are characterized by interconnectedness, complicatedness, uncertainty, ambiguity, conflict, and societal constraints. Kuhn (1970, ch. 6) characterizes scientific advance during periods of crisis as involving anomalies, problems not well handled by established paradigms, that have these same characteristics.

Strategy structures and directs manager attention to relevant aspects of an otherwise undefined environment (Weick 1977). Similarly, the information contained in a paradigm "provides a map whose details are elucidated by mature scientific research. And since nature is too complex and varied to be explored at random, that map is as essential as observation and experiment to science's continuing development" (Kuhn 1970, 109). Kuhn's notion of scientific revolutions and the paradigm formation process go a step beyond an incremental, logistical positivistic approach to science. Science is reinterpreted as a social as well as a rational and individualistically phenomenological process. "The transfer of allegiance from paradigm to paradigm is a conversion experience that cannot be forced" (Kuhn 1970, 151). However, this process is viewed as being conducted largely with a particular scientific community (Kuhn 1970, 176–87).

A Pragmatic, General Systems Philosophy of Science

Another degree of openness, not well developed in the philosophy of science, goes beyond the scientific community to include other parties. Taking the philosophy of science this next step involves placing the scientific process in the context of political, economic, and cultural forces that are only hinted at by Kuhn. Recognizing that the effects of such contextual factors are mediated by social actors who have different interests in the scientific process, the nature of social science changes. The social scientist becomes an actor in a large scale Hegelian dialectic of not just logical thesis and antithesis, but also value-linked thesis and countervalue-linked antithesis. The social scientist is seen in a position similar to that of a senior executive trying to generate a synthesis and working consensus having both value and information elements as part of a system open to a turbulent environment of competing social actors.

Applying a strategic planning analogy to the scientific process makes two modifications to social philosophies of science. One modification transforms the analysis of science from a social system theory analysis to a general system theory analysis (Miller 1971, Von Bertalanffy 1968). Science is thus viewed as a political process transacted by individuals and cliques whose attitudes and actions implicitly represent the interests of a broad set of "stakeholders" in the scientific process. These stakeholders are assumed to affect the scientific process by exerting coercive control through manipulating resources, and, possibly, normative control by directly shaping researcher attitudes.

The second modification is consistent with traditional American pragmatism (James 1907, Peirce 1878). The contribution of a philosophical perspective or research approach does not depend on its objective accuracy in comparison to competing approaches. All philosophies and theories are, at some relatively short term point, philosophies in action. A stakeholder perspective on the philosophy of social science is only successful if it changes the behavior of scientists and the stakeholders they implicitly represent. The SAST process conducted at the present leadership symposium was directed toward promoting an explication of who are the stakeholders in leadership research and what assumptions leadership researchers are making about their probable actions.

An Adapted SAST Process

In attempting to apply the preceding considerations to the problem of promoting development in the leadership field, several assumptions were made. A process for facilitating development in the leadership field—or other fields of organizational science—should have several characteristics. First, several rationalistic characteristics often tried in the past are not likely to be constructive. An effective approach should avoid trying to obtain agreement about terms throughout the field. It should avoid establishing a "meta theory" intended to provide a single definition of leadership and a "unifying" framework within which all parties will placidly interact.

Instead, a more effective approach requires a sophisticated form of process consultation. The goals should be to save researchers' time and generate increased resources for each of several conflicting views. It should promote collaboration among individuals who hold compatible views of leadership research to increase the pace with which that view's implications are clarified. It should promote an explication of assumptions and evaluation criteria by parties inside and outside the field who control resources—including potential collaboration opportunities—that are of interest to leadership researchers. Adapting Mason and Mitroff's (1981, 43) definition of organizational stakeholders, stakeholders in the leadership field may be defined as follows: "Stakeholders are all those claimants inside and outside the [leadership research field] who have a vested interest in the problem and its solution."

Process consultation for leadership researchers should promote paradigm evangelism and paradigm competition to reveal more of the underlying assumptions made about stakeholders than is revealed in formal article reviews. It should encourage actions by individuals and research groups to maximize resources of all kinds, and minimize time wasted on low probability ventures that are likely to be scuttled by unsupportive stakeholder response.

An adapted SAST process was carried out; the purposes were described to symposium participants as follows.

1. To meet in working groups that will explore different perspectives with regard to leadership theory
2. To surface the assumptions underlying each group's perspective by means of the concept of stakeholders
3. To show the relative importance and certainty of assumptions by means of a simple graphic plot
4. To prepare and present to a plenary session the assumptions upon which each group's perspective rests
5. To debate similarities and differences in the assumptions surfaced by the exercise

The history of science suggests that it is difficult to draw boundaries around a set of adherents to a paradigm or to unambiguosly specify the rules defining a paradigm (Kuhn 1970, 43–44). However, a process was attempted for the SAST session to place participants into groups such that the underlying paradigm rules and supporting social structures would be reasonably compatible within each group.

Groups had been formed in advance of the session following a two-step process. In the first step, participants were asked to describe the most significant issues in the leadership field at present. This was done either prior to arriving at the symposium, or during the first day. Participants submitted comments varying from key descriptive words and phrases, to up to two pages of comments. The two session chairs used these comments to subjectively induce some of the most critical qualities differentiating sets of researchers.

Based on these responses, the session chairs identified five topics that, taken together, were expected to separate the forty participants into subgroups that were each more internally homogenous in theoretical and research orientation than was the larger group as a whole. The participants were then asked to answer a series of questions concerning their attitudes or positions regarding these topics. Based on answers to both sets of questions, as well as the session chairs' observations of the attitudes about leadership research that participants expressed throughout the symposium, five groups were formed.

The process of creating these groups indicated that several perspectives on leadership were not represented at the symposium in proportion to recent leadership publications. In particular, no group distinctly represented the laboratory experimental tradition, although some groups did represent an individual, positivistic view of research more nearly than did others. No group represented structured observation methods, although some represented more unstructured observation approaches. No group expressed clear identification with Fiedler's contingency theory, the Vroom/Yetton/Jago decision theory model (Jago and Vroom 1980, Vroom and Yetton 1973), or Graen's vertical dyad linkage model (Graen 1976, Wakabayashi and Graen 1984). These are perspectives that would probably have been represented by at least some participants in leadership symposia in the recent past.

The process the session followed is summarized in table 11–1. The session purposes, as previously described, were reviewed orally with the participants at the beginning of the session (Briefing" in table 11–1). A description of what the various events involve in a more extended strategic planning application is provided in Mason and Mitroff (1981, 37–57).

Table 11–2 provides detail of the five groups that emerged through the use of the group formation procedures. Of particular interest are the names which they selected for themselves, and the manner in which the various nationalities within the symposium were distributed between the groups. Groups 1 and 5 were composed almost entirely of North Americans. The Traditional Applied Empiricists had the oldest average age and were all male. The Data-Enhanced Theorists, although also largely North American, were somewhat younger and more identified with recent attempts to draw upon cognitive conceptions of social process.

The remaining three groups were composed predominantly of researchers from the other parts of the world, and they included all but one of the eleven women. These groups favored either a research strategy addressing more macroscopic levels of analysis or else an integration of levels of analysis. True to their own views of research priorities, they were much more resistant to

Table 11–1
Leadership SAST Schedule

1.45–2:00	Step 1:	Briefing
2:00–2:20	Step 2:	Establishment of group identities (identifying the group's perspective, selecting a name)
2:20–2:40	Step 3:	Identifying stakeholders
2:40–3:15	Step 4:	Assumption surfacing
3:15–3:35	Step 5:	Rankings of important assumptions
3:35–3.45	Step 6:	Preparations of presentations
3:45–4:00	Break	
4:00–5:30	Group presentations and general discussion	

Table 11–2
The Groups and Their Composition

Group	Rationale Provided	Self-Selected Name	Composition
1	Progress will be made only through better quantified data	"Traditional Applied Empiricists"	5/6 North American
2.	Better theory, integrating different levels of analysis	"Oklahoma"	3/6 North American
3	Work at the macro level, to include conceptualization of leaders, followers, and a wide variety of situational variables	"Social Constructors of Multiple Realities"	1/6 North American
4	Work at the macro level, focusing more specifically on leader behavior, particularly at more senior levels (modified by the group to "at all levels")	"Impatto Internationale"	2/6 North American
5	Work at the micro level, with particular emphasis on followers' cognitions, attributions, and experiences	"Data-enhanced Theorists"	6/7 North American

the quantitative elements in the approach used to form groups for the present exercise. Accordingly, two of these groups chose names for their groups that were at least partly facetious.

Each of these five groups was asked to identify its principal stakeholders, in line with the instructions provided in table 11–3. The stakeholders identified by each group are shown in table 11–4.

Following this, they debated assumptions they might make about future behavior of these stakeholders (see table 11–5). In the plenary session which followed, it emerged that the five groups had identified substantially different stakeholders, making the assumptions surfaced about the behaviors of those stakeholders difficult to compare. For example, the Traditional Applied Empiricists identified a trio of high-status journals as a prime stakeholder in their view of the field.

In contrast, the Social Constructors of Multiple Realities identified funding agencies as a key stakeholder. There was little disagreement among participants that the publication policies of key journals in accepting empiricist papers and the funding policies of key agencies in denying funds to non-empiricist theorists was likely to continue. Thus it proved to be the diversity of their stakeholders which differentiated the symposium members, more than the assumptions which each group might make about the stakeholders' future behavior.

Table 11–3
Stakeholders and Stakeholder Assumptions

Stakeholders are parties who would be affected if your group's preferred perspective were to become (or continue to be) a key one in the leadership field, or parties who would need to support your perspective in order for it to become a key one. Stakeholders are those who have a vested interest in your leadership perspective.

Please identify one especially important stakeholder in each of the following categories.

1. A theorist or established group of theorists (e.g., Fred Fiedler, implicit leadership theory researchers, etc.)

2. A journal or other dissemination medium (e.g., the *ASQ* editorial board, John Wiley publishers, American Management Association conference organizers, etc.)

3. Academic or research institutions (e.g., business schools, Survey Research Center, tenure committees, psychology departments)

4. Funding agencies (e.g., NSF, client organizations, resources of a university or a major consulting organization, etc.)

5. Major users or categories of users (e.g., Fortune 500 CEOs, human resources managers of manufacturing companies, U.S. military, free-lance consultants, etc.)

6. A second key example of one of the above, or another kind of stakeholder who can be described in one of the following ways. Someone who:

   Is *affected* by the leadership perspective

   Has an interest in the perspective and its outcomes

   Can affect the perspective's acceptance, development, and application

   Has expressed an interest in the issues involved

   Because of his or her dependence on leadership or other characteristics, *ought* to care or *might* care about the perspective

Other Stakeholder Examples

1. Financial support sources:
   Federal agencies
   Private foundations
   User organizations
   University centers

2. Research assistants:
   Graduate students, doctoral and masters
   Junior consultants

3. Dissemination media:
   Academic journals
   Practitioner journals
   Magazines
   Newspapers

4. Middlemen:
   Consultants
   Human resources practitioners

Table 11–4
Stakeholders Identified

Group 1: Traditional Applied Empiricists:
Theorists
Journals and publication companies
Business schools (as research institutions)
Business schools (as teaching institutions)
Military (as a funding source)
Academics and researchers
Leadership training clients
Followers in general

Group 2: Oklahoma
The Leadership Symposium
General systems theorists
Marxists
Political theorists
Social psychologists
Authors of political history biographies
Social movement groups
Qualitative/clinical methodologists
Federal government funding agencies

Group 3: Social Constructors of Multiple Realities:
Main stakeholder categories: enemies, friends, and bystanders

Enemies: Gatekeepers in:
    a. dissemination media
    b. funding agencies
    c. academic departments
Summary or enemies: "All adherents of the dominant scientific mode of knowledge production; those who are guided by the technical interest, and believe in one objective reality, for example, powerholders."

Supporters:
    a. Sage Press (reflecting demand for critical theorists)
    b. Ford Foundation (funding in response to interest in critical theorists)
    c. Bystanders (who affect institutional policies)

Ourselves:
    a. (Implicitly, people already pursuing critical theory)

Group 4: Impatto Internationale:
Peter Drucker
Harvard Business Review
Organizational behavior departments (vis-à-vis executive development emphasis)
McKinsey Consulting Group
CEOs generally (that can affect their organization)
Other special interest groups outside business and government (that affect the fortunes of an organization)

Table 11–4 (Continued)

Group 5: Data-enhanced Theorists:

Likert-type researchers and theorists

Journals: *Administrative Science Quarterly, Journal of Personality and Social Psychology, Organizational Behavior and Human Decision Processes*

Professional peers

Army Research Institute/clients/SSHRC

Managers and educators

"Children": the next generation

Table 11–5
Examples of Critical Stakeholder Assumptions

Research sites as stakeholders (as relevant to micro-emphasis field researchers)

Assumption: Research sites will cooperate with the increasingly demanding methodological requirements imposed by peer-reviewers for (1) considering multiple predictors, contingencies, and criteria, (2) obtaining independent data sources, (3) including sufficient sample sizes to permit complex multivariate statistical tests, and (4) including multiple data waves to permit causal analysis.

Counterassumptions: Potential research sites will conclude that data collection costs exceed probable benefits and that promoting academic work has insufficient inherent value to justify participation. Alternative sources of any benefits that micro-field research previously provided will be found in in-house and less-obtrusive consulting company data collection programs.

Publication outlets as stakeholders (as relevant to qualitative field researchers)

Assumption: A sufficient number of publication outlets viewed as credible by university tenure and promotion committees will be found that an entrenched network of qualitative workers can develop within academia:

Counterassumption: Few established journals will accept qualitative methods, and those that do will decline in credibility, roughly in proportion to that acceptance of this research.

Funding agencies as stakeholders (as relevant to structured field observation researchers)

Assumption: Sufficiently persuasive findings will be generated by structured field observation that major funding agencies will be willing to accept the high cost of the method compared to other methods.

Counterassumption: Initial structured observational field studies will encounter sufficient logistical, data management, and data analysis difficulties that major funding agencies will be unwilling to accept the risks involved.

Publication outlets as stakeholders (as relevant to laboratory researchers)

Assumption: A sufficient number of credible publication outlets will maintain a review policy accepting the external validity of laboratory research to organizational settings that such methods can prosper.

Counterassumption: Publication outlets that attempt to support laboratory methods will lose readership and thus lose resources from an impatiently pragmatic, business-school-dominated academic audience.

Table 11-5 (Continued)

Senior executives as stakeholders (as relevant to top management researchers)

Assumption: A sufficient pool of executives will make themselves available to the more competent researchers that publishable results will be produced.

Counterassumption: The population of chief executives is sufficiently small, their ability to evaluate researchers sufficiently limited, and the quantity of requests sufficiently great that they will not make themselves available as data sources for useful research endeavors.

Executive trainees as stakeholders (as relevant to training-oriented leadership research)

Assumption: Executives will continue to finance executive-oriented research by purchasing pragmatic books and attending conferences requiring substantial fees, because they accept the legitimacy of the researchers.

Counterassumption: Executives will require sufficient documentation and public verification of executive-oriented research that proprietary use and sale of the research becomes impossible.

Academic Dialogue versus Stakeholder Analysis

The Mason and Mitroff technique envisions that substantial subsequent time be spent in debating between groups the validity of varying assumptions and counter-assumptions about the future behavior of groups' stakeholders. Within the symposium there was only limited time or enthusiasm for such a debate. We wish here to argue that this unwillingness itself provides evidence as to constraints upon future development of research into leadership, and indeed of academic research more generally.

Presentations to the symposium by each group evoked the reaction that the analysis presented was clear but depressingly familiar. What we accomplished was a formal presentation of issues that are extensively discussed at almost any academic conference. On such occasions colleagues talk about the reactions of different universities and departments to varying kinds of publications and professional activities, especially as these reactions are expressed at salary, tenure, and promotion evaluation times. Close colleagues talk about transitions in journal policies. Very close colleagues talk about funding opportunities by various federal and private foundations, or research and change opportunities within corporations. Programs such as SAST formalize such informal processes. The SAST process, if broadly practiced, might open up some areas that researchers treat as the most proprietary.

Should projections about stakeholder actions be discussed openly? Perhaps, yes. Doing so could provide information to newer or less well connected researchers that would contribute to the development of the field. To the extent that stakeholder analysis is important yet proceeds informally, interpersonal skills and political processes among researchers take on increased importance compared to more technical professional skills.

But perhaps, no. Explicating information about parties controlling resources would negate much informal prescreening by information centers, the "powers to be" in a field. If practitioner stakeholders and funding agencies are not capable of screening for quality as well as are the informal cliques of leaders in a field, perhaps it is desirable to leave informal the process of information control about stakeholders. One could only justify a "yes" answer rather than a "no" if the SAST process can be conducted in a manner that facilitates development of the field, rather than merely illuminating a deadlocked debate.

Researchers' Norms and Stakeholder Debate

As a step in this direction let us examine again the differences between corporate strategic planners and leadership researchers. Leadership researchers do not perceive themselves as being functionally interdependent. They are less like functional department heads than division directors. The parties have little reason, or perceive little reason, to come to any consensus, or even to interact regularly. And they are less like division directors than independent entrepreneurs.

Further, norms of depersonalized evaluation, such as refereed review processes for funding and dissemination, can be invoked when threatening evaluations are required. Other complex and unexplicated norms limit the explicit attention that can be given to various stakeholders—especially textbook writers, consultants (middlemen), ultimate users, and business funding sources—which implicitly and substantially affect researchers' time allocation. Time spent giving explicit attention to federal and foundation agencies and journal review boards is more consistently considered legitimate.

The goals of leadership researchers are targeted toward overcoming two pervasive forces—mistaken judgment and action, and disorder. These are substantial challenges; indeed they can seem so overwhelming that researchers on occasion transfer their zeal from these targets to one another. The need to do so may stem from the diffuseness of an academic's identity.

Tajfel's (1978, 1981) theory of intergroup relations proposes that one's identity is established through such opposition. In his model, one's identity resides in a membership group which is favorably compared with relevant outgroups. Both in an academic field and a work organization, a series of groups can be interrelated in a manner where some groups are of a continuingly higher status than others.

Under such circumstances, Tajfel (1981) proposes that the low-status groups will seek to change the basis of social comparison between the groups to one more advantageous to their own position. Experimental studies within the Tajfel tradition (e.g., Lemaine 1974) have provided supportive evidence. In line with such models, we may anticipate a continuing diversification among leadership research subgroups in conflicting bases of comparison.

Conventional wisdom concerning intergroup relations has been much influenced by the classic Sherif and Sherif (1953) studies of boys at summer camp. The view generated by these studies has been that in the absence of compelling superordinate goals, hostile intergroup relations will develop where groups are in competition with one another. More recently, critics have suggested that the external validity of such studies is limited by the fact that the Sherif groups were newly composed ones and that the role of the experimenters in influencing the experimental outcome in the desired direction was substantial (Billig 1976). Studies with long-established scout troops at summer camp (Tyerman and Spencer 1983) have shown that competitive activities were carried through within a framework of conflict-regulating norms.

The Tyerman and Spencer study provides us with a more appropriate model of relationships between researchers in the leadership field, and may help to explain the manner in which the SAST exercise worked out. Disagreements between leadership researchers favoring differing research strategies are regulated by a variety of emergent social processes. These include the anonymity of journal review procedures, differential selection of which sessions to attend at large conferences, and reliance upon the stakeholders who support one's view of the field as sponsors of smaller, more specialist conferences. The absence of most of those who are most strongly committed to laboratory experimentation from the present symposium also illustrates how a series of symposia that has given stronger emphasis to theoretical development and innovation may also set in motion self-fulfilling conference member selection processes.

SAST and Its Alternatives

Can a stakeholder orientation to facilitating the development of the leadership field help overcome these basic difficulties? The answer is not clear. The SAST process follows a Hegelian logic, and is probably realistic as a means to speeding movement—possibly even progress—in a direction that would otherwise be taken more slowly. Although intergroup relations may provide us with a model of the inevitability of a continuing diversity of viewpoints, it is the ebb and flow in the numbers of adherents to each of these views which marks the outcome of the dialectic between them. Stakeholder analysis has the potential to affect this ebb and flow.

However, the SAST exercise is explicitly designed around propositions about social processes that are better approximations of organizational processes than of social science field dynamics. The SAST process is designed to produce cohesion within groups to encourage the open advocacy of a position that clearly diverges from that of other groups. One model of commitment suggests that commitment depends on the explicitness, visibility, volitionality, and irrevocability of attachment to an object (Salancik 1977). In commitment terms, establishing groups for an SAST process makes explicit and visible an identification that may previously have been implicit and personal. It then provides social support to encourage participants to increase the explicitness, experienced volitionality, and irrevocability of one's commitment to a group position. It encourages people to accept personal ownership of the position, and to support one another in doing so.

Participants in the SAST process resisted commitment. During the debriefing, some participants indicated that they had been assigned to a group the consensus of which did not reflect their personal beliefs. Others indicated an unwillingness to evaluate the assumptions about stakeholders that were made by other groups. The Traditional Applied Empiricists identified themselves as "the good old boys," and seemed to be the focus of some "we-they" feeling with respect to other groups. However, the process of promoting cohesion within groups to encourage debate with other groups was not overwhelmingly successful.

Is it possible to derive better ways of confronting the apparent norm among leadership researchers that clear alliance with any one research approach is undesirable? What is required is a procedure that does not deny the importance of the current norms of the leadership research community, but that also allows fuller exploration of relations between each view of the field and its related stakeholders. Several possibilities are apparent. One would be to reduce the threat to one's own identity through the use of the Nominal Group Technique (Van de Ven and Delbecq 1974). A second would be to provide a more substantial time period for the exercise. Each group could be provided time within which to prepare structured proposals as to how they might address themselves to the stakeholders considered most important by *other* groups. A third would be to allow groups to trade members who felt that they were misplaced, once each group had established for itself an identity. A fourth would be to form a larger number of even more homogenous groups.

Such approaches will require testing in further symposium settings. The present procedure had value in that it opened up issues concerning processes of academic debate that have implications far beyond the area of leadership research. Examples of stakeholder assumptions worthy of debate are provided in table 11–5. Publically addressing these assumptions would be desirable. Doing so would promote the initiation and socialization of researchers new to the field by providing them with information relevant to their work, but not readily available.

It would help researchers sharing compatible perspectives to begin to seek alternative sources of resources of all kinds to continue their work. It would also focus controversies about the leadership field as a whole, and particular perspectives within it, on a broad set of issues likely to affect paradigm adherence, rather than on particular theories and methods viewed abstractly from a strictly scientistic standpoint. It is disheartening to see one's colleagues, especially doctoral students and recent Ph.D.'s, living in a "fool's paradise," earnestly pursuing very rational objectives, but not realizing that they have little or no chance of accruing the social, financial, and organizational supports necessary to achieve them.

Epilogue

Given the very modest success of the SAST session conducted at the leadership symposium, what is the status of the pragmatic general system philosophy of science that the session implicitly reflected? The internally consistent criteria for evaluating success have already been stated—has it changed behavior, and is it likely to do so? Although the proposed philosophy of science has not been well articulated in the past, actions in organization behavior reflect its implicit influence. The doctoral consortia at the annual Academy of Management meetings occasionally devote time to some form of stakeholder analysis, although that label is rarely used. Recent books concerning the research and publication process (e.g., Cummings and Frost 1985) reflect increasing recognition of obvious stakeholders on the edge of the scientific community.

Also, despite frustration with the session itself, a practical majority of the editors of the present book were persuaded that the underlying logic has sufficient merit to be exposed to more public scrutiny. It will be instructive to see if and how a pragmatic general system philosophy of science is reflected in future leadership symposia, future organization behavior conferences, and future "scientific" and "non-scientific" work of other kinds. In general, to the extent that stakeholders outside the leadership field continue to support non-scientific management models over scientific models, the scientific community is likely to be forced to explicitly recognize the significance of stakeholders outside the field.

> Genuine philosophical problems are always rooted in urgent problems outside philosophy, and they die if these roots decay.
> —Popper (1963, 72)

12
Reading Leadership as a Form of Cultural Analysis

Marta B. Calas
Linda Smircich

Recently a considerable number of books and articles have appeared that question what the field of leadership research has attained. There is widespread discontent with the knowledge accumulated, expressed in feelings of stagnation, regret over the unfulfilled promise of social science, and in desires for different paradigms to revitalize the field.

This discontent and questioning has been well documented by the recent Leadership Symposia books. The opening pages of *Leadership: Beyond Establishment Views* (Hunt, Sekaran, and Schriesheim 1982) presented the leadership field as a cultural space in dispute, discontent, and dismay. (See figure 12–1 for a depiction of the cultural space of leadership literature.) "Sharp splits" are prevalent in the literature, "the researcher/practitioner split" being one of the most dramatic," but there are others. The "leadership establishment" is characterized by "many scholars" (unnamed) as producers of models that are "narrow, highly deterministic, rigidly delineated." A second group accuses the establishment of being "responsible for current dismay with the leadership literature" because its narrow models "screen out" . . . "most of the potentially interesting and important things that occur in leadership in the real world."

Hunt, Sekaran, and Schriesheim (1982) placed themselves between two distasteful alternatives: "defending to the death rigor/emphasizing scientific canons" and "complete scrapping of this emphasis." Their position was "we need to get beyond" but we cannot "throw out the baby with the bath water." There was interest in putting some distance between themselves and "the establishment," but there was also concern about going too far.

The editors saw themselves and the field of leadership as running both a risky and conservative course, bounded on one extreme by the dictates of the scientific method and on the other by something that is unnamed—its only distinguishing feature is that it is *not* science. One alternative was a well-known quantity, despite its failure to deliver; the other alternative was so unarticulated as to be no alternative at all!

Where would the field move? To something more pluralistic, free-market,

```
------------------------------------------------        ------------------------------------------------
LEADERSHIP ESTABLISHMENT,
known for its narrow,
highly deterministic,                                                        ????????
rigidly delineated models
------------------------------------------------        ------------------------------------------------



                        ------------------------------------------------------
                                  BEYOND ESTABLISHMENT
                                          VIEWS
                        ------------------------------------------------------
```

Figure 12–1. Cultural Space of Leadership Literature According to Hunt, Sekaran, and Schriesheim 1982

anything-goes, consumer-oriented, and fun, proclaimed Hunt, Sekaran, and Schriesheim. Diversity was treated as so much product. *Everything* was okay.

With the 1984 symposium book (Hunt et al. 1984), there was a change in this self-understanding. The unnamed alternative of the 1982 book still had no name, but the diversity in the field was understood as deeply signif-icant—evidence of conflicting paradigms and competing values. The opposi-tion for self-understanding was no longer "establishment/beyond establish-ment" but "status quo/paradigm shift." The editors noted little evidence of a paradigm shift in the North American literature, nor was it clear what a par-adigm shift would really mean for leadership research and researchers. But they acknowledged that their earlier position was untenable: "It is impossible to value all perspectives, methodologies, and the like as being of equal value."

With this chapter we enter the dialogue in the leadership field. Our wish to join the conversation springs from reading the accounts of our colleagues, sharing their frustration and disenchantment, and desiring to contribute our efforts. Much of what we "academics" produce is irrelevant to the pressing problems of the world. What can we do? How can the organizational scholar go forward and feel valuable in the world? What kind of leadership are we to practice?

Too often our solution to problems is the one proposed for the unfortu-nate Humpty-Dumpty—"more horses, more men." We propose rather than going forward with more horses and more men (a technical solution akin to more of the same), that we not go forward at all, but that we stop—to give attention to what it is that we are doing, how we are doing it, and why.

One way out of our stagnation is to reexamine what we have taken for granted as we have produced the academic leadership literature. By so doing we acknowledge that the organizations and the leaders we portray in our writing are our own creations, that as leadership writers/researchers, critics, and teachers (along with the popular business press and leadership training industry) we have created leadership in our discourse. Our proposal to include ourselves as subjects stems from the belief that the phenomenon of leadership as demonstrated by human beings in organizations cannot be understood in isolation from the discursive practices which are present and possible at any given time in a culture, because practices of writing and talking leadership "make" leadership as much as those who "do" leadership.

Literature as Our Central Cultural Practice

When anthropologists seek to learn about a community they take up residence with the natives and proceed to learn about their ways of life. We, however, are not anthropologists seeking to learn about the exotic life of a remote group. Instead we are investigating our own community, a community of scholars, to better understand what we do and what other alternatives may be open to us.

How is one to learn about the academic culture and its worlds of possibility? We argue that the key lies in our literature. It is absolutely central to the identity of the academic culture. It is who we are and what we do.

To substantiate our point, we call attention to how we spend of lot of time reviewing each others' writing to judge whether it should become part of the "literature." We make constant reference to the "literature" to locate our arguments, legitimate our claims, and rationalize our actions. Furthermore, status is achieved by being a published author (preferably frequently and in the "right" places). And at the very least in many situations being part of the "literature" constitutes a requirement for continued employment ("publish or perish"). Thus, writing literature, as well as reading it, reviewing it, and knowing it are favored and important cultural practices.

In this chapter we take the leadership literature itself as a cultural indicator, a manifestation of cultural dynamics. We treat the leadership literature as a series of messages. We examine these messages for clues as to why there is discontentment with the leadership literature. We want to know what are the messages *about the ways we think about organizational life and its possibilities* that are embedded in the leadership literature? We ask, what is it communicating and how? What is it not communicating and why not? In so doing we are performing a cultural analysis on ourselves as cocreators of a narrative inscribed in our organizational literature.

As organizational researchers we are used to investigating the details of organizational life. But how shall we conduct research on our literature?

The Paradigm of Reading

As researchers we strive to know the organizational world through a series of empirical methods. But in our lives as "regular" citizens we gain knowledge in other ways. We know through direct participation in events and situations—that is, we know *through experience.* We also participate symbolically and come to know through interpreting the experiences of others. One way we do this is through reading; by reading the words of others we gain knowledge through symbolic representation.

As researchers, if we are going to be consistent in our endeavors, the epistemological position that we take and the methodology that we use have to be congruent with the nature of what we want to know. Since what we want to know about is literature, and the phenomenon is manifest in writings, it can only be uncovered by reading.

What is reading? This is one of our most taken for granted activities. We seldom question how we are able to read, short of saying that we can understand the words we see in print: how they sound and what they mean. However, perhaps we should be amazed by the fact that we are able to read at all! Consider what we read. The markings on a page are mere graphics with no sounds at all, unless we have agreed upon the sounds that they should have. More important, we should have also agreed as to the meanings of those markings. And the meanings change, also by agreement, depending on the way the markings are put together in form and context. In other words, reading is a negotiated cultural practice.

Furthermore, since there are many ways to understand that which is written (we have been unable to negotiate a unique and definite meaning for all that we read, the same way that it is impossible to negotiate a unique and definite meaning for all that we do), then reading is not only understanding but interpreting what we read. In this sense, reading allows not only for multiple interpretations but also for the "authority" of the reader and the critic, which goes well beyond the "authority" of the writer.

We can then say reading is the realization of a text through its interpretation. Here we go beyond asking how reading is possible and are concerned with how interpretation is possible. That is, how do we understand a string of markings? What is there, in our community, that permits us to make sense of them? Why may others in our community make sense of these same markings in a different way? In asking this we are no longer asking, what do we *mean,* but how do we *signify?* And what we are discussing is not how we give meaning to words but how we signify with our texts.

This brings us to a specialized type of reading: the *semiotics* of literature. Semiotics attempts to discover the conventions, the codes, which make meaning possible. A semiotic reading is centered on readers because they are the repository of the codes which account for the intelligibility of texts. Only their reading can make a text intelligible since an unread text, for all practical purposes, does not exist. Semiotic reading involves making explicit the implicit cultural knowledge which enables signs to have meaning. By reading the leadership literature this way we go beyond understanding *what* we say, to understanding ourselves as members of a particular community, *as social and cultural beings* (Culler 1981).

How do we do semiotic reading? The notion of semiotic structures as systems of oppositions or differences is fundamental to this type of reading (Eco 1984). To describe a system of relations, such as markings on a page, is to identify the oppositions that combine to differentiate the phenomenon in question. This idea can be extended to understand a whole body of literature by examining the key oppositions that underlie its intelligibility.

Another important concept is "horizon of expectations," a frame of reference without which experiences, observations, and the like would have no meaning (Culler 1981). There are three principal elements in the idea: One, the reader has previous understanding of the genre in question. For example, the reader can tell the difference between a novel and a journal article. Two, the form and theme of earlier works is assumed to be known. The reader knows, for example, that he or she is about to encounter suspense since he or she is reading a detective novel. Three, the reader can discern the cultural codes of the text. The reader can tell "what is going on" beyond the written word because there are a series of cultural conventions "pointed at" by the language used. Thus "the sound of footsteps behind the bedroom door" brings a series of images to the reader's mind in the context of an Agatha Christie story that are different from the images triggered when reading a Harold Robbins novel.

These elements do not imply that every reader will have an identical "horizon of expectations" and will, therefore, interpret a text in the same manner. Two reasons account for this: "intertextuality" and "readerly competence." Intertextuality poses that every text is "made up" of other texts with which the reader is acquainted. A text can be read only in relation to other texts "which provide a grid through which it is read and structured, by establishing expectations which enable one to pick out salient features and give them structure" (Kristeva 1969). Any reading experience becomes "a grid of signification," "a weaving of meanings" brought about by the different texts, which existed previously in the experience of the reader. Therefore, rather than expecting identical interpretations, intertextuality provides grounding for the plurality of interpretations which are possible in one culture.

A second reason for nonidentical interpretations is varying readerly competence. Readers have learned a "grammar of responses" which enables them to choose relevant structures of meaning from an otherwise amorphous mass of details so they know the "conventions of plausibility" (Culler 1975).

However, there are limitations to possible interpretations. Not "anything goes." These limitations are established by the cultural and "literary" codes of any one community at any one point in time. Thus, a deep semiotic reading should be able to make explicit those limitations by uncovering the beliefs and values of the community. By doing so, not only is the possible acknowledged but the "world of possibilities" may be extended into that which is presently impossible.

Reading the Field of Leadership

Informed by the philosophical/theoretical position of the semiotics of literature and the operational paradigm of reading, we are now ready to read the current literature of leadership, to find out how it signifies and about the beliefs and values of the academic leadership research community.

We searched the *Business Periodicals Index* and the *Social Sciences Index* for the 1983–1984 leadership literature published in the major academic journals in management. This resulted in a total of twenty-three articles from *Academy of Management Journal, Academy of Management Review, Administrative Science Quarterly, Journal of Applied Psychology, Journal of Management,* and *Organizational Behavior and Human Performance.* We chose this current literature as representative of the valued products of the scholarly community we are investigating. We assume it reflects the most recent influences and issues of importance within the field. To have appeared in these journals the papers must have been subjected to testing against the standards of the community (Cummings and Frost 1985).

Authors of these twenty-three articles are: Adams, Rice, and Instone (1984); Carbonell (1984); Dobbins, et al. (1982); Frost (1983); Graeff (1983); Heilman, et al. (1984); Jones (1983); Kenny and Zaccaro (1983); Knight (1984); Knight and Saal (1984); Larson, Lugle, and Scerbo (1984); McElroy and Downey (1983); Phillips (1984); Pierce, Dunham, and Cummings (1984); Podsakoff, et al. (1984); Podsakoff, Todor, and Schuler (1983); Rice, Instone, and Adams (1984); Seers and Graen (1984); Sheridan, Vredenburgh, and Abelson (1984); Singh (1984); Smith and Simmons (1983); Vecchio and Göedel (1984); and Wofford and Srinivasan (1983).

We read this literature with three questions in mind:

1. *How* does this literature (or text) signify/communicate/mean?

2. *What* does this literature/text signify/communicate/mean? (meta-meaning)

3. What is missing and why? What *worlds of possibility* are excluded by this literature/text?

Let us clarify that this is not a standard review of the literature. Our task is more archeological—to uncover the signifying processes, to uncover the values and visions of the world portrayed.

How: Codes of Signification

Our first reading of the literature is directed to the question of *how* this literature signifies what it is: to uncover the codes of signification. Codes are abstractions that contain the logical operations, the conventions, that make meaning possible through reading. They are taken for granted so that when we read we do not even notice how they are functioning in the construction of meaning. They are intermediary between "the thing itself" (i.e., symbols on pages) and the individual interpreter. Thus, to point to the codes of signification of any literature is to uncover the basic elements that make that literature what it claims to be. It is possible to discern the codes because we are members of the cultural community that has produced these texts. We have been acculturated so that our horizon of expectations "prepares" us for reading organizational literature.

Even though we have not exhausted the possible codes in this literature, the following appear to account for what our literature is.

Themes chosen. Most themes are not "fresh." Papers begin with a statement indicating that a particular question has been investigated before and the authors want to further that line of inquiry. All the expressions introducing the theme of the paper come with references to others who have done similar work. This serves to authorize the theme as appropriate and legitimate.

Lexical expression. The papers are written in neutral, highly specialized language. Instead of "plain English" there is a technical language that implies precision. This may serve to mystify the discussion so that the people who are actually being described in the text would not recognize themselves in the descriptions.

Form of the text. Papers have multiple parts and these parts have common labels. For example, *introduction* or opening statements, *method, results, discussion, implications,* and *conclusions.* All of the parts except the introduction are signaled by headings.

Rhetorical modes. Although argument is done differently in the different parts of the text, the overall tone of communication is rational, logical, with incremental steps of reasoning. The *introductory* section substantiates and legitimates what follows by linking it to the work of others. The writing style is emphatic and persuasive. The *methods* and *results* sections rely on the power of numbers as a rhetorical strategy. Terms such as *instrument, measurement, manipulations,* and *hypothesis testing* signal that a particular kind of technology has been applied to produce a certain kind of knowledge statement. The term *sample* communicates representativeness and the term *reliability* communicates consistency, lending further persuasive power to the words and numbers that follow. The typical results section has powerful abstract visual displays such as graphs or charts in which the rows and columns portray a world that looks neat and clean and precise. Judging by the amount of space devoted to the different parts of the papers, the methods and results sections are clearly the most important: over 50 percent of the total length of each paper is taken up by these two sections. By comparison the discussion and conclusion sections are generally brief. They often restate the opening argument. Claims and persuasive appeals are on the basis of "the evidence." Arguments are made on the basis of abstract, generalized hypotheses as opposed to details. In contrast to the assertive openings of most papers, the endings are the domain of humility. Most speculation, if any, is couched in terms such as "it seems reasonable to assume"; the words *hunch* and *intuition* do not appear. The endings of papers are usually cautious, with hedging statements. These provide a kind of "safety valve," for authors know their argument has areas of weakness. There is never a total resolution at the end of a paper. There is always openness—"more research is needed." Most endings communicate "we know very little for sure."

References. The presence of references is also a rhetorical strategy and a signifying code. Nine of the twenty-three articles ended their first sentences with citations. Fifteen out of the twenty-three had citations in the first paragraph. The citations show connections to the knowledge base of the community and provide evidence for the claims that follow.

Support and acknowledgments. Acknowledgments at the bottom of the first page of articles express gratitude to others who helped in the research. The authors of one paper thanked the president and vice president of the company where the research was done; another thanked those who had served as experimenters. Interestingly, no one thanked the people who served as the subject of their research. Of the twenty-three articles, ten acknowledged receipt of financial support from institutions; five of them were funded by military sources. The acknowledgments point to the historical situation of the work; they provide traces of the influences on the thinking of the authors, give clues as to what audience(s) the paper was intended for, demonstrate links with institutions and people, and bid for legitimation by citing past acceptance at conferences and funding agencies. Overall, they point to political and social networks.

Institutional affiliation. Underneath the author's name is printed an institutional affiliation, most often a university, but in the case of these twenty-three papers, sometimes the name of a corporation or governmental agency. University affiliation signals that one is legitimately based in the academic environment and has the right credentials. What would the unemployed author do?

Context. Each article signifies by virtue of its location in a scholarly journal. All of the journals carry editorial statements which indicate what the journal aims to print. These serve as a frame for the work that appears within their covers.

An Example

To demonstrate the functioning of these codes of signification, we will illustrate how we read one article. The reading shows how this article signifies to other members of the community.

When we open up *Organizational Behavior and Human Performance (OBHP),* volume 31 (February 1983), to read about leadership, we come upon an article called "Role Perceptions and Behavior of the Immediate Superior: Moderating Effects on the Prediction of Leadership Effectiveness." Under the title we see "Dean E. Frost, Duquesne University," followed by a summary in small print, then the formal beginning of the article.

We do not know Dean E. Frost personally or even impersonally. In fact, we arbitrarily selected this article to illustrate a point. Why should we accept anything that is said in it? On what basis is this text to have value for us? By what "authority" does it speak?

The first sentence gives some clues: "Research on the effects of role perceptions on organizational effectiveness has produced a large body of empirical data since the national survey reported by Kahn, Wolfe, Quinn, Snoek, and Rosenthal (1964)." Thus, this text speaks with the weight of history. The work that has gone before has established a tradition of meaningfulness for terms such as "role perceptions" and "organizational effectiveness." In fact, in this article references are made to twenty-four different works "author-ized" by thirty-five different people. Frost's work therefore proceeds in extension from the work of others. The references to past work serve to praise and criticize, and to differentiate his work from others. However, perhaps most importantly, they serve to legitimate the author as a "worthy speaker" by demonstrating that he fits into a "research tradition" or a "stream of inquiry" that has been "authorized" for some time. Thus, one reason we may conclude that this text has value for us is its connection to other texts in which we have been interested.

Although the text by Frost speaks with the authority of a research tradition, we have never heard of Frost and when we look at the bottom of the first page we see the words: "This research was conducted while the author was a doctoral candidate at the University of Washington . . ." These words might give us reason to pause; after all these are just the ideas of a graduate student (low ranking on our status hierarchy). Dean Frost may be at Duquesne now (but what do we know of Duquesne? . . . except phenomenology . . . and *OBHP* is definitely not phenomenological!), but this is the work of a graduate student; why should it have value for us? If we continue to read we see "and was supported by a grant from the Defense Advanced Research Projects Agency to Fred E. Fiedler." More clues. Since we are competent readers of the leadership literature, we know of Fiedler that he has been a prolific researcher for about thirty years and that he has had many publications, many awards, and many grants. Thus, not only does Frost's text have a stream of research behind it, it has Fred E. Fiedler behind it, as well as money provided by the Defense Advanced Research Projects Agency— two more bids for legitimacy and signs of competence.

But other articles appear in *OBHP* without benefit of Fiedler and funding and we still read them and attribute value to them, even if they are written by someone we do not know—for *OBHP* is a *scientific* journal specializing in "fundamental research and theory in applied psychology." Each article appearing pledges allegiance to the canons of scientific inquiry as well as the scientific writing style. When we read "Role Perceptions and Behavior of the Immediate Superior: Moderating Effects on the Prediction of Leadership Effectiveness," we give its words value and authority because IT IS SCIENCE SPEAKING. Even if Dean E. Frost were *still* a graduate student his words could have value for us, not because he is Dean E. Frost, but because he is speaking in the voice of science.

Scientific Discourse

The operations described previously on reading the Frost article resemble the implicit logic underlying the decoding of it as a scientific piece. The codes enable the paper to communicate its scientific nature.

Our reading illustrates the claim that scientific knowledge is a kind of discourse with specific rules/conventions of signification (Lyotard 1984). Lyotard summarizes the special nature of scientific discourse and likens it to Wittgenstein's notion of "language game." That is, different modes of discourse have different rules that specify their properties, just as the game of chess is defined by rules determining the way different pieces may be moved. These moves make the game what it is. Lyotard summarizes the "moves" in science as:

1. One is "learned" if one can produce a true statement about a referent. One is a "scientist" if one can produce verifiable or falsifiable statements about referents accessible to the experts. A statement's truth-value is the criterion of acceptability.
2. Those speaking a particular language game consolidate themselves into separate institutions. Scientific knowledge is set apart from the language

games of everyday life. The scientist does not speak in the everyday language of society.

3. The adequacy of scientific work depends on the competence of the sender of the communication. There are still measures applied to determining whether someone may be a scientific speaker. The referent, the speaker's subject, is external to the communication between speaker and reader (addressee). In fact, a person (the subject of the scientist's speech) does not have to know how to be what knowledge says he or she is.

4. Science implies a memory and a project. The current sender of a scientific statement is supposed to be acquainted with previous statements concerning its referent (bibliography) and only proposes a new statement if it is different.

5. One's project gains validity not by virtue of its existence but because it is verifiable through argumentation and proof. Validity comes from a connection with or building on previous statements, either supporting, challenging, or refuting them. Any new statement that contradicts a previously approved statement can be accepted as valid only if it refutes the previous statement by producing arguments and proofs (Lyotard 1984, 25–26).

These are the well-known properties of science, moves we take for granted when we act as speakers or as addressee in the discourse of organizational research. At one level this is *how* our literature signifies.

How: Oppositions

Another level of semiotic reading, the identification of oppositions, is needed to show how this literature is structured and therefore intelligible as a specific kind of scientific literature, the leadership literature.

Some of the oppositions on which the twenty-three articles relied to establish meaningfulness were:

Male/Female

Internal attribution/External attribution

Ability/Performance

Initiating Structure/Consideration

Autocratic/Participative

Actual leader behavior/Rater perceptual bias

Leader structure/Substitute structure

Situational variables/Leader traits and behavior

Leader sex/Follower sex

High LPC/Low LPC

Deep/Surface

It is likely that competent readers of leadership will be able to recognize the main topics of these articles just by looking at their oppositions. These oppositions have been intersubjectively negotiated by a particular "interpretive community" (Valdes and Miller 1985), and through their activation the world of academic leadership is charted and known, and made intelligible.

How: Webs of Signification

At this point we can see that our codes and oppositions show our literature to be a well-defined and well-chartered territory. The questions to ask at this level of our reading are: How was such definition possible? And what does such definition mean?

Earlier, we mentioned intertextuality as central to our ability to read. It entails the possibility of "making a reading" because we bring to bear over the present text our previous knowledge and experiences of other texts (not necessarily in a conscious manner). Thus, intertextuality is not produced by the citations provided by the author (with which the reader might or might not be acquainted) but by the readers when they give an identity to each text as it means to them.

On the other hand, basic competence in our academic community is acquired through "reading the literature." These readings usually have developed shared intertextuality whereby any reading, by any members of the community, elicits similar meanings. And the more this literature is deemed distinct and separated from other forms of discourse (for example scientific leadership literature versus mystery novels), the less likely the possibility of multiple meaningful readings. This process creates closure not only for the readers as readers, but also for the readers as writers. What is possible becomes well identified by a well-knitted web of signification. And this brings again to the foreground the notion of horizon of expectations.

Think of a horizon as a line in the distance that permits us to locate and orient ourselves. However, most people using the horizon will want to move beyond their current location once they know where they are. In this sense, moving beyond will accomplish gaining new ground and obtaining a new horizon. With these ideas we can picture intertextuality as either a web of signification that permits us to "catch" new meanings and move forward or as a spiderweb where we are trapped without hope to advance or escape.

We did our reading of the twenty-three articles trying to uncover only the intertextuality permitted by our field. We considered each article as an

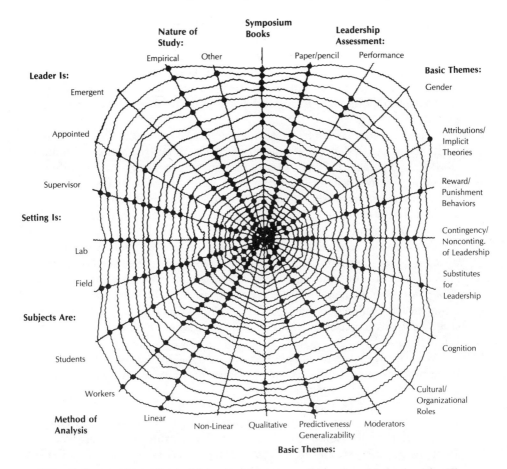

Note: Each strand (wavy lines) of the web represents one of the reviewed journal articles. The points on the axes represent the meaning-making activities which locate the articles inside the web.

Figure 12–2. Web of Signification

important contribution that would advance knowledge about leadership and that would move our horizon. At the end of this exercise we were left with the web in figure 12–2. The possible meanings were meager, and we felt trapped.

What Is, What Is Not, and Why

We have been reading the current leadership literature to find out *how* it signifies. Three elements: codes of signification, structure of oppositions, and web of signification account for how the literature communicates. If all this seems self-evident, that is exactly our point. We are surfacing the taken-for-granted operations of the community over its texts.

Our second and third questions are even more important to our exploration into our field's discontent: *What* does the literature communicate/signify/mean? What is *missing* and *why*? What *worlds of possibility* are excluded?

The sheer volume of literature and ubiquity of interest communicate the centrality of leadership as an issue for organizational researchers (Meindl, Ehrlich, and Dukerich 1985). One reading of this literature indicates that it communicates the scientific achievements of researchers, that it advances knowledge about leadership, and that it is still in search of better methods to grasp the phenomena of leadership in all their manifestations. But this is only a partial reading of the situation.

Consider the academics doing leadership literature. There are many of them, and they are smart. Almost all of them, however, have been overheard to say at one time or another: "All those studies and what do we really know about the phenomenon?" "We're trying to advance knowledge" they proclaim, but at conferences they confess "we're not getting very far," as they cast a sideways glance at their former colleagues who are making it big on the best-seller list.

Why are these smart people beating their heads against a wall? They claim they are not getting very far with what they have been doing, yet they are redoubling their efforts and trying even harder. There must be some other way to understand this behavior.

Perhaps leadership research is a form of artistic expression, an end in itself. Perhaps, like some artists, we want our work to be appreciated, admired, understood, and loved. Or, perhaps, leadership research is like a jigsaw puzzle. You work for a long time to put the pieces together yet you only look at the completed puzzle for a few minutes since, after all, the fun was in the doing.

Nonetheless it is clear that typical academic leadership literature producers work very hard to maintain the claim that they are scientists. However, we are going to deny the hegemony of science as *the* definition of the situation. We contend that "science" is only one explanation of what is happening and that "science" is one of the reasons we are so frustrated in our endeavors.

What moves us to do something so radical? Recent literature on the nature of knowledge and the relationship of science to knowledge has influenced us (Fisher 1984, Geertz 1983, Harding and Hintikka 1983, Keller 1985, Lyotard 1984, Morgan 1983). One way of understanding our research is to consider that humans, in their actions and practices, are essentially story telling animals (Fisher 1984). Narration is their common mode of being, represented by symbolic action-words that have sequence and meaning for those who live, create, and interpret them. Thus, the scientific point of view is subsumed under the narrative perspective; it is but one way to tell the story of how persons reason together in certain settings. The scientific form does not represent the totality of knowledge. It exists together with the narrative form, which is "the quintessential form" of customary or traditional knowledge (Lyotard 1984). In fact, much current activity in the wider intellectual community consists of critiques of the incompleteness and one-sidedness of scientific knowledge (Harding and Hintinkka 1983, Keller 1985, Kellerman 1984).

Narrative Discourse

Like science, the narrative form has its constitutive rules. These, of course, are quite different from the rules of science:

1. Popular stories recount what could be called positive apprenticeships (successes) or negative apprenticeships (failures). Narratives allow the society in which they are told to define its criteria of competence and to evaluate performance according to those criteria.

2. The narrative form lends itself to a great variety of language games. Denotative statements and prescriptive statements are included, as are interrogative statements and evaluative statements. The areas of competence whose criteria the narrative supplies or applies are thus tightly woven together in the web it forms, ordered by the unified viewpoint characteristic of this kind of knowledge.

3. The narration usually obeys rules that define the pragmatics of its transmission. The narrative "posts" (sender, addressee, hero) are so organized that the narrator's only claim to competence for telling the story is the fact that the narrator has heard it her or himself. The current narratee gains potential access to the same authority simply by listening. The speech acts relevant to this form of knowledge are performed not only by the speaker, but also by the listener as well as by the third party referent. What is transmitted through these narratives is the set of pragmatic rules that constitutes the social bond.

4. A collectivity that takes narrative as its key form of competence has no need to remember its past. It finds the raw material for its social bond not only in the meaning of its narratives, but in the reciting of them. The narrative's reference may seem to belong to the past, but in reality it is always contemporaneous with the recitation.

5. A culture that gives precedence to the narrative form has no need for special procedures to authorize its narratives. The narratives themselves have this authority; but people are their actualizers by putting them into "play" by

assigning themselves the posts of narrator, narratee, and audience (Lyotard 1984, 22–23).

According to Lyotard it is impossible to judge the validity of scientific knowledge on the basis of narrative knowledge, and vice versa, since the relevant criteria are different. But although narrative knowledge approaches scientific knowledge with tolerance, by considering its discourse a variant in the family of narrative cultures, the opposite is not true: the scientist questions the validity of narrative statements, and denies their status as knowledge (Ingersoll and Adams 1983).

What we are claiming, with tolerance, is that when we read the leadership literature we are entering a narrative culture that has "scientific knowledge" as its preferred mode of discourse. The leadership literature (or any other organizational literature that calls itself "scientific") forms a story that goes beyond its "scientific" nature and tells us about the epic of the society that produced it.

We now turn to examine the story embedded in the narrative or current leadership literature. A note of caution: In telling a tale that portrays what leadership researchers have been researching, we are aware that it is very much our own tale that we are telling, done with the purpose of liberating LEADERS from the context they have been placed in by the researchers. But please note, the phrases in quotes are the researchers' own words.

A Saga of LEADER

Saga: (1) A medieval Scandinavian story of battlers, customs, and legends, narrated in prose and generally telling the traditional story of an important Norse family; (2) any long story of adventure or heroic deeds.

This is the story of LEADER as told by a community of his researchers.

Researchers' Tale

What it tells us about the community

LEADERSHIP is a good and worthy subject.

The saga is not about the legitimacy or desirability of LEADERSHIP within this culture. The domination implied in the oppositions leader/subordinate, leader/member, leader/follower is never questioned; instead these oppositions are treated as the "natural" elements of hierarchical organizations.

Researchers' Tale	*What it tells us about the community*
(continued)	*(continued)*

The LEADER's quest is to have effects over others.

The researcher shares this same quest by seeking to explain the sources of variance in the life-world of LEADER and to predict and have effects in that life-world.

The character appears in different roles, but is very often cast by the researchers in the role of "organizational manager."

The casting of LEADER in the role of manager is nonproblematic. Researchers assume a manager must be a leader; otherwise he would not have been able to become a manager. The saga is not about the possibility that manager — LEADER because of his placement in an organizational position that brings with it certain powers to make things happen.

Four themes seem to be intertwined in the story: (1) the struggle of LEADERS to have their leadership behavior recognized by non-leaders, (2) the concern of some narrators to identify what LEADER is like, (3) the importance of gender in the life-world of LEADER, and (4) the potency of LEADER.

Theme 1: The Struggle for Recognition

Researchers' Tale	*What it tells us about the community*

The LEADER exhibits particular behaviors that are representative of his leadership. But non-leaders constantly avoid recognizing them when given the opportunity to rate the LEADER.

Most of this research has been concerned with *the problem with non-leaders that prevents them from seeing real leadership* as defined by the researchers' community (usually via the LBDQ); and how to correct "the problem."

Theme 1: The Struggle for Recognition (continued)

Researchers' Tale (continued)	*What it tells us about the community (continued)*
Non-leaders have trouble remembering leader-relevant information. There is a pervasive bad influence called "implicit theories of leadership" which impedes the identifications of "real," "objective," "true" leadership behavior. Implicit theories of leader behavior pose a significant threat to the validity of questionnaire-based leader behavior rating. This is "troublesome" and "devastating" to the researcher. Furthermore, non-leaders also attribute behaviors to LEADER based on things like success and failure of performance outcomes where LEADER was involved.	The whole issue of the problems with attribution and implicit theories of leadership makes it clear that there has seldom been any attempt to identify a legitimate notion of "leadership" as understood *outside* of the researcher's community.
One solution to this problem is to do more research, applying attribution theory to leadership research. Another solution is to train non-leaders to evaluate leadership correctly, being sure that such a program "systematically structures appropriate cognitive categories for observers . . . rather than relying on their 'naive' prototypes." However, such attempts will be effective only to the extent that they "are compatible with the cognitive mechanisms associated with observers' abilities to accurately remember leader-relevant information."	Instead, researchers assume that "true leadership behavior" exists separate from the responses of those who share the LEADER's life-world. Researchers have a preconceived notion about what LEADER behavior is. What is problematic is getting respondents to distinguish between outcome performance cues and real behavior. Researchers feel somewhat thwarted because the unruly mental processes of non-leaders have gotten in the way of their efforts. Some researchers are concerned with training away the "naive" responses of non-leaders in order to keep their research enterprise alive. Thus, this community of researchers is at odds with the wider society in that they are in a battle with observers of LEADERS and are set apart from them. To accept implicit theories and attributions as normal human behavior that makes the world what it is would imply that the researchers must reconsider their whole approach to investigations and their role in the world.

Theme 2: Quest for Leader's Identity

Researchers' Tale	*What it tells us about the community*

Although some researchers are hard at work figuring out ways to get observers to recognize the LEADER's behavior, others are still concerned with describing what leaders are like. Some say, "A major psychological function the leader performs for subordinates is reducing their role stress." The leader is somebody "who is highly competent in reading the needs of their behavior to more effectively respond to these needs." Yet, "leaders are caught in a bind. Before acting, they have to decide who they want to impress and in what way. They cannot be all things to all people." And: Beliefs about effective leader behavior include good upward and downward communication, positive leader responses to subordinate performance, elicitation compliance because of personally maintained bases of power, and positive forth-right forms of social influence."

This theme shows the weight of tradition on the research community. The questions of "LEADER effectiveness," and the importance of traits versus situations are the most ancient ones in this community. The community knows that there are no answers to these questions. However, asking them permits the perpetuation of leadership research under the legitimacy of tradition.

There is honor in being associated with the most important character in the organizational literature.

But this tradition implies that certain questions such as the following will not be asked: How is the action of "leadering" possible? Who does it serve? What do the myths of leadership tell us about our cultural norms and organizational life? How does the imagery of leadership traits serve to oppress organizational members?

Theme 3: The Search for Gender Differences

Researchers' Tale	*What it tells us about the community*

How does sex enter the saga? LEADER is typically male, but some researchers have cast females in the lead. Researchers believe that there are differences when sex enters the LEADERS saga; for example, "female leaders may respond to all

This is a newer theme in response to a mandate outside the community [Equal Employment Opportunity Commission, (EEOC)] and the women's movement, an indication of followership rather than leadership in the community.

Theme 3: The Search for Gender Differences (continued)

Researchers' Tale (continued)	*What it tells us about the community (continued)*

poor performers equally whereas male leaders may alter their corrective actions based upon cause for the subordinate's failure." So, in spite of negligible results supporting this statement, sex prototypes should be included "to adequately predict and explain the corrective actions taken by a leader."

When no differences between male and female leaders are found, researchers seek to explain "factors that give significance to the failure to detect strong and replicable leader sex effect."

Cultural stereotypes are alive in the research community. Finding no differences between males and females is so surprising that it has to be defended energetically.

We can also learn about the community by noticing that it does not ask why there are so few women in its samples of LEADERS nor why there are few women researchers. The range of questions around gender is limited. There is research into male and female tasks, which takes

cultural stereotypes for granted, but none on the gender of organizations or of organizational research. For example, assuming that organizations are "neutral" or "androgynous" precludes investigation of women's experiences in organizations. It also prevents investigating more "female type" issues such as leaders' development of nurturing environments, and the importance of feelings in leadership.

Theme 4: The Measure of Potency

Researchers' Tale	*What it tells us about the community*

When LEADER was effective he was "able to analyze the deficiencies in the follower's ability, motivation, role perception, and work environment that inhibited performance, and to take action to eliminate those deficiencies." But

LEADER's status as a central figure in this cult(ure) would lead us to expect great things from him. But LEADER's potency is in debate, and this provides a good clue to the heart of LEADER's saga. His aim is not, apparently, to undo some sort of

Theme 4: The Measure of Potency (continued)

Researchers' Tale (continued)	*What it tells us about the community (continued)*
that was more like his dream. Others posed that contextual influences, task characteristics, and environmental influences can be important elements in supplementing or substituting the leader's effects.	wrong to make a better world, as most hero figures in traditional tales seem to do. Rather, he is struggling to have his potency acknowledged, that is, to have his effects measured. Some researchers have even abandoned him because they were unable to measure his effects.
Some researchers have thought it might be better to subsume LEADER and environmental influences under the single rubric "management" since management structures all that can be called "the work situation," in which case they would be writing the drama of MANAGEMENT instead of saga of LEADER. But they changed their minds because "management" would reflect regression to a construct, which many believe has outlived its utility in a *science* (or emphasis) of behavior in organization. Management becomes, simultaneously, everything and yet provides little or no guidance for untangling the sources of variance in employee affect and behavior.	But the abandonment has been only temporary. Even if measuring the "leadership effects" is difficult, leadership remains a useful notion as one more place to impute variance. The paradox is that this literature first equates manager with leader, then it measures the leadership of the manager, and when little is found, it finds ways to substitute for leadership and also to do away with management. It seems to signal a trend toward the non-human organization.
	With this line of reasoning, learning about leadership from the "whole" rather than from the "parts" becomes a logical possibility.

Only one article in the group analyzed showed any closeness to the LEADER and to the complex world of lived leadership. Thus, it did not enter the story formed by the other articles. It was bold enough to sound like a narrative and not measure anything. It presented the LEADER as a real person in his native surroundings with all his strengths and weaknesses. It dared to suggest that stories could serve as research methods uncovering deeper levels of organizational consciousness. No pretentions of "Science" here. Just pure "Narrative." But for the same reason, the tale was very foreign and out of the social bond that forms the traditional community of academic researchers of leadership.

Meta-Perspectives on the Saga

At one level an argument can be made that the researchers' tale (the left-hand side of the page) is scientific discourse and that it represents "doing science." But we are arguing that it is "doing" much more. The researchers' tale contains the narrative knowledge necessary to sustain the community. Later we will argue that the boundaries of this narrative are too constraining and function to keep us from expanding our horizons. But first let us clarify how the researchers' tale functions as narrative knowledge.

We propose that the researchers' tale forms a narrative that defines the criteria for a competent performance within this culture (Lyotard's point 1). Its main task is to socialize others into what is permissible or desirable to say. Statements of truth and generalizability are valued, as are the abilities to predict, control, and untangle variance: in short, as if science were spoken and scientists were the speakers. There are a variety of language games at play in this narrative, not only the denotative language games of science (Lyotard's point 2). That is, leadership researchers speak in the verifiable/falsifiable language of science but their discourse is also heavily laced with prescriptive and evaluative statements. The unified view contained in the tale is: "This is scientific work" and "What is said should be expressed this way."

In this saga, as in any other narrative, the right to occupy the post of sender is based on having occupied the post of addressee and by the ability to recount the story (Lyotard's point 3). The present narrators were the addressees during their period of apprenticeship (where they learned how to recount the saga: formal education in this "field of expertise"). They may have been the referent by virtue of participating as subjects in experimental studies during this period. Now, while recounting the saga, they implicitly position themselves as the hero (LEADER). For example, in most experimental studies of this topic, the researcher appoints the LEADER. By doing this he is really appointing himself (through his confederates and manipulations of the experiment) to a post of leadership. Also, the researcher defines what leadership should be like, and quarrels when the resulting responses do not identify LEADER behavior as expected. Thus Researcher and LEADER are two manifestations of the same character from a culture that values orderliness, predictability, and control. The researcher has cast the LEADER in his or her own (wished for) image—a person who can decipher, manipulate, structure, and control. They share a quest for mastery, to be LEADER-master of the situation, master of the laws of behavior.

The literature continues to be important and publishable within this culture, in spite of claims that "leadership doesn't exist" or that the research "is going nowhere," because this culture finds its social bond not only in the content of its narrative, but in the *act of reciting it* (Lyotard's point 4). Producing the narrative and telling it are how we stay connected to each other.

Finally the culture actualizes the narratives, that are now authorized, by putting them into play in their institutions (e.g., journals, leadership symposia, etc.) and assigning themselves the post of narrator, heroes, and audience (Lyotard's point 5). So, different from "science," this "narrative of science" is only of the community and for the community. The subjects and objects of these investigations are only abstractions of the wider society. For example, laboratory studies use students as subjects and videotaped cases as "stimuli" but pretend to be about "real organizational leadership;" and when "true" managers are investigated, the research is so sanitized that they would not recognize what is happening as pertaining to themselves and their organizational life.

Further Reflections on the Saga

In an earlier leadership symposium book Karl Weick, in the midst of a response to Chris Argyris's work, tossed off this aside:

> I am not so sure that people are currently debating whether to do away with science or not . . . , but rather that what they are doing is working toward a new understanding of science and what it can and cannot do. From this standpoint we may have to learn to discriminate good from bad poetry rather than good from bad research. If inquiry looks more like appreciation or enrichment or description then this does not mean that we forego criticism. It means instead that we simply use a different kind of criticism (Weick 1979b, 90–91).

In this chapter we have aimed to do a different kind of criticism of ourselves and of our community's cultural codes, based on what we have learned when trying to attain a new understanding of science. Our approach arose from a commitment to the pleasures and pains of self-knowledge as a source of energy for good work and as fundamental to informed practice. Self-knowledge is critical to our taking personal responsibility for the worlds we are making. Thus, our vision of scholarship is explicitly emancipatory; we sought to liberate leaders and ourselves from the constraints that limit what is possible.

After doing the readings our original optimism about the leadership research community waned somewhat. We started with the assumption that there is despair in the field and that this despair is about feelings of stagnation and of lack of relevance. We further assumed that a reexamination of the community's achievements in literature would bring an awareness of its limitations and would point toward ways of transcending them. Our present pessimism arises from the following.

If the community was doing science, but doing it poorly, the readings would have helped to point out how to get back on the "right track" of scientific discourse. If the community was doing narrative, but was doing poor narrations, the readings would have helped to point out how to get back on the "right track" of narrative discourse. But what should we think about a community that does narrations whose content is scientific discourse? How can that community get back on the "right track"?

Our first thought was to correct our assumptions and treat the literature as purposive acts of mystification done solely to preserve a stronghold of academic domination. The (ab)use of this literature as an instrument for determining who should be included in the community also entered our minds. This was a repugnant thought because we know that some individuals' livelihoods depend on being included (receiving tenure), and inclusion may depend on speaking the "right language" and publishing in the "right places." We also thought that the literature represents the community's search for unattainable certainty and shows its inability to tolerate an ambiguous world. But these thoughts reveal our own frustrations in a moment of tiredness. We prefer to hold on to our original assumptions that the community wants to be relevant and contributed its efforts to the pressing problems of the world.

From this perspective, the Saga of the LEADER as told by this literature strikes us as the quest of the Researcher-LEADER to break "the code of leadership" and unlock its secrets. As the proverbial Rosetta Stone promised, breaking this code may mean fame and fortune for the one who does it. It is a fascinating topic because on it rests the whole structure of Western Culture, which some claim is disintegrating because of "a crisis of leadership." Thus, the community views the quest as not only important for organizational research but as important for *society*. And since the community seems to firmly believe that *society* puts a premium on and legitimizes "science" as the only way to be told what to do, the efforts to break the codes have to appear "scientific."

But the task is very elusive, so more and more effort is put into it. The assumption that subcodes should lead to the main code is so prevalent that most efforts have been put into dividing "all that should be leadership" into more and more pieces. As a result, the main code has disappeared and what is left is so antiseptic that LEADER is nowhere to be seen. Kept this way, it will be impossible to put Humpty-Dumpty together again.

Looking at Ourselves

Expanding Our Horizons

What do we need? What can we do? Our first proposition: We cannot go anywhere unless we take a very good look at ourselves. But in order to do that we have to achieve a different vantage point, one that allows us to see within and without at the same time. We have to learn about the practices of other communities not only to understand ourselves better but to enrich what we do. A program such as this requires that we first reeducate ourselves and then educate others (the way we form the bonds of the community) in a wider variety of subjects and topics, as well as in alternative ways of knowing.

For example, multivariate statistics could be learned not only from the perspective of the statistician but also with broader questions that come from philosophy and sociology of science. (How much philosophy is taught to those who attain a Doctor of Philosophy degree in Business Administration?) Literary criticism, feminist theory, and critical theory may enable us to develop not only richer readings of our texts but incorporate pluralistic views and deeper, more critical questioning. Cultural anthropology may foster sensitivity to the variety of human practices of organizing. These examples illustrate that we may be able to (1) ask different questions that come from standing in different vantage points, and (2) gain a broader range of discursive practices.

With these two achievements our narratives will become true narratives since we will not be constrained by having only the "discourse of science" as content: the vicious circle of science will be broken. This is another way of saying that we can develop broader intertextuality and break loose from a meager web of signification. We can knit a more complex web, one that will permit us to "catch" new meanings for our practices, because we now know where we stand and can proceed from there.

Connecting to the World

Other, more important, things may happen under this program for building our community. One of our main problems is the isolation of our research community from the rest of the world. This isolation is apparently our own making.

Researchers are participating less in the teaching of those who are not graduate students. Often we educate Ph.D. candidates who will never go outside of the community. A large proportion of those who become managers have learned from many other sources. Some organizations also now prefer to hire from outside business schools because, as one prominent manager said, "liberal arts graduates [have the] ability to continue learning how to learn."

Furthermore, actual organizational managers develop ideas from many others who are not within the community of academic leadership researchers. Many may go for what we call "fads," but we know for sure that they are not reading us. Why? An executive's comment: "As I read many of the articles I kept getting the impression that the research was done without a sincere interest and desire to understand behavior in organizations" (Price in Cummings and Frost 1985, 130).

Thus, we propose that we must reeducate ourselves to be able to talk in multiple languages and with multiple communities. Reconnecting to society should be fairly easy once we can do this. The point we are making is not to connect with other communities to influence or gain power, but to be able to participate more fully in making the world we all live in: A true act of leadering. We know that the problems we are talking about are not only ours. Other groups in our society may be facing a similar situation. But we do not belong to the other groups. We belong to this one.

Learning for Ourselves

We started this chapter saying that we were going to learn about ourselves from our academic literature. But what about learning from our own actual practice of leadering? We have organized leadership symposia, edited journals, chaired departments, directed graduate programs, served as deans. How do we, academics of leadership, do leadership beyond the literature? What can we learn (and write) about leadership from our actual leading? Can we get published in THE JOURNALS if we write from our own experience? Can we speak with our own voices? Is is worth trying, not only to help others, but ourselves as well?

Conclusion

We finally come to what is for us the logical conclusion of our analysis. We are perched on the brink of naming the unnamed alternative, and filling in the box containing question marks in figure 12–1 with the word "Narrative," and acknowledging, with tolerance and appreciation, that we researchers are storytellers and culture-makers. Perhaps we have privileged scientific knowledge for fear that we would lose our honored place in society if we admitted to being just "storytellers," but this is because we have not understood the transforming capacities of narrative. We have undervalued the skills of narration in favor of technical skills.

A great story speaks to hearts and souls in a way that science does not. Narration frees us to have a different relationship with organizational life. Through narrative we can build a social bond on the basis of insight and imagination and inspiration. We make our world through the tales we tell. The questions we need to address now are: What kind of tales will we tell? What kind of world will we make?

13
Commentary on Part III

Chapter 10 Commentary:
On Extending Leadership Theory:
Leadership Attributions and Beyond

Torodd Strand

The McElroy and Hunger chapter states flatly that leadership variables fail to explain much and it offers attempts at explaining this sad state of affairs with a psychological theory. For a Scandinavian such a statement does not shake any intellectual and ideological foundations. Leadership is little talked about and has no particular place in academic curricula. In fact I know few Scandinavian colleagues, if any, who would call themselves leadership theorists or researchers. After serving some years with leadership development activities, I myself have a feeling that the theoretical foundations have been insufficient and general psychology and social science have been more helpful than leadership theory.

McElroy and Hunger suggest that leadership theories can be seen as a series of developing but not very useful theories of performance. They apply attribution theory as an explanatory device for the leadership theorists' stubborn adherence to a concept that fails to be very useful, and this is their starting point for classifying theories and explaining their development.

This book on leadership is marked by an urge to go beyond what are perceived as the mainstream approaches to leadership studies—hence the rather extensive remarks of a philosophy of science nature found in much of its content. These remarks may open up people's thinking. Chapter 10 is helpful for this purpose as well. The authors argue that the general concept of leadership is unduly restricting and that methodological refinement without careful and unorthodox causal modeling is of questionable value. By being explicit about the causal models and their assumptions, McElroy and Hunger pick up the challenge from Pfeffer (1977), who points to the futility of relying on leadership as a major explanation in general concerning organizational performance. McElroy and Hunger help clarify the different causal paths which lie implicit or explicit in present traditions when these are seen as different theories of (organizational ?) performance.

Clearly there is an attributional danger in associating immediately measurable results with leadership behavior, thus losing a wider perspective and short-circuiting the causal connection. The assumed simple connection between leader behavior and performance is naive and unhealthy. McElroy and Hunger spell out the development from such a simple notion, where leadership is seen as the only explanation through the inclusion of other factors to the present questions of whether leadership should be seen as a result rather than a cause.

As I see it there is a need for pushing the debate in a direction where we can find common ground between the leadership theorists (mostly psychologists) and organization theorists and others, and avoid the pitfalls and professional narrowmindedness which may lead to attributional errors in one camp and lack of interest in the questions of leadership and intervention in the other.

McElroy and Hunger address themselves to broad and important questions by arguing that performance is the master variable from where research should start; by showing that despite growing sophistication, leadership theory overemphasizes leadership and fails to explain performance to a significant degree; and by highlighting assumptions of the theories and offering an explanatory scheme for why we have not been able to shift paradigms.

It is exciting to see a bold attempt at explaining intellectual positions and developments by psychological theory that points to the obvious assumption that individuals need cognitive coherence. The concept certainly appears promising in an area of study where the actors (the leaders themselves), and maybe the researchers, have good reasons for attributing causality to leadership—serving to keep leaders in power and creating meaning for organizational action (Meindl, Ehrlich, and Dukerich 1985, Pfeffer 1977), and to a varying degree serving to ensure the success of the organization (Salancik and Meindl 1984).

Attributions are defined as interpretations of the causes of behavior. Individuals have an inherent need to explain, and the cognitive process of assigning causes to events is called the attribution process. Depending on information available and the degree to which this information has qualities of consensus, consistency, and distinctiveness, the attributor will select types of explanations on the internal-external, stable-variable combinations.

To continue further with their proposal, the authors need to work on two levels: (1) spell out the theory and illustrate its use in leadership theory, and (2) apply the concepts on a meta-level using analysis of information available to the researchers to explain why they choose certain explanations, that is, attribute certain causes. The authors carefully state that no attempt has been made to survey leadership theorists concerning their personal attributional assumptions underlying their theories. Instead the theories themselves are taken as public statements of perceived causality. Attributional approaches have helped us understand some aspects of leadership (Meindl, Ehrlich, and Dukerich 1985). But in this case attribution is only partially helpful for the second part of the analysis since it is not carried through by the help of basic concepts like consensus, consistency, and distinctiveness. But in the process many of the hidden assumptions of leadership theory are made clear and the causal structures are revealed and classified in four groups—a very useful and revealing undertaking.

The general statement that leadership theorists overemphasize the causal weight of leadership and that leadership theories restrict themselves in the types of questions they pose is convincingly argued. Attributional theories propose that in an achievement-related context, success and failure need to be attributed to single factors such as effort and ability. If researchers live in this particular context, they may be prone to feedback into their theorizing data that possibly support such a notion and devote great effort to refine methods and measures that make the theory likely and justifiable.

Other theories relying on one broad concept have shown a similar faith. In political science and policy analysis, the politics variable, operationalized as party groupings and strengths, failed to add much information about public policy output, and in the area of public and private planning a strong faith in rationality and predictability has produced an imagery that has not fared well as a causal description. According to my reasoning, the basic beliefs were democracy as party politics and rationality as planning. The parallel to leadership is interesting. Democracy and rationality can be thought of as highly legitimate types of interventions in social processes with a built-in need to appear efficient.

The theory about the two phenomena, like leadership theory, fails to produce a grounded set of concepts about how the institutional context tempers the process and how the decision processes themselves unfold in their complexity (Rakhof and Shaefer 1970). These instances may or may not be examples of attributional mechanisms at work but it seems that researchers and planners were caught in their basic assumptions.

The cultural context of theories and the specific rewards researchers obtain may provide a broader explanation of particular instances, such as rationality and oversight in the Soviet Union, democracy in the West, and individual achievement in the United States—combined with the fact that the knowledge concerning cultural context and specific rewards researchers obtain has a high market value and the profession is thriving on that value.

The authors have some suggestions about implications of their findings. They argue for starting anew with questions of performance and refining the descriptions of relevant leadership behaviors. They hope to be able to reveal the proportion of variance which leadership can account for when trying to explain performance.

What should justify an interest in leadership if not an interest in its impact? It may be a narrow track. At the very least, the performance variables need to be elaborated, distinctions need to be made between intermediate versus long-term results, and the multiplicity of measures must be recognized. It may well be typical of leadership theory that McElroy and Hunger mention group performance as their dependent variable. In fact there is little unity among leadership researchers concerning the nature of the dependent variables, the range from individual mobility to group acceptance to satisfaction and task completion. Rarely does performance in an organizational sense appear to occur as a main concern.

As in the case of planning and policy studies, advanced measurement techniques and demands to define the dependent variables have highlighted the big question marks over the theory, tradition and its assumptions. (Meindl, Ehrlich, and Dukerich 1985, Samuelson, Gailbraith, and McGuire 1985).

The development of leadership theory from emphasis on stable internal factors to focus on variability and external circumstances parallels the development in organization theory (Scott 1981). The two theory tracks departed some time after Chester Barnard. It seems to me that some of the developments in organization theory have led to lasting improvements and insights whereas leadership theory has moved in rather narrow circles. The initial common interest was that of how to govern organizations and to understand the role of important actors—managers or leaders—in this process. In organization theory some of the following problems have been dealt with successfully, although their implications for leadership theory have not been explored fully.

The inhibiting but also instrumental nature of organizations in relation to actors. (Possible implication: Even powerful actors or leaders may have little leeway; changing the organization may be an almost impossible task.)

The fundamentally political nature of organizations and thus the multiplicity of goals and interests to be dealt with (The need to negotiate goals and a working order).

The variety and development of structures and cultures. (These change over time; they can be more or less well understood; they emerge partly as results of leadership activities.)

The dependence of organizations on a wider environment conceived as semipermeable domains. (Organizations vary as to their dependence on and understanding of their environment; what is the role of leader as mediating agent?)

The recognition of limitations, contradictions, and ambiguities in decision processes. (Instrumentality, rationality, and the impact of leadership are doubtful in spite of an appearance symbolizing effectiveness.)

Let me add that in organization theory, although focusing strongly on actors, the leader more or less got lost in the field's development. Organization theory usually turns a cold shoulder to leadership themes—by relegating them to oblivion or in pursuing analyses designed to show the insignificance of the phenomena. There are approaches in organization theory which reject the assumption of voluntarism and theories vary as to the level—from micro to macro—on which they focus. (Astley and Van de Ven 1983).

Only within a framework that allows for a voluntaristic orientation and a micro-level focus is it possible to conceive of management or leadership that is proactive and thus visible, meaningful to observers, and potentially useful as explanation. Among other things, the merit of such a mapping of theories is that the possibility of nonexisting, inactive, or merely reactive leadership is left open and we are urged to specify the circumstances under which leadership is a meaningful category. Omitting leadership is a danger in modern organization theory; but romanticizing it is a pitfall in any undertaking that starts with the assumption that leadership makes a difference.

Suppose one starts with broad questions of what makes organizations work well. The answers are almost trivial and relate to:

Order and coordination

Skills and technology

Commitment and the raising of members to make them adhere to values

Adaptability and growth

There is little room for the heroic leader. Actually the leader cannot be sorted out as a separate semiautonomous force, but appears as a potential contributor and an important inhabitant who works with those basic functions, but in a manner that evades straightforward description. Organizations might be seen as mediating elements between a society and the individual or the group. As Hosking and Morley (chapter 6) suggest, leadership is possibly the vital, conscious and so perceived, core of organized and organizing activity.

Leaders are partly caught in the organization and the environment in which it operates. They are often selected and socialized so that they are indistinguishable from each other; one vice president is like another. Leaders without organizations provide little meaning and organizations may be viewed as tool kits which are there initially for some powerful reasons. The leader is not a free agent; he or she must come to grips with the organization, and live there. The leader may be the possessor of the most operative organization theory of all the members, and he or she may represent the values of the organization and be expected to promote them.

To the extent that leadership theory needs to move from an area where stable and internal factors are considered to fields where variable circumstances external to the actors are operating also, organization theory may offer some of the concepts.

There seems to be some common ground for the psychological approach, which may lead to attributional errors but retains the person and actor, and a sociological approach with its systems emphasis, namely the notion of basic requirements which have to be fulfilled to secure the survival of an organization and roles that reflect these requirements. We can start looking for actors or roles in the organization that seem to address themselves to such functions as creating and maintaining order, integrating the orientations of the members into a common understanding of things, goal achievement and productivity, and adapting the organization to its environment. We may benefit from identifying such behavior as potential leadership behavior and be aware of the variety of theories and orientations which are needed to obtain a well-rounded understanding (Quinn 1984).

Theories have professional and cultural biases. Quinn argues that theorists tend to have blind spots; they often cover two or three of the areas or functions, rarely all. One can think of leadership as an embodiment of organizational characteristics and values, and managers as representatives.

Leadership, however, will exhibit itself differently in different organizational contexts and cultures. Organization theory may provide perspectives and concepts for the analysis of powerful actors. This theory tradition, however, provides primarily an analytical description of the machinery, including its limitations. Leadership theory points directly to handles but often the machinery does not move. Its basic orientation is toward action and intervention.

Conclusion

McElroy and Hunger have shown us the attributional pitfalls in leadership research and they inspire the discussion of new strategies in research around the phenomenon of leadership.

A couple of advantages of an attributional emphasis to leadership in organizational studies have been the direct focus on actors and the more or less implicit promise that intervention and conscious change is possible. The uncertain results so far may encourage a rejection and a concentration on a higher level of social organization where the actors are lost sight of.

But analysis of powerful actors could be fruitfully combined with concepts of organizations and environment. Statistical analysis of the proportion of variance such actors account for may be useful in, for example, determining the importance of selecting certain types of leaders.

But further appreciation of the significance of leaders and leadership may suffer in such an approach, particularly if quantitative measures of organizational output, sales growth, and the like are focused on. One should recognize the dynamic relationship between actors and structures. Actors such as leaders take part in shaping structures and other lasting conditions, particularly if they for some reason are not selected and socialized to be images of some of the upper echelons of an organization, but bring in tension and deviant behavior.

Rather than asking if the functioning of leaders is determined by organizational demands or the other way around, the evolving process should be studied. Rather than focusing solely on quantitative output measures, one should ask questions about how high-ranking personnel as well as other members of an organzation contribute to solving important problems in an organization's life—surviving and adapting, creating and maintaining the social order, achieving its goals and committing its members to the organization.

Leadership in this perspective does not appear as an ultimate cause, but an acting force and also a result of circumstances. To uncover the leadership processes and to understand them we need to design strategies where the impact over time can be accounted for and typical leadership features of different types of organizations can be mapped.

Leadership roles may differ in terms of their impact and their visibility. Leadership may function differently according to organizational type, the stage in an organization's life cycle, as discussed in chapter 8, by Baliga and Hunt, the nature of the environment, and other factors. And it may seemingly be substituted for. The question of legitimate visibility adds another dimension to the problem. We may ascribe meaning to leadership when it is visible and refute it when it is hidden, thus disregarding the factual impact of leadership variables.

Chapter 12 Commentary: Reading Leadership with Structural Lenses

Walter Nord

I hope Calas and Smircich's chapter is read (and reread) by students of leadership; it makes a very useful contribution. My comments on it will be of three sorts, beginning with some general reactions. Second, most of my reactions will focus on specific points in their chapter that, although I generally agree with, I think need qualification. The third set of comments, guided by the spirit that emerges from their work, will develop some additional implications.

Overall, the chapter adds some important dimensions to this book, and improves the study of leadership more generally. It does this in at least two ways. First, it stimulates what Alvin Gouldner (1970) termed *reflexive* social science. It calls attention to the fact that social scientists are human beings whose product—social science—is influenced by their own understanding (and lack of understanding) of themselves. Second, we need models for being reflexive and Calas and Smircich provide one. More than merely asserting the need to do reflexive work, as many are prone to, they do reflexive social science and, in so doing, provide one clear model for others to examine. Although they recognize it is a preliminary model and they did not provide enough detail so that one could do narrative analysis from their account, narrative analysis seems to be a potentially useful tool to help social scientists understand their enterprise.

Moreover, the style of presentation is engaging. I found myself analyzing the data with them. Although I did not always agree with their interpretations, I found myself participating in the process. Most of my disagreements involved their conclusions about the research community from the "Researchers' Tale." "The Researchers' Tale" is their description of the scientific text that they analyze using textual analysis in order to reveal the "real meaning." The real meaning includes accounting for why the tale has the contents it does and what it leaves out.

I wish to thank Elizabeth Doherty for extremely helpful comments on an earlier draft of this commentary.

In short, my overall reaction is very positive. Calas and Smircich point to the need for reflexivity, they do reflexivity, and they provide one framework to help others do reflexivity. My general enthusiasm about their chapter is dampened only a little by a few concerns.

The first concern involves absence of a fully self-reflexive approach. The authors recognize that they are telling "their own tale," but do not analyze the effects of their own background and context. It is not clear where they see themselves. They describe a community of scientists they seem to belong to and then analyze some members of the community and not others. To me, their critique seemed selective—they analyzed only members of the community who live "across the tracks" from them, not themselves or their neighbors. To a degree this point may be a bit unfair; they did not intend to do a fully reflexive piece. The label reflexive is mine, not theirs.

Second, although I have only a few minor problems in following their deductions from what is said in the "Researchers' Tale," I have more difficulty understanding how one can determine what has been left out from narrative analysis by itself. To talk about what is left out implies some basis for knowing what properly should be included. Even though I agree with their conclusions, I was not able to determine their basis for the so-called omissions. I doubt if they can be determined from narrative analysis—they seem to depend on some (unstated in the chapter) a priori assumptions. A more complete self-reflexivity would have stimulated them to make these assumptions explicit.

Most of my other reactions fall under one of two headings—concerns about their diagnosis of the problems in the study of leadership and a parallel set of issues concerning the therapy they proposed. Underlying both sets is the view that their diagnosis and therapy for leadership research are almost exclusively psychological. Primarily they want to change us as individuals; I propose the need for structural therapy as well.

Diagnosis

Calas and Smircich see many shortcomings with normal science. They see many problems in existing knowledge about leadership as stemming from the limitations inherent in normal science. They make a persuasive argument against what, at least in their view, is normal science. I am also persuaded by many of their conclusions about what has been left out and what questions and directions are needed. On the other hand, they did not address the positive roles normal science has played in the past and might play in the future. (Even if normal science provides nothing but a thesis for critics to attack, it plays an essential role in enhancing knowledge.) The chapter seems to imply that normal science has less of a productive role than I think it has.

Second, Calas and Smircich's rejection of normal science leads them to reject the common belief that a major cause of the problems of leadership research is too few resources. Although they recognize that part of the problem may stem from the fact that what we are seeing is bad science, their major emphasis is on the inappropriateness of normal science for the study of leadership. Consequently, they reject the value of doing additional normal science. They warn us that the model is inappropriate; in their words, "more horses and more men" will not help.

I suggest that such rejection is premature. There are many reasons why knowledge about social phenomena is thin—one very plausible one is that we have too few horses and people. As Staw (1982) suggested, our field is understaffed for the questions we are attempting to answer. I think understaffing is a serious problem. Because we do not have the necessary resources, some very fundamental questions never get attention. For example, consider Campbell and Pritchard's (1976) chapter on motivation in Dunnette's *Handbook of Industrial and Organizational Psychology*. They show quite persuasively how poor our constructs are and how imprecise we have been in efforts to operationalize some of the central constructs about work motivation such as performance. The amount of work that would be necessary to respond to their concerns is awesome.

Extending this argument to leadership, suppose (and I am using this as an example rather than offering a serious hypothesis) that charismatic leadership involves a pattern of subtle verbal and nonverbal cues that trigger certain deep psychological characteristics or human emotions. And then suppose those emotions could be measured psychologically by galvanic skin responses, eye-blink rates, pupil dilations, and so on. It would be very possible to get some precise micro-measures of the traces charismatic leaders leave upon those who are following them. Suppose that charisma needs to be understood at that level. Would we have the resources or enough people with the inclination to examine phenomena at that particular level? If these types of variables are important, we do need more horses and more men. In short, although I like the spirit of the Calas and Smircich chapter, I am not as ready to abandon the need for more science.

Third, their attempt to deliberately abandon the scientific paradigm was only partially successful. Somewhat paradoxically they were successful in getting new insights, but less successful in their ability or willingness to step far enough away from the paradigm itself to avoid some of its trappings. It seems more accurate to say that they criticized a part of what we talk about as normal science and then performed another act of science—the inductive act—than to say they abandoned science. In short, rather than seeing that they abandoned science, I see them as emphasizing one particular part—to be sure a part that often is obscured by those who write on the scientific method.

Similarly, (and I will return to this in my comments on their proposed therapy), they wrote mainly *as* normal scientists. Their chapter describes how science is done and how scientific papers are written—with brief introductions, modest methodology sections, long results sections, short discussion and conclusions, and long lists of references. Despite their intent to abandon the scientific methodology, Calas and Smircich use almost an identical format. At a process level then, their chapter is very consistent with articles that appear in most journals.

This fact points to personal and structural dilemmas we face in being truly reflexive—our training and professional outlets constrain our ability to use radically different approaches. At the personal level, because we are trained as scientists, we have a trained incapacity to abandon the approach. The scientific paradigm is so strongly ingrained in us that we are not free to not use it. Even when we try to abandon it, we still find ourselves writing in that tradition. Although this point is consistent with their diagnosis, I will suggest later that it causes problems for their therapy, because their therapy is directed at changing individuals in the established scientific community.

At a structural level, had they strayed too far from the normal scientific format, the chances that their chapter would have been accepted into this book or other creditable outlets in the field seem remote. To the degree that effective reflexivity requires the abandonment of the scientific paradigm, we appear to face a "catch-22."

Another issue I wish to raise about their diagnosis concerns the degree of negative impact existing research or leadership has had on larger society. Calas and Smircich assert that leadership research creates an image of leadership for our own community, that is, for students of leadership. Undoubtedly, this is true. However, they also assert that the community we are addressing and influencing is more broad—we are having an impact on society. At present, I think it is easier to show the impact leadership research has had on the scientific community than on society at large. However, many of the dysfunctional results that concern them most deal with the impact on society at large.

How much harm have we done? To do harm, we must have had an impact. Suppose we compare the impact children's stories, movies, television programs, and newspaper accounts have had on how people think about leadership with the influence social science research has had. I suspect the impact of the latter is comparatively small. Therefore, how serious a problem is it if we do not know what we are doing or if we have studied the wrong things? I speculate that society at large may be well protected from our research *because* of some of the very problems Calas and Smircich note. The research we "yogis" provide is based on such narrow premises that the "commissars" find it relatively useless and give it only peripheral attention.

A couple of other diagnostic matters. First, Calas and Smircich drew mainly on academic journals for their data. Consequently, their sample contains the work of only one segment of the community. It is, of course, quite likely that the same people who wrote the articles Calas and Smircich cited may have written of the other dimensions of their work (perhaps the very ones that Calas and Smircich say are missing) and published it elsewhere. Alternatively, other people have drawn on the academic research in writing for other audiences and addressing other issues.

Finally, and this may be a lack of understanding on my part, I have difficulty with the notion that somehow narrative analysis reduces the importance of grounding understanding in an historical context. If I have interpreted the argument correctly, I disagree with it. Although it is a small point in the chapter, I raise it here because I think one of the most important omissions in the study of leadership is historical grounding. For some reason, little attention is given to existing macro-level, historical events that were present when data were collected.

It does not seem to make any difference whether the data were collected in a declining industry or in a rapidly growing one, during a depression/recession or economic prosperity, during a war or a prolonged period of peace. (Such variables are seldom reported in journal articles. They would seem to be at least as important as some of the information that is often reported—for example, whether a questionnaire was administered in a group setting or on company time.) It seems to me that concern with these aspects of historical context is important if we are to build a body of knowledge.

Therapy

My analysis of Calas and Smircich's diagnosis leads me to a parallel approach to their proposals for change. Although they do recognize that the development of science is a community activity, the major thrust of their therapy relies on getting us as individuals to reeducate ourselves by expanding our own personal intellectual roots. I agree that this would certainly make it possible for us to ask new questions and to expand our roots in related disciplines. I am very enthusiastic about the goal and I think that these would be very important steps. However, I have some reservations about those tactics that do not give fuller attention to the structural aspects of social science.

My concern stems from the question: How much can very many of us know really well? In fact, the effort we make to include so many specialties in our individual work may contribute to some of the problems we have in our discipline. We try to include a bit of everything that appears to be relevant. For example, someone says culture is important and then many of us feel compelled to go out and learn some anthropology and try to introduce this knowledge in our work. Somebody else says that general systems theory is important so we learn a little bit about general systems theory and we try to mix that in too. As a result we talk about a number of things with little precision and depth.

Still, I believe such multidisciplinary knowledge is needed, but I would propose an alternative model. We need high levels of integration and differentiation, but rather than restricting our emphasis to developing individuals who only have an elementary knowledge of many areas, we also need to find structures to integrate experts.

For example, only a few social scientists can also be first rate philosophers or historians—but we need first-rate philosophy and history in our work. Perhaps we can find ways to work with those in other disciplines to use their differentiated knowledge. We need to redesign some of our institutions to support such developments.

If progress requires an integrated division of labor, we need to take differentiation and integration (Lawrence and Lorsch 1967) of our own enterprise, applied social science, as problematic. Viewed this way, science is accomplished through the efforts of a number of different people performing at least four complementary operations. There ought to be optimal structures to facilitate such progress (Nord 1985). Yet scientists in a given field seldom design their structures deliberately. Structures that generate appropriate differentiation and integration do not develop. We need novel ideas and paradigms. We need people to design and build technology, people to operate technology, and people to translate into practice the results of running the technology.

I think those are four important roles that have to be played to advance knowledge. Often they can be played best by different types of people, but most of our structures seem to run against this specialization. We seem to assume they all must go together in one person.

I suggest we need to work at the structural level. In particular, instead of giving exclusive attention to selecting/developing people who can play all four roles, we need to create structures that integrate the efforts of specialists in each of the roles on a continuing basis. We need to legitimate individuals who play only one of these roles. For example, we need people who do excellent translations from the research journals for those who can benefit from the knowledge. We need to find ways to legitimate all of these different roles being played within the research community.

As it now stands, individuals who do only one of these have little standing and are driven out of the community. It is important to find mechanisms that support getting all the specialized tasks accomplished using the needed degree of specialization. Such individuals have to be supported, not only in terms of outlets, but in terms of faculty positions and tenure decisions.

What are some of the things that we might want to do differently? I have already indicated that I think we need to find ways to support diversity—diversity for the different functions which together make up the community of knowledge. We need to examine aspects of our own relationships with our community and our subject matter. On another level, we may need some ways to develop special research structures that are not governed by the academy with its procedures and rules for awarding tenure. Maybe we need some new social structures. One that comes to mind is the Center for Creative Leadership. At least from the outside, this center seems to facilitate some integrated inquiry on a specific subject. Inquiry is both traditional and innovative and both theoretical and applied. It also seems to disseminate knowledge effectively to practitioners and thereby supports its long-term research mission. We need structures that support long-term inquiry relatively unconstrained by short-term perspectives.

Conclusions

Calas and Smircich's chapter provides an extremely useful reading of leadership with a psychological focus. However, some of the study of leadership and other topics in organizational behavior may be due to the way we structure ourselves, rather than to failure of scientific methods or narrowly trained individuals. Adopting their spirit and rereading leadership with structural lenses may generate a useful, complementary set of tactics.

Part IV
Overviews

James G. Hunt
B.R. Baliga
H. Peter Dachler
Chester A. Schriesheim

The two chapters in this part attempt a broad overview of the state of leadership research in general and the messages implied by the contents of this book in particular. The task of both chapters was to analyze the general state of dissatisfaction in the leadership literature as well as the problems raised during the leadership symposium on which this book is based. In addition, these overviews were meant to comment on available approaches to overcome what many see as a crisis in leadership research. Clearly the two chapters comprising this part are based upon very different perspectives and suggest very different solutions to the current problems in leadership research.

Chapter 14, "Leadership Research: Some Forgotten, Ignored, or Overlooked Findings," by Robert J. House, attributes this so-called crisis in leadership theory and research to the fact that many well-supported findings available in the leadership literature have been forgotten or overlooked. Thus, in fact we know more about leadership than is implied by the concerns expressed about the problematic state of leadership theory. In this sense, House sees no fundamental problems in the state of leadership theory and research and therefore sees no reason to change our basic paradigmatic approaches to leadership, although improvements in the specifics of doing research are of continued concern to him.

Chapter 15, by H. Peter Dachler, "Constraints on the Emergence of New Vistas in Leadership and Management Research: An Epistemological Overview," uses the search for new leadership vistas suggested by the title of this book and its implied dissatisfaction with the traditional perspectives of leadership and management as its starting point. In contrast to House's assessment of the problems in leadership research, Dachler very definitely sees a major crisis in this area of social science. He shows the origin of this crisis to lie in both the implicit epistemological assumptions that guide the majority of leadership and management writings as well as in the content assumptions made about the leadership and management phenomenon as such and about the social system of which it is an integral part. Dachler maintains that a way out of this crisis can be achieved only through making explicit the often implicitly held assumptions and then systematically questioning them with respect to their usefulness and meaning within current socially constructed interpretations of the leadership and management reality.

House looks at four issues in leadership research: (1) whether leaders have an impact on performance; (2) whether past research has yielded an important amount of useful theoretical knowledge; (3) whether normal science can be used to study the leadership phenomenon; and (4) the role of qualitative research in the study of leadership or organizational behavior in general.

House refers to comprehensive literature reviews and other sources to take an affirmative stance on each of the first three issues. In addressing the last issue, he first looks briefly at the use of qualitative research outside the traditional scientific paradigm. Then he examines a number of uses of it within the dominant paradigm of leadership research.

Considering Dachler's overview, at first glance one might wonder whether the two overviews are discussing the same topic. They definitely are. Whereas House takes the dominant assumptions as given, Dachler argues that they are simply one construction of social knowledge in general and of leadership and management in particular, whose explanatory usefulness and meaning may increasingly decline in view of what is currently experienced and constructed as our social-organizational world. Dachler contrasts the currently used realist ontology of scientific inquiry regarding leadership with an ontological view in which science is informed by the meaning-based construction in the observation process.

Contrary to the realist perspective on the basis of which House presents his arguments, the view of leadership and management developed in Dachler's overview chapter is based on the assumption that leadership is a phenomenon that is created by the inquiry process in the context of our culture. Leadership therefore cannot be something which is *knowable* independently of the observer. It cannot be informed objectively by the world out there, since that world is in principle not knowable independent of the interpretative processes inherent in observation.

Dachler next goes on within this context to examine constraints he sees to "real" as opposed to "marketing-oriented" conceptions of emerging vistas. He then analyzes the emerging vistas demonstrated in the chapters of this book within the two epistemological perspectives and concludes with a discussion of the ethical issues involved in the two epistemological perspectives.

As a package, these overviews stir up as much controversy as we as editors had hoped. Whether such controversy will in fact be useful in moving leadership and management research in new directions and in overcoming what many experience as a crisis is left to the future and to the readers of this book.

14
Leadership Research: Some Forgotten, Ignored, or Overlooked Findings

Robert J. House

This symposium book has raised (at least by implication) several contentious issues. These concern:

1. Whether leaders have effects on organizational, group, or individual performance. Some have argued that leaders have little or no effects on performance, especially organizational performance.
2. Whether past research has yielded a significant amount of useful theoretical knowledge. Some believe that after several years of scientific research little is known about the leadership phenomenon.
3. Whether the leadership phenomenon can be studied scientifically—that is, within the physical science paradigm.
4. The role of qualitative research in the study of leadership, or more broadly in the study of organizational behavior.

In this overview I address each of these issues. Having been involved in leadership research for the past twenty-five years, I do not pretend to be unbiased. Rather, I intend to take a position on each issue. I believe I will be able to marshal sufficient evidence for my positions to demonstrate that they are not without empirical support, and in some cases are also based on sound theoretical reasoning.

Does Leadership Make a Difference?

The first contentious issue raised on which I wish to focus concerns the effects of leaders. For example, Baliga and Hunt (this book, ch. 8) argue that leaders have a substantial impact throughout the life cycle of an organization. In

This chapter was made possible by Grant #3-17-207-70 from the Social Sciences Humanities Research Council of Canada.

contrast, Pfeffer (1977) raises the question of whether leadership makes a difference to organizational functioning and performance.

Pfeffer argues that there are several reasons why the observed effects of leaders on organizational outcomes would be small. First, the selection process is constrained by the internal system of influence in the organization. Norms concerning age, gender, education, and experience are likely to be applied in the selection process. Selection, as a critical decision, is also affected by the internal power distribution of the organization as well as critical contingencies facing the organization.

The selection of persons to leadership positions is affected by self-selection processes as well. One consequence of these processes is the selection of homogeneous managers with respect to background, values, attitude, and behavior. Thus, by the time a leader is selected into the position of chief operating officer, that leader will likely have similar attitudes, values, and behaviors to those in the organization at that time.

Pfeffer also argues that the leader is embedded in a social system that constrains behavior. The leader has a role set in which members have expectations for appropriate behavior. Pressures to conform to the expectations of peers, subordinates, and superiors are all relevant in the determination of actual behavior. Accordingly, leader behavior is also constrained by both the demands of others in the role set and by organizationally prescribed limitations on the sphere of activity and influence.

Pfeffer further contends that leaders are constrained by the external environment in which the organization operates. He argues that costs are largely determined by the operation of commodities and labor markets and demand is largely affected by external factors such as interest rates, availability of mortgage money, and economic conditions that are affected by governmental policies over which the executive has little control.

Finally, Pfeffer argues that leader success or failure may be partly due to circumstances unique to the organization but still outside the leader's control. Thus, the choice of a new executive does not fundamentally alter the market and financial position that has developed historically over several years.

Research on the effects of executive succession are relevant to this issue. Two hypotheses concerning executive succession are the resource dependency hypothesis and the population ecology hypothesis. According to resource dependence theory (Pfeffer and Salancik 1978), environmental contingencies affect the selection and removal of top managers. This process theoretically keeps organizations aligned with the demands of their environments by importing new information and perspectives into the organization. I refer to this hypthesis as the succession-adaptation hypothesis.

However, this succession-adaptation hypothesis stands in direct opposition to the succession-crisis hypothesis of population ecology theory (e.g., Carroll 1984). According to this theoretical perspective, organizational survival is age dependent. That is, survival is a function of the age of the organization, among other factors. Specifically, it is argued that newly founded organizations suffer from a liability of newness (Carroll and Delacroix 1982; Freeman, Carroll, and Hannan 1983, Stinchcombe 1965). Accordingly, new organizations face four kinds of problems in their early years. These are internal socialization and coordination, need for favorable exchanges with environmental actors, and the need to establish legitimacy.

Population ecology theory asserts that executive succession "sets back the liability of newness clock" (Hannan and Freeman 1984, 159–60; Carroll 1984) because such succession is likely to be followed by a period of internal confusion similar to that experienced by newly founded organizations. During this period the succeeding executive adjusts to the organization, and introduces new strategies, procedures, and structures. Internal communication and coordination are assumed to suffer, unity of command is temporarily lost, work routines change, and employee insecurity runs high (Carroll 1984). Accordingly, Carroll (1984) argues that this reasoning suggests that managerial succession creates a crisis that lowers organizational performance, and the likelihood of survival. This argument is referred to by Carroll as the succession-crisis hypothesis.

Carroll (1984) provides us with a literature review that demonstrates that the effects of executive succession are not consistent across studies. As Carroll has pointed out, the effect of succession on organizational performance and survival is sometimes deleterious, sometimes beneficial, and sometimes irrelevant. Carroll argues that these findings are likely due to failure to control other relevant variables such as the context of the succession, the timing of the succession relative to the organizational life cycle, the type of transfer, and the degree to which the control structure of the previous organization differs from the control structure of the recruiting organization.

A study by Smith, Carson, and Alexander (1984) not included in Carroll's review is informative. Smith and associates studied a random sample of fifty ministers, stratified by length of tenure. Data for this sample of ministers were collected over a twenty-year period, from 1961 to 1980. For each of the twenty years, the specific church congregations associated with each of the ministers were identified and objective measures of organizational performance concerning financial and membership affairs for each church were recorded. The performance variables consisted of attendance, membership, property value, general assembly giving, total giving, and salary. Smith and his colleagues also collected information concerning the United Methodist Women's giving. This variable was included as a control variable which was not expected to be affected by leadership.

The study involved two phases, the identification of effective leaders and an estimation of the leaders' impact on the preceding criterion variables. Salary received by the ministers was treated as an objective performance appraisal measure, since salary increases reflect prior performance appraisals by the membership. Ministers were identified who, for the entire twenty-year period, consistently had tenure-adjusted standardized salaries above the mean, and in addition had salaries at or above the standard deviation above the mean for eight or more assignments. This criterion resulted in seven of the fifty ministers being labeled as high-performing ministers. A step-wise regression analysis was conducted separately for each of the performance variables. Adding minister performance status (effective versus ineffective) contributed significantly to the prediction for all criterion variables except the United Methodist Women's giving, as predicted. The analysis indicated that the performance of the churches with effective ministers improved when these ministers took charge and that these churches consistently performed higher than others. Smith and his associates also conducted an analysis of the main effects of the succession event without controlling for leader effectiveness status. The authors found that leadership change does not in and of itself account for immediate or delayed variation in organizational performance, positive or negative.

Thus, the preceding findings suggest that when the effects of succession are adequately studied, it is possible to show that leaders do make a difference to the organizations they manage. In addition to the findings of Smith and his associates, there are a vast number of studies that have shown leaders to have an effect on followers and on group performance (House and Baetz 1979). I believe we can safely conclude that leaders can and do make a difference, but that leaders' effects will be conditional on several factors such as the leader's ability, follower's ability, organizational form, technological constraints, and environmental demands.

Leadership Research and Useful Knowledge

It is popular to begin articles on leadership with quotes such as, "Probably more has been written and less known about leadership than any other topic in the behavioral sciences" (Bennis 1959, 259); "After 40 years of accumulation, our mountain of evidence about leadership seems to offer few clear-cut facts" (McCall 1976); "It is difficult to know what, if anything, has been convincingly demonstrated by replicated research. The endless accumulation of empirical data has not produced an integrated understanding of leadership" (Stogdill 1974, vii).

Straw men, such as the fruitlessness of prior leadership research, set the stage for an attack and permit catchy and interest-arousing introductions to articles. However, I believe that such statements also misrepresent the current state of leadership knowledge, underestimate the amount of knowledge produced to date, suggest that we should engage in handwringing despair, and cast doubt on whether or not leadership research should continue to be conducted.

I refer the reader to two literature summaries to which I shall refer throughout this chapter. These are Gary Yukl's book entitled *Leadership in Organizations* (1981) and the review paper Mary Baetz and I coauthored entitled "Leadership: Some Empirical Generalizations and New Research Directions" (House and Baetz 1979). In addition, I will cite other sources of evidence as my argument develops.

In the following sections the state of leadership knowledge is discussed under the following topics: leadership trait research, leadership behavioral research, current theories, and situational moderators of the relationship between leadership traits and/or behavior, and relevant criterion variables. I address each of the remaining contentious issues in subsequent sections.

Leadership Trait Research

In the House and Baetz paper, we reviewed evidence relevant to leadership traits and their relationship to leadership effectiveness and emergence. Based on a review of the studies conducted to that date, including studies reviewed by Stogdill (1948, 1974), we concluded that (1) traits can, and often do, have main effects with respect to nontrivial criterion variables such as measures of performance, effectiveness, emergence and succession rate; and (2) many traits likely interact with situational variables to produce effects on such criterion variables.

Stogdill (1948) is usually referred to as having summarized evidence to the effect that trait research should be abandoned. What Stogdill said was the following.

see also pg. 52

> It becomes clear that an adequate analysis of leadership involves not only a study of leaders, but also situations . . . The findings suggest that leadership is not a matter of passive status, or of the mere possession of some combination of traits. It appears rather to be a working relationship among members of a group, in which the leader acquires status through active participation and demonstration of his capacity for carrying cooperative tasks through to completion. Significant aspects of this capacity for organizing and expediting cooperative effort appear to be intelligence, alertness to the needs and motives of others, and insight into situations, further reinforced by such habits as responsibility, initiative, persistence, and self-confidence (Stogdill 1974, 65).

Thus, rather than recommending the abandonment of trait research, Stogdill advocated continued research on traits in interaction with situational variables.

It is my opinion that currently traits are alive and well. And by current theoretical reasoning they should be. First, let me develop the argument as to why, theoretically, we should expect traits to have effects on leader criterion variables. Then I will cite some recently published evidence relevant to leadership traits that have not been considered in the mainstream of leadership research to date.

Traits are stable characteristics of individuals. Traits are unobservable, measured indirectly by some test, and represent predispositions, disinhibitors, or abilities of individuals. One class of traits, personality traits, is assumed to predispose individuals to engage in certain behaviors. Such traits may be reflections of needs or motives, reflections of kinds of abilities, reflections of prior learning, and/or reflections of habits and their strengths. Need for achievement and need for power are examples of traits assumed to be motives or needs. Cognitive complexity is an example of an ability trait. Locus of control, authoritarianism, dogmatism, and Machiavellianism are traits that theoretically reflect prior cognitive learning and are likely to be a mixture of both motivational and ability components.

According to social learning theory (Mischel 1973), traits serve to stimulate and guide behavior under a couple of conditions. First, there are situational factors that emphasize the salience of influence, leadership, or control. Second, there are few other clear-cut situational rules, cues, constraints, incentives, or guides to induce a person to behave in specific ways.

Thus, according to this theoretical reasoning, certain kinds of behavior are instrumental to the satisfaction of individual needs. The traits associated with those behaviors will predispose or disinhibit the individual such that the individual will engage in that behavior more than if he or she did not have that trait. However, this can only occur when there are few or no other constraints on the individual's behavior. Such constraints limit behavioral variability and thus suppress the behavioral effects of traits.

Consider these two propositions. The first is illustrated by studies by Megargee, Bogart, and Anderson (1966). These authors studied the interaction between leader dominance and situational cues in the prediction of emergent leaders.

Leader dominance, a trait that had positive, negative, and nonsignificant associations with leadership in the studies reviewed by Stogdill, has been found in the emergent leadership literature (Rohde 1951) and in experimental studies (e.g., Berkowitz and Haythorn 1955) to be rather consistently predictive of leadership. The mixed findings concerning dominance as a trait associated with leadership can be explained by consideration of the measures used in the situation. Several of the findings reviewed by Stogdill are based on measures of the degree to which the leaders were observed as being bossy or domineering. However, when dominance is defined as the leader's predisposition to be ascendant or assertive, as measured by the Dominance Scale of the California Personality Inventory, and when the situation calls for one person to assume the role of leadership, dominance is highly predictive of individual leader behavior as demonstrated by Megargee, Bogart, and Anderson (1966).

These researchers asked pairs of high and low dominance subjects to work together on a manual task requiring one person to verbally communicate instructions to the other. When leadership was emphasized in the experimental instructions to the subjects, the dominant subjects assumed the leadership role in fourteen of sixteen pairs. When the task was emphasized and leadership was deemphasized, there was no association between dominance and the assumption of the leadership role.

The limiting effects of constraints on behavioral variability have been shown by Monson, Hesley, and Chernick (1982). These authors conducted two studies in which the participants were placed in either of three experimental conditions: forced extroversion, forced introversion, or neutral. Subject's talkativeness was measured in each condition. As predicted, variance in talkativeness among subjects was significantly higher in the neutral condition than in the forced-introversion or the forced-extroversion condition.

In the second study, Monson, Hesley, and Chernick (1982) asked participants to indicate the probabilities that they would engage in various behaviors in each of four hypothetical situations. They were also asked to determine the probabilities that other individuals would exhibit the behaviors. On average, individuals were perceived to be most likely to exhibit extroverted behaviors when there were perceived situational pressures to do so, and least likely when such situational pressures were lowest. Correlations were also calculated between the participants' self-ratings of extroversion and the likelihood of exhibiting extroverted behavior in each of the conditions.

Again, the correlation was found to be an inverse function of the degree of situational pressure. These findings support Mischel's (1973) general argument that individual differences will be most predictive of behavior when environmental conditions are unstructured and offer little behavioral guidance to the individual. Although this evidence supports the general argument advanced by Mischel, there remains a need to demonstrate specifically how it applies to leader behavior in complex organizations.

The limiting effects of situational constraints is also illustrated by the work by John Miner concerning managerial motives to manage. Miner (1978) has advanced a role-motivational theory of leadership and he has specified the domain of the theory.

> In many respects each managerial position is unique in the demands it makes on its incumbents. Certainly role prescriptions can differ considerably from one organization to another. Yet there do seem to be some requirements which appear again and again in association with a great variety of managerial positions. And it is one such set of requirements that has been incorpo-

rated in the present theory. Primary stress is placed on certain components which contribute to what amounts to a common variance, or perhaps it would be better to speak of a general factor which operates across a great many managerial positions. There is no reason to believe that all of these role prescriptions will be present everywhere in management, however. Some may well be lacking at a given hierarchic level or in a particular type of organization or in a specific job. Nevertheless, they are presumed to occur with relatively high frequency, and across a considerable range of positions and organizations.

The role requirements which have been identified are assumed to be among those which occur with high frequency in business firms organized in accordance with the scalar principle. It is entirely possible that the theory is applicable to managerial or administrative jobs in other types of organizations, but it was not devised with these positions in mind. Where there is characteristically a considerable departure from this type of hierarchic structure, and from the value system that typifies the modern business organization, the theory would be expected to have only minimal applicability. When family membership, religious affiliation, sales ability and the like are the crucial bases for reward within the managerial components of an organization, the theory is not pertinent.

Those individuals who repeatedly associate positive rather than negative emotion with the various role prescriptions which have been identified as generally characteristic of managerial positions would tend to meet existing organizational criteria of effectiveness. Those in whom negative emotional reactions predominate should be defined as relatively ineffective (Miner 1978, 740–741).

The research carried out to evaluate the effectiveness of managerial role-motivation theory has indicated positive effects in twenty of twenty-one instances, as well as construct validity of the Miner Sentence Completion Scale. Five of the twenty-one positive studies are predictive. Similar studies conducted in nonbureaucratic organizations, and therefore outside of the domain of theory, have uniformly failed to produce significant results.

Miner argues that the role-motivation theory applies in bureaucratic organizations. The boundaries of the theory can be interpreted as situational moderators of the effects of managerial role motivation.

The studies by Megargee and by Miner illustrate the fruitfulness of considering trait by situational interactions. Let us now return to the conclusions drawn by Stogdill based on his 1948 and 1970 reviews. Stogdill concluded that there is a set of task-related characteristics and a set of social characteristics associated with effective leadership.

The leader is characterized by a strong drive for responsibility and task completion, vigor and persistence in pursuit of goals, venturesomeness and originality in problem solving, drive to exercise, initiative in social situations, self-confidence and sense of personal identity, willingness to accept consequences of decision and action, readiness to absorb interpersonal stress, willingness to tolerate frustration and delay, ability to influence other persons' behavior, and capacity to structure social interaction systems to the purpose at hand (Stogdill 1974, 81).

It may be concluded that these clusters of characteristics differentiate (1) leaders from followers, (2) effective from ineffective leaders, and (3) higher echelon from lower echelon leaders. In other words, different strata of leaders and followers can be described in terms of the extent to which they exhibit some of the preceding characteristics (Stogdill 1974, 81).

If one considers the nature of leadership activity, it seems to me that it becomes clear why these classes of traits make theoretical sense. Leadership is a social activity involving informal or formal status differences between the leader and the follower, usually face-to-face communication, exertion of social as well as informational influence, usually but not always involving relationships between a leader and a group of subordinates or between a leader and a number of individuals in multiple dyads. Given this description of the leadership process, it seems to me that it is obvious that several traits should be theoretically predictive of emergent and effective leadership.

First, leadership always takes place with respect to others. Therefore, social skills are likely always to be needed if attempted influence acts are to be viewed as acceptable by followers. Such skills as speech fluency and such traits as personal integrity, cooperativeness, and sociability are thus prime candidates for the status of leadership traits.

Second, leadership requires a predisposition to be influential. Therefore, such traits as dominance or ascendance, need for influence (Ulman 1972), and need for power (McClelland 1961) are also likely to be associated with leadership.

Third, leadership almost always takes place with respect to specific task objectives or organizational goals. Consequently, such traits as need for achievement, initiative, tendency to assume personal responsibility for outcomes, desire to excel, and task-relevant ability are also associated with leadership.

Leadership Behavioral Research

It is my contention that we also know a fair amount about the specific leader behaviors that contribute to leader effectiveness, leader success, effective decision making, and followers' satisfaction and performance. Although space limitations prohibit a detailed explication of the state of knowledge with respect to leader behavior, I am willing to assert that the leader behaviors listed in table 14–1 usually, but not always, have a positive effect on the normal criterion variables associated with leadership. These leader behaviors are leader initiating structure (as measured by Form XII of the Ohio State

Table 14–1
Leader Behavior and Relevant Theories

Behaviors	Relevant Theories	Author
Initiation of structure, consideration, path-goal clarification	Path-goal theory, substitutes theory, LEFI theory	House 1971, Kerr and Jermier 1978
Goal emphasis, goal setting, contingent reward and punishment	Substitutes theory, LEFI theory	Kerr and Jermier 1978, Wofford 1983
Participation	Vroom-Yetton theory	Vroom and Yetton 1973
Use of intelligence and experience	Human resource utilization theory	Fiedler 1985
Leader-member exchange	Vertical dyadic theory	Graen 1978
Leader goal contributions	Idiosyncracy theory	Hollander 1960
Ideological goal articulation showing high confidence and performance expectation, role modeling, goal articulation, and motive-arousing behaviors	Charismatic and transformational theory	House 1976, Avolio and Bass, this book Sashkin and Fulmer, this book

Leader Behavior Description Questionnaire), leader consideration, leader expectations toward followers, participative decision making, goal emphasis and goal setting, contingent reward and punishment, path-goal and role clarification, ideological goal articulation, role modeling behavior, and leader expressions of confidence in followers.

These behaviors have been shown in a number of studies to be positively related to leadership criterion variables such as turnover, satisfaction, leader emergence, leader effectiveness, and work group performance and cohesiveness.

The magnitude of the correlation between these behaviors and criterion variables varies between 0.3 and 0.5. I would expect that multiple correlations combining the effects of several of these behaviors would be in the range of 0.5 or better. Thus there is a very practical body of knowledge with respect to leader behavior. It is practical in the sense that such knowledge can be used to guide leadership selection, development, and placement endeavors. I believe it would be practically useful for all leaders to have these behaviors in their repertoire.

Situational Moderators

There are several ways in which situational variables interact with traits and with behaviors to produce effects that are different from the main effects described previously. First, situational factors arouse specific motives. Second, such factors provide guidance, constraints, and reinforcement for both leaders and followers. Path-goal theory (House 1971), leadership sub-stitutes theory (Kerr and Jermier 1978), and a recent extension of path-goal theory, the leader environment follower interaction theory (LEFI theory) (Wofford and Srinivasan 1983), all assert that situational variables can serve as substitutes for leadership. That is, to the extent that followers obtain either guidance or satisfaction from situational factors, such followers will not need guidance or support from leaders. To the extent that the task is intrinsically motivational, or to the extent that reward and punishment con-tingencies are clear and consistently applied by system factors as in the case of piece-work, the leaders' efforts to motivate followers is unnecessary. Thus, the task or the system can serve as substitutes for leadership with respect to motivation.

With respect to arousal, it has been demonstrated repeatedly that need for achievement and need for power are arousable by situational stimuli in laboratory experiments. The need for achievement is aroused by social cues that imply that the task is a measure of excellence and presents the individual with an opportunity to achieve an objective above and beyond that which has been achieved in the past. Need for power is aroused by social cues that threaten the individual, illustrate the application of power, or by circum-stances that permit the individual to engage in the exercise of power. The study by Megargee and his associates, cited previously, demonstrates that situational cues that make salient issues of leadership, control, or influence arouse the dominance need.

The constraining effect of situational factors is illustrated by Miner's theory and findings with respect to the conditions under which the theory applies. Other substitutes for leadership have been described and empirically verified by Kerr and Jermier (1978).

Situational stress has been shown to moderate the relationship between intelligence and/or experience and leader effectiveness. Fiedler (1985) has shown how stress moderates the relationship between leader LPC and sub-ordinate performance. Fiedler's findings demonstrate that under conditions of high stress individuals rely on experience to guide their behavior. Under conditions of low stress individuals rely on intelligence. Finally, loss of situa-tional control, or inability to influence others, has been shown to cause indi-viduals with high needs for power to experience signficiantly more stress than individuals with low need for power.

Thus, as with traits and with leader behaviors, there is a rather long list of situational factors that have been shown to moderate relationships between traits and behavior or between leader behavior and effects.

Current Theories

Thus far we have identified a number of traits, a number of behaviors, and a number of situational factors that moderate relationships between traits, behaviors, and relevant criterion variables. What is obviously needed is a theory, or a number of theories, that deal with these variables in a more integrative and parsimonious manner.

Gary Yukl's book (Yukl 1981) goes a long way toward accomplishing this. There are also a number of less ambitious theories. These theories are listed in table 14–1. The theories are listed beside the relevant behavioral dimensions to which they refer. These theories have been tested and show a substantial amount of promise. In addition to the theories listed here, there also is Fiedler's contingency theory, which specifies the relationship between leader and preferred coworker, a personality trait, and group performance. Recent meta analyses have demonstrated that Fiedler's hypothesized bow-shaped curve relating LPC to performance has been empirically established and is quite generalizable across both laboratory and field studies (Fiedler 1985).

Hollander's theory of idiosyncrasy credits also deserves mentioning. Although this theory was originally published in 1960, and has since been somewhat forgotten by current writers, it has been the subject of a number of studies that have shown support (House and Baetz 1979).

Path-goal theory, substitutes theory, and LEFI theory are essentially of the same class and deal with the effect of the leader on the follower welfare or performance under conditions where situational factors moderate the relationship between leader behavior and follower performance. This class of theory essentially argues that it is the role of the leader to compliment the situation such that the follower has sufficient guidance and support to carry out his or her work.

Participation theory, authored by Vroom and Yetton (1973), deals with a different dependent variable than the preceding theories and therefore is not in competition with them.

Charismatic leadership (House 1977) and transformational leadership (this book, ch. 3) deal with different independent and dependent variables from those discussed previously. The dependent variables and performance beyond expectations, extremely heightened motivation, involvement in the mission, trust in the leader, and follower self-esteem. The independent variables are leader's show of expectations toward followers, leader's show of confidence in followers, leader's articulation of ideological goals, and role modeling of values. This class of theory attempts to explain why some leaders are not merely effective but rather are "great leaders." Finally, the human resource utilization theory offered by Fiedler (1985) relates the leader's use of intelligence and experience, in interaction with situational factors, to predict small group performance.

Although there is certainly room for integration of the propositions of the several theories, each purports to explain a different aspect of the leadership phenomenon and therefore these theories are not in direct competition with each other. It is interesting to note that with the exception of Hollander's idiosyncrasy theory, all of these theories have been developed within the last fifteen years. To me this is a promising sign because it indicates that the study of leadership has become less characterized by dust bowl empiricism or exploratory investigations and more characterized by theoretical analyses coupled with empiric testing.

Can Leadership Be Studied within the Scientific Paradigm?

The third contentious issue I wish to address concerns whether the leadership phenomenon can be studied scientifically. Some argue that the social sciences are qualitatively different from physical sciences and for that reason it is not possible to study social behavior using the physical science paradigm. I would argue that when studying at the genotypic level, the physical and social sciences are not qualitatively different. For example, there is substantial evidence that the need for achievement is a learned phenomenon, but that once learned it operates the same way in multiple cultures. McClelland has demonstrated this with respect to underdeveloped nations (McClelland 1961). He was able to predict the industrial development of a number of nations using measures of need for achievement expressed in children's storybooks.

There are also a number of studies from several different nations that illustrate that stress induces authoritarianism and induces expectations by followers to accept authoritarian leaders. This finding has been demonstrated in a number of western societies (Mulder, Ritsema, and De Jong 1970; Mulder and Stemerding 1963; Sales 1972). However, the effects of stress have not been demonstrated to date, in eastern societies. It would be interesting to follow this line of research to see whether the phenomenon described previously is culture bound. It is my belief that the closer we get to the study of physiological variables, the more likely we are to be studying at the genotypic level. However, I do not believe we are necessarily restricted to physiological phenomena to study at the genotypic level.

One criticism of research in the social sciences is that the objects of research, namely people, are reactive. The argument is that when we observe an individual, that individual changes as a result of the observation and therefore a valid measurement cannot be obtained. This argument is correct if the individuals under study are aware of the phenomenon being studied. That is, it is possible that individuals may respond to questionnaires or interviews by giving socially desirable answers which do not reflect their own behavior, perceptions, or attitudes. Psychologists figured that out a long time ago and refined the practice of writing cover stories. Psychologists are very good playwriters; they are scriptwriters; they lie to their subjects; the subjects do not know what is being observed. This practice allows psychologists to get at the phenomenon of study without having a reaction on the part of the subject. But we cannot do this all of the time and should not do it at all some of the time. There are ethical limitations.

An alternative to lying to subjects concerns unobtrusive measurement. To the extent that individuals can be observed without knowing that they are being observed, or to the extent that the product of their behavior can be identified in the form of traces or accretions, it is possible to measure without affecting the object of study.

Finally, it is possible to find ways to discount the effects of observation on the subject. Psychologists do this when they use lie scales or social desirability scales. If the lie scale indicates that the respondent is not telling the truth, then the respondent's data can be either discounted or eliminated from the study. Social desirability scales give the researcher an estimate of the degree to which individuals are biased toward giving socially desirable answers. The social desirability score can then be used as a moderator variable or a weighting variable to increase the amount of variance in dependent variables accounted for. This is not different from what is done in physics. If a physicist wants to take the temperature of a body of water, the physicist will insert a thermometer into it. If the physicist wants to be precise, he or she will take the temperature of the thermometer first, and then measure the body of water, discounting the measurement by the initial temperature of the thermometer. Although our methods of controlling for subject reactivity are still crude, they have been shown to be extremely useful in social science research.

The Role of Qualitative Research

Qualitative research is the fourth and final contentious issue to be examined. It can be used for many reasons beyond the scientific paradigm. Qualitative research can and should be used to develop case studies for instruction, to illustrate or describe conflict, control, and suppression for emancipatory purposes, to describe to organizations how they operate, or to describe to society how organizations operate. Such studies are socially relevant and I believe should not be discouraged in any way. In the following discussion, I am not referring to such studies; however I am referring to the use of qualitative research within the scientific paradigm only.

Within the scientific paradigm qualitative research is most effectively used when we have little knowledge about the phenomenon under study. Under these conditions is is necessary to allow the environment to teach us because we do not have an adequate framework, we do not have hypotheses, we do not have a clear idea as to what the critical variables are, and we have little ability to measure them. Observation, interviews, critical incidents, and historical analyses are especially relevant at this stage of the development of a body of knowledge. These qualitative methods have been used effectively in the past for purposes of generating hypotheses, specifying variables, and providing rich and detailed insights concerning the subject.

Another occasion that frequently calls for qualitative research concerns unexpected results from prior research. When prior research generates inconsistent findings or dilemmas, qualitative research can give us insights into the causes of such inconsistencies.

Qualitative research can be used to elaborate quantitative findings. If I assert that the relationship between path-goal clarification and subordinate performance is moderated by task structure, one might ask what the qualitative nature of path-goal clarification is. That is, what do people do when they engage in this behavior? How do they act toward subordinates? How do they use their nonverbal behavior? What do we mean by task structure? What are the structuring aspects of the task that cause people to respond to questionnaires by saying such things as, "My task is predictable, I know what to do, it is highly structured, I do not have to rely on instructions from others." These questions might be better answered by qualitative interviewing and observation. This may give us insights into the nature of path-goal clarification and task structure that cannot be gained by quantitative research.

Qualitative research can be used to illustrate generalizations for expository or for teaching purposes. One can pick a number of instances of a generalization and develop scenarios to explain how the generalization operates.

Qualitative research is also useful in operationalizing variables in a rigorous manner. We cannot really operationalize variables like task structure without observing tasks. We cannot sit in our laboratories or in our offices and write questionnaire items and be sure that we have an adequately descriptive scale. We need to interview and observe. We need to make up some items, feed them back to the people whom we interviewed, and ask them whether the items reflect what we intended them to mean.

Finally, qualitative research is useful in the development of technologies. In order to translate theories of leader behavior into statements that are meaningful to laypersons, it is necessary to use scenarios, role-playing exercises, management simulations, and/or introspective exercises. Such teaching technologies require that the developer of the technology have enriched knowledge of the way in which the theory operates. Such knowledge is likely to be gained by qualitative research.

I see the role of qualitative research as quite important in the development of the social sciences. There is both bad qualitative and bad quantitative research in our literature. It seems to me that we need to develop a set of norms to guide us in conducting qualitative research. Such a set of norms is already developed and in place for quantitative research. Without such norms, we will not have criteria on which to judge the research as adequate or not. Other social sciences or non-physical science-based disciplines have to some extent developed norms for qualitative research. Journalism requires that the writer obtain corroborating evidence for any statement that the writer claims to be true. Law requires that attorneys develop their arguments on the basis of evidence rather than theories or polemics alone. Some anthropologists engage in back-translation when they describe a society. They go into a society, try to picture and describe what is going on, write it down, put it into the language of the natives, and ask the natives if the account is accurate. Although there is some controversy over this method, it is an example of the use of a rigorous standard against which to measure the acceptability of qualitative research. It is a rigorous check and it is still qualitative.

I see the possibility of qualitative research being rigorous. I do not see why it has to be casual or uncontrolled observation. Although it is harder to have controls for qualitative research, I believe it is not impossible. I would further be more tolerant of less controls in qualitative than quantitative research.

Conclusion

In conclusion I would like to stress my belief that the study of leadership has yielded a number of empirically supported generalizations and a number of promising theories. I am optimistic about the future. I see promise and progress in leadership research and theory.

15
Constraints on the Emergence of New Vistas in Leadership and Management Research: An Epistemological Overview

H. Peter Dachler

Such metaphors as "emerging leadership vistas," "the cutting edge," "new frontiers," and "beyond establishment views" have been included in the titles of many of the recent leadership symposia books. These offer a promise of breaking out of established boundaries, if not conceptual prisons, and of coming closer to making the dream of exploring new leadership territory a reality. On the one hand, this obligates us to think about what it means to dream of new directions in leadership research and about freedom from establishment views regarding leadership and management.[1] On the other hand, the implied promise of outlining new vistas of leadership in this book requires questioning whether we have been able to construct new vistas of leadership and management insights or not. Perhaps the promise may be but a dream, a myth that has more to do with marketing considerations for the distribution of the book than with demonstrating viable alternative insights about the meaning of the obviously ambiguous notions regarding leadership and management anchored in our culture.

Some Thoughts on the Meaning of Scientific Progress and New Directions in Leadership

Science Based upon a Realist Ontology

From the chapters in this book at least two major conceptions are discernible of the outcomes we can imagine when new vistas or new directions are sought and what is meant by progress in leadership conceptions and research. These

I am very much indebted to my colleagues Klaus Bartölke, Ken Gergen, Gareth Morgan, Gilbert Probst, Ben Schneider, and Linda Smircich for their insightful comments and helpful suggestions. I also gained much from the often critical discussion of an earlier draft of this chapter with my colleagues Emil Walter-Busch, Thomas Dyllick, and Rüdiger Klimecki during a doctoral seminar that I conducted together with them.

two conceptions are in fact based on very different assumptions about the nature of the scientific enterprise.

Without much elaboration of the fairly extensive literature on this topic (e.g., Burrell and Morgan 1979, Feyerabend 1976, Gergen 1982, Habermas 1971, 1973, Kuhn 1970, Morgan 1983), some of the chapters in this book are based on the positivistic, empiricist tradition of social science scholarship. This perspective of science, on the basis of which scientific progress is evaluated and criteria are established for defining "new directions" in leadership, basically adheres to the ontological assumption that the reality to be investigated is concrete and objective in its structure and process (Morgan and Smircich 1980).

Leadership and management, whether these phenomena are culture produced or emerge on the basis of inherited individual differences that preordain some individuals as leaders, are seen as a reality that exists "out there," as an "object" separate from the scientist who observes "leadership." However the scientist decides to observe leadership, on a micro or macro level, with a narrow or broad focus, he or she does so independently of the object of observation, in order to get a better picture of the facts inherent in leadership and management.

The main task of leadership researchers according to this paradigm (well articulated in House's overview chapter in this book) is to search for facts, for *natural* facts, since a fact is only a fact by being "unambiguously" informed through the concrete and objective leadership reality. There are only "facts as natural objects" (Krippendorff 1985, 6) which allow for manipulation through various analysis methods in order to discover true or valid insights about the leadership phenomena "out there."

Within this reigning perspective true insights as opposed to subjective, contaminated, illusion-based, and value-riddled prejudgments are objective because the observer is separated through all our methodological sophistication from what is observed. Thus we are informed by a priori and physically independently existing facts inherent in the leadership phenomena "out there."

At the same time, within this perspective, seeking new vistas of leadership means the discovery of new facts and of new relationships among the facts. The goal implied by searching for new frontiers is to find new points of view based on additional variables or new combinations of variables. The hope for a resulting better understanding of leadership is coupled with the hope that the improved understanding may provide a means for improved prediction and control of an already predefined and objectively existing leadership and management reality.

Scientific progress, therefore, means the accumulation of isolated facts. Attempts are made to aggregate these facts within the ever-increasing complexity of their interrelationships, in order to move closer to the ontological goal of knowing as completely as possible the "real" nature of leadership and management. The question "what is leadership" is answered through the authority of science.

Science Informed by the Meaning-based
Construction in the Observation Process

A second set of chapters in this book to a greater or lesser degree is embedded in different ontological assumptions. This set of assumptions regarding the nature of the scientific enterprise provides a different basis for evaluating the meaning of scientific progress and for defining what is meant by seeking new directions in leadership research. In contrast to the "realist" concerns (Burrell and Morgan 1979) of the traditional paradigm whose focus is on the question of what leadership is in the world "out there," there is an emerging set of assumptions about the nature of science.

The main focus is on epistemological processes in leadership research. Of interest in this perspective in general are the processes by which we come to *know* leadership and management phenomena. The ontological emphasis is on leadership as something that cannot be known independently and "outside" of the scientific observer. In this sense it does not exist previous to the act of observation, and it does not inform the observer objectively.

On the contrary, in line with what people like Neisser (1976) or Piaget (1970) have shown for cognition and Krippendorff (1985) or Watzlawick, Beavin, and Jackson (1967) have demonstrated for communication processes, Varela (1984) has suggested for visual perception, and Hanson (1958), or Von Foerster (1981) have suggested about the process of observation in scientific inquiry, "seeing" and being informed require an active construction of the reality of leadership by the observers. As a consequence, what is "seen" is the leadership reality we as leadership observers have constructed.

House's contribution to this book, for example, provides an upbeat review of "truths" about leadership. He assigns these remarkable accomplishments to the careful empirical accumulation of objective facts. What House seems to overlook, however, is the fact that as members of our culture we define and ask questions sensible in the context of the way our culture has evolved the concept of leadership.

More specifically, he clearly neglects to consider that within the "realist" leadership paradigm, we reduce the inherent ambiguity of leadership processes: to those aspects that fit our dominant everyday theoretical *pre*conceptions; and to what our methodological capabilities define as acceptable. What we accept as objective facts are then actually nothing more than what we have collectively constructed within our discipline in the context of our culture.

Thus, only questions sensible to the constructed leadership reality are asked and, therefore, only answers are possible within the domain of the general assumptions that guide the questions. Other, potentially equally informing questions are not asked, and a wide range of possible answers are made unavailable. That is precisely what reality construction entails. It is this unavoidable process that renders the concept of an objective reality to be discovered "out there" at best a "half truth," if not a myth!

To avoid misunderstandings, it is important to emphasize that the issue raised here is not one of truth or falsity regarding what we have so far constructed as the scientifically "discovered" leadership reality. The concern is to question the concept of an objective leadership reality which through natural facts informs our knowledge.

For example, it is astounding the degree to which the review of "true" leadership traits in House's chapter is a description, nearly a caricature, of the dominating, competitive, aggressive, manipulating, and achievement-driven male. The "problem" of women as leaders, for example, is then a problem because male traits as predictors of effective leadership are so unquestioningly accepted as the objective "God-given" reality.

The historical or evolutionary "accident" of male dominance is one of many possible social constructions, and evidence of a different reality within the social situation of female leadership is beginning to emerge. For instance, an investigation of Swiss female chief executives suggests that, at least in this cultural context, women top managers are effective and successful by approaching leadership problems much more holistically than is implied by the analytical and competitive processes inherent in the "true" leadership traits and behaviors reviewed by House (Preuss 1986).

The dominance of male leadership researchers within a culture where leadership is already constructed in the image of the male, must result in the prevalence of questions regarding "male" traits as opposed to other possible aspects of people we think of as leaders. What narratives about the characteristics of leaders (cf. Calas and Smircich in this book) would our literature contain if we asked questions about whether managers are afraid or lack courage (Kanter 1984), cooperate, rather than compete (Kohn 1986), or frame problems according to the way they interpret themselves and their social context (Smith and Simmons 1983).

And what kind of image or mental map of a leader would be implied by such questions in contrast to the "macho-male" picture that seems to underlie House's literature review of "true" leadership traits? Interestingly, within the currently hot topic of organizational culture, leaders seem suddenly to be seen not so much as competitive, achievement-driven, and task-oriented, but as managers of meaning and symbols (Pfeffer 1981), as people who help create visions and resist an addiction to established procedure and current consensus (Schein 1985).

Is it reasonable to say that such different "knowledge" about the characteristics of leaders is informed by a different or changed objective reality? Or is it possible that, based upon different perspectives implied by the concept of organizational culture and its implicit assumptions regarding the nature of people and social systems, a different *pre*conception of leaders emerges which now makes sensible a whole set of questions that could not be asked meaningfully within the traditional leadership perspective?

Thus, what House in his overview sees as established knowledge of leadership is not an objective and value-free "known" reality. It is a reflection of what leadership research as a discipline in the context of western cultures has constructed as its reality, which is but one of many possible leadership realities that could be imagined.

Leadership research is both cause and consequence of observation. This is an issue which systems-generated epistemology refers to as self-referential (cf. Von Foerster 1981, Krippendorff 1985, Luhmann 1977, Spencer-Brown 1979, Varela 1975). Not any constructed reality of leadership is sensible or useful. As Krippendorff (1985, 22) suggests, "we know nothing about reality external to us except when our constructions fail in some respects." The empirical referent of constructed realities is a crucially important issue to be raised in this context. However, for the point I am raising here it may suffice to refer the reader to writers such as Bateson (1972), Gergen (1982), Von Glasersfeld (1981, 1984), and Krippendorff (1985).

The desire to seek new leadership vistas and the criteria to evaluate scientific progress in leadership and management research takes on a different meaning within an epistemology that acknowledges explicitly the social and subjective processes of interpretation when observing reality. This alternative epistemological "paradigm" is emerging in various corners of the social sciences. It is based upon a fundamental dissatisfaction with and realization of the untenable root assumptions on which the empiricist position is based.

Thus the title of *Emerging Leadership Vistas* must be taken in its literal sense. The metaphor of "vistas" refers to perceptual, conceptual, and interpretation processes. It does not imply a search for new variables and new relationships among "facts" delivered by an observer independent and value-free—that is, objective leadership reality. Rather, it implies a search involving a systematic questioning of the processes by which we see and know.

The aim is to understand the processes by which we learn to understand ourselves as researchers, as an organized social system in search of the meaning of leadership in its socially constructed context. New vistas or perspectives imply a fundamental change in the basic assumptions made about ourselves as observers and our interactions with what we observe. New leadership and management vistas also imply a fundamental change in the basic assumptions we make about the phenomena of leadership and management and the contexts in which they unfold their attributes and consequences.

Also, with respect to criteria of progress in leadership research, the "social construction" paradigm leads to different conclusions than the "objective reality" perspective of science. Rather than thinking of knowledge as an increasingly accurate map of an objective territory that is knowable without valuation and interpretation, the social construction perspective accepts the existence of multiple realities. Some of these realities are experienced as more viable or meaningful than others.

The issue is not that one constructed reality will ultimately prove to be the "correct" or objective one, that exists apart from our values and preconceptions. The issue is to understand the way different leadership realities are constructed. Such construction involves understanding the various and complex social-political processes by which some constructions are retained as sensible and useful whereas others in the context of different social and historical events begin to lose their interpretative usefulness.

Fundamental to this perspective of scientific progress is that knowledge is dynamic. Based on complex cultural-social-political processes, different constructions of realities emerge, serve as means of interpreting the world, and contribute to the emergence of a social order. They often disappear again as the patterns and substance of relationships in a society or in some collectivity change.

Understanding leadership does not progress to an ultimate and objective truth. Understanding leadership and management is a continuous and unpredictable pattern of emerging constructions of realities. Through the emerging patterns of new reality constructions, the complexity of the social situations can be interpreted, reinterpreted, and found meaningful within given contexts. Alternatively, such complexity can be found useless or meaningless for the interpretations of a constructed social order.

Within such an epistemological perspective it becomes a crucial concern to question the implicit assumptions that are made: about the process of gaining knowledge, about the nature of man and social institutions, and about leadership and management in particular. It is then on the basis of finding certain assumptions wanting in light of changed social realities that new assumptions can be generated that provide new constructions of leadership and management.

The crucial concern of this overview is to draw attention to the fallacy that fundamental new directions, new constructions of the way in which we "see" leadership and management, can be developed without basic questioning of the meaningfulness of our root assumptions and investigation of the way in which we come to know through the process of inquiry.

I count myself among those who are very concerned about the debilitating constraints of the empiricist tradition in leadership research. Because I cannot see how the increasingly vociferous critique regarding the relevance of traditional leadership theory and research can be met effectively within the traditional empiricist construction of leadership reality, I focus my overview on: (1) the extent to which this book has produced some new leadership vistas, or at least first steps in that direction; (2) what some of the constraints might be that discourage the use of our imaginative potential in constructing and making more explicit alternative leadership and management realities; and, (3) what our ethical responsibilities as leadership and management researchers might be by adhering to the traditional construction of leadership or by constructing alternative leadership and management realities.

Emerging Leadership Vistas and Their Constraining Assumptions

Basically, my thesis is that there are clearly some emerging leadership vistas recognizable in various chapters in this book. However, the potential of constructing new leadership and management realities on the basis of these emerging perspectives is constrained by currently insufficient analysis of the underlying assumptions. Many of these remain entrenched in the existing "realist" leadership paradigm.

Thus, the possibility is reduced of realizing some new leadership realities from the emerging vistas. Such realities might provide a different and perhaps more relevant perspective for the complexity of the "problems" our societies are facing. I would like to review the nature of these constraints, then discuss the emerging leadership vistas. Finally, I will try to illustrate the extent to which some of these constraints may hinder the full realization of some of the emerging leadership vistas presented in this book.

Constraints on Emerging Leadership Vistas

We can distinguish three basic sets of constraints inherent in the seldom explicitly stated root assumptions that guide to a greater or lesser extent the development of the conceptual basis underlying most of the chapters in this book.

Natural Mental Properties of the Individual as the Basic Unit of Analysis in Leadership Research. There are two basic and widely held assumptions in current leadership and management research that are of concern here. One is that for any question regarding leadership or management phenomena the basic unit of analysis is some individual. This is so regardless of the questions asked: about attributes or behaviors of either a designated or emergent leader, about questions concerned with followers, or about moderating or direct effects on leadership of certain "distilled" variables from the complex environment.

A second assumption is that the individual as the main unit of analysis is of prime concern because individuals possess natural mental elements which causally determine their behavior and thus their leadership or management effectiveness. Although the first assumption is accepted readily and understood within most of this literature, the second assumption has only recently been reintroduced. It has been brought back into the consciousness of the research community by writers such as Gergen (1984a, 1984b, 1982, 1985), Mummendey (1984), and Shotter (1975) and may require some elaboration.

All of the concepts about individual attributes that have been used in leadership chapters in this book are hypothetical constructs. They are linguistic constructions, interpretative symbols that have been invented to stand for or make sense of certain experiences that we have defined to be of some significance within certain leadership contexts. It is understandable that the ontology of such mental constructs is tied to what is phenomenologically given, to systematic observation and logical inference.

Although the hypothetical nature of mental traits is readily recognized in leadership research, it is commonly accepted that psychological conditions are a result of drawing inferences from careful and systematic observation. With accumulating research we learn to infer the existence of various needs, motives, goals, intentions, and predispositions of leaders or managers. For example, Gergen (1982) shows clearly that in principle there are various reasons why our linguistic constructions of mental traits cannot be anchored in or constrained by observation. For instance, any identification of some action is subject to infinite kinds of revisions, depending on the narrowness or breadth of the retrospective as well as emergent context in which some action has been observed. There are no empirical absolutes on the basis of which one can decide in which context some action is to be identified as an indicant of some trait assumed to be possessed by an actor.

Furthermore, any action is subject to multiple identifications. There are no empirical criteria on the basis of which one could decide that some action is more appropriately designated as "supportive" as opposed to "manipulative," for example (cf. Gergen 1982, ch. 2). Finally, mental categories frequently have been shown to reflect cultural ideologies and various indications of historical and cultural variations in the assumed contents of mind help show the cultural relativity of mental assumptions (Gergen 1985).

The concern raised here is twofold. First, it is doubtful whether leadership traits and behavioral tendencies can be unambiguously identified by careful and systemic observation, as if leaders possessed natural mental traits. Second, there is mounting evidence that people's attributes may be part of a linguistic process in which the actor and the observers interepret the social context and cultural rules that govern the network of relationships in which an actor is embedded (Gergen 1984a, 1984b; Smith 1982).

Consistent with arguments made by Austin (1962) and Searle (1970), Gergen (1984b, 3), for example, maintains that, "mental talk is largely performative—that is, it does not mirror or map an independent reality but is a functioning element in social process itself." What Gergen tries to show is that in an attempt to make sense of and deal with the daily social relations, a language of psychological dispositions emerges:

> Such a language is necessitated by the human incapacity to cement linguistic integers to the proteanlike activity of the human body. As this language of dispositions is expanded and reified, the "inner value" of psychology becomes an accepted reality, part of the common sense world of daily relations (Gergen 1985, 119).

A convincing explanation of how the construction of mental elements develops is certainly missing. However, there seems to be sufficient reason to begin questioning the usefulness of the traditional assumption that interpretative linguistic symbols such as intelligence, motives, needs, trustworthiness, and cognitive schemata are indicative of natural mental elements individuals possess.

As we look through many of the contributions to this book or read House's overview chapter, the traditional implicit assumption is clearly recognizable. Certain traits characterize "effective" leaders as do certain behavioral repertoires, which we have come to label as "task-oriented" or "employee-oriented," for example. These are assumed to be inherent properties of the individuals on whom such mental elements are "measured," as if they are natural attributes such as height or weight. Based on a systematic questioning of the traditional assumptions underlying the individual trait approach to leadership and management and within the emergent alternative assumptions regarding the ontology of psychological dispositions briefly outlined previously, we can construct a rather different perspective of leadership and management. Rather than thinking of leadership and management as individual phenomena, we could conceptualize this perspective as a product of complex social relationships. Such accounts of leadership processes may possess enormous potential that has been largely overlooked.

As an example, Smith (1982) and Kanter and Stein (1979) show convincingly the very different realities constructed by groups that take up different positions within a power hierarchy (i.e. uppers, middles, and lowers). As these "groups" interact with each other and as individuals interact within groups they actively construct their own reality vis-à-vis other groups. All are in the context of a constructed social order.

These insights applied to leadership phenomena could raise the question of the degree to which upper management constructs a reality of subordinates as those with lesser qualities, knowledge, or experience. To what extent is the construction of this reality of groups in lower power positions a part of self-referential interaction circles through which subordinates are "kept" somewhat incompetent so that they actually see themselves as always having too little information, for example?

Through this construction of reality imposed on subordinates, managers legitimatize withholding information because it cannot be understood effectively and handled by the less "competent." Such constructions make it appear rational to usurp more power. Alternatively, managers may jealously guard the status quo of power and influence differential for the benefit of helping, guiding, and controlling in management's eyes those who are in some ways less competent.

Thus, mental elements of managers and subordinates emerge on the basis of relations and the meaning such relations have within the context of social systems. Mental elements in this view are not determined by some identifiable "outside" factor and thus "possessed" by individuals. They are complex indicants and symbols of reality constructions that emerge from relationships. It seems very difficult to explain under the assumption of natural individual dispositions the processes by which: (1) some social order is constructed; and (2) structurally differentiated groups emerge who proceed to perceive each other's "qualifications" within constructed realities that become operative through the relationships inherent in or constitutive of social order.

The meaning of such constructed "qualifications" must be explainable on the basis of the interactive relationships that direct their own processes. Relationships, not individuals and their natural mental properties, should be our main unit of analysis in leadership and management research. This brings me to the second constraint on the emergence of new leadership vistas.

Social Systems as Monocentrically Controlled and Designed Aggregates of Individuals. Leadership and management as concepts are meaningless outside the context of a social system. The assumptions made about the nature of organized human collectiveness are essential to any understanding of leadership or management phenomena. Nevertheless, much current leadership and management research is undertaken without explicitly and critically analyzing the theoretical assumptions invariably made about the larger social context giving leadership and management their constitutive meanings, What are the main implicit assumptions about the larger organizational and cultural context underlying most current leadership conceptions?

As argued earlier, in the majority of leadership and management research the individual and his or her natural properties usually serve as the basic unit of analysis. The consequent assumptions regarding the nature of social systems as wholes are in one way or another based on aggregations of individuals and their natural mental properties. Leaders as individuals are either: (1) predefined on the basis of their particular positions in some existing hierarchical structure; or (2) in the case of emergent leaders, individuals are defined as leaders on the basis of some characteristic indicative of superiority relative to the attributes or resources of others.

The questions implied in such a construction of leadership imply some of the following assumptions about social systems:

1. They represent some form of weighted sum of attributes of individuals.

2. They have a structure based upon differentiated realities of "competence" and consequently differentiated kinds and amounts of resources and influencing potential.

3. They are controlled, designed, and changed monocentrically by some powerful individual or coalition within a given structure, usually at the top.

4. They have objectives and goals existing a priori to the development of means for goal achievement on the basis of rational analysis by some powerful individual or coalition.

5. They have problems and consequently decision contents that exist objectively; that is, on the basis of the nature of the objective observer-actor independently existing in organizational and environmental reality.

The preceding is only an oversimplified summary of a complex set of assumptions about social systems necessary if the kinds of conceptions of leadership and management contained in many of the chapters of this book are to make sense. Space constraints do not allow a more detailed analysis of these implicit assumptions. Later, I will show some of the underlying social system assumptions in selected chapters and their possible constraining effects on the emergence of new vistas.

Given the previous arguments about the constraining effects of the "objective reality" assumptions of science and viewing individual natural elements as the main unit of analysis in leadership research, the social system assumptions outlined previously lead to serious contradictions. Many legitimate questions cannot be raised or answered within the framework of these assumptions.

The aggregation assumptions stand in contradiction to the old insight that social systems are more than the sum of their parts. We have spent hardly any effort in trying to build conceptual frameworks that take this idea seriously and look at the consequences for the way we think about the nature of social systems.

Clearly, individuals in social systems must act. They do so rationally and in goal-directed ways. Contrary to the idea that individuals' dispositions represent the final objective reality to be inferred from their actions, their behavior is a consequence of as well as an input to the way they interpret themselves and the context in which they act. This constructed reality emerges from the usually intertwined relations actors have with other people as well as with objects and value—or ideological systems. Thus actions are embedded in constructed realities in which certain goals become meaningful or sensible whereas others do not. Their rationality is informed by the constructed reality imposed on their experiences.

Rather than goals being a reflection of natural mental properties such as needs, motives, and values, goals are a reflection of the interwoven relationships in which people enact and interpret the meaning of the reality emerging within a web of relationships (Weick 1979). The autonomous and self-referential interaction processes between management and subordinates with different constructed realities based upon the interactions between "uppers" and "lowers" lead to different interpretations of each group's needs and values. Goals constructed by the individuals in the different groups differ. They differ because of the meaning of the jointly or in interaction constructed reality.

Managers construct goals regarding design, control, and development of interaction patterns among those of assumed lesser competence. In contrast, within subordinates' constructed reality, more meaningful goals may emerge regarding search for additional information and for providing optimistic success stories to management. Selective perception and information withholding about failures may be involved. These are all action goals and intentions that provide a better interpretation of the different socially constructed realities than the notion that everyone is pulling together toward the same end.

There is considerable evidence of such "irrational" behavior on the part of employees (e.g., Whyte 1956). Rather than assuming employees are inherently less rational than managers—that is, that they possess lesser amounts of the relevant natural mental elements—a whole set of different questions become meaningful to pursue, if mental elements and their related goals and intentions are thought of as an outcropping of the nature of relationships within the overall social order constructed in our culture and in business organizations.

Within such a perspective it should be possible to understand Hayek's (1967) argument that social systems are the result of human action, but not of human design. Through multiple constructed realities that emerge on the basis of autonomous and self-referential processes inherent in the social-political multilogue in organizations, yet unbracketed flows of events and information are differentially punctated, to use Weick's (1979a) terminology.

Thus, the nature of the social system, its structure, its goals, its actions, is not the direct result of any particular monocentrically thinking and acting powerful person or coalition. It is something that emerges: (1) from the interpretations and actions of many complexly interdependent individuals; and

(2) from "self-organizing" and self-referential processes whose "output" cannot in principle be the linear sum of the actions and attributes of the participants.

The structure of an organization cannot be seen only as a rational means (that is, based upon known causal and objective determinants) toward some predefined goals. The structure or social order of a social system is also a constructed reality. That reality is not that of some person, but of the pattern of relations that is enacted within an organization as well as with other "stakeholders" of the social system (Mitroff 1983).

For similar reasons, goals and perceived problems in need of solution, and the kinds of solutions implied by the way something is constructed as a problem, are not inherent in the objective, observer-independent reality of social systems. They are a reflection of the social reality construction processes that constitute social systems.

To summarize with the paraphrased arguments of Gergen (1984b, 15), relationships precede the ontology of the individual and the collectivity. Prior to relationships there is little sense in which there is a concept of the leader or manager as individual, that is, the independent leader-self. It is as if we have currently at our disposal a rich language for characterizing rooks, pawns, and bishops, with kings and queens as leaders. However, we have yet to discover the *game* of chess.

Leadership and Management as Applied Social Science. The third set of constraints has less to do with assumptions about leadership and management, than with the origin of what are seen as important research problems to be addressed within leadership and management phenomena. These constraints I see in some of the chapters in this book when leadership or management research is thought of as applied social science. This implies that terms, conceptions, and methods, as well as the basic problems addressed in many of the chapters, have their direct origin in some theoretical or methodological problem of interest to the *discipline of psychology.*

In contrast, one could ask, how many chapters in this book or current leadership studies in the leading journals use concepts, analogies, metaphors, or experienced leadership or management "problems" as interpreted by the actual actors in the practical world? How much leadership and management research comes from the *phenomenology* of practicing managers, politicians, third-world country leaders, or symphony conductors. How much research comes from all manner of groups directly or indirectly affected by what in our society is signified as leadership and management?

Typically we see our work as taking some isolated leadership "problem" from our culture, as for example, the ubiquitous concern with tying leadership to organizational effectiveness and small group productivity. Then we reduce it to the available theoretical frameworks, paradigm assumptions, and methods contained in the "grab bag" of psychology. The resulting construction of leadership and management phenomena must seriously be constrained. The problem again is one of self-referential processes usually ignored in the assumptions we make about how we come to "know" leadership and management phenomena.

In "applying" psychology to the culturally constructed phenomena of leadership and management, we operate under assumptions Krippendorff (1984, 23) designates as "a one-way process of communication from an unvarying and disinterested object (e.g., leaders, followers) to an intelligent and interested observer (researcher)." In other words, the researcher, based upon the prescriptions and acceptable concepts of the reigning paradigm in psychology, decides for the research subject what the relevant questions, problems, and relevant answer alternatives are (e.g., in the case of questionnaires).

Alternatively, one can imagine an inquiry process as a transdisciplinary social science of social processes constituting social systems as wholes. The origin of the questions of what is seen as something worth knowing better is no longer located in any particular theory, concept, root assumption, or method within the paradigm of *one specific discipline*.

Instead, questions emerge on the basis of a dialogue or multilogue among the constructions of those who see themselves as leaders or managers or those who are affected by them and the multiple perspectives of a transdisciplinary language which one could designate as *systems thinking* (cf. Checkland 1981, for example). Calas and Smircich (this book, ch. 12) refer to a similar issue with their concern that there is too little emphasis on understanding leadership outside the researchers' community.

Toward Realizing Emerging Leadership Vistas

I have now laid the groundwork for analyzing: (1) what new leadership vistas have emerged in the chapters of this book; and (2) whether the constraints outlined previously might prevent some of these emerging leadership vistas from becoming a more meaningful or sensible "reality" within current interpretations of our social world. There is only space for an outline and some examples of the main theses contained in the emerging perspectives.

We must distinguish between the two different kinds of interpretations of new leadership vistas on the basis of the two epistemological perspectives of leadership and management research discussed earlier. In some chapters, new "leadership vistas" are primarily based upon the traditional positivist assumptions. They describe expansions of existing leadership models through integration of additional variables (e.g., Avolio and Bass, Sashkin and Fulmer). Or they try to integrate models of leadership with specific theoretical assumptions regarding motivation (e.g., expectancy theory, Avolio and Bass) or certain aspects of organization theory (e.g., Baliga and Hunt).

These chapters implicitly accept scientific progress as getting closer to some ultimate leadership reality. Such closeness is based on the discovery of additional facts (variables) and relationships among facts (causal relationships) within an observer-independent objective leadership and management reality. Such conceptions of scientific progress strain the metaphor of "emerging leadership vistas," since they essentially ask for more of the same with respect to the fundamental root assumptions.

They will not be discussed further in any detail, especially in view of the fact that House's overview emphasizes the "realist ontology" (Burrell and Morgan 1979) of progress in leadership and management knowledge. Concerning the criteria of progress as seen from the "social construction of reality" perspective of science, several major themes are discernible and can be seen as emerging leadership vistas.

Leader and Manager Construct Meaning for the Followers. Boal and Bryson's contribution on a phenomenological and structural approach to charismatic leadership maintains that "[charismatic leaders] appear to be intimately and unusually involved in the creation of a new or different 'world'—or interpretation scheme(s)—for their followers that is cognitively, emotionally, behaviorally, and consequentially 'real' for them" (p. 3).

Avolio and Bass argue, while building upon existing models of leadership which have dealt primarily with relatively short term leader-follower relations, that they are presenting "a new paradigm of leadership" that "attempts to explain how leaders draw attention of their subordinates to an idealized goal and inspire them to reach beyond their grasp to achieve that goal" (p. 3).

Explicitly in the Boal and Bryson chapter and somewhat between the lines in the Avolio and Bass contribution is the important suggestion that leadership may have relatively little to do with direct influence on followers' specific behaviors and on their natural mental characteristics. Instead, leadership may have more of a bearing on the way people interpret themselves as well as the meaning of their work and general social world.

One could argue that the whole interest in charismatic or transformational leadership is based upon the recognition that leaders do not directly cause certain a priori defined behaviors (such as productivity). Leadership may have a bearing on such behaviors on the basis of helping people to interpret, to perceive and think about themselves and the meaning of their world.

Implicit in such arguments is that charisma is a *relational* concept, not a trait concept. Rather than speaking about some observer-independent, objective leadership and follower reality, the basic arguments underlying charismatic leadership imply that the leader, within his or her relationships with followers and relevant other groups, is part of a social construction process of the followers' reality. On the basis of that reality *he or she is interpreted as being charismatic*. Similar processes must be involved in the reality the person who is experienced as charismatic constructs for him or herself.

Boal and Bryson argue that people must see their behavior in terms of the fulfillment of some underlying purpose, meaning, or value that goes beyond the particulars of the moment, if they are to experience their leaders as charismatic. Charismatic leaders do not possess charisma as a natural mental element. They are interpreted (constructed) as charismatic out of the reality that emerges through the multilogue between people in the context of a particular social-political situation, and in which our cultural understanding of charisma seems to be a sensible conception of the nature of that reality.

Boal and Bryson, with their concept of "crisis-produced charismatic leaders," do seem to recognize that charisma may be a phenomenon that emerges within particular kinds of situations. But based upon statements, like "crisis-produced charismatic leaders handle a crisis situation through detailing the actions to be taken and the expected consequences of those actions" (p. 9), Boal and Bryson seem to be back to the implicit assumption that it is the leader who constructs reality through essentially a "monologue" from leaders to others.

The Boal and Bryson chapter clearly contains a leadership vista that in principle could question many of the traditional leadership and management assumptions. It would allow different perspectives of what is "worth" knowing in leadership and management phenomena. But if we look at the graphically illustrated frameworks in both chapters (Avolio and Bass; Boal and Bryson), for example, they still seem to contain many of the constraining assumptions discussed earlier which may hinder the full realization of a new perspective both chapters seem to pursue.

It is the leader and the leader's followers as individuals who are given additional natural mental elements, which are at least partially ignored in other leadership models. Relationships are argued on the basis of these individual properties in the same way a chemist explains chemical reactions on the basis of the properties of the interacting elements within established general laws of nature.

Furthermore, the inherent assumption regarding the monocentric-design-and-control nature of organizations allows Boal and Bryson and particularly Avolio and Bass to argue so positively that it is the inherent "superiority" of leaders or managers that enables them to construct a reality *for* the subordinates. This reality is constructed as if the relationship between leader and followers is a "one-way-street."

Finally, as is clearly evident from the terms and concepts included (and excluded) in their figures, both chapters argue on the basis of a conception of leadership and management research as applied psychology. The mutual or social interpretation processes and resulting socially constructed realities as central processes get lost within the remaining traditional implicit assumptions about individuals and organizations.

Leadership as Social Processes Constituting Social Systems. Perhaps the most potentially far-reaching and provocative leadership vista contained in this book is the idea that leadership and management are not properties of some a priori designated person whose relevance is confined to the context of the leader-subordinate influence relationship. Nor is there in this view of leadership research the discovery of some objective phenomena which are given and which inform the researcher independently of the observer's own reality constructions.

Instead, leadership and management are *social processes* defining attributes of social systems as wholes. Such wholes can be work organizations or entire cultures whose meanings change as the web of relationships constituting social systems changes. The most explicit and elaborated statements in this book about understanding leadership as processes that define social systems are made in Hosking and Morley's chapter on the skills of leadership.

They state that a truly social-psychological approach to leadership, to the skills involved in leadership and to the organizational consequences requires premises and arguments concerning the theoretically interrelated issues of participants, processes, and contexts.

Hosking and Morley base their central arguments on the assumption that "participants [are] leaders when they (1) *consistently* make *effective* contributions to social order, and (2) are both *expected* and *perceived* to do so by fellow participants." According to these authors, many people can make contributions to leadership within a particular context. What is important in the view of Hosking and Morley is the necessity to study "the process by which particular acts come to be perceived as contributions to social order and therefore, come to be perceived as leadership acts."

Thus, leadership is seen as an emergent phenomenon, not something that by definition is inherent or even constitutive of formal positions in an organizational hierarchy. Leadership processes are seen as a kind of organizing activity which the authors designate as political decision making in the widest sense. The effect is "of constructing more or less stable social orders which, in turn, are more or less effective in protecting and promoting the values [and the power relations] of the participants."

With respect to the organizational context of leadership, Hosking and Morley, since they define leadership as a special kind of organizing activity, claim that "'organization' is found in the cognitive-social and social-political processes through which leaders and groups enact, socially construct, and influence their social order, and that of interdependent others."

The previous insights come from the important recognition that very little leadership research has dealt with the inevitable embeddedness of leadership processes in the macro organizational system. Organizations have been treated as "entitative," that is in the "condition of being organized." "Organization is treated as a macro object which exists independently of the activities, interactions, and evaluations of participants."

It is on the basis of this critique of a fundamental assumption in traditional leadership research, which is in line with similar arguments in the literature (e.g., Dachler 1984, 1985a, 1985b; Meyer 1975; Smith 1982), that Hosking and Morley develop their "process" conception of organization as an integral part of leadership. Such fundamental questioning of the implicit assumptions in traditional leadership and management approaches is an absolute prerequisite for the development of alternative and perhaps more "meaningful" perspectives of leadership and management realities.

The core of their chapter is a general model of social skills based on the argument that social skills characterize leadership process. According to the authors:

> Skilled leadership depends on skilled perceptions: . . . [leaders are skilled, in part] through contributing higher-order constructs which help systematically to organize understandings of the environment, and how to work in it. What this amounts to, is that leadership involves the management of meaning. Leaders promote persuasive scripts that help others to interpret actions, and events, in relation to the "core values" of their social order (pp. 143–144).

Hosking and Morley also elaborate the components and interdependencies among the components of social skills. The authors take a cognitive and symbolic interactionist perspective in trying to show how cognitive processes, networking processes, and the functions and processes of negotiations within the leader's group and between this and other groups can help the leader understand the social-political situation of his or her systemic context. On the basis of that understanding leaders can be effective in framing issues, in providing scripts for others to effectively orient themselves and to develop a meaning for inherently ambiguous, dilemma-riddled situations. The aim is to reduce complexity of interchange, to engage central values, and to suggest approaches for mobilizing resources "to protect a stake or gain a prize."

Clearly Hosking and Morley provide an initial, still sketchy framework with considerable potential for constructing new vistas of leadership. These authors do question some of the basic implicit assumptions of current leadership research in the literature. They then use these assumptions for a search of alternative assumptions that may be more meaningful in light of the complexity of leadership in today's highly intertwined and dynamic organizations. However, there is a whole set of additional assumptions in the traditional leadership perspective whose status is not clear in the Hosking and Morley chapter.

Space does not allow a specific discussion of all of these issues. An illustration, however, might help show how some unquestioned implicit assumptions might constrain the full realization of new leadership vistas. Hosking and Morley leave unclear what epistemological assumptions are implicit in their framework and what assumptions they make about the status of natural mental properties of "leaders" and "non-leaders" as well as about the nature of relationships.

They refer to many kinds of relationships, such as leaders as negotiators or leadership as the management of meaning. But they leave unaddressed: (1) whether relations are assumed to depend upon the properties of the interacting individuals (as is the case in most of traditional social psychology research, (2) or whether the nature of relations is based upon *common rules* of interpretation of both the situation and the respective reality of the interacting partners. Thus, it is very difficult to avoid the impression that the managing of meaning is something an emergent leader does for or does to other members of his or her group.

The authors, at the beginning of their chapter, clearly state that leadership can only be understood through the processes by which "social order" is constructed and changed. However, in their delineation of various kinds of skill-induced processes there is repeatedly the implication that some people (leaders) are more involved, more skillful, more in control of these processes than others. The approach to leaders as those who exert more influence or are "better" in some sense than their counterparts has been singularly unsuccessful. It should be noted, however, that the issue is *not* that all actors are equal or that some people do not exert more influence or are better than others on some dimension.

The issue is, that when some people are experienced as better, more skillful, or exerting more influence, this is *not* an issue of only the leader's attributes or skills and a *one-way* relation the leader has with others. Rather, the entrenched idea of "more than others," which is used to define leaders, is a resultant of the *nature* of the multilateral relationships between the leader and his or her counterparts and the meaning such relationships have within a particular constructed social context.

Hosking and Morley discuss many issues that characterize leaders but relatively little is said about the "game rules" by which *all* relevant actors play and which form the "social-interpretative cosmos" out of which the reality of the leader, of his or her counterparts, and the meanings of their interactions emerge. The "more than others" of the leader is an emergent phenomenon of *collectively* constructed social reality, an outcropping of issues such as self-referential and autonomous communication processes (cf. for example, Krippendorff 1985).

Crouch and Yetton (ch. 7) also emphasize the *process nature* of leadership, particularly with respect to reaching dynamic equilibrium states within work groups. They develop some components toward new leadership and management vistas. They attempt to illustrate some manager-subordinate processes, among other and related processes that are imaginable which sustain or prevent the reaching of equilibria states within such work groups.

Given these processes whose emergence depends on the interdependence of managers and subordinates, Crouch and Yetton raise interesting questions about traditional team development strategies and the effects of changes in group membership on group effectiveness. Space precludes detailed discussion of the emerging leadership vistas in the Crouch and Yetton chapter. Discussion of the Hosking and Morley chapter should serve as an example, on the basis of which the constraining assumptions might be recognized in the Crouch and Yetton contribution.

The basic constraining issue in the Crouch and Yetton perspective of leadership and management is that there is a fundamental contradiction between the explicit arguments made about the leadership processes that may sustain or prevent equilibria states within work groups and the implicit root assumptions on which the perspective of this chapter rests. These implicit assumptions for the most part are rooted in the realist ontology and content assumptions of the positivist tradition in psychology. Probst's commentary on the Crouch and Yetton chapter outlines further constraining assumptions that emerge on the basis of general systems thinking.

Some Emerging Vistas on the Epistemology of Leadership and Management Research. Three chapters focus totally or in part on the epistemology of leadership and management research. These chapters are by McElroy and Hunger, Peterson and Smith, and Calas and Smircich. Rather than concentrating on the question of what is leadership and management, these chapters deal with *how we come to know* leadership and management phenomena. All three of these chapters merit a discussion of their root assumptions and ways in which these have the potential for new leadership vistas or, alternatively, implicitly continue to sustain the status quo of the dominant epistemology in current leadership research. But space constraints allow only an illustrative discussion of one of these contributions. Because the chapter of Calas and Smircich has particularly far reaching epistemological implications, I will restrict my comments to crucial points made there.

Before discussing the Calas and Smircich chapter, I would like to note that, even though the particular approach employed by Peterson and Smith in chapter 11 was not overly successful, their central premises are ones that need to receive a great deal more attention in social science research in general and leadership and management research in particular. The research community as a social system with all its constituting processes and dynamics and the *nature* of such a system with its enormous bearing on the way we do research, on what questions are selected for study, and on which ones are (one could sometimes even say negligently) ignored, are all phenomena that have been sadly left unexplored in the leadership and management area.

One answer always has been that as leadership researchers we collect facts. We leave the reflection of what we do, its larger societal meanings and the underlying philosophies, and certainly the way we manage and *lead* ourselves as leadership researchers, to the sociologists of science, the philosophers or historians and other disciplines that make commentary about science.

I would like to submit that this view is a particularly narrow, uninformed, and incredibly confining one. Given the fact that our mission has as its central core the "production" of knowledge, refusing to reflect on the *way* such knowledge is produced and the processes by which the "outcomes" are evaluated, is an approach which in the analogue of a business or other work organization none of us would judge to be very effective.

The issues raised by Calas and Smircich in many ways overlap the concerns of Peterson and Smith. Calas and Smircich base their central theme on the assumption that "as leadership writers/researchers, critics, and teachers (along with the popular business press and leadership training industry) we have created leadership in our discourse." They write: "the phenomenon of leadership as demonstrated by human beings in organizations cannot be understood in isolation from the discursive practices which are present and possible at any given time in a culture, because practices of writing and talking leadership 'make' leadership as much as those who 'do' leadership" (p. 203).

They analyze the current professional leadership literature, not on the basis of categorizing approaches, variables, and methods used by leadership researchers, but on the basis of the semiotics of literature which is a particular practice of literary analysis. The aim is to uncover the nature of the communication or "story telling" processes within the field of leadership and management. They want to find out how the field is constructed and rendered meaningful through the social practices and corresponding communicative conventions, codes, and norms inherent in the language of the traditional scientific paradigm within our culture.

Calas and Smircich's central point is consistent with the issues raised in this overview. The dream of new leadership vistas can be realized by first uncovering and making explicit the many hidden and implicit values, assumptions, and ideologies inherent in the scientific discourse on leadership and management. The meaningfulness and appropriateness of these assumptions have to be questioned as a basis for constructing alternative perspectives that remain hidden or impossible to articulate within the constraints of the current culture of scientific inquiry.

The aim is to construct a leadership reality which is more sensible or meaningful, not with respect to only the current culture of "science," but also with respect to the urgent problems we experience in the larger community in which we all live. The authors argue that we as researchers have seldom identified a notion of "leadership" outside our researchers' community.

Calas and Smircich, on the basis of their semiotic reading of the leadership literature, identify a number of major themes of the story embedded in the narrative of the literature. They also analyze what these various themes uncover about the nature of the leadership research community. The crucial aspect of that chapter is the usually completely ignored insight that the research community is as much a social system embedded in our culture as the organizations in which we try to discover the nature of leadership. Furthermore, within the processes defining the research community in the context of our history and our culture lies the crucial origin of "what is leadership?" It is not in some "objective" reality.

The more we learn about the way our leadership stories emerge and are narrated, the better we can understand what we as a research community mean when we are dissatisfied and confused about the fleeting nature of leadership and management phenomena. Calas and Smircich illustrate the constraints imposed on us as a research community by telling our stories solely by the "rules of science" and ignoring the rules of the narrative form of knowledge.

Since we make our world through the stories we tell, many opportunities of insight, of meaning, and of new perspectives are therefore excluded. According to Calas and Smircich, the rules of knowledge within the scientific form of literature have produced "the assumption that subcodes should lead to the main code . . . [so that] most efforts have been put into dividing 'all that should be leadership' into more and more pieces. As a result, the main code has disappeared and what is left is so antiseptic that LEADER is nowhere to be seen" (p. 224).

One could hardly be more descriptive of what is so confining in the way the current leadership research community tells the "leadership story." Calas and Smircich's proposals of ways of looking at ourselves are steps toward identifying the forces behind the dream for new vistas of leadership.

However, we are only at the beginning of a systematic cultural analysis of the leadership and management research culture. Many complexities, in part discussed earlier in this chapter, will need to be understood to realize new vistas of leadership and management which are more meaningful and relevant to the profound uncertainties in our current societies.

On the Ethics of Constructing Leadership and Management

The subjectivist or social construction perspective of knowledge about leadership and management implies some difficult-to-handle ethical considerations, which do not seem a pressing problem in the "realist" perspective of science. Since this perspective separates the scientist, his or her values, prejudices, ideologies, and norms from the object of investigation, there is no ethical responsibility attached to the discovery of facts informed by the objective reality. Ethical considerations in the "realist" view of science, therefore, can be restricted to how facts are discovered, (i.e., the ethics of doing research) and how discoveries are used in our society.

During the discussion of his overview at the symposium, House, referring to the division of labor in our society, maintained that the scientist is the discoverer of objective facts. However, the scientist is ill-equipped to deal with the political nature of the societal consequences created by the application or use of such facts. The professional societies, according to House, clearly carry such political responsibilities. However, these political and ethical considerations have no bearing on "calling the shots" as informed by the objectivity of the reality "out there."

Although such a position is "sensible" within a "realist" perspective of science, from a "social constructivist" perspective such a position on the ethics of knowing is untenable. This point has to be made because of the undeniable fact that through the myth of value-free, that is observer-independent discovery of a "God-given" reality, a vast amount of knowledge is constructed by leadership science with far-reaching consequences.

These consequences relate: (1) to the way we explain or see ourselves as a scientific community (as discussed by Calas and Smircich); (2) to the way the "non-scientific" communities see us as providers of leadership realities; and (3) and, most important, to our intimate involvement in the construction of meaning people, as managers, and those interdependent with managers, attach to their world and themselves in that context.

We must begin to realize that the questions we ask, the concepts we invent, the methods we use are not objectively given by nature. They are constructions and inventions we choose to select from many possible interpretations which the inherent ambiguity of the products of culture allows. Thus, science and its individual practitioner are not absolved from carefully questioning the ethical implications of the constructions the practitioner helps to design. This design is imparted through the terms, concepts, metaphors, variables, and methods he or she chooses within the framework of science to use in telling a story about leadership phenomena.

Clearly the kind of leadership traits we choose to investigate, and the methods we use to measure them, tell a story about how we as intelligent and knowledgeable researchers see the subjects we are investigating. What is important for leaders to be (and what is not important) is implied by the fact that we ask questions about such traits as: (1) the tendency to use and manipulate people; (2) aggressiveness and ability to get one's views accepted in competition with those of others; (3) including the views of others through participation when circumstances for achieving organizationally-defined effectiveness are "right"; and (4) visions or symbolic outcomes as a means to reach performance beyond expectations.

When people are classified as high or low on the preceding characteristics, the experts contribute to the subject's own reality constructions as a human being who possesses such traits. Such contribution implies absoluteness and inevitability of these, through the "power" of science-established truths. There have been repeatedly demonstrated processes of self-fulfilling prophecies. In these prophesies, ethnomethodologists and others have shown in the areas of education, medicine, and the field of mental health (e.g., Watzlawick 1978) that measured traits communicated to the person can lead to a reality construction and corresponding actions in line with those traits.

The crucial ethical problem in such self-fulfilling prophecies is raised precisely because within the "realist" perspective of science, traits are considered to be empirically validated truths. And the person who is assessed to possess such traits has to live or attempt to change them. The reality thus constructed, together with the person, is as much an invention of the "science" which established the truth value of such traits as it were a reflection of the person's circumstances and cultural embeddedness.

Nobody doubts the *descriptive* truth of the statistical relationships to which House, in his overview chapter, confidently points in outlining what we know about leadership. However, these descriptions simply reflect one possible *interpretation* of our culture which we have constructed through the vagaries of history and the social-political processes referred to earlier. Based upon: (1) the root assumptions of psychology, and (2) the fact that mostly male researchers choose certain issues as important to describe in a primarily male leadership and management population, a choice is made regarding what is "worthy" or "interesting" or "profitable" or "status enhancing" to be described in the leadership and management world.

Since these are choices we are free to make upon reflection, the claim that we are simply investigating the objective facts of our current society is a myth. To put it bluntly, the claim is an unreflected half-truth. This half-truth contributes (for some perhaps conveniently) to a perpetuation of current ways of thinking about ourselves and the world in which we live.

In this sense then, leadership researchers, whether they adhere to a "realist" perspective or not, are involved in political activities, like it or not. One might even use the term "arrogant," if we remain secure in the myth of describing and explaining some objective reality, for fear of the painful self-questioning about the societal consequences of the way we ask questions about leadership and management. There can no longer be a comfortable acceptance of the dominant paradigm in leadership and management research, or any other perspective, for that matter.

Only with systematic uncovering of: (1) the underlying root assumptions; (2) their implied values and ideologies; and (3) their possible consequences for maintaining what we, together with our "research subjects," consider to be useful and meaningful in the social world as we currently interpret it, can we as scientists consciously and on the basis of our ethical responsibilities *choose* to accept the current constructed reality of leadership and management.

Alternatively we can choose an emphasis on realizing new leadership and management vistas, if, on the basis of our dialogue with the "research subjects" and our explicit analyses of our root assumptions, we realize that the dominant constructions of leadership and management phenomena are not meaningful in the current social-political context. With respect to these ethical considerations, there can be no division of labor in the way House described it.

These arguments should not be misunderstood as implying that the "realist" perspective of science is a less ethical point of view than any other epistemology. However, within the social constructivist epistemology a number of crucial ethical issues emerge which cannot be ignored by *any* perspective of science. Through the systematic questioning of our ways of knowing and the meaning of "knowledge" in society, it becomes possible to ask whether in the dominant positivistic perspective there is an inherent inequality in the way reality is constructed between the informed and intelligent researcher and the passive and less knowledgeable research subject who only responds to the researcher's questions. This inequality leads Krippendorff (1985) to formulate an ethical imperative which demands, "when involving others in your constructions, always grant the same autonomy you practice in constructing them" (p. 35).

This ethical imperative turns the one-way communication between subject and observer into a dialogue with all of the meanings attached to this concept. Multiple realities of researcher and subject, including their respective value bases, can evolve into a collective reality. Different values and conceptions are reflected on the basis of the experienced or interpreted meaningfulness of a collectively constructed reality in the current cultural context. Thus, the dream of realizing emerging leadership vistas involves more effort and harder, more painful questions than is implied by a search for new traits, variables, methods, and generalized statistically significant empirical relationships. These are the "costs" future leadership symposia have to be willing to bear, if, to remain viable, their longstanding dream about new leadership and management realities is to be realized.

Note

1. Throughout the chapter, I consider leadership and management as conceptually separate but closely interdependent phenomena. Although the topic of management versus leadership is a frequently discussed one, a meaningful analysis of this issue is beyond the scope of this chapter. Some initial suggestions are outlined in Dachler (1984).

References

Abelson, R.P. (1983). Whatever became of consistency theory? *Personality and Social Psychology Bulletin* 9:37–54.

Ackoff, R.L. (1981). *Creating the corporate future.* New York: Wiley.

Adair, J. (1984). *The skills of leadership.* Aldershot: Gower.

Adams, J., Rice, R.W., and Instone, D. (1984). Follower attitudes toward women and judgments concerning performance by female and male leaders. *Academy of Management Journal* 27:636–43.

Argyle, M. (1969). *Social interaction.* London: Tavistock.

——— (1978). *The psychology of interpersonal behaviour.* Harmondsworth, U.K.: Penguin.

——— (1984). A look at functionalism as an alternative approach to studying leadership. In J.G. Hunt, D.M. Hosking, C.A. Schriesheim, and R. Stewart (eds.), *Leaders and managers: International perspectives on managerial behavior and leadership* (95–99). Elmsford, N.Y.: Pergamon.

Argyris, C. (1951). *The impact of budgets on people.* New York: Controllership Foundation.

——— (1979). How normal science methodology makes leadership research less additive and less applicable. In J.G. Hunt and L.L. Larson (eds.), *Crosscurrents in leadership* (47–63). Carbondale, Ill.: Southern Illinois University Press.

Argyris, C., and Schon, D.A. (1978). *Organizational learning.* Reading, Mass.: Addison-Wesley.

Astley, G.W., and Van de Ven, A.H. (1983). Central perspectives and debates in organization theory. *Administrative Science Quarterly* 28:243–73.

Austin, J. (1962). *How to do things with words.* Cambridge, Mass.: Harvard University Press.

Avolio, B.J., Waldman, D.A., Einstein, W.O., and Bass, B.M. (1985). Transformational leadership and organizational effectiveness. Unpublished manuscript. School of Management, State University of New York at Binghamton.

Bakan, D. (1966). *The duality of human existence.* Chicago: Rand-McNally.

Bales, R.F. (1953). The equilibrium problem in small groups. In T. Parsons, R.F. Bales, and E.A. Shils (eds.), *Working papers on the theory of action* (pp. 111–16). New York: Free Press.

Barber, J.D. (1977). *The presidential character* 2d ed. Englewood Cliffs, N.J.: Prentice-Hall.

Bartölke, K., Bergmann, T., and Liegle, L. (eds.) (1980). *Integrated cooperatives in the industrial society: The example of the Kibbutz.* Assen: Van Gorcum.

Bartölke, K., Eschweiler, W., Flechsenberger, D., Palgi, M., and Rosner, M. (1985). *Participation and control—A comparative study about industrial plants in Israeli Kibbutzim and the Federal Republic of Germany.* Spardorf: Verlag Rene' F. Wilfer.

Bass, B.M. (1960). *Leadership, psychology and organizational behavior.* New York: Harper.

—— (1981). *Stogdill's handbook of leadership.* New York: Free Press.

—— (1983). *Organizational decision making.* Homewood, Ill.: Irwin.

—— (1985a). *Leadership and performance beyond expectations.* New York: Free Press.

—— (1985b). Leadership: Good, better, best. *Organizational Dynamics* (Winter): 26–40.

Bass, B.M., Avolio, B.J., and Goodheim, L. (1987). Biography and the assessment of transformational leadership at the world-class level. *Journal of Management.* 13: 7–20.

Bass, B.M., Cascio, W.F., and O'Connor, E. (1974). Magnitude estimations of frequency and amount. *Journal of Applied Psychology* 59:313–20.

Bass, B.M., Valenzi, E.R., Farrow, D.L., and Solomon, R.J. (1975). Management styles associated with organizational, task, personal, and interpersonal contingencies. *Journal of Applied Psychology* 60:720–29.

Bateman, T.S., and Organ, D.W. (1983). Job satisfaction and the good soldier: The relationship between affect and employee citizenship. *Academy of Management Journal* 26:587–95.

Bateson, G. (1972). *Steps to an ecology of mind.* New York: Ballantine.

Batstone, E., Boraston, I., and Frenkel, S. (1977). *Shop stewards in action.* Oxford: Blackwell.

Bazerman, M.H., and Lewicki, R.J. (eds.) (1983). *Negotiating in organizations.* Beverly Hills, Calif.: Sage.

Benne, K.D. and Sheats, P. (1948). Functional roles of group members. *Journal of Social Issues* 4:41–49.

Bennis, W.G. (1959). Leadership theory and administrative behavior: The problems of authority. *Administrative Science Quarterly* 4:259–301.

—— (1982). Leadership transforms vision into action. *Industry Week* (31 May): 54–56.

—— (1984). The four competencies of leadership. *Training and Development Journal* 38(8): 14–19.

Bennis, W.G., and Nanus, B. (1985). *Leaders.* New York: Harper & Row.

Berger, P.L., and Luckmann, T. (1966). *The social construction of reality.* Garden City, N.Y.: Irvington.

Berkowitz, L., and Haythorn, W. (1955). *The relationship of dominance to leadership choice.* Unpublished Report CRL-LN-55-8. Crew Research Laboratory, AF Personnel and Training Reserve Center, Randolf AF Base, San Antonio, Tex.

Berlew, D.E. (1974). Leadership and organizational excitement. In A. Kolb, M. Rubin, and J.M. McIntyre (eds.), *Organizational psychology: A book of readings* 2d ed. (265–77). Englewood Cliffs, N.J.: Prentice Hall.

Berne, E. (1961). *Transactional analysis in psychotherapy.* New York: Grove.

Bernstein, R. (1976). *The structuring of social and political theory.* Philadelphia: University of Pennsylvania Press.

Bertalanffy, L. von (1968). *General system theory.* New York: George Braziller.

Bettman, J.R., and Weitz, B.A. (1983). Attributions in the board room: Causal reasoning in corporate annual reports. *Administrative Science Quarterly* 28:165–83.

Beyer, J.M. (1981). Ideologies, values, and decision making in organizations. In P.C. Nystrom and W.H. Starbuck (eds.), *Handbook of organizational design* vol. 2. (166–202). London: Oxford University Press.

Billig, M. (1976). *The social psychology of intergroup relations.* London: Academic Press.

Bishop, Y.M.M., Fienberg, S.E., and Holland, P.W. (1975). *Discrete multivariate analysis: Theory and practice.* Cambridge, Mass.: MIT Press.

Blair, J.D., and Hunt, J.G. (1986). Getting inside the head of the management researcher one more time: Context free and context specific orientations in research. In J.G. Hunt and J.D. Blair (eds.), *1986 Yearly Review of Management of the Journal of Management* 12:147–66.

Blake, R.R., and Mouton, J.S. (1962). The developing revolution in management practices. *Training Directors Journal* 16(7): 29–52.

Blake, R.R., and Mouton, J.S. (1964). *The managerial grid.* Houston: Gulf Publishing.

Blauner, R. (1964). *Alienation and freedom.* Chicago: University of Chicago Press.

Blumer, H. (1969). *Symbolic interactionism: Perspective and method.* Englewood Cliffs, N.J.: Prentice-Hall.

Bolan, R.S. (1980). The practitioner as theorist: The phenomenology of the professional episode. *Journal of the American Planning Association* 46:261–74.

Bradley, R. (1984 August). Charisma's structural foundation: A relational approach. Symposium on Rethinking Charisma: Structure, Process, and Consequences. 44th Annual Meeting of the Academy of Management, Boston.

Brehm, J. (1966). *A theory of psychological reactance.* New York: Academic Press.

Brickman, P. (1978). Is it real? In J.H. Harvey, W. Ickes, and R.F. Kidd (eds.), *New directions in attributional research* vol. 2 (5–34). Hillsdale, N.J.: Lawrence Erlbaum Associates.

Brown, M.H., and Hosking, D.M. (1986). Distributed leadership and skilled performance as successful organization in social movements. *Human Relations* 39: 65–79.

Bryson, J.M. (1981). A perspective on planning and crisis in the public sector. *Strategic Management Journal* 2:181–96.

Bryson, J.M., and Kelley, G. (1978). A political perspective on leadership emergence, stability, and change in organizational networks. *Academy of Management Review* 3:713–23.

——— (1981). Leadership, politics and the functioning of complex organizational and interorganizational networks. In A. Negandhi, G. England, and B. Wilpert (eds.), *The functioning of complex organizations* (203–36). Cambridge, Mass.: Oelgeschalger, Gunn and Hain.

Burns, J.M. (1978). *Leadership.* New York: Harper & Row.

Burrell, G., and Morgan, G. (1979). *Sociological paradigms and organizational analysis.* London: Heinemann.

Business Week (26 May 1980). Bracing for baby bell (110–15).

Business Week (16 July 1984). GM Moves into a new era: No longer cautious it goes on a high-tech kick and looks beyond cars (48–52, 54).

Butterfield, D.A. (1972). Leadership and organizational effectiveness. In P. Mott (ed.), *The characteristics of effective organizations* (117–49). New York: Harper & Row.

Campbell, J.P., and Pritchard, R.D. (1976). Motivation theory in industrial and organizational psychology. In M.D. Dunnette (ed.), *Handbook of industrial and organizational psychology* (63–130). Chicago: Rand McNally.

Cannon, W.B. (1929). *Bodily changes in pain, hunger, fear and rage* (2d ed.). New York: Appleton Century.

Carbonell, J.L. (1984). Sex roles and leadership revisited. *Journal of Applied Psychology* 69:44–49.

Carr, D. (1970). Translation of Edmund Husserl's *The crisis of European sciences and transcendental philosophy.* Evanston, Ill.: Northwestern University.

Carroll, G.R. (1984). Dynamics of the publisher succession in newspaper organizations. *Administrative Science Quarterly* 29:93–113.

Carroll, G.R., and Delacroix, J. (1982). Organizational mortality in the newspaper industries of Argentina and Ireland: An ecological approach. *Administrative Science Quarterly* 27:169–98.

Carrol, S.J., and Tosi, H.L., Jr. (1977). *Organizational behavior.* Chicago: St. Clair.

Checkland, P.B. (1981). *Systems thinking, systems practice.* Chichester, U.K.: Wiley.

Child, J., and Hosking, D.M. (1979). Model building and contributions to understanding. In J.G. Hunt and L.L. Larson (eds.), *Crosscurrents in leadership* (148–55). Carbondale, Ill.: Southern Illinois University Press.

Churchman, C.W. (1971). *The design of inquiring systems.* New York: Basic Books.

Clark, P.A. (1984). Part 5 integrative comments: Leadership theory: The search for reformulation. In J.G. Hunt, D.M. Hosking, C.A. Schriesheim, and R. Stewart (eds.), *Leaders and managers: International perspectives on managerial behavior and leadership* (375–81). Elmsford, N.Y.: Pergamon.

Clore, G.L., and Ortony, A. (1984). Some issues for a cognitive theory of emotion. *Cahiers de Psychologie Cognitive* 4:53–57.

Coch, L., and French, J., Jr. (1948). Overcoming resistance to change. *Human Relations* 1:512–32.

Cook, T., and Campbell, D. (1976). The design and conduct of quasi-experiments and true experiments in field settings. In M.D. Dunnette (ed.), *Handbook of industrial and organizational psychology* (223–26). Chicago: Rand McNally.

Cowan, T.A. (1965). On the very general character of equilibrium systems. *General Systems* 8:125–28.

Crouch, A.G.D. (1982). Psychological climate, behaviour, satisfaction and individual differences in managerial work groups. Unpublished doctoral dissertation, University of New South Wales, Australia.

Culler, J. (1975). *Structural poetics.* Ithaca, N.Y.: Cornell University Press.

——— (1981). *The pursuit of signs.* Ithaca, N.Y.: Cornell University Press.

Cummings, L.L., and Frost, P. (eds.) (1985). *Publishing in the organizational sciences.* Homewood, Ill.: Irwin.

Dachler, H.P. (1984). On refocusing leadership from a social systems perspective of management. In J.G. Hunt, D.M. Hosking, C.A. Schriesheim, and R. Stewart (eds.), *Leaders and managers: International perspectives on managerial behavior and leadership* (100–08). Elmsford, N.Y.: Pergamon.

—— (1985a). Der Widerspruch zwischen individual-partikularistischem und ganzheitlich-systemischem Denken uber Humansysteme: Konsequenzen fur Management- und Fuhrungsprobleme auf der Mikroebene [The contradiction between individual-concrete and wholistic-systematic thinking about human systems: Consequences for management and leadership problems at the micro level]. In G.J.B. Probst and H. Siegwart (eds.), *Integriertes management* (351–64). Bern, Switzerland: Haupt.

—— (1985b). Allgemeine Betriebswirtschafts- und Managementlehre im Kreuzfeuer verschiedener sozialwissenschaftlicher Perspektiven [Organization and management theory at the crossroads of different perspectives in the social sciences]. In R. Wunderer (ed.), *Die betriebswirtschaftslehre als management- und fuhrungslehre* (203–35). Stuttgart, West Germany: Poeschel.

Dalton, G., Thompson, P., and Price, R. (Summer 1977). The four stages of professional careers—A new look at performance by professionals. *Organizational Dynamics* 6:19–42.

Dansereau, F., Graen, G., and Haga, W.J. (1975). A vertical dyad linkage approach to leadership within formal organizations. *Organizational Behavior and Human Performance* 13:46–78.

Dansereau, F., Alluto, J.A., and Yammarino, F.J. (1985). *Theory testing in organizational behavior: The varient approach.* Englewood Cliffs, N.J.: Prentice-Hall.

Davis, T., and Luthans, F. (Summer 1980). Managers in action: A new look at their behavior and operating models. *Organizational Dynamics* 9:64–80.

Dobbins, G.H., Pence, E.C., Orban, J.A., and Sgro, J.A. (1983). The effects of sex of the leader and sex of the subordinate on the use of organizational control policy. *Organizational Behavior and Human Performance* 32:325–43.

Douglas, T. (1983). *Groups: Understanding people gathered together.* London: Tavistock.

Dow, T. The theory of charisma. (1969). *Sociological Quarterly* 10:306–18.

Drenth, P.J.D., and Koopman, P.L. (1984). A contingency approach to participative leadership: How good? In J.G. Hunt, D.M. Hosking, C.A. Schriesheim, and R. Stewart (eds.), *Leaders and managers: International perspectives on managerial behavior and leadership* (303–15). Elmsford, N.Y.: Pergamon.

Drucker, P.F. (1970). *The effective executive.* London: Pan Business Management.

Dubin, R. (1979). Metaphors of Leadership: An overview. In J.G. Hunt and L.L. Larson (eds.), *Crosscurrents in leadership* (225–38). Carbondale, Ill.: Southern Illinois University Press.

Eco, U. (1979). *The role of the reader.* Bloomington, Ind.: Indiana University Press.

—— (1984). *Semiotics and the philosophy of language.* Bloomington, Ind.: Indiana University Press.

Eden, D., and Ravid, G. (1982). Pygmalion vs. self-expectancy: Effects of instructors and self-expectancy on trainee performance. *Organizational Behavior and Human Performance* 30:351–64.

Eden, D., and Shani, A.B. (1982). Pygmalion goes to boot camp: Expectancy, leadership and trainee performance. *Journal of Applied Psychology* 67:194–99.

Eiser, J.R. (1961). Emergent leadership and social influence. In L. Petrullo and B.M. Bass (eds.), *Leadership and interpersonal behavior* (30–47). New York: Holt, Rinehart & Winston.

Eiser, J.R. (1980). *Cognitive social psychology.* New York: McGraw-Hill.

Emery, F.E. (1977). *Futures we are in.* Leiden, The Netherlands: Martinus Nijhoff.

Erikson, E. (1964). Inner and outer space: Reflections on womanhood. *Daedalus* 93: 582–606.

Etzioni, A. (1961). *A comparative analysis of complex organizations.* New York: Free Press.

——— (1975). *A comparative analysis of complex organizations* 2d ed. New York: Free Press.

Evans, M.G. (1970). The effects of supervisory behavior on the path-goal relationship. *Organizational Behavior and Human Performance* 5:277–98.

——— (1974). Extensions of a path-goal theory of motivation. *Journal of Applied Psychology* 59:172–78.

Farris, G.F. and Butterfield, D.A. (1973). Are current theories of leadership culturebound? An empirical test in Brazil. In E.A. Fleishman and J.G. Hunt (eds.) *Current developments in the study of leadership* (105–38). Carbondale, Ill.: Southern Illinois University Press.

Farris, G.F., and Lim, F.G. (1969). Effects of performance on leadership, cohesiveness, influence, satisfaction and subsequent performance. *Journal of Applied Psychology* 53:490–97.

Feldman, M., and March, J. (1981). Information in organizations as signal and symbol. *Administrative Science Quarterly* 26:171–86.

Feyerabend, P.K. (1976). *Against method.* New York: Humanities Press.

Feyerabend, P.K. (1984). *Wissenschaft als kunst.* Frankfurt, West Germany: Suhrkamp.

Fiedler, F.E. (1967). *A theory of leadership effectiveness.* New York, McGraw-Hill.

Fiedler, F.E. (1985 August). *A human resource utilization theory of leadership.* Presented at Academy of Management Meetings, San Diego.

Fiedler, F.E., and Chemers, M.M. (1974). *Leadership and effective management.* Glencoe, Ill.: Scott, Foresman.

——— (1984). *Improving leadership effectiveness: The leader match concept.* 2d ed. New York: Wiley.

Fisher, W.R. (1984). Narration as a human communication paradigm: The case of public moral arguments. *Communication Monographs* 51:7–22.

Fleishman, E.A. (1953). Leadership climate, human relations training, and supervisory behavior. *Personnel Psychology* 6:205–22.

Fleishman, E.A., and Harris, E.F. (1962). Patterns of leadership behavior related to employee grievances and turnover. *Personnel Psychology* 15:43–56.

Frankl, V. (1959). *Man's search for meaning.* New York: Simon & Schuster.

Freeman, J., Carroll, G.R., and Hannan, M.T. (1983). Age dependence in organizational death rates. *American Sociological Review* 48:692–710.

French, J.R.P., and Raven, B.H. (1959). The bases of social power. In D. Cartwright (ed.), *Studies in social power* (150–67). Ann Arbor, Mich.: Institute for Social Research.

Frieze, I.H. (1976). Causal attributions and information seeking to explain success and failure. *Journal of Research in Personality* 10:279–92.

Frost, D.C. (1983). Role perceptions and behaviors of the immediate superior moderating effects on the prediction of leadership effectiveness. *Organizational Behavior and Human Performance* 31:123–42.

Garfinkel, H. (1967). *Studies in ethnomethodology.* Englewood Cliffs, N.J.: Prentice-Hall.

Geertz, C. (1973). *The interpretation of cultures.* New York: Basic Books.

——— (1983). Blurred genres: The refiguration of social thought. In C. Geertz (ed.), *Local knowledge* (19–35). New York: Basic Books.

Gergen, K.J. (1982). *Toward transformation in social knowledge.* New York: Springer.

——— (1984a). Aggression as discourse. In A. Mummendey (ed.), *The social psychology of aggression* (51–68). New York: Springer.

——— (1984b Summer). *Toward self as relationship.* Plenary talk given at the Conference on Self and Identity, Cardiff, Wales.

——— (1985). Social pragmatics and the origins of psychological discourse. In K.J. Gergen and K.E. Davis (eds.), *The social construction of the person* (111–28). New York: Springer.

Giddens, A. (1979). *Central problems in social theory: Action, structure and contradiction in social analysis.* Berkeley, Calif.: University of California Press.

Gioia, D., and Poole, P.P. (1984). Scripts in organizational behavior. *Academy of Management Review* 9:449–59.

Glauser, M.J. and Bednar, D.A. (1986 August). Work unit representation: Constraint development and measurement. Academy of Management Meetings, Chicago.

Goodman, P.S., and Pennings, J.M. (eds.) (1977). *New perspectives on organizational effectiveness.* San Francisco: Jossey-Bass.

Gouldner, A.W. (1970). *The coming crisis of western sociology.* New York: Basic Books.

Graeff, C.L. (1983). The situational leadership theory: A critical view. *Academy of Management Review* 8:285–91.

Graen, G. (1976). Role-making processes within complex organizations. In M.D. Dunnette (ed.), *Handbook of industrial and organizational psychology* (1201–45). Chicago: Rand McNally.

Graen, G., and Cashman, J.F. (1975). A Role-making model of leadership in formal organizations: A developmental approach. In J.G. Hunt and L.L. Larson (eds.), *Leadership frontiers.* (143–65). Kent, Ohio: Comparative Administration Research Institute, Kent State University.

Graham, J.W. (1982 August). Leadership: A critical analysis. Paper presented at the 42nd Annual Meeting of the Academy of Management, Organizational Behavior Division, New York.

——— (1985). An enquiry concerning organizational citizenship. Working paper University of British Columbia, Faculty of Commerce and Business Administration, Vancouver, BC.

Greene, C.N. (1973). A longitudinal analysis of relationships among leader behavior and subordinate performance and satisfaction. *Academy of Management Proceedings:* 433–41.

——— (1979). Questions of causation in the path-goal theory of leadership. *Academy of Management Journal* 22:22–41.

Greiner, L.E. (1972). Evolution and revolution as organizations grow. *Harvard Business Review* (July–August): 37–46.

Greller, M.M. (1980). Evaluation of feedback sources as a function of role and organizational development. *Journal of Applied Psychology* 65:24–27.

Grieco, M.S., and Hosking, D.M. (1985 June). *Networking, exchange, and skill.* Paper presented at the 7th E.G.O.S. Colloquium, Sweden.

Gupta, A.K., and Govindarajan, V. (1984). Business unit strategy, managerial characteristics, and business unit effectiveness at strategy implementation. *Academy of Management Journal* 27:25–41.

Habermas, J. (1971). *Knowledge and human interests.* Boston: Beacon Press.

——— (1973). *Theory and practice.* Boston: Beacon Press.

Hackman, J., and Lawler, E. (1971). Employee reactions to job characteristics. *Journal of Applied Psychology Monograph* 55:259–86.

Hackman, J., and Oldham, F. (1976). Motivation through the design of work: Test of a theory. *Organizational Behavior and Human Performance:* 250–79.

Haldane, E.S., and Ross, G.R.T. (1955) (translation). *The philosophical works of Descartes.* New York: Dover.

Hall, B. (1976). *The development of consciousness.* New York: Paulist.

Hall, J. and Donnell, S.M. (1979). Managerial achievement: The personal side of behavioral theory. *Human Relations* 32:77–101.

Hannan, M.T., and Freeman, J. (1984). Structural inertia and organizational change. *American Sociological Review* 49:149–64.

Hanson, N.R. (1958). *Patterns of discovery.* London: Cambridge University Press.

Harding, S., and Hintikka, M.B. (1983). *Discovering reality: Feminist perspectives on epistemology, metaphysics, methodology, and philosophy of science.* Boston: D. Reidel.

Hayes, R.H., and Abernathy, W.J. (1980). Managing our way to economic decline. *Harvard Business Review* (July–August): 67–77.

Hebb, D.O. (1969). Hebb on hocus-pocus: A conversation with Elizabeth Hall. *Psychology Today* 3(3): 20–28.

Hedberg, B. (1981). How organizations learn and unlearn. In P.C. Nystrom and W.H. Starbuck (eds.), *Handbook of organizational design* vol. 1 (3–27). London: Oxford University Press.

Heider, F. (1958). *The psychology of interpersonal relations.* New York: Wiley.

Heilman, M.E., Cage, J.H., Hornstein, H.A., and Herschlag, J.K. (1984). Reaction to prescribed leader behavior as a function of role perspective: The case of the Vroom-Yetton model. *Journal of Applied Psychology* 69:50–60.

Heller, F.A. (1984). The role of longitudinal method in management decision-making studies. In J.G. Hunt, D.M. Hosking, C.A. Schriesheim, and R. Stewart (eds.), *Leaders and managers: International perspectives on managerial behavior and leadership* (283–302). Elmsford, N.Y.: Pergamon.

Hersey, P., and Blanchard, K.H. (1969). Life-cycle theory of leadership. *Training and Development Journal* 23(5): 26–34.

——— (1982). *Management of organizational behavior* 4th ed. Englewood Cliffs, N.J.: Prentice-Hall.

Hewitt, J.P., and Hall, P.M. (1973). Social problems, problematic situations, and quasi-theories. *American Sociological Review* 38:367–74.

Hinings, C.R., Hickson, D.J., Pennings, J.M. and Schneck, R.E. (1974). Structural conditions of intraorganizational power. *Administrative Science Quarterly* 19: 22–44.

Hofer, C.W., and Davoust, M.J. (1977). *Successful strategic management.* Chicago: Kearney.

Hollander, E.P. (1960). Competence and conformity in the acceptance of influence. *Journal of Abnormal and Social Psychology* 61:365–69.

——— (1978). *Leadership dynamics.* New York: Free Press.

——— (1979). What we study and where we study it: Leadership research in the laboratory and field. In J.G. Hunt and L.L. Larson (eds.), *Crosscurrents in leadership* (99–102). Carbondale, Ill.: Southern Illinois University Press.

Hollander, E.P. (1979). Leadership and social exchange processes. In K. Gergen, M.S. Greenberg, and R.H. Willis (eds.), *Social exchange: Advances in theory and research* (103–18). New York: Winston-Wiley.

Holsti, O. (1970). The "operational code" approach to the study of political leaders: John Foster Dulles' philosophical and instrumental beliefs. *Canadian Journal of Political Science* 3:123–57.

Homans, G.C. (1951). *The human group.* London: Routledge & Kegan Paul.

Hosking, D.M. (1983a, October 4–7). *Leadership and the effective negotiation of design processes.* Presented at the Third Organization Development World Congress, Inter-University Centre Dubrovnik, Yugoslavia.

——— (1983b, November 3–5). *Leadership skills and organisational forms: The management of uncertainty.* Presented at the 6th E.G.O.S. colloquium, "New movements and change in organizational forms," Florence, Italy.

——— (In press). Leadership and organisational skills. In A. Keiser, G. Reber, and R. Wunderer (eds.), *Encyclopaedia of leadership* Stuttgart, West Germany: Poeschel.

Hosking, D.M., Hunt, J.G., Schriesheim, C.A., and Stewart, R. (1984). Conclusions: On paradigm shifts in studying leadership. In J.G. Hunt, D.M. Hosking, C.A. Schriesheim, and R. Stewart (eds.), *Leaders and managers: International perspectives on managerial behavior and leadership* (417–24). Elmsford, N.Y.: Pergamon.

Hosking, D.M., and Morley, I.E. (1983). *Leadership and organization: The negotiation of order.* Birmingham, U.K.: University of Aston Working Paper Series, no. 249.

——— (1985). *Leadership and organization: Processes of influence, negotiation, and exchange.* Coventry, U.K.: University of Warwick.

House, R.J. (1971). A path-goal theory of leader effectiveness. *Administrative Science Quarterly* 16:321–338.

——— (1977). A 1976 theory of charismatic leadership. In J.G. Hunt and L.L. Larson (eds.), *Leadership: The cutting edge* (189–207). Carbondale, Ill.: Southern Illinois University Press.

——— (1985). Research contrasting the behavior and the effect of reputed charismatic versus reputed non-charismatic leaders. *Paper presented at the annual meeting of the Administrative Science Association of Canada,* Montreal.

House, R.J., and Baetz, M.L. (1979). Leadership: Some empirical generalizations and new research directions. In B.M. Staw (ed.), *Research in organizational behavior* vol. 1 (341–423). Greenwich, Conn.: JAI Press.

House, R.J., and Mitchell, T.R. (1974). Path-goal theory of leadership. *Journal of Contemporary Business* 3(4): 81–97.

Howell, J.M. (1985). *An experimental test of the theory of charismatic leadership.*

Paper presented at Annual Meeting of the Administrative Science Association of Canada, Montreal.

Huff, A.S. (1984). Situation interpretation, leader behavior, and effectiveness. In J.G. Hunt, D.M. Hosking, C.A. Schriesheim, and R. Stewart (eds.), *Leaders and managers: International perspectives on managerial behaviour and leadership* (253–62). Elmsford, N.Y.: Pergamon.

Hunt, J.G. (1984). Leadership and managerial behavior. J.E. Rosenzweig and F.E. Kast (eds.), *Modules in management.* Chicago: Science Research Associates.

Hunt, J.G., Hosking, D.M., Schriesheim, C.A., and Stewart, R. (eds.) (1984). *Leaders and managers: International perspectives on managerial behavior and leadership.* Elmsford, N.Y.: Pergamon.

Hunt, J.G. and Larson, L.L. (eds.) (1975). Leadership frontiers. Kent, Oh.: Comparative Administration Research Institute, Kent State University.

Hunt, J.G., and Larson, L.L. (eds.) (1977). *Leadership: The cutting edge.* Carbondale, Ill.: Southern Illinois University Press.

—— (eds.) (1979). *Crosscurrents in leadership.* Carbondale, Ill.: Southern Illinois University Press.

Hunt, J.G., and Osborn, R.N. (1982). Toward a macro-oriented model of leadership: An odyssey. In J.G. Hunt, U. Sekaran, and C.A. Schriesheim (eds.), *Leadership: Beyond establishment views* (196–221). Carbondale, Ill.: Southern Illinois University Press.

Hunt, J.G., and Schuler, R.S. (1976). *Leader reward and sanctions behavior relations to criteria in a large public utility.* Department of Administrative Sciences, Carbondale, Ill.: Southern Illinois University at Carbondale.

Hunt, J.G., Sekaran, U., and Schriesheim, C.A. (eds.) (1982). *Leadership: Beyond establishment views.* Carbondale, Ill.: Southern Illinois University Press.

Iacocca, L., and Novak, W.L. (1984). *Iacocca: An autobiography.* New York: Bantam.

Ilgen, D.R., and Knowlton, W.A. (1980). Performance attributional effects on feedback from supervisors. *Organizational Behavior and Human Performance* 25: 441–56.

Ingersoll, V.H., and Adams, G.B. (1983). Beyond organizational boundaries: Exploring the managerial metamyth. Paper presented at the Organizational Folklore Conference, UCLA, Los Angeles.

Jablin, F.M. (1979). Superior-subordinate communication: The state of the art. *Psychological Bulletin* 6:1201–22.

Jacobs, T.O. (1971). *Leadership and exchange in formal organizations.* Alexandria, Va.: Human Resources Research Association.

Jaques, E. (1956). *The Measurement of responsibility.* London: Tavistock.

—— (1961). *Equitable payment.* London: Heinemann.

—— (1964). *Time-span handbook.* London: Heinemann.

—— (1976). *A general theory of bureaucracy.* New York: Halsted.

—— (1979). Taking time seriously in evaluating jobs. *Harvard Business Review* 57(5): 124–32.

—— (1985). *Stratification of cognitive complexity.* Unpublished report, U.S. Army Research Institute for the Behavioral and Social Sciences, grant number DAJA37-80-C-007. Alexandria, Va.

Jago, A.G. (1982). Leadership: perspectives in theory and research. *Management Science* 28:315–36.

Jago, A.G., and Vroom, V.H. (1980). An evaluation of two alternatives to the Vroom/Yetton normative model. *Academy of Management Journal* 23:347–55.

James, W. (1907). *Pragmatism: A new name for some old ways of thinking.* New York: Longmans, Green.

——— (1950). *The principles of psychology* vol. 2. New York: Dover. (Original work published in 1890.)

Janis, I.L. (1982). *Groupthink.* Boston: Harcourt Brace.

Janis, I.L., and Mann, L. (1977). *Decision-making: A psychological analysis of conflict, choice, and commitment.* New York: Free Press.

Jermier, J. (1985). When the sleeper wakes: A short story illustrating themes in radical organizational theory. *Journal of Management* 11(2): 67–80.

Jervis, R. (1972). *Perception and misperception in international politics.* Princeton, N.J.: Princeton University Press.

Johnson, B. (1977). *Communication: The process of organizing.* Boston: Allyn and Bacon.

Johnson, D.W. (1981). *Reaching out* 2d ed. Englewood Cliffs, N.J.: Prentice Hall.

Jones, E.E., and Nisbett, R.E. (1972). The actor and the observer: Divergent perceptions of the causes of behavior. In E.E. Jones, D.E. Kanguse, H.H. Kelley, R.E. Nisbett, S. Valins, B. Weiner, (eds.), *Attribution: Perceiving the causes of behavior* (79–94). Morristown, N.J.: General Learning Press.

Jones, G.R. (1983). Forms of control and leader behavior. *Journal of Management* 9: 159–72.

Kahn, R.L., Wollfe, D.M., Quinn, R.P., and Rosenthal, R.A. (1964). *Organizational stress: Studies in role conflict and ambiguity.* New York: Wiley.

Kanter, R.M. (1984). *The change masters: Corporate entrepreneurs at work.* London: George Allen & Unwin.

Kanter, R.M., and Stein, V.A. (eds.) (1979). *Life in organizations.* New York: Basic Books.

Kaplan, R.E. (1979). The conspicuous absence of evidence that process consultation enhances task performance. *Journal of Applied Behavioral Science* 15:346–60.

——— (1984). Trade routes: The manager's network of relationships. *Organizational Dynamics* 12(spring): 37–52.

Katz, D., and Kahn, R.L. (1966, 1978). *The social psychology of organizations.* New York: Wiley.

Kaufman, H. (1960). *The forest ranger.* Baltimore: Johns Hopkins Press.

Keller, E.F. (1985). *Reflections on gender and science.* New Haven: Yale University Press.

Kellerman, B. (ed). (1984). *Leadership: Multidisciplinary perspectives.* Englewood Cliffs, N.J.: Prentice-Hall.

Kelley, H.H. (1967). Attribution theory in social psychology. In D. Levine (ed.), *Nebraska Symposium on Motivation* (192–238). Lincoln: University of Nebraska Press.

Kelman, H.C. (1958). Compliance, identification, and internalization: Three processes of attitude change. *Journal of Conflict Resolution* 2:51–60.

Kelvin, P. (1970). *The bases of social behavior.* New York: Holt, Rinehart & Winston.

Kenny, D.A., and Zaccaro, S.J. (1983). An estimate of variance due to traits in leadership. *Journal of Applied Psychology* 68:678–85.

Kerr, S. (1983). Substitutes for leadership: Some implications for organizational design. In J.R. Hackman, E.E. Lawler III, and L.W. Porter (eds.), *Perspectives on behavior in organizations* (515–22). New York: McGraw-Hill.

Kerr, S., and Jermier, J.M. (1978). Substitutes for leadership: their meaning and measurement. *Organizational Behavior and Human Performance* 22:375–403.

Kerr, S., and Slocum, J., Jr. (1981). Controlling the performances of people in organizations. In P.C. Nystrom and W.H. Starbuck (eds.), *Handbook of organizational design* vol. 2 (116–34). London: Oxford University Press.

Kimberly, J.R., and Quinn, R.E. (1984). *Managing organization transitions.* Homewood, Ill.: Irwin.

Kluckhohn, C. (1951). Values and value orientation in the theory of action. In T. Parsons and E.A. Shils (eds.), *Toward a general theory of action* (388–433). Cambridge, Mass.: Harvard University Press.

Knight, P.A. (1984). Heroism vs. competence: Competing explanations for the effects of experimenting and consistent management. *Organizational Behavior and Human Performance* 33:307–22.

Knight, P.A., and Saal, F.E. (1984). Effects of gender differences and selection agent expertise on leader influence and performance evaluations. *Organizational Behavior and Human Performance* 34:225–43.

Koestler, A.J. (1948). A summing up. London: Hutchinson.

Koehler, W. (1930). *Gestalt psychology.* London: G. Bell.

Kohlberg, L. (1969). State and sequence: The cognitive-development approach to socialization. In D. Goslin (ed.), *Handbook of socialization theory and research* (347–480). Chicago: Rand-McNally.

Kohn, A. (1986). *No contest: The case against competition.* New York: Houghton Mifflin.

Kotter, J.P. (1982). *The general managers.* New York: Free Press.

Kotter, J.P., and Lawrence, P. (1974). *Mayors in action: Five studies in urban governance.* New York: Wiley.

Krippendorff, K. (Summer 1984). An epistemological foundation for communication. *Journal of Communication* 21–36.

Krippendorff, K. (1985 May). *On the ethics of constructing communication.* Presidential address given at the International Communication Association Conference on Paradigm Dialogues. Honolulu, Hawaii.

Kristeva, J. (1969). *Semiotike: recherches pour une semalyse* (p. 146). Paris: Editions du Seuil. As quoted by J. Culler (1975) in *Structural poetics* (p. 139). Ithaca, N.Y.: Cornell University Press.

Kuhn, T.S. (1970). *The structure of scientific revolution* 2d ed. Chicago, Ill.: University of Chicago Press.

Lammers, C.J., and Hickson, D.J. (eds.) (1979). *Organizations alike and unlike.* London: Routledge & Kegan Paul.

Larson, J.R., Lugle, J.H., and Scerbo, M.M. (1984). The impact of performance cues on leader-behavior ratings: The role of selective information availability and probabilistic response bias. *Organizational Behavior and Human Performance* 33:323–49.

Lau, R.R., and Russell, D. (1980). Attributions in the sports pages. *Journal of Personality and Social Psychology* 39:29–38.

Lawrence, P.R., Dyer, D. (1983). *Renewing American industry: Organizing for efficiency and innovation.* New York: Free Press.

Lawrence, P.R., and Lorsch, J. (1967). *Organization and environment.* Cambridge, Mass.: Harvard Business School.

Lazarus, R. (1964). *Leaders, groups and influence,* New York: Oxford University Press.

——— (1984). On the primacy of cognition. *American Psychologist* 39:124–29.

——— (1968). Emotions and adaptations. Conceptual and empirical relations. In W.J. Arnold (ed.), *Nebraska symposium on motivation* (175–266). Lincoln: University of Nebraska Press.

Lemaine, G. (1974). Social differentiation and social originality. *European Journal of Social Psychology* 4:17–52.

Lewin, K., Lippitt, R., and White, R.K. (1939). Patterns of aggressive behavior in experimentally created social climates. *Journal of Social Psychology* 10:271–301.

Lewin, K. (1948). *Resolving social conflicts.* G.W. Lewin (ed.), New York: Harper & Brothers.

Lewis, M. (1985). Sourcing workplace cultures: Why, when and how. In R. Kilmann, M. Saxton, and R. Serpa (eds.), *Gaining control of the corporate culture* (126–36). San Francisco: Jossey-Bass.

Libby, R., and Lewis, A. (1982). Human information processing research in accounting: The state of the art in 1982. *Accounting, Organizations, and Society* 7: 231–85.

Lieberson, S., and O'Connor, J.F. (1972). Leadership and organizational performance: A study of large corporations. *American Sociological Review* 37:117–30.

Likert, R. (1961). *New patterns of management,* New York: McGraw-Hill.

Lippitt, G.L., and Schmidt, W.H. (1967). Crises in a developing organization. *Harvard Business Review* (March–April): 102–12.

Loomis, C.P., and Loomis, Z.K. (1965). *Modern social theories* 2d ed. Toronto: Van Nostrand.

Lord, R.G., Binning, J.F., Rush, M.C., and Thomas, J.C. (1978). The effect of performance cues and leader behavior on questionnaire ratings of leadership behavior. *Organizational Behavior and Human Performance* 21:27–39.

Lord, R.G., Foti, R.J., and Phillips, J.S. (1982). A theory of leadership categorization. In J.G. Hunt, U. Sekaran, and C.A. Schriesheim (eds.), *Leadership: Beyond establishment views* (104–21). Carbondale, Ill.: Southern Illinois University Press.

Lovejoy, A. (1950). Terminal and adjectival values. *Journal of Philosophy* 47: 593–608.

Lowin, A., and Craig, J.R. (1968). The influence of level of performance on managerial style: An experimental object-lesson in the ambiguity of correlational data. *Organizational Behavior and Human Performance* 3:440–58.

Lowin, A., Hrapchak, W.J., and Kavanaugh, M.J. (1969). Consideration and initiating structure: An experimental investigation of leadership traits. *Administrative Science Quarterly* 14:238–53.

Luhmann, N. (1977). *Zweckbegriff und systemrationalitat* [The concept of purpose and systems rationality] 2d ed. Frankfurt, West Germany: Suhrkamp.

Luthans, F., and Kreitner, R. (1975). *Organizational behavior modification.* Glenview, Ill.: Scott, Foresman.

Lyotard, J. (1984). *The postmodern condition: A report on knowledge.* Minneapolis: University of Minnesota Press.

McCall, M.W., Jr. (1976). Leadership research: Choosing gods and devils on the run. *Journal of Occupational Psychology* 49:139–53.

——— (1983). Leaders and leadership: Of substance and shadow. In J.R. Hackman, E.E. Lawler, and L.W. Porter (eds.), *Perspectives on behavior in organizations* (476–85). New York: McGraw-Hill.

McCall, M.W., Jr., and Lombardo, M.M. (eds.) (1978). *Leadership: Where else can we go?* Durham, N.C.: Duke University Press.

——— (1983). *Off the track: Why and how successful executives get derailed.* Technical Report no. 21. Greensboro, N.C.: Center for Creative Leadership.

McClelland, D.C. (1961). *The achieving society.* Princeton, N.J.: Van Nostrand.

——— (1975). *Power: The inner experience.* New York: Irvington.

McClelland, D.C., and Burnham, D.H. (1976). Power is the great motivator. *Harvard Business Review 54* (March–April): 100–10.

McClelland, D.C., Davis, W.N., Kalin, R., and Warner, E. (1972). *The drinking man.* New York: Free Press.

McClelland, D.C., and Winter, D.G. (1969). *Motivating economic achievement.* New York: Free Press.

McElroy, J.C., and Downey, H.K. (1983). Rater involvement as a moderator of performance cues and leader behavior descriptions. *Journal of Management* 9: 41–54.

McGregor, D. (1960). *The human side of enterprise.* New York: McGraw-Hill.

Maier, N.R.F. (1948). A human relations program for supervisors. *Industrial and Labor Relations Review* 1:443–64.

——— (1967). Assets and liabilities in group problem solving: The need for an integrative function. *Psychological Review* 74:239–49.

Malik, F., Probst, G.J.B. (1984). Evolutionary management. In H. Ulrich, G.J.B. Probst (eds.), *Self-organization and management of social systems* (105–20). Heidelberg, West Germany: Springer.

Mann, F.C. (1965). Toward an understanding of the leadership role in formal organization. In R. Dubin, G.C. Homans, F.C. Mann, and D.C. Miller (eds.), *Leadership and productivity* (68–103). San Francisco: Chandler.

——— (1968). The researcher and his working environment: Research findings and their application. In D.L. Arm (ed.), *Vistas in science* (25–27). Albuquerque: University of New Mexico Press.

Mann, R.D. (1959). A review of the relationships between personality and performance in small groups. *Psychological Bulletin* 56:241–70.

March, J.G., and Simon, H.A. (1958). *Organizations.* New York: Wiley.

Marrow, A. (1974). *The failure of success.* New York: American Management Association.

Martin, J., Sitkin, S. and Boehm, M. (1983 August). Riding the wave: The culture creation process. Paper presented at the Academy of Management meeting. Dallas.

Martinko, M., and Gardner, W. (1984). The observation of high performing managers: Methodological issues and managerial implications. In J.G. Hunt,

D.M. Hosking, C.A. Schriesheim, and R. Stewart (eds.), *Leaders and managers: International perspectives on managerial behavior and leadership* (142–62). Elmsford, N.Y.: Pergamon.

Mason, R.O., and Mitroff, I.I. (1981). *Challenging strategic planning assumptions: Theory, cases, and techniques.* New York: Wiley.

Mawhinney, T.C., and Ford, J.D. (1977). The path-goal theory of leader effectiveness: An operant interpretation. *Academy of Management Review* 2:398–411.

Megargee, G.I., Bogart, P., and Anderson, R.A. (1966). Prediction of leadership in a simulated industrial task. *Journal of Applied Psychology* 50:292–95.

Meindl, J.R., Ehrlich, S.B., and Dukerich, J.M. (1985). The romance of leadership. *Administrative Science Quarterly* 30:78–102.

Melcher, A.J. (1977). Leadership models and research approaches. In J.G. Hunt and L.L. Larson (eds.), *Leadership: The cutting edge* (94–108). Carbondale, Ill.: Southern Illinois University Press.

Merleau-Ponty, M. (1962). *Phenomenology of perception* (trans. Colin Smith). London: Routledge & Kegan Paul.

Meyer, M. (1975). Leadership and organization structure. *American Journal of Sociology* 81:514–42.

Miller, D., and Frisen, P. (1980). Archetypes of organizational transition. *Administrative Science Quarterly* 25:268–99.

Miller, J.G. (1971). The nature of living systems. *Behavioral Science* 16:278–301.

Miner, J.B. (1965). *Studies in management education.* Atlanta, Ga.: Organizational Measurement Systems Press.

———— (1975). The uncertain future of the leadership concept: An overview. In J.G. Hunt and L.L. Larson (eds.), *Leadership frontiers* (197–208). Kent, Ohio: Comparative Administration Research Institute, Kent State University.

———— (1978). Twenty years of research on the role-motivation theory of managerial effectiveness. *Personnel Psychology* 31:739–60.

Minsky, M., and Papert, S. (1972). Research at the laboratory in vision, language, and other problems of intelligence. *Artificial Intelligence Progress Report. Artificial Intelligence Memo. No. 252.* Massachusetts Institute of Technology.

Mintzberg, H. (1975). The manager's job: Folklore and fact. *Harvard Business Review* 53(4): 49–61.

———— (1983). *The structuring of organizations.* Englewood Cliffs, N.J.: Prentice Hall.

Mischel, W. (1973). Toward a cognitive social learning reconceptualization of personality. *Psychological Review* 80:252–83.

Mitchell, T.R. (1982). Attributions and actions: A note of caution. *Journal of Management* 8:65–74.

Mitchell, T.R., Larson, J.R., and Green, S.G. (1977). Leader behavior, situational moderators, and group performance: An attributional analysis. *Organizational Behavior and Human Performance* 18:254–68.

Mitroff, I.I. (1983). *Stakeholders of the organizational mind.* San Francisco: Jossey-Bass.

Monson, T.C., Hesley, J.W., and Chernick, L. (1982). Specifying when personality traits can and cannot predict behavior: An alternative to abandoning the attempt to predict single act criteria. *Journal of Personality and Social Psychology* 6: 385–499.

Morgan, G. (1983). *Beyond method*. Beverly Hills, Calif.: Sage.

Morgan, G., and Smircich, L. (1980). The case for qualitative research. *Academy of Management Review* 5:491–500.

Morley, I.E. (1981a). Negotiation and bargaining. In M. Argyle (ed.), *Social skills and work* (84–115). London: Methuen.

——— (1981b). Bargaining and negotiation. In C.L. Cooper (ed.), *Psychology and management* (95–130). London: Macmillan/British Psychological Society.

——— (1982b). Strategies for dealing with different processes in different contexts. In J.G. Hunt, U. Sekaran, and C.A. Schriesheim (eds.), *Leadership: Beyond establishment views* (151–56). Carbondale, Ill.: Southern Illinois University Press.

——— (1983 July 19–22). What skilled negotiators do. Paper presented at Sixth Annual Scientific Meeting of the International Society of Political Psychology, Oxford, U.K.

Morley, I.E., and Hosking, D.M. (1984). Decision making and negotiation: Leadership and social skills. In M. Gruneberg and T. Wall (eds.), *Social psychology and organizational behavior* (71–92). Chichester, U.K.: Wiley.

——— (1986). The skills of leadership. In G. Debus and H.W. Schroiff (eds.), *The psychology of work and organization* (273–80). Amsterdam, The Netherlands: North Holland.

Morley, I.E., and Stephenson, G.M. (1977). *The social psychology of bargaining*. London: George Allen & Unwin.

Mowday, R.T. (1983). Beliefs about the causes of behavior: The motivational implications of attribution processes. In R.M. Steers and L.W. Porter (eds.), *Motivation and work behavior* 3d ed. (352–75). New York: McGraw-Hill.

Mowday, R.T., Porter, L.W., and Steers, R.M. (1982). *Employee-organization linkages: The psychology of commitment, absenteeism, and turnover*. New York: Academic Press.

Mulder, M., Ritsema, J.R., and de Jong, R.D. (1970). An organization in crisis and non-crisis situations. *Human Relations* 24:19–51.

Mulder, M., and Stemerding, A. (1963). Threat, attraction to group and need for strong leadership. *Human Relations* 16:317–34.

Mummendey, A. (ed.) (1984). *The social psychology of aggression*. New York: Springer.

Nance, J.J. (1984). *Splash of colors: The self destruction of Braniff International*. New York: Morrow.

Neisser, U. (1976). *Cognition and reality*. San Francisco: Freeman.

Neuberger, U. (1984). *Führung*. Stuttgart, West Germany: Ferdinand Enke Verlag.

Newcomb, T. (1953). An approach to the study of communication. *Psychological Review* 60:393–403.

Newcomb, W.W., Jr. (1980). *The Indians of Texas*. Austin: University of Texas Press.

Nicholson, N. (1984). Organizational culture, ideology, and management. In J.G. Hunt, D.M. Hosking, C.A. Schriesheim, and R. Stewart (eds.), *Leaders and managers: International perspectives on managerial behavior and leadership* (263–68). Elmsford, N.Y.: Pergamon.

Nidditch, P.H. (1979). Translation of John Locke's (1960) *An essay concerning human understanding*. New York: Oxford University Press.

Nisbett, R., and Ross, L. (1980). *Human inference: Strategies and shortcomings of social judgment.* Englewood Cliffs, N.J.: Prentice-Hall.

Nord, W.R. (1985). Looking at ourselves as we look at others: An exploration of the publication system for organization research. In L.L. Cummings and P.J. Frost (eds.), *Publishing in the organizational sciences* (76–88). Homewood, Ill.: Irwin.

Nystrom, P.C., and Starbuck, W.H. (1984). To avoid organizational crises, unlearn. *Organizational Dynamics* 12(Spring): 53–65.

——— (1984). Managing beliefs in organizations. *Journal of Applied Behavioral Science* 20:277–87.

Oberg, W. (1972). Charisma, commitment, and contemporary organization theory. *Business Topics* 20(2): 18–32.

Oldham, G.R. (1976). The motivation strategies used by supervisors. *Organizational Behavior and Human Performance* 15:66–86.

O'Reilly, C., and Chatman, J. (1984 July). The bases of organizational commitment: The effects of compliance, identification, and internalization on prosocial behavior. Working Paper. University of California, Berkeley.

Ouchi, W.G. (1980). Markets bureaucracies and clans. *Administrative Science Quarterly* 25:129–41.

——— (1981). Theory Z: *How American business can meet the Japanese challenge.* Reading, Mass.: Addison-Wesley.

Parsons, T. (1937). *The structure of social action.* New York: Free Press.

——— (1951). *The social system.* New York: Free Press.

——— (1960). *Structure and process in modern societies.* New York: Free Press.

Parsons, T., Bales, R.F., and Shils, E.A. (1953). *Working papers in the theory of action.* New York: Free Press.

Peirce, C.S. (1878). How to make our ideas clear. *Popular Science Monthly* 12: 286–302. (Reprinted in Peirce, C.S. (1957). *Essays in the philosophy of science* (31–56). New York: Liberal Arts Press.

Perrow, C. (1970). *Organizational analysis.* Monterey, Calif.: Brooks/Cole.

Peters, L.H., Hartke, D.D., and Pohlmann, J.T. (1985). Fiedler's contingency theory of leadership: An application of the meta-analysis procedures of Schmidt and Hunter. *Psychological Bulletin* 91:274–85.

Peters, T., and Austin, N. (1985). *A passion for excellence: The leadership difference.* New York: Random House.

Peters, T., and Waterman, R.H., Jr. (1982). *In search of excellence.* New York: Harper & Row.

Pfeffer, J. (1977). The ambiguity of Leadership. *Academy of Management Review* 2: 104–12.

——— (1981). Management as symbolic action. The creation and maintenance of organizational paradigms. In L.L. Cummings and B.M. Staw (eds.), *Research in organizational behavior* vol. 3 (1–52). Greenwich, Conn.: JAI Press.

Pfeffer, J., and Salancik, G. (1978). *The external control of organizations: A resource dependence perspective.* New York: Harper & Row.

Phillips, J.S. (1984). The accuracy of leadership ratings: A cognitive categorization perspective. *Organizational Behavior and Human Performance* 33:125–38.

Phillips, J.S., and Lord, R.G. (1981). Causal attributions and perceptions of leadership. *Organizational Behavior and Human Performance* 28:143–63.

Piaget, J. (1970). *Genetic epistemology.* New York: Columbia University Press.

Pierce, J., and Dunham, R. (1976). Task design: A literature review. *Academy of Management Review* 1:83–97.

Pierce, J., Dunham, R.B., and Cummings, L.L. (1984). Sources of environmental structuring and employee reactions. *Organizational Behavior and Human Performance* 33:214–42.

Pleck, J., and Sawyer, J. (eds.) (1974). *Men and masculinity.* Englewood Cliffs, N.J.: Prentice-Hall.

Podsakoff, P.M., and Schriesheim, C.A. (1985). Field studies of French and Raven's bases of power: Critique, reanalysis, and suggestions for future research. *Psychological Bulletin* 97:387–411.

Podsakoff, P.M., Todor, W.D., Grover, R.A., and Huber, V. (1984). Situational moderators of leader rewards and punishment behaviors: Fact or fiction? *Organizational Behavior and Human Performance* 34:21–63.

Podsakoff, P.M., Todor, W.D., and Skov, R. (1982). Effect of leader contingent and non-contingent reward and punishment behaviors on subordinate performance and satisfaction. *Academy of Management Journal* 25:810–21.

Polanyi, M. (1966). *The tacit dimension.* New York: Doubleday.

Popper, K.R. (1959). *The logic of scientific discovery.* New York: Basic Books.

———(1963). *Conjectures and refutations: The growth of scientific knowledge.* New York: Harper & Row.

Porter, L., and Lawler, E. (1968). *Managerial attitudes and performance.* Homewood, Ill.: Irwin.

Preuss, E. (1986). *Die frau im management: Vorurteile, fakten und erfahrungen* [Women in management: Prejudices, facts and experiences]. München, West Germany: AWi-Druck.

Price, R.L. (1985). A customer's view of organizational literature. In L.L. Cummings and P. Frost (eds.), *Publishing in the organizational sciences* (125–32). Homewood, Ill.: Irwin.

Probst, G.J.B., and Scheuss, R. (1984). Die ordnung von sozialen systemen-Resultat von organisieren und selbstorganisation. *Zeitschrift fuer Fuehrung und Organisation* 53:480–88.

Pugh, D., Hickson, D., Hinings, C., and Turner, C. (1969). The context of organizational structures. *Administrative Science Quarterly* 14:91–114.

Quinn, R.E. (1984). Applying the competing values approach to leadership: Towards an integrative framework. In J.G. Hunt, D.M. Hosking, C.A. Schriesheim, and R. Stewart (eds.), *Leaders and managers: International perspectives on managerial behavior and leadership* (10–27). Elmsford, N.Y.: Pergamon.

Quinn, R.E., and Cameron, K. (1983). Organizational life cycles and the criteria of effectiveness. *Management Science* 29:33–51.

Quinn, R.E., and Rohrbaugh, J. (1983). A spatial model of effectiveness criteria: Towards a competing values approach to organizational analysis. *Management Science* 29:363–77.

Rackham, N., and Carlisle, J. (1978a). The effective negotiator—Part 1: The behavior of successful negotiators. *Journal of European Industrial Training* 2(6): 6–10.

——— (1978b). The effective negotiator—Part 2: Planning for negotiations. *Journal of European Industrial Training* 2(7): 2–5.

Rakhof, S.H., and Shaefer, R. (1970). Politics, policy and political science. Theoretical alternatives. *Politics and Society* 1(1).

Rauch, C.F., and Behling, O. (1984). Functionalism: Basis for an alternate approach to the study of leadership. In J.G. Hunt, D.M. Hosking, C.A. Schriesheim, and R. Stewart (eds.), *Leaders and managers: International perspectives on managerial behavior and leadership* (45–62). Elmsford, N.Y.: Pergamon.

Reitz, H.J. (1971 August). Managerial attitudes and perceived contingencies between performance and organizational response. Paper presented at the Academy of Management Meeting. Atlanta, Ga.

Rest, J. (1979). *Revised manual for the defining issues test: An objective test of moral judgment development.* Minneapolis, Minn.: Moral Research Projects.

Rice, R.W. (1981). Leader LPC and follower satisfaction: A review. *Organizational Behavior and Human Performance* 28:1–25.

Rice, R.W., Instone, D., and Adams, J. (1984). Leader sex, leader success and leadership process: Two field studies. *Journal of Applied Psychology* 69:1–12.

Ridder, H.G. (1986). Grundprobleme einer ethisch-normativen betriebswirtschaftslehre. In R. Pfriem (ed.), *Okologishe unternehmensplanung.* Frankfurt, West Germany: Campus.

Riley, P., and Finney, M. (1986). Culture change: The case of resistant cultures. Paper prepared for the Organizational Culture Conference, Montreal.

Roberts, N. (1985). Transforming leadership: A process of collective action. *Human Relations* 38:1023–46.

Rohde, K.J. (1951). *Dominance composition as a factor in the behavior of small leaderless groups.* Doctoral dissertation, Northwestern University, Evanston, Ill.

Rokeach, M. (1973). *The nature of human values.* New York: Free Press.

Rotter, J. (1966). Generalized expectancies for internal versus external control of reinforcement. *Psychological Monographs* 80:1–28.

Rousseau, D. (1977). Technological differences in job characteristics, employee satisfaction, and motivation: A synthesis of job design research and sociotechnical systems theory. *Organizational Behavior and Human Performance* 19:18–42.

Rush, M.C., Phillips, J.S., and Lord, R.G. (1981). The effects of a temporal delay in rating on leader behavior descriptions: A laboratory investigation. *Journal of Applied Psychology* 66:442–50.

Rush, M.C., Thomas, J.C., and Lord, R.G. (1977). Implicit leadership theory: A potential threat to the internal validity of leader behavior questionnaires. *Organizational Behavior and Human Performance* 20:93–110.

Salancik, G.R. (1977). Commitment and the control of organizational behavior and belief. In B.M. Staw and G.R. Salancik (eds.), *New directions in organizational behavior* (1–53). Chicago: St. Clair.

Salancik, G.R., and Meindl, J.R. (1984). Corporate attributions as strategic illusions of management control. *Administrative Science Quarterly* 29:238–54.

Salancik, G.R., and Pfeffer, J. (1977a). The bases and use of power in organizational decision making: The case of a university. *Administrative Science Quarterly* 22:427–56.

Saleh, S., and Hoset, J. (1976). Job involvement: Concepts and measurements. *Academy of Management Journal* 19:213–24.

Sales, S. (1972). Authoritarianism: But as for me, give me liberty, or give me maybe, a great big, strong, powerful, leader I can honor, admire, respect, and obey. *Psychology Today* 6(6): 94–98, 140–42.

Samuelson, B.A., Gailbraith, C.S., and McGuire, J.W. (1985). Organizational performance and top management turnover. *Organizational Studies* 6:275–91.

Sanders, P. (1982). Phenomenology: A new way of viewing organizational research. *Academy of Management Review* 7:353–60.

Sashkin, M. (1985a). *Trainer guide: Leader behavior questionnaire.* Bryn Mawr, Pa.: Organization Design and Development.

——— (1985b). Why public bureaucracies cannot be excellent. Unpublished manuscript, U.S. Department of Education, Washington, D.C.

——— (1985c August). Creating organizational excellence: Developing a top management mind set and implementing a strategy. Paper presented as part of a symposium, Achieving Excellence, at the annual meeting of the Academy of Management (Organization Development Division), San Diego, Calif.

Sayles, L. (1964). *Managerial behavior: Administration in complex organizations.* New York: McGraw-Hill.

——— (1979). *Leadership: What effective managers really do . . . and how they do it.* New York: McGraw-Hill.

Schacter, S., and Singer, J.E. (1962). Cognitive, social and physiological determinants of emotional state. *Psychological Review* 69:379–99.

Scheff, T. (1967). Toward a sociological model of consensus. *American Sociological Review* 32:32–46.

Schein, E.H. (1985). *Leadership and organizational culture.* San Francisco: Jossey-Bass.

Scherer, K.R. (1982). Emotion as process: Function, origin and regulation. *Social Science Information* 21:555–70.

Schermerhorn, J.R., Jr., Hunt, J.G., and Osborn, R.N. (1985). *Managing organizational behavior* 2d ed. New York: Wiley.

Schiffer, I. (1973). *Charisma: A psychoanalytic look at mass society.* Toronto: University of Toronto Press.

Schutz, A. (1967). *The phenomenology of the social world.* Evanston, Ill.: Northwestern University Press.

Scott, W.C., Jr. (1977). Leadership: A functional analysis. In J.G. Hunt and L.L. Larson (eds.), *Leadership: The cutting edge* (84–93). Carbondale, Ill.: Southern Illinois University Press.

Scott, W.R. (1981). *Organizations. Rational, natural, and open systems.* Englewood Cliffs, N.J.: Prentice-Hall.

Searle, J.R. (1970). *Speech acts.* London: Cambridge University Press.

Seashore, S. (1954). *Group cohesiveness in the industrial work group.* Ann Arbor: University of Michigan Press.

Seers, A., and Graen, G.B. (1984). The dual attachment concept: A longitudinal investigation of a combination of task characteristics and leader-member exchange. *Organizational Behavior and Human Performance* 33:283–306.

Seligman, M. (1975). *Helplessness.* San Francisco: Freeman.

Selznick, P. (1957). *Leadership in administration.* Evanston, Ill.: Row, Peterson.

Sheridan, J.E., Vredenburgh, D.J., and Abelson, M.A. (1984). Contextual model of leadership influence in hospital units. *Academy of Management Journal* 27:57–78.

Sherif, M., and Sherif, C. (1953). Groups in harmony and tension. New York: Harper & Row.

Shils, E.A. (1965a). Charisma. In D. Sills (ed.), *International encyclopedia of the social sciences* vol. 2 (386–90). New York: Free Press.

—— (1965b). Charisma, order, and status. *American Sociological Review* 30: 199–213.

Shotter, J. (1975). *Images of man in psychological research.* London: Metheun.

Shweder, R.A., and Miller, J.G. (1985). The social construction of the person: How is it possible? In K.J. Gergen and K.E. Davis (eds.), *The social construction of the person* (41–72). New York: Springer.

Simon, H. (1976). *Administrative behavior* 3d ed. New York: Free Press.

Sims, H.P. (1977). The leader as manager of reinforcement contingencies: An empirical example and a model. In J.G. Hunt and L.L. Larson (eds.), *Leadership: The cutting edge* (121–37). Carbondale, Ill.: Southern Illinois University Press.

Singer, E.A., Jr. (1924, reprinted 1980). *Mind as behavior and studies in empirical idealism.* New York: AMS Press.

Singh, R. (1983). Leadership style and reward allocation: Does the LPC scale measure task and relation orientation? *Organizational Behavior and Human Performance* 32:178–97.

Smircich, L. (1983). Concepts of culture and organizational analysis. *Administrative Science Quarterly* 28:339–58.

Smircich, L., and Morgan, G. (1982). Leadership: The management of meaning. *Journal of Applied Behavioral Science* 18:257–73.

Smith, B.J. (1985). *An initial test of a theory of charismatic leadership based on the responses of subordinates* Doctoral dissertation, University of Toronto.

Smith, C.A., Organ, D.W., and Near, J.P. (1983). Organizational citizenship behavior: Its nature and antecedents. *Journal of Applied Psychology* 68:653–63.

Smith, C.A., and Ellsworth, P.C. (1985). Patterns of cognitive appraisal in emotion. *Journal of Personality and Social Psychology* 48:813–38.

Smith, J.E., Carson, K.P., and Alexander, R.A. (1984). Leadership: It can make a difference. *Academy of Management Journal* 27:765–76.

Smith, K.K. (1982). *Groups in conflict—Prisons in disguise.* Dubuque, Iowa: Kendall/Hunt.

Smith, K.K., and Simmons, V. (1983). A rumplestiltskin organization: Metaphors on metaphors in field research. *Administrative Science Quarterly* 28:377–92.

Snyder, G.H., and Diesing, P. (1977). *Conflict among nations: Bargaining, decision-making and system structure in international crises* Princeton, N.J.: Princeton University Press.

Spector, P., and Suttell, B.J. (1975). An experimental comparison of the effectiveness of three patterns of leadership behavior. Technical Report Contract NONR 89003. Washington, D.C.: American Institute for Research.

Spencer-Brown, G. (1979). *Laws of form.* New York: Dutton.

Starbuck, W.H. (1982). Congealing oil: Inventing ideologies to justify acting ideologies out. *Journal of Management Studies* 19:3–27.

Starbuck, W.H., Greve, A., and Hedberg, B.L.T. (1978). Responding to crises. *Journal of Business Administration* 9:111–37.

Staw, B.M. (1977). The experimenting organization: Problems and prospects. In B.M. Staw (ed.), *Psychological foundations of organizational behavior* (33–54). Pacific Palisades, Calif.: Goodyear.

—— (1980). Rationality and justification in organizational life. In B.M. Staw and L.L. Cummings (eds.), *Research in organizational behavior* vol. 2 (45–80). Greenwich, Conn.: JAI Press.

—— (1982). Some judgments on the judgment calls approach. In J.E. McGrath, J. Martin, and R.A. Kulka (eds.), *Judgment calls in research* (119–27). Beverly Hills, Calif.: Sage.

Stein, R.T., Hoffman, L.R., Cooley, S.J., and Pearse, R.W. (1979). Leadership valence: Modeling and measuring the process of emergent leadership. In J.G. Hunt and L.L. Larson (eds.), *Crosscurrents in leadership* (126–47). Carbondale, Ill.: Southern Illinois University Press.

Steinbruner, J. (1974). *The cybernetic theory of decision.* Princeton, N.J.: Princeton University Press.

Stewart, R. (1976). *Contrasts in management: A study of the different types of managers' jobs, their demands and choices.* New York: McGraw-Hill.

—— (1982). *Choices for the manager.* Englewood Cliffs, N.J.: Prentice-Hall.

Stinchcombe, A.L. (1965). *Organizational and social structure.* In. J.G. March (ed.), *Handbook of Organizations* (142–93). Chicago: Rand-McNally.

Stogdill, R.M. (1948). Personal factors associated with leadership: A survey of the literature. *Journal of Psychology* 25:35–71.

—— (1972). Group productivity, drive, and cohesiveness. *Organizational Behavior and Human Performance* 8:26–43.

—— (1974). *Handbook of leadership.* New York: Free Press.

Szilagyi, A.D., Jr., and Schweiger, D.M. (1984). Matching managers to strategies: A review and suggested format. *Academy of Management Review* 9:626–37.

Tajfel, H. (1978). Differentiation between social groups. New York: Harper and Row.

Tajfel, H. (1981). *Human groups and social categories.* Cambridge, U.K.: Cambridge University Press.

Thompson, J.D. (1967). *Organizations in action.* New York: McGraw-Hill.

Thompson, V. (1961). *Modern organizations.* New York: Knopf.

Thorndike, E. (1911). *Animal intelligence.* New York: Macmillan.

Tichy, N.M. (1983). *Managing strategic choice.* New York: Wiley Interscience.

Tichy, N.M., and Ulrich, D. (1984). The leadership challenge: A call for the transformational leader. *Sloan Management Review* 26:59–68.

Tosi, H.J., Jr. (1982). Toward a paradigm shift in the study of leadership. In J.G. Hunt, U. Sekaran, and C.A. Shriesheim (eds.), *Leadership: Beyond establishment views* (222–23). Carbondale, Ill.: Southern Illinois University Press.

Türk, K. (1981). *Personalfuhrung und soziale kontrolle.* Stuttgart, West Germany: Ferdinand Enke Verlag.

Turner, J. (1978). *The structure of sociological theory.* Homewood, Ill.: Dorsey Press.

Tyerman, A., and Spencer, C. (1983). A critical test of the Sherifs' Robber's Cave Experiment: Intergroup cooperation and competition between groups of well-acquainted individuals. *Small Group Behavior* 14:515–32.

Ulman, J.S. (1972). The need for influence: Development and validation of a measure, and comparison of the need for power. *Genetic Psychology Monographs* 85:157–214.

Ulrich, H. (1984). Management—A misunderstood societal function. In H. Ulrich, G.J.B. Probst (eds.), *Self-organization and management of social systems* (80–93). Heidelberg, West Germany: Springer.

Valdes, M.J., and Miller, O. (1985). *Identity of the literary text.* Toronto: University of Toronto Press.

Varela, F.A. (1975). Calculus for self-reference. *International Journal of General Systems* 2:1–25.

——— (1984). The cybernetics of autonomy. Address given at the annual meeting of the American Society for Cybernetics, Philadelphia.

Vecchio, R.P., and Goedel, B.C. (1984). The vertical dyad linkage model of leadership: Problems and prospects. *Organizational Behavior and Human Performance* 34:5–20.

Van de Ven, A., and Delbecq, A. (1974). The effectiveness of Nominal, Delphi, and interacting group decision making processes. *Academy of Management Journal* 17:605–21.

Von Foerster, H. (1979). Cybernetics of cybernetics. In K. Krippendorff (ed.), *Communication and control in society* (5–8). New York: Gordan and Breach.

——— (1981). *Observing Systems.* Seaside, Calif.: Intersystems.

——— (1985). On constructing a reality. In P. Watzlawick (ed.), *The invented reality* (41–45). New York: Norton.

Von Glasersfeld, E. (1981). Einfuhrung in den radikalen konstruktivismus [Introduction to radical constructivism]. In P. Watzlawick (ed.), *Die erfundene wirklichkeit* (16–38). Muenchen, West Germany: Piper Verlag.

——— (1984). *Konstruktion der wirklichkeit und des begriffs der objektivitaet.* Muenchen, West Germany: Siemens.

——— (1984). Knostruktion der wirklichkeit und des begiffes der objektivitat [Construction of reality and the concept of objectivity]. Working paper. University of Georgia, Department of Psychology, Athens, Ga.

——— (1985). An introduction to radical constructivism. In P. Waltzlawick (ed.), *The inverted reality* (17–40). New York: Norton.

Von Hayek, F.A. (1967). *Studies in philosophy, politics and economics.* London: Routledge & Kegan Paul.

——— (1967). The theory of complex phenomena. *Studies in philosophy, politics and economics.* London: Routledge & Kegan Paul.

Vroom, V., and Yetton, P.W. (1973). *Leadership and decision making.* Pittsburgh: University of Pittsburgh Press.

Waldman, D.A., Bass, B.M., and Einstein, W.O. (1985). Effort, performance and transformational leadership in industrial and military service. Working paper 85-80, School of Management, SUNY Binghamton.

Wakabayashi, M., and Graen, G.B. (1984). The Japanese career progress study: A 7-year follow-up. *Journal of Applied Psychology,* 69:603–14.

Walton, R.E., and McKersie, R.B. (1966). Behavioral dilemmas in mixed-motive decision-making. *Behavioral Science* 11:370–84.

Watzlawick, P. (1978). *The language of change: Elements of therapeutic communication.* New York: Basic Books.

——— (ed.) (1985). *The invented reality.* New York: Norton.

Watzlawick, P., Beavin, J.H., and Jackson, D.D. (1967). *Pragmatics of human communication: A study of interactional patterns, pathologies, and paradoxes.* New York: Norton.

Weber, M. (1947). *The theory of social and economic organization.* (A.M. Henderson and T. Parsons, translators) T. Parsons (ed.). New York: Free Press.

Weick, K.E. (1977). Enactment processes in organizations. In B. Staw and G. Salancik (eds.), *New directions in organizational behavior.* (267–300). Chicago: St. Clair.

——— (1978). The spines of leaders. In M. McCall and M. Lombardo (eds.), *Leadership: Where else can we go* (37–61). Durham, N.C.: Duke University Press.

——— (1979a). *The social psychology of organizing.* Reading, Mass.: Addison-Wesley.

——— (1979b). Some thoughts on normal science and Argyris' model I and model II. In J.G. Hunt and L.L. Larson (eds.), *Crosscurrents in leadership* (88–99). Carbondale, Ill.: Southern Illinois University Press.

Weiner, B., Frieze, I.H., Kukla, A., Reed, L., Rest, S., and Rosenbaum, R.M. (1972). Perceiving the cause of success and failure. In E.E. Jones, D.E. Kanoose, H.H. Kelley, R.E. Nisbett, S. Valins, and B. Weiner (eds.), *Attribution: Perceiving the causes of behavior* (95–120). Morristown, N.J.: General Learning Press.

Weiss, H.M. (1977). Subordinate imitation of leaders' behavior: The role of modeling in organizational socialization. *Organizational Behavior and Human Performance* 19:89–105.

Welford, A. (1980). The concept of skill and its application to social performance. In W. Singleton, P. Spurgeon, and R. Stammers (eds.), *Social skills.* New York: Plenum.

White, R. (1959). Motivation reconsidered: The concept of competence. *Psychological Review* 66:297–333.

Whyte, W.H. (1956). *The organization man.* New York: Simon & Schuster.

Wildavsky, A.B. (1972). *The politics of the budgetary process.* Boston: Little, Brown.

Winkler, J.T. (1974). The ghost at the bargaining table: Directors and industrial relations. *British Journal of Industrial Relations* 12:191–212.

Wissema, J.G., Van Der Pol, H.W., and Messer, H.M. (1980). Strategic management archetypes. *Strategic Management Journal* 1:37–47.

Wofford, J.C. (1982). An integrative theory of leadership. *Journal of Management* 8: 27–47.

Wofford, J.C., and Srinivasan, T.N. (1983). Experimental test of leader-environment-follower interaction theory of leadership. *Organizational Behavior and Human Performance* 32:35–54.

Wrapp, H.E. (July–August 1984). Good managers don't make policy decisions. *Harvard Business Review* 8–21.

Wright, P.L., and Taylor, D.S. (1984). *Improving leadership performance.* Englewood Cliffs, N.J.: Prentice-Hall International.

Yankelovich, D., and Immerwahr, J. (1983). *Putting the work ethic to work* New York: Public Agenda Foundation.

Yukl, G.A. (1981). *Leadership in organizations.* Englewood Cliffs, N.J.: Prentice-Hall.

Yukl, G.A., and Nemeroff, W. (1979). Identification and measurement of specific categories of leadership behavior. In J.G. Hunt and L.L. Larson (eds.), *Crosscurrents in leadership* (164–200). Carbondale, Ill.: Southern Illinois University Press.

Zajonc, R.B. (1980). Feeling and thinking: Preferences need no inferences. *American Psychologist* 35:151–75.

——— (1984). On the primacy of affect. *American Psychologist* 39:117–23.

Zaleznik, A. (1977). Managers and leaders: Are they different? *Harvard Business Review* (May–June): 67–78.

Zaltman, G., and Duncan, R. (1977). *Strategies for planned change.* New York: Wiley.

Zartman, I.W. (1977). Negotiation as a joint decision making process. In I.W. Zartman (ed.), *The negotiation process: Theories and applications* (67–86). Beverly Hills, Calif.: Sage.

Zey-Ferrell, M., and Aiken, M. (eds.) (1981). *Complex organizations: Critical perspectives.* Glenville, Ill.: Scott, Foresman.

Name Index

Abelson, M.A., 206
Abelson, R.P., 39
Abernathy, W.J., 143
Ackoff, R.L., 161
Adair, J., 156
Adams, G.B., 216
Adams, J., 206
Aiken, M., 93
Alexander, R.A., 180, 247
Alluto, J.A., 35
Anderson, R.A., 250, 251
Argyle, M., 95
Argyris, C., 15, 16, 89, 112, 146, 156, 223
Astley, G.W., 27n3, 232
Austin, J., 269
Austin, N., 78
Avolio, B.J., 6, 7, 8, 9, 44, 46, 68, 73, 74, 76, 77, 78, 79, 135, 136, 137, 274, 275

Baetz, M.L., 54, 174, 248, 249
Bales, R.F., 57, 60, 109
Baliga, B.R., 86, 87, 183, 234, 245, 274
Barber, J.D., 70
Barnard, C., 231
Bartölke, K., 86, 87, 151, 261n
Bass, M., 6, 7, 8, 9, 29, 30, 32, 34, 35, 36, 37, 42, 44, 46, 47, 48, 51, 68, 70, 73, 74, 76, 77, 78, 79, 103, 135, 136, 137, 143, 155, 169, 174, 274, 275
Bateson, G., 265
Batstone, E., 100
Bazerman, M.H., 154
Beavin, J.H., 263

Bednar, D., 136
Behling, O., 107
Ben-Gurion, D., 46
Benne, K.D., 61
Bennis, W.G., 6, 38, 52, 62, 64, 68, 78, 80, 81, 82, 133, 134, 248
Bergmann, T., 151
Berkowitz, L., 250
Berlew, D.E., 16
Berne, E., 78
Bettman, J.R., 172
Beyer, J.M., 17
Billig, M., 197
Binning, J.F., 181
Bishop, Y.M.M., 116
Blair, J.D., 165
Blake, R.R., 36, 60, 61, 119, 174
Blanchard, K.H., 36, 57, 58, 175
Blauner, R., 25
Blumer, H., 27n3
Boal, K.M., 5, 6, 7, 8, 9, 67, 68, 71, 275, 276
Boehm, M., 82
Bogart, P., 250, 251
Boraston, I., 100
Bradley, R., 25
Brehm, J., 25
Brickman, P., 12, 13, 14, 18, 20n
Brown, C., 147
Brown, M.H., 92, 96, 99, 104
Browning, R., 29
Bryson, J.M., 5, 6, 7, 8, 9, 16, 67, 68, 71, 275, 276
Burnham, D.H., 54, 55
Burns, J.M., 6, 29, 33, 34, 52, 70, 80

Burrell, G., 27n3, 262, 263, 275
Butterfield, D.A., 7, 71, 178, 184

Cage, J.H., 206
Calas, M.B., 87, 166, 167, 168, 235, 236, 237, 239, 241, 264, 274, 280, 281, 282, 283
Cameron, K., 129, 130
Campbell, D., 27n4
Campbell, J.P., 237
Carbonell, J.L., 206
Carlisle, J., 98
Carr, D., 185
Carroll, G.R., 246, 247
Carroll, S.J., 149
Carson, K.P., 180, 247
Cascio, W.F., 35
Cashman, J.F., 30, 107, 112
Chatman, J., 75
Checkland, P.B., 274
Chemers, M.M., 176
Chernick, L., 251
Child, J., 89
Churchman, C.W., 161
Clark, P.A., 106
Clore, G.L., 39
Cook, R., 170n
Cook, T., 27n4
Cooley, S.J., 91
Coons, A., 52, 60
Cowan, T.A., 163
Craig, J.R., 112, 178
Crouch, A., 85, 86, 87, 88, 114, 158, 159, 160, 164, 279, 280
Culler, J., 205
Cummings, L.L., 76, 79, 165, 199, 206, 226

Dachler, H.P., 87, 151, 163, 165, 243, 244, 278, 285n
Dansereau, F., 35, 112, 179
Davis, T., 103
Davoust, M.J., 177
deButts, J., 147
Deising, P., 101
De Jong, R.D., 257
Delbecq, A., 198
Derickson, U., 69
Dobbins, G.H., 206
Doherty, E., 235
Donnell, S.M., 61
Douglas, T., 90

Dow, T., 37
Downey, H.K., 206
Drenth, P.J.D., 94
Drucker, P.F., 98, 193
Dubin, R., 5, 90
Dukerich, J.M., 11, 73, 79, 182, 214, 229, 231
Duncan, R., 25
Dunham, R.B., 24, 25, 76, 206
Dunnette, M.D., 237
Dyer, D., 145
Dyllick, T., 261n

Eco, U., 205
Eden, D., 41
Ehrlich, S.B., 11, 73, 79, 181–182, 214, 229, 231
Einstein, W.O., 44
Eiser, J.R., 98
Ellsworth, P.C., 39, 40, 41
Emery, F.E., 161
Eschweiler, W., 151
Etzionni, A., 155
Evans, M.G., 30, 175

Farris, G.F., 112, 178
Farrow, D.L., 32, 35
Feldman, M., 103
Feyerabend, P.K., 152, 262
Fiedler, F.E., 36, 51, 57, 58, 71, 107, 129, 144, 176, 177, 179, 181, 190, 210, 255, 256
Fienberg, S.E., 116
Finney, M., 80
Fisher, W.R., 214
Flechsenberger, D., 151
Fleishman, E.A., 60
Ford, G., 46
Ford, J.D., 175
Frankl, V., 23
Freeman, J., 247
French, J.R.P., 74, 75
Frenkel, S., 100
Friesen, P., 130
Frieze, I.H., 170, 172
Frost, E., 209, 210
Frost, P., 165, 199, 206, 226
Fulmer, R.M., 6, 7, 9, 80, 81, 82, 136, 137, 274

Galbraith, C.S., 231
Gandhi, M., 33, 46

Gardner, W., 94
Garfinkel, H., 27n3
Geertz, C., 214
Gergen, K.J., 162, 261n, 262, 265, 268, 269, 273
Giddens, A., 18, 19, 83
Gilroy, F.D., 27n2
Gioia, D., 97
Göedel, B.C., 206
Golembiewski, R., 109
Goodheim, L., 46
Goodman, P.S., 186
Gouldner, A., 235
Govindarajan, V., 177
Graeff, C.L., 206
Graen, G., 30, 107, 112, 179, 190, 206
Graham, J.W., 7, 8, 73, 74, 75, 76
Green, S.G., 181
Greene, C.N., 178, 107 ???
Greiner, L.E., 129
Greller, M.M., 32
Greve, A., 158
Grieco, M.S., 96, 100, 104
Grover, R.A., 206
Gupta, A.K., 177

Habermas, J., 27n3, 262
Hackman, J.R., 24, 25
Haga, W.J., 112, 179
Haldane, E.S., 185
Hall, B., 23
Hall, J., 60, 61
Hall, P.M., 17
Halsey, W.F., 27n2, 11
Hammarskjold, D., 46
Hannan, M.T., 247
Hanson, N.R., 263
Harding, S., 214, 215
Harris, E.F., 60
Hartke, D.D., 58
Harvey, J.H., 14, 15
Hayes, R.H., 143
Haythorn, W., 250
Hebb, D.O., 37
Heckhausen, H., 170n
Hedberg, B.L.T., 17, 27n5, 158
Heider, F., 170, 171
Heilman, M.E., 206
Heller, F.A., 94, 107
Herschlag, J.K., 206
Hersey, P., 36, 57, 58, 175

Hesley, J.W., 251
Hewitt, J.P., 17
Hickson, D.J., 25, 113, 153
Hinings, C.R., 25, 113
Hintikka, M.B., 214, 215
Hitler, A., 46
Hofer, C.W., 177
Hoffman, L.R., 91
Holland, P.W., 116
Hollander, E.P., 30, 91, 107, 256, 257
Holsti, O., 97, 103
Homans, G.C., 100, 108, 109
Hornstein, H.A., 206
Hosek, J., 24
Hosking, D.M., 85, 86, 87, 89, 92, 93, 96, 97, 98, 99, 100, 103, 104, 106, 107, 151, 154, 155, 156, 165, 166, 202, 232, 277, 278, 279
House, R.J., 7, 12, 18, 19, 20n, 30, 35, 37, 39, 47, 54, 58, 68, 73, 77, 81, 107, 129, 174, 175, 243, 244, 248, 249, 255, 256, 262, 263, 264, 265, 275, 283, 284
Howell, J.M., 37
Hrapchak, W.J., 178
Huber, V., 206
Huff, A.S., 97, 98, 107
Hunger, J.D., 70, 165–167, 228, 229, 233, 280
Hunt, J.G., 8, 30, 67, 74, 75, 85, 86, 87, 90, 91, 92, 107, 130, 136, 151, 165, 166, 201, 202, 234, 245, 274

Iacocca, L., 41, 69, 145
Ickes, W., 14, 15
Ilgen, D.R., 32
Immerwahr, J., 32, 43
Ingersoll, V.H., 216
Instone, D., 206

Jablin, F.M., 112
Jackson, D.D., 263
Jacobs, T.O., 8, 74
Jago, A.G., 74, 75, 190
James, W., 39, 188
Janis, I.L., 99, 109
Jaques, E., 52, 55, 56, 130
Jermier, J.M., 27n3, 58, 79, 177, 255
Jones, E.E., 178
Jones, G.R., 206

Johnson, D.W., 109
Julian, J.W., 107

Kahn, R.L., 51, 52, 55, 61, 74, 77, 129, 209
Kanter, R.M., 95, 106, 146, 264, 269
Kaplan, R.E., 126
Katz, D., 51, 52, 55, 61, 74, 77, 129
Kaufman, H., 17
Kavanaugh, M.J., 178
Keller, E.F., 214, 215
Kellerman, B., 215
Kelley, H.H., 171
Kelman, H.C., 75
Kelvin, P., 92, 98, 99
Kennedy, J.F., 70
Kennedy, R.F., 11
Kennedy, T., 11, 27n1
Kenny, D.A., 206
Kerr, S., 19, 58, 79, 169n, 177, 184, 255
Kidd, R.F., 14, 15
Kimberly, J.R., 129, 130
Klimoski, R., 261n
Kluckhohn, C., 155
Knight, P.A., 206
Knowlton, W.A., 32
Koehler, W., 185
Koestler, A.J., 160
Kohlberg, L., 23
Kohn, A., 264
Koopman, P.L., 94
Kotter, J.P., 95, 98, 99, 100, 103
Kreitner, R., 30
Krippendorff, K., 262, 263, 265, 274, 279, 285
Kristeva, J., 205
Kuhn, T.S., 185, 186, 187, 189, 262
Kukla, A., 170, 172

Lammers, C.J., 153
Larson, J.R., 181, 206
Larson, L.L., 67, 91, 92, 165, 166
Lau, R.R., 172
Lawler, E.E., 23, 24
Lawrence, P.R., 95, 103, 145, 240
Lay, B., 27n2
Lazarus, R., 28n7, 39
Lewicki, R.J., 154
Lewin, K., 52, 64, 80, 81, 160, 174
Lewis, A., 112
Lewis, M., 82
Libby, R., 112

Lieberson, S., 180
Liegle, L., 151
Likert, R., 109
Lim, F.G., 112
Lippitt, G.L., 129, 174
Lombardo, M.M., 38
Loomis, C.P., 109
Loomis, Z.K., 109
Lord, R.G., 181
Lorsch, J., 240
Lovejoy, A., 92
Lowin, A., 112, 178
Lugle, J.H., 206
Luhmann, N., 265
Luthans, F., 30, 103
Lyotard, J., 210, 211, 214, 215, 216, 222, 223

McCall, M.W., Jr., 38, 178, 248
McClelland, D.C., 52, 54, 55, 253, 257
McElroy, J.G., 70, 165–167, 206, 228, 229, 233, 280
McGregor, D., 174
McGuire, J.W., 231
McKersie, R.B., 101
Maier, N.R.F., 58
Malik, F., 163
Mann, R.D., 51, 52, 55
Mann, L., 99
March, J.G., 16, 103
Marrow, A., 145
Martin, J., 82
Martinko, M., 94
Mason, R.O., 166, 186, 188, 189, 195
Maturana, H., 162
Mawhinney, T.C., 175
Megargee, G.I., 250, 251
Meindl, J.R., 11, 73, 79, 181, 214, 229, 231
Melcher, A.J., 86
Merleau-Ponty, M., 185
Messer, H.M., 177
Mayer, M., 92, 278
Meyer, W., 170n
Miller, D., 130
Miller, J.G., 187
Miller, O., 212
Miner, J.B., 11, 54, 67, 179, 251, 252, 255
Minsky, M., 94, 97
Mintzberg, H., 51, 129, 140, 178

Mischel, W., 250, 251
Mitchell, T.R., 30, 58, 129, 180, 181
Mitroff, I.I., 166, 186, 188, 189, 195, 273
Monson, T.C., 251
Morgan, G., 27n3, 97, 261n, 262, 263, 275
Morley, I.E., 85, 86, 87, 92, 93, 96, 97, 98, 100, 106, 151, 154, 155, 156, 232, 277, 278, 279
Morrow, P., 169n
Mouton, J.S., 36, 60, 61, 119, 174
Mowday, R.T., 24, 171, 179
Mulder, M., 257
Mummendey, A., 268

Nance, J.J., 143
Nanus, B., 6, 62, 68, 78, 133, 134
Near, J.P., 76, 77
Neisser, U., 100, 263
Nemeroff, W., 60
Neuberger, U., 153
Newcomb, T., 14
Newcomb, W.W., 152
Nidditch, P.H., 185
Nisbett, R., 100, 178
Nord, W.R., 240
Novak, W.L., 145
Nystrom, P.C., 158

Oberg, W., 37
O'Connor, E., 35
O'Connor, J.F., 180
Oldham, F., 24, 25
Oldham, G.R., 30
Orban, J.A., 206
O'Reilly, C., 75
Organ, D.W., 76, 77
Ortony, A., 39
Osborn, R.N., 8, 85, 92, 130, 136
Ouchi, W.G., 62, 82, 154

Palgi, M., 151
Papert, S., 94, 97
Parsons, T., 56, 57, 58, 59, 63, 64, 109
Pearse, R.W., 91
Peery, N., 11n
Peirce, C.S., 188
Pence, E.C., 206
Pennings, J.M., 113, 186
Perrow, C., 57
Peters, L.H., 58

Peters, T., 48, 78, 158, 183
Peterson, M.F., 166, 167, 183, 280
Piaget, J., 263
Pierce, J., 24, 25, 76, 79, 206
Pfeffer, J., 11, 113, 158, 169, 177, 178, 180, 228, 229, 246, 264
Phillips, J.S., 181, 206
Podsakoff, P.M., 30, 32, 75, 206
Pohlmann, J.T., 58
Polanyi, M., 185
Poole, P.P., 97
Popper, K.R., 199
Porter, L., 23, 24
Preuss, E., 264
Probst, G.J.B., 87, 88, 163, 261n
Pritchard, R.D., 237
Pugh, D., 25

Quinn, R.E., 129, 130, 233

Rackham, N., 98
Rakhof, S.H., 230
Rauch, C.F., 107
Raven, B.H., 74, 75
Reed, L., 170, 172
Reitz, H.J., 30
Rest, S., 170, 172
Rice, R.W., 206
Ridder, H.G., 156
Riley, P., 7, 9, 80
Ritsema, J.R., 257
Robbins, H., 205
Roberts, N., 17
Rohde, K.J., 250
Rohrbaugh, J., 130
Rokeach, M., 23, 155
Roosevelt, E., 46
Roosevelt, F.D., 35
Rosenbaum, R.M., 170, 172
Rosner, M., 151
Ross, G.R.T., 185
Ross, L., 100
Rotter, J., 25
Rousseau, D., 25
Rush, M.C., 181
Russell, D., 172

Saal, F.E., 206
Salancik, G.R., 113, 180, 198, 229, 246
Saleh, S., 24
Sales, S., 257
Samuelson, B.A., 231

Sanders, P., 18, 27n3
Sashkin, M., 6, 7, 9, 62, 63, 64, 68, 80, 81, 82, 136, 137, 184, 274
Sayles, L., 95, 104
Scerbo, M.M., 206
Schacter, S., 39
Scheff, T., 15
Schein, E.H., 56, 57, 64, 264
Scherer, K.R., 39
Schermerhorn, J.R., Jr., 136
Scheuss, R., 163
Schiffer, I., 52
Schmidt, W.H., 129
Schneck, R.E., 113
Schneider, B., 261n
Schon, D.A., 15, 16, 146
Schriesheim, C.A., 75, 90, 91, 92, 107, 151, 165, 166, 184, 201, 202
Schuler, R.S., 30, 206
Schutz, A., 27n3
Schweiger, D.M., 176
Scott, W.C., 175, 231
Searle, J.R., 269
Seashore, S., 26
Seers, A., 206
Sekaran, U., 90, 91, 92, 165, 166, 201, 202
Seligman, M., 16, 25
Selznick, P., 97
Sgro, J.A., 206
Shaefer, R., 230
Shani, A.B., 41
Sheats, P., 61
Sheridan, J.E., 206
Sherif, C., 197
Sherif, M., 197
Shils, E.A., 37, 57, 81
Shotter, J., 268
Simmons, V., 206, 264
Simon, H.A., 16, 130
Sims, H.P., 30, 175
Singer, E.A., 161
Singer, J.E., 39
Singh, R., 206
Sitkin, S., 82
Skov, R., 30, 32
Slocum, J., 19
Smircich, L., 87, 97, 158, 166, 167, 168, 235, 236, 237, 239, 241, 261n, 262, 264, 274, 280, 281, 282, 283
Smith, B.J., 37

Smith, C.A., 39, 40, 41, 76, 77
Smith, J.E., 180, 247
Smith, K.K., 206, 264, 268, 269, 278
Smith, P.B., 166, 167, 183, 280
Snyder, G.H., 101
Solomon, R.J., 32, 35
Spector, P., 30
Spencer, C., 197
Spencer-Brown, G., 265
Srinivasan, T.N., 206, 255
Starbuck, W.H., 158
Staw, B.M., 19, 24, 161, 237
Steers, R.M., 24
Stein, R.T., 91
Stein, V.A., 269
Steinbruner, J., 94, 100
Stemerding, A., 257
Stephenson, G.M., 101
Stewart, R., 95, 98, 107, 130, 133, 151, 165, 166, 202
Stinchcombe, A.L., 247
Stogdill, R.M., 26, 52, 53, 54, 55, 56, 59, 60, 70, 248, 249, 250, 252, 253
Stone, R., 224
Strand, T., 166
Suttell, B.J., 30
Szilagyi, A.D., 176

Tajfel, H., 196
Taylor, D.S., 95
Thomas, J.C., 181
Thompson, J.D., 24, 57, 63, 134
Thompson, V., 25
Thorndike, E., 23, 69
Tichy, N.M., 68, 135, 140, 146
Todor, W.D., 30, 32, 206
Tosi, H.L., Jr., 133, 149, 178, 180
Türk, K., 154
Turner, C., 25
Tyerman, A., 197

Ulman, J.S., 253
Ulrich, D., 68
Ulrich, H., 160

Valdes, M.J., 212
Valenzi, E.R., 32, 35
Van Der Pol, H.W., 177
Van de Ven, A.H., 27n3, 198, 232
Varela, F.A., 263, 265
Vecchio, R.P., 206

Von Bertalanffy, L., 187
Von Foerster, H., 162, 263, 265
Von Glasersfeld, E., 162, 265
Von Hayek, F.A., 164, 272
Vredenburgh, D.J., 206
Vroom, V., 36, 107, 129, 175, 190, 256

Wakabayashi, M., 190
Waldman, D.A., 44
Walter-Busch, E., 261n
Walton, R.E., 101
Waterman, R.H., 48, 78, 158, 183
Watzlawick, P., 162, 263, 284
Weber, J.F., 37
Weber, M., 11, 52, 56, 80, 81
Weick, K.E., 102, 187, 223, 272
Weiner, B., 170, 172
Weiss, H.M., 112
Weitz, B.A., 172
Welch, J.F., 36
White, R., 25, 174

Whyte, W.H., 272
Wildavsky, A.B., 16
Wissema, J.G., 177
Wofford, J.C., 179, 206, 255
Wrapp, H.E., 93, 98
Wright, P.L., 95

Yammarino, F.J., 35
Yankelovich, D., 32, 43
Yetton, P.W., 36, 85, 86, 87, 88, 107, 129, 158, 159, 160, 164, 175, 190, 256, 279, 280
Young, A., 46
Yukl, G., 11n, 37, 60, 179, 256

Zaccaro, S.J., 206
Zajonc, R.B., 28n7, 40
Zaleznik, A., 133
Zaltman, G., 25
Zartman, I.W., 93
Zey-Ferrell, M., 93

Subject Index

Absenteeism, 180
Academy of Management Journal, 206
Academy of Management Review, 206
Action: theories of, 17
Action framework, 57, 63
Activation: level of, 41
Adaptation, 59, 63
Administration, 55
Administrative Science Quarterly, 206
Aggressiveness, 54
Altruism, 76
Ambiguity: conditions of, 17
Applied psychology, 276
Arab Oil Embargo of 1973, 145
Assumptions: epistemological, 1; of researchers, 165; about leadership and management, 273–275
Attention: focusing of, 62; mentioned, 40, 64
Attitudes: behavior and, 24
Attribution process, 170, 229
Authority and power, 155
Automotors: subordinates as, 7

Behavior: an equilibrium model of, 108–109; followers, 19; leadership and, 59–65; mentioned, 52
Behavioral variability: constraints on, 251
Behavior modification, 175
Behavior patterns, 180
Business Periodicals Index, 206
Business Week, 147

Casual attributions: the nature of, 170–172
Center for Creative Leadership, 241
Centralization, 25

Charisma: as a person variable, 7; at all organizational levels, 37–38; cognitive process view of, 39–41; defined, 34; emphasis on, 7; in executive leadership behavior, 61–64; existence for, 81; in followers, 77; forms of, 12; viewed as gift or relationship, 8; mentioned, 137
Charisma leaders: visionary and crisis-produced, 16–18
Charismatic leader: influence on followers, 38–39; mentioned, 276
Charismatic leadership: approach to study of, 6; crisis-produced, 6; defined and measured, 37–39; discussed, 5; essence of, 62; essential function of, 12; explored for operation and executive leadership, 6; House's theory of, 77; model of, 12, 18–26; pattern for, 237; primary function of, 26–27; primary impact of, 19; propositions on, 22–26; requirements for, 16; research needed on, 70–71; theory of, 67–72; types of, 16–18; mentioned, 2, 137, 256
Charismatic leadership scale, 35
Charismatic relationship, 41–42
Charismatic theory, 174
Citizenship behavior, 7
Cognition, 263
Cognitive ability, 55
Cognitive complexity, 250
Cognitive development, 55
Cognitive dimensions: defined, 40
Cognitive frameworks, 97

Cognitive sociology, 97
Command: unity of, 247
Communal interchange, 162
Communication: one-way process of, 274; mentioned, 63, 95
Communication processes, 263
Compliance: followers', 75
Concepts: considered for leadership, 283
Conceptual framework: model of, 80–82
Concern, 63
Conduct: evaluation of, 18
Conflict legitimacy, 109, 114, 160, 164
Consensus, 171, 229, 230
Consideration, 36, 38, 60
Consistency, 63, 171, 229, 230
Constraints: conclusions on basic sets of, 267–274; mentioned, 141
Constructivism, 162
Contingency Model, 57
Contingency variables, 94
Contingent reinforcement: strategy of, 32; mentioned, 30
Contingent reward, 30, 43, 137
Coordination, 56, 57, 59, 63, 247
Co-orientation: detailed, 15; in group behavior, 14–15; within group of followers, 16; mentioned, 12
Core processes, 97
Core problems: defined, 101
Corporate strategic planners, 196
Correspondence: internal and external, 13–14. *See also* External correspondence; Internal correspondence
Crisis-produced behavior, 19
Crisis-produced charisma, 25
Crisis-produced leadership, 68, 69
Crisis situation: leader in a, 24; mentioned, 8
Criterion variables, 247–249
Criticism, 223
Crosscurrents in Leadership, 91
Cultural dynamics, 203
Cultural space: leadership field as a, 201
Culture: function of, 9; mentioned, 80

Decision making: demands of, 98–99; studies of, 94–95; mentioned, 96, 99, 155, 175

Decision-making Theory, 175
Decision processes: recognition of, 231
Defense Advanced Research Projects Agency, 210
Demands, choices, and constraints: discussion on, 133–135; linked to life cycle, 138–148
Differentiation, 240
Discourse analysis, 83
Discretion: time span of, 55
Discretionary leadership, 8
Dominance Scale of the California Personality Inventory, 250

Effective culture, 63
Effective leaders: identification of, 247–248; mentioned, 54
Effective leadership: components of, 82; functions of, 81; summarized, 64; mentioned, 73, 97, 252
Effective performance, 79
Effort: anticipated levels of, 40
Emotional arousal, 40
Emotions: viewed, 39–40
Environment: leadership in, 56
Environmental variables, 22, 23, 69
Environmental processes: policy generated by, 186–187
Environmental scannings, 136
Epistemological concerns, 7, 82
Epistemological implications, 280
Epistemological issues, 3
Epistemology: leadership and management research, 280–282
Equilibrium: concept of, 109
Equilibrium model: about stable and unstable state in an, 113–114; on changes in team membership of an, 118–123
Ethics: considered for constructing of leadership and management, 282–285
Executive behavior, 51
Executive leader: and the creating of a "culture," 63; summarized, 59
Executive leadership: charisma in, 81; macro variables of, 56–57
Executive succession: effects of, 246
Expectations: horizon of, 205
External correspondence: condition for, 19; factors affecting, 25; heightened for individual followers,

16; high degree of, 22; mentioned, 18

External validity, 17

Extraordinary vision, 5

Extrinsic validity: experience of, 23; mentioned, 12, 13, 14, 19, 68

Family-based employment networks, 104–105

Fiedler's Least Preferred Coworker (LPC), 143

Follower autonomy, 73, 77

Follower characteristics, 12, 22

Follower free choice, 76–78

Follower perception, 19

Followers: emotional arousal in, 40; emotional effect on, 39; effective performance by, 79

Followers behavior: charismatic leadership with respect to, 275–280

Followers performance: nature of, 75–76

Foreign competition, 145

Formalization, 25

Formal negotiation, 96

Gender differences: search for, 219–220

Generalized compliance, 76

General systems theory, 239–240

General system thinking, 280

Goal attainment, 57, 59, 63–64

Great-man theory, 174

Group cohesion, 177

Group performance and cohesiveness, 26; mentioned, 79

Group productivity, 273

Handbook of Industrial and Organizational Psychology, 237

Handbook of Leadership, 70

Horizons: expanding our, 224–225

Hypothesis testing, 207

Identification, 75

Ideological goal: on the articulation of an, 19–20

Ideology: concept of, 23

Independent variables, 256

Individual attributes, 268

Individual: natural mental properties of the, 267–270

Individualized consideration: definition of, 34; mentioned, 38, 77, 137

Influence process, 149

Initiating structure, 60

Initiation, 36

Inspirational leadership, 37

Integration, 57, 63, 240

Intellectual persuasion, 38

Intellectual stimulation: defined, 34; mentioned, 41, 77, 137

Intelligence, 164

Interaction: on group, 59

Interactions and relations, 163–164

Interactive behavior, 61

Interface management, 136

Intergroup relations, 196–197

Internal action, 56

Internal communication, 247

Internal correspondence: condition for, 19; heightened, 16; high degree of, 22; low task scope and, 25; need for, 69; on factors that influence, 23–24; mentioned, 18

Internalization, 75

Interpretations: plurality of, 205; mentioned, 284

Interpretative scheme, 6, 16

Interpretists orientation, 9

Interpretist views, 7

Intertextuality, 205

Intraorganizational power; theory of, 113

Intrinsic validity: experience of, 23; mentioned, 12, 13, 14, 17, 19, 68

Isolation: about community research, 8, 225

Job involvement, 24

Job role uncertainty, 30, 32

Job satisfaction, 30

Job scope: low, 24

Journal of Applied Psychology, 206

Journal of Management, 206

Journal of Personality and Social Psychology, 170n

Law of Effect, 69

Leader: about training of, 155–157; characterization of a, 252–253; charismatic qualities attributed to a, 5; concept of a, 155; effects of, 245–246; exchange with subordinates, 30; from a

Leader (*continued*)
transforming perspective, 38; gifted with charisma, 11; on significance of, 234; operational and executive, 6; primary role of, 139; role of the charismatic, 12–13; time span of, 55–56

Leader authority, 58

Leader behavior: in relation to subordinate performance, 60; meaning of, 9; on proportion of variance in, 180–181; mentioned, 18, 178

Leader Behavior Description Questionnaire (LBDQ—Form III), 36, 62

Leader characteristics, 18

Leader dominance, 250. *See* Dominance Scale of the California Personality Inventory

Leader effectiveness: criterion for, 139; status, 248; mentioned, 36, 43, 129, 255

Leader environment: follower interaction theory (LEFI theory), 255

Leader-follower relations: definition of, 74–75; mentioned, 29

Leader-follower relationship, 51

Leader-member relations, 58

Leader-member relationships, 88

Leader performance, 23, 69

Leader's identity: quest for, 219

Leader's personality: function of, 5; interaction of, 176

Leadership: academic culture of, 203; analysis of, 249; artform of, 82; causal attributions used in study of, 169–170; concept of, 3, 90, 91, 93, 170–180, 228; conception of, 87; conceptual framework of, 7; on controversy for studying, 11; core processes of, 92; *crisis-produced,* 11; distinctiveness, 171, 229, 230; diversity in 240; as a dominant role, 181–182; in dynamic organizational setting, 85–88; epistemological assumptions in study of, 1; on the exchange models of, 29; field of, 201; focused on *in context,* 8; about functional terms of, 153; gestation-to-birth transition,

139–141; and group members, 74; image created for, 238; limitations of normal science in, 236–239; marginal utility of, 180–181; paradigm of, 29–30; participants of, 90–91; perspectives of, 2; perspectives on, 178–179; on problems in the study of, 236; process aspects of, 86; process nature of, 279; reading the field of, 206–207; on research around the phenomenon of, 233; skills of, 96–102; social construction of, 156–157; social reality a part of, 151; substitutes for, 177; as Superior/Subordinate influence, 135; systematic approach to, 158–159; theories detailed for, 228–234; theory of, 9

Leadership activity; nature of, 253

Leadership behavior: current models of, 36; description of, 230–231; evaluation of, 46; mentioned, 148, 149

Leadership Behavioral Research: overview on, 253–254

Leadership-by-contingent reinforcement: effectiveness of, 30

Leadership concept: value of, 89

Leadership effectiveness: defined, 93–94; mentioned, 58, 129

Leadership establishment, 201, 202

Leadership Frontiers, 67

Leadership: The Cutting Edge, 67

Leadership literature, 214

Leadership processes: analyses of, 90; aspects of, 2; an overview given on, 277–280; mentioned, 269

Leadership proposition: birth stage, 141–142; growth stage, 142–144; maturity stage, 144–145

Leadership reality, 262

Leadership research: on leader and subordinate, 29; on new directions in, 261–267; about new directions in, 263–267; new focus in, 5; state of turmoil in, 1; questionable, 245–248; as revealed in a complex social system, 1–2

Leadership roles, 234

Leadership skills: significance of, 85; a theory of, 156

Leadership skills model: implementation of, 102–105
Leadership substitutes theory, 255
Leadership theory: causal explanations given for, 172–178; on the crisis in, 243; explanation of, 67–72; performance outcome played in, 169; mentioned, 9, 189
Leadership Trait Research, 249–253
Leadership traits, 52–54, 283
Leadership variables: impact of, 234
Leadership vistas: constraints on emerging new, 267–282; mentioned, 274–275
Lexical expression, 207
Life cycle: on phases of organizations, 129–149; phases of, 139–148
Linguistic process, 268

Macro leadership: versus micro leadership, 1; mentioned, 56, 86
Macro vs micro skills, 95
Management: leadership researched in, 11; about leadership theory in, 169
Management-by-exception: defined, 35; mentioned, 30, 43, 137
Management team: behavioral characteristics of the, 107–108; building and changes in membership of a, 123–125; on building and process training of, 126–127
Managerial behavior: studies of, 90, 95–96
Managerial effectiveness: defined, 134
Managerial goals, 272
Managerial role-motivation theory, 252
Managerial work team: survey done on, 114–115
Managers: dynamic process of, 3; as effective leader, 133–135; about mental elements of, 270; mid-level and supervisory-level, 143, 144, 146
Manager-subordinate exchange, 107
Manager-subordinate performance, 109–113, 116–118
Manager-subordinate relations, 91
Manipulation, 155, 207
Manipulative leadership, 32
Measure of Potency, 220–221
Metabehaviours versus variables, 7

Micro leadership: contrasts between macro and, 1; mentioned, 56, 86
Micro-Variables: identified, 57–59
Military leadership: studies of, 42
Miner Sentence Completion Scale, 252
Morale, 140, 142, 144
Motivation: concept of, 54; mentioned, 25, 140, 142, 144, 237
Motivation theory, 23
Multifactor Leadership Questionnaire (MLQ—Form 5), 35
Multiple identification, 268

nAch, 54
n(Pow), 54, 55
Natural mental properties, 272
Negotiation: process of, 92, 98; mentioned, 105
Negotiation skills, 153–155
Network development and support, 136
Networking: context of, 98; explanation for, 100–101
New Directions in Attribution Research, 14n, 15n
Nominal Group Techniques, 198
"normal science" approach, 3
Novelty, 40

Objectivist research, 7
Observations: as related to leadership, 265
Ohio State Leader Behavior Description Questionnaire, 254
Openness: element of, 185; mentioned, 187
Operant conditioning theory, 175
Operational leadership behaviors, 60–61
Oppositions: identification of, 211–212
Order: on patterns of, 163–164
Organizational advocacy, 136
Organizational behavior: study of, 67; theories of effectiveness in, 161; mentioned, 241, 244
Organizational Behavior and Human Performances (OBHP): an article on leadership in, 209–210
Organizational citizenship: criteria for, 75–76; research of multidimensional measure in, 76; mentioned, 7, 74

Organizational commitment, 24
Organizational culture: on creating, 62; creation of an, 60; of executive leaders, 81; importance of, 57; spotlight on, 83; mentioned, 56
Organizational demands, 234
Organizational effectiveness, 73, 145, 209, 273
Organizational leadership theory, 51–52
Organizational life cycle: crisis path of the, 145–146; leadership aspects in the, 135–138; manager's role in an, 133–135; about the phases of an, 130–133; proactive path of the, 147–148
Organizational literature: themes chosen for, 207
Organizational performance, 228, 245, 247–248
Organizations: leadership in, 88; structure of, 273
Organization start-ups, 140–141
Organization theory, 231–233
Organization variables, 92
Orientation: voluntaristic, 232

Path-goal clarification, 259
Path-goal theory, 30, 47, 58, 175, 255
Pedagogy, 83
Performance: causation, 177–178; causes of, 173; focus on, 167; high, 63; higher order change in, 47; impact on, 244; leader as primary determinant of, 174–176; leader's role in, 177; a master variable, 229; on questions of, 230; on theories of, 180; mentioned, 44, 160
Persuasion, 155
Person, 52
Personality: in leader behavior, 59–60
Phenomenological validity: discussed, 12–15; emphasis on different aspects of, 16–18
Piagetian theory, 55
Plausibility: conventions of, 205
Political decision making, 91
Political psychology, 97
Policy formulation, 62
Population ecology theory, 246–247
Power: exercise of, 18; mentioned, 164
Power and value: systems of, 93

Power bases, 75
Power-orientation, 54
Pro-organizational actions, 55
Pseudocrisis, 8
Punishment: fear of, 74; mentioned, 57

Qualitative research: role of, 245 258–260

Radial constructivism, 162
Rationalism: Descartes', 185
Reading leadership: frame of reference within, 205; narrative discourse reviewed for, 215–216; paradigm of, 204–206; a saga of LEADER as told citing, 216–221; a study, 235–241; web of significance in, 212–213
Realist ontology, 261–263
Reality: constructing a, 162; explanation of socially constructed, 152–155; as in social science, 265
Reality construction, 284–285
Recognition: struggle for, 217–218
"Researchers' Tale," 216–221, 235, 236. See also Saga of LEADER
Reflexive social science, 235
Relationship-centered behavior, 63
Representation behavior, 136
Residual effort, 48
Resource aquisition, 136
Responsibility for events, 40
Rewards: form of, 32; promise of, 74
Reward systems, 19
Rhetorical modes, 207
Risks: calculated, 62
Role-making processes, 107
Role perceptions, 209
Role requirements, 252
Routineness, 177
Rules theory, 83

Saga of LEADER: Meta-Perspectives on, 222–223; reflections on the, 223–224; as written, 216–221
Science nature: philosophy of, 228
Scientific discourse, 210–211
Scientific inquiry: on process of observation in, 263
Scientific paradigm: leadership within questioned, 257–258

Self-confidence: subordinates, 36; mentioned, 47
Self-knowledge, 223
Semiotic reading, 204–206, 211, 281
Serial interdependence, 24
Signification: codes of, 207–209; web of, 213
Situation, 52
Situational approaches, 129
Situational control factors, 40
Situational interactions, 252
Situational Leadership Theory, 57, 175
Situational moderators, 254–255
Situational pressure, 251
Situational stress, 255
Situational task, 22
Situational variables: as given in *Quadrant III,* 176–177; mentioned, 12, 249, 255
Skills: significance of, 89
Social action, 92
Social cognition, 83
"Social construction of reality" perspective, 3
Social control: mechanisms of, 155
Social identity, 98
Social learning theory, 250
Social life: fundamental elements of, 18
Social order: core values of, 97; flexible, 98, 99, 102; mentioned, 85, 90, 92, 94
Social power, 74
Social reality: conceptualization of, 151
Social sciences: development of, 259–260; epistemological perspectives of, 3; a major crisis in the area of, 243; the structural aspects of, 239–241
Social Sciences Index, 206
Social skill: approaches to, 93–96; approach to study of, 98–99; dilemmas fundamental to an understanding of, 99; a general model of, 96; on the components of, 278; use of, 105; mentioned, 97, 253
Social structure: changes in the, 108; process issues in, 107
Social systems: about the management of, 159–160; context of, 270–273; impersonal properties of, 19;

leadership processes in, 277–280; nature of, 161, 265; observations on, 162–163; order in, 163; overview on the, 265–267; philosophy of, 185–186; as result of human action, 272
Stability and change: of team performance and behavior, 108–109
Stagnation, 202
Stakeholders: analysis of leadership research, 183–199; identified, 193; of the social system, 273; mentioned, 166. *See* Organizational Life Cycle Approach
Standardization, 25
Status competition, 91
Strategic apex: demands in life cycle use of, 138–149; demands on the, 142; on a framework termed, 129–130; mentioned, 136
Strategic apex leader: demands on the, 140–141, 142; in Japanese organization, 143
Strategic Assumption Surfacing and Testing (SAST): and its alternatives, 197–199; summarized, 188–195; usefulness of, 195–196; mentioned, 166, 186
Strategic planning, 186–187
Strategy structures, 187
Stress and ambiguity: conditions of, 17
Structuration: concept of, 18; mentioned, 83
Structurational analysis, 19
Styles-of-behavior theory, 174
Subordinate capability, 58
Subordinate performance, 30, 129
Subordinates: on affect of leadership on, 47; charisma, cognition and emotional arousal role in, 39–42; feedback for the, 32; leadership research on leader and, 29; link to organizations, 75–76; influence on leaders, 88; and taking risks, 48
Subordinate satisfaction, 43
Superior-subordinate behavior: expanding of, 136–138
Supervision, 74
Support, 160
Supportive leadership, 76–77
Supportiveness, 109, 114
Symbolic interactionism, 97

Systematic statements, 171
Systematic thinking, 87
System effectiveness: elements of, 15;
    for groups of followers, 16;
    mentioned, 12, 68

Task autonomy, 24
Task design, 19
Task information, 109
Task objectives, 253
Task-oriented activity, 63
Task performance, 75, 113
Task significance: for the follower, 25
Task structure, 58, 59
Task variables, 69
Team performance: an equilibrium
    model of, 108–109
Theoretical knowledge, 244
Thought processes, 165
Time span, 56
Traits and behavior, 255–257
Trait theory, 174
Transactional leadership: basis for, 30;
    measured, 6; problems with, 32; in
    parallel to transformational
    leadership, 7; tested, 44–45;
    mentioned, 137
Transcendental goals, 6, 33
Transformational leader: achievements
    of the, 33–34; on changes brought
    about by, 33–34; defined, 6;
    discussed, 5; expanding boundaries
    for, 35–39; factors in, 77–78; and

fostering of follower autonomy, 73;
    measurements for, 34–35;
    subordinates efforts for, 43; use of
    longitudinal designs in, 47;
    mentioned, 2, 137, 142
Transformational leadership behaviors,
    146, 147; mentioned, 256
Trustworthiness: in manager-
    subordinate relations, 112–113;
    mentioned, 109, 160, 164
Turnover, 180

Uncertainty, 40

Variables: in an equilibrium model,
    109–113
Versatility: levels of, 60–61
Vertical dyad linkage approach,
    179–180
Vision and goals: articulation of, 16
Visionary charisma, 25
Visionary charismatics, 25
Visionary leadership, 12, 16, 68, 69,
    137
Visual perception, 263

Women: as leaders, 264
Women's groups, 104
Work teams, 158
World-class leaders: psychohistorical
    analysis of, 46–47

"Z" cultures, 82

About the Contributors

Bruce J. Avolio is Assistant Professor of Management, State University of New York at Binghamton.

B.R. Baliga is Associate Professor of Management, Texas Tech University, Lubbock.

Klaus Bartölke is Professor of Business Administration, University of Wuppertol, West Germany.

Bernard M. Bass is Regents Distinguished Professor of Management, State University of New York at Binghamton.

Kimberly B. Boal is Associate Professor of Management Sciences, University of Nevada-Reno.

John M. Bryson is Associate Professor of Public Affairs, Hubert H. Humphrey Institute of Public Affairs, University of Minnesota, Twin Cities.

D. Anthony Butterfield is Professor of Management, University of Massachusetts-Amherst.

Marta B. Calas is Assistant Professor of Management, University of Massachusetts-Amherst.

Andrew Crouch is Senior Lecturer, Graduate School of Management, University of Melbourne, Australia.

H. Peter Dachler is Professor of Management, Saint Gall Graduate School of Economics, Law, Business, and Public Administration, Switzerland.

Robert M. Fulmer is Director of Executive Education, School of Business Administration, Emory University, Atlanta.

Jill W. Graham is Assistant Professor of Management, Loyola University, Chicago.

Dian-Marie Hosking is Lecturer in Organizational Behaviour, University of Aston Management Centre, United Kingdom.

Robert J. House is Shell Professor of Organizational Behavior, University of Toronto, Canada.

J. David Hunger is Professor of Management, Iowa State University, Ames.

James G. (Jerry) Hunt is Paul Whitfield Horn Professor of Management, Texas Tech University, Lubbock.

James G. McElroy is Associate Professor of Management, Iowa State University, Ames.

Ian E. Morley is Senior Lecturer in Psychology, University of Warwick, United Kingdom.

Walter Nord is Professor of Organizational Psychology, Washington University, St. Louis.

Mark F. Peterson is Associate Professor of Management, Texas Tech University, Lubbock.

Gilbert J.B. Probst is Professor of Management, Saint Gall Graduate School of Economics, Law, Business, and Public Administration, Switzerland.

Patricia Riley is Associate Professor of Speech Communication, University of Southern California, Los Angeles.

Marshall Sashkin is Senior Associate, Office for Educational Research and Improvement, U.S. Department of Education, Washington, D.C.

Chester A. Schriesheim is Professor of Management and of Psychology, University of Miami, Florida.

Linda Smircich is Associate Professor of Management, University of Massachusetts-Amherst.

Peter B. Smith is Lecturer in Management, University of Sussex, United Kingdom.

Torodd Strand is Research Director, Administrative Research Foundation, Bergen, Norway.

Philip Yetton is Professor of Management, Australian Graduate School of Management, New South Wales, Australia.